Microsoft

PROGRAMMING
MICROSOFT
DIRECTSHOW
FOR DIGITAL VIDEO
AND TELEVISION

Mark D. Pesce

PUBLISHED BY
Microsoft Press
A Division of Microsoft Corporation
One Microsoft Way
Redmond, Washington 98052-6399

Library of Congress Cataloging-in-Publication Data
Pesce, Mark.
    Programming Microsoft DirectShow for Digital Video and Television / Mark D. Pesce.
        p. cm.
    Includes index.
    ISBN 0-7356-1821-6
    1. Digital video.   2. Microsoft DirectShow.   3. Video recording.   4. Computer animation.
    I. Title.

  TK6680.5.P5   2003
  621.388'332--dc21   2003042172

Printed and bound in the United States of America.

1 2 3 4 5 6 7 8 9   QWE   8 7 6 5 4 3

Distributed in Canada by H.B. Fenn and Company Ltd.

A CIP catalogue record for this book is available from the British Library.

Microsoft Press books are available through booksellers and distributors worldwide. For further information about international editions, contact your local Microsoft Corporation office or contact Microsoft Press International directly at fax (425) 936-7329. Visit our Web site at www.microsoft.com/mspress. Send comments to: *mspinput@microsoft.com*.

Acquisitions Editor: Juliana Aldous Atkinson
Project Editor: Barbara Moreland
Technical Editor: Dail Magee Jr.

Body Part No. X08-95171

Table of Contents

Part II   Capture and Editing

Acknowledgments

A book is rarely written alone; although a title might have one author, there are a host of midwives who help it into being. First and foremost, thanks go to the Microsoft DirectShow team, who created this technology, and especially to the following members who contributed specifically to this project: Syon Bhattacharya, John Carothers, Alok Chakrabarti, Ben Ellett, Glenn Evans, Dennis Evseev, Stephen Estrop, Dennis Flanagan, Matthijs Gates, David Goll, Jay Kapur, Tuan Le, Danny Miller, Stan Pennington, Michael Savage, Robin Speed, Gary Sullivan, and E-Zu Wu.

Michael Blome and Mike Wasson of the DirectShow Documentation team at Microsoft provided vital input into the design of the book, and their timely and thoughtful review of each chapter helped immeasurably. (They also contributed several of the sample programs discussed in the text.) Jay Loomis on their team provided helpful input on the Microsoft Windows Media chapter, and their manager, Peter Turcan, deserves a tip of the hat as well, for giving them the resources and time they needed to assist me in this project. Ross Cutler from Microsoft Research contributed the filter wizards—many thanks to him for those.

At Microsoft Press, Barbara Moreland and Juliana Aldous Atkinson were patient, tireless, and hard workers who kept me well informed throughout the whole process of making this book happen, and they were responsive to my needs as they developed. Everyone at Microsoft Press did a wonderful job: from the art design, through the editing, and to production, everything went smoothly. The big boss, publisher Don Fowley, deserves a big "thank you" for managing such a great team.

This book required a few media samples. I'd like to thank Brian Tibbetts and Liam Gowing of John Boy 9 for their song, "Foggy Day," which is included on the CD (and used in several of the examples). The "Sunset" movie was shot with the help of the peerless Steven Piasecki. Finally, I'd like to thank Jeff Cain, who put up with my 20-hour days as this book neared deadline.

Introduction

During the 1990s, the personal computer underwent a radical transformation, entering the decade as an information processing device, suitable only for word processing and spreadsheets. By the turn of the century, the PC had become a media machine, playing music and movies, games, DVDs, and streaming news reports, live from CNN. Part of the reason for this reimagining of the possibilities of the PC came from the exponential growth in processing power, memory, and storage, courtesy of Moore's Law, which effectively states that computers double in CPU speed every 18 months.

Although Moore's Law might have enabled the age of PC-as-media-machine, it took an entirely new class of peripherals—items such as PDAs, webcams, digital cameras and camcorders, MP3 players, and snazzy cell phones—to make the age of media computing absolutely inevitable. Before the digital camcorder, only folks like Steven Spielberg and George Lucas had the resources and capability to edit films on a computer. Today just about any PC users can make their own movies using Microsoft Windows Movie Maker, Adobe Premiere, or any of a hundred other applications. These films can be posted to a Web site, enclosed within an e-mail message, or even distributed on DVDs—with cinema-quality images and full surround sound, making it increasingly easy to create "Hollywood" movies at home.

In this revolution of media machines, nothing's changed as radically as recorded music. In 1990, the compact disc was still coming into its own. A decade later, CDs seem to be on their way out (for music, anyway), having been supplanted by newer formats such as MP3, Windows Media, and RealAudio, which deliver the same sound quality with a lot less storage. An album that used to take up 700 MB on a CD can be "ripped" into a 64-MB MP3 or Windows Media file, written out to a flash memory card, and popped into a computer, PDA, or MP3 player. As MP3s caught on as a format to encode and exchange music, song-swapping services such as Napster and Gnutella began to appear—

to the consternation of record companies around the world. Music has become so easy to transport that even downloading it over a dial-up modem (which isn't fast by today's standards of connectivity) happens millions of times each day.

A lot of software underlies this revolution in the way PCs deal with media. It's software that captures video or audio data, stores it, encodes it in bandwidth-intensive or bandwidth-sparing formats, and allows it to be edited and viewed. Without that layer of software, your computer would behave very much as it did in 1990 (albeit many times faster), confined to the dull tasks of mincing words and balancing books.

The internal details of many media formats are closely guarded pieces of information (for competitive purposes), and they're also not all that easy to understand. Nearly every encoding method employs sophisticated techniques of mathematical analysis to squeeze a sound or video sequence into fewer bits. In the early days of media programming for the PC, you'd have to master these techniques for yourself—a process that could take months, or even years.

It would be vastly preferable if the PC itself offered a set of services to handle the details of capturing, encoding, editing, decoding, and playback of audio and video signals. With that kind of help, a programmer could focus on the details of a media application without having to worry about endless, detailed specifics that could slow the job of writing an application to a crawl.

I confronted just this conundrum in October 2001. I had a great idea: I wanted to write some code that could transform a standard consumer-level digital camcorder into a backup device for my PC. The miniDV tapes used by these camcorders can store up to 18 GB of data—the equivalent of nearly 30 CDs!

When I started to work on my project, I had no idea how to use software to control my digital camcorder, nor how I could read data from the camcorder into the computer or write it out. I studied the documentation for Microsoft DirectX—a collection of multimedia technologies distributed as core parts of the operating system—and found that most of the problem had already been solved for me. Microsoft DirectShow—a set of DirectX interfaces designed specifically for video and audio—provided everything I needed to control my digital camcorder. Because of DirectShow, I could focus on the unique part of my application—writing data from the disk to the camcorder and restoring it—while DirectShow handled all the communication with my camcorder. I'd originally estimated that the job would take two months to complete. Instead, I finished in just two weeks! With a working prototype of my original idea, I could begin the process of patenting my invention. (With a bit of luck, in a few years, I'll have been granted a patent on the idea.)

Although DirectShow is very useful, the documentation included with the DirectX Software Development Kit (SDK) is quite technical, designed for the advanced user of DirectShow, rather than the rank novice. Therefore, I spent more time puzzling my way through the documentation than I did writing code. I realized that the perfect complement to the Microsoft documentation would be a book that could lead a programmer into DirectShow step-by-step, with useful examples presented as a "cookbook" of different techniques. So, here it is, *Programming Microsoft DirectShow for Digital Video and Television*. (I guess Microsoft Press thought it was a good idea, too.)

The Evolution of DirectShow

In the early 1990s, after the release of Windows 3.1, a number of hardware devices were introduced to exploit the features of its graphical user interface. Among these were inexpensive digital cameras (known as webcams today), which used charge-coupled device (CCD) technology to create low-resolution black-and-white video. These devices often connected to the host computer through the computer's parallel port (normally reserved for the printer) with software drivers that could handle data transfer from the camera to the computer. As these devices became more common, Microsoft introduced Video for Windows (VFW), a set of software application program interfaces (APIs) that provided basic video and audio capture services that could be used in conjunction with these new devices. Although VFW proved to be sufficient for many software developers, it has a number of limitations; in particular, it's difficult to support the popular MPEG standard for video. It would take a complete rewrite of Video for Windows to do that.

As Windows 95 was nearing release, Microsoft started a project known as "Quartz," chartered to create a new set of APIs that could provide all of Video for Window's functionality with MPEG support in a 32-bit environment. That seemed straightforward enough, but the engineers working on Quartz realized that a much broader set of devices just coming to market, such as digital camcorders and PC-based TV tuners, would require a more comprehensive level of support than anything they'd planned to offer in a next-generation tool. Everywhere they looked, the designers of Quartz realized they couldn't possible imagine every scenario or even try to get it all into a single API.

Instead, the designers of Quartz chose a "framework" architecture, where the components can be "snapped" together, much like LEGO bricks. To simplify the architecture of a complex multimedia application, Quartz would provide a basic set of building components—known as *filters*—to perform essential functions such as reading data from a file, playing it to the speaker, rendering it to the screen, and so on.

Using the newly developed Microsoft Component Object Model (COM), Quartz tied these filters together into *filter graphs*, which orchestrated a flow of bits—a *stream*—from capture through any intermediate processing to its eventual output to the display. Through COM, each filter would be able to inquire about the capabilities of other filters as they were connected together into a filter graph. And because Quartz filters would be self-contained COM objects, they could be created by third-party developers for their own hardware designs or software needs. In this way, Quartz would be endlessly extensible; if you needed some feature that Quartz didn't have, you could always write your own filter.

The developers of Quartz raided a Microsoft research project known as "Clockwork," which provided a basic framework of modular, semi-independent components working together on a stream of data. From this beginning, Quartz evolved into a complete API for video and audio processing, which Microsoft released in 1995 as ActiveMovie, shipping it as a component in the DirectX Media SDK. In 1996, Microsoft renamed ActiveMovie to DirectShow (to indicate its relationship with DirectX), a name it retains to this day.

In 1998, a subsequent release of DirectShow added support for DVDs and analog television applications, both of which had become commonplace. Finally, in 2000, DirectShow was fully integrated with DirectX, shipping as part of the release of DirectX 8. This integration means that every Windows computer with DirectX installed (and that's most PCs nowadays) has the complete suite of DirectShow services and is fully compatible with any DirectShow application. DirectX 8 also added support for Windows Media, a set of streaming technologies designed for high-quality audio and video delivered over low-bandwidth connections, and the DirectShow Editing Services, a complete API for video editing.

Microsoft bundled a new application into the release of Windows Millennium Edition: Windows Movie Maker. Built using DirectShow, it gives novice users of digital camcorders an easy-to-use interface for video capture, editing, and export—an outstanding demonstration of the capabilities of the DirectShow API. In the two years after the release of DirectX 8, it's probably safe to say that most of the popular video editing applications have come to use DirectShow to handle the intricacies of communication with a wide array of digital camcorders. Those programmers of these applications made the same choice I did, using DirectShow to handle the low-level sorts of tasks that would have consumed many, many hours of research, programming, and testing.

With the release of DirectX 9 (the most recent, as this book is written), very little has changed in DirectShow, with one significant exception: the Video Mixing Renderer (VMR) filter. The VMR allows the programmer to mix multiple video sources into a single video stream that can be played within a window or applied as a "texture map," a bit like wallpaper, to a surface of a 3D object created in Microsoft Direct3D.

Nearly any Windows application or tool that records or plays audio and/or video can benefit from DirectShow. The list of uses for DirectShow is lengthy, but the two most prominent examples are Windows Movie Maker (mentioned previously) and Windows Media Player. Both have shipped as standard components of Microsoft operating systems since Windows Millennium Edition, and tens of millions of people use them each day.

DirectShow Capabilities

DirectShow capabilities can be separated into three broad areas, which reflect the three basic types of DirectShow filters. First are the capture capabilities. DirectShow can orchestrate capture of audio from the microphone or from a line input, can control a digital camcorder or D-VHS VCR (a nifty new kind of VCR that stores video digitally in high resolution), or can capture both audio and video from a live camera, such as a webcam. DirectShow can also open a file and treat it as if it were a "live" source; this way, you can work on video or audio that you've previously captured.

Once the media stream has been captured, DirectShow filters can be used to transform it. Transform filters have been written to convert color video to black-and-white, resize video images, add an echo effect to an audio stream, and so on. These transform filters can be connected, one after another, like so many building blocks, until the desired effect is achieved. Streams of audio and video data can be "split" and sent to multiple filters simultaneously, as if you added a splitter to the coaxial cable that carries a cable TV or satellite signal. Media streams can also be multiplexed, or *muxed*, together, taking two or more streams and making them one. Using a mux, you can add a soundtrack to a video sequence, putting both streams together synchronously.

After all the heavy lifting of the transform filters has been accomplished, there's one task left: rendering the media stream to the display, speakers, or a device. DirectShow has a number of built-in render filters, including simple ones that provide a window on the display for video playback. You can also take a stream and write it to disk or to a device such as a digital camcorder.

Most DirectShow applications don't need the full range of DirectShow's capabilities; in fact, very few do. For example, Windows Media Player doesn't need much in the way of capture capabilities, but it needs to be able to play (or render) a very wide range of media types—MP3s, MPEG movies, AVI movies, WAV sounds, Windows Media, and so on. You can throw almost any media file at Windows Media Player (with the notable exception of Apple QuickTime and the RealNetworks media formats), and it'll play the file without asking for help. That's because Windows Media Player, built with DirectShow, inherits all of DirectShow's capabilities to play a broad range of media.

On the other hand, Windows Movie Maker is a great example of an application that uses nearly the full suite of DirectShow capabilities. It's fully capable of communicating with and capturing video from a digital camcorder (or a webcam). Once video clips have been captured, they can be edited, prettied up, placed onto a timeline, mixed with a soundtrack, and then written to disk (or a digital camcorder) as a new, professional-looking movie. You can even take a high-resolution, high-bandwidth movie and write it as a low-resolution, low-bandwidth Windows Media file, suitable for dropping into an e-mail message or posting on a Web site. All of these capabilities come from Windows Movie Maker's extensive use of DirectShow because they're all DirectShow capabilities.

The flexibility of DirectShow means that it can be used to rapidly prototype applications. DirectShow filters can be written quickly to provide solutions to a particular problem. It's widely used at universities and in research centers—including Microsoft's own—to solve problems in machine vision (using the computer to recognize portions of a video image) or for other kinds of audio or video processing, including the real-time processing of signals. It's easy to write a DirectShow filter (at least, it'll seem easy once you've read this book); many people with a background in C++ have written their own filters.

There are some tasks that DirectShow can't handle well, a few cases in which "rolling your own" is better than using DirectShow. These kinds of applications generally lie on the high end of video processing, with high-definition video pouring in at tens of millions of bits per second or multiple cameras being choreographed and mixed in real time. Right now these kinds of applications push even the fastest computers to the limits of processor speed, memory, and network bandwidth. That's not to say that you'll never be able to handle high-definition capture in DirectShow or real-time multicamera editing. You can write DirectShow applications that edit high-definition images and handle real-time multicamera editing. However, can you get a computer fast enough to run these DirectShow programs? You might, if you wanted to spend $15,000 on a dual-processor Pentium 4 system running at 3 GHz. (And if you're interested that kind of high-performance work, you might have that kind of budget to throw around.)

In any case, DirectShow isn't magic; working with video is both processor-intensive and memory-intensive, and many DirectShow applications will use every computing resource available, up to 100 percent of your CPU. So when you make the decision to use DirectShow for a project, set your expectations appropriately. DirectShow is an excellent architecture for media processing, but it isn't perfect. It's up to you to determine whether you're asking too much of DirectShow.

Hardware and Software Requirements

Although DirectShow applications should run across a broad range of computers, for the purposes of this book, I'll make some very specific recommendations about the kinds of components, both hardware and software, that you should have while working on the example code in this book. Although you don't absolutely have to have the configuration as I'll give it, the more you differ from this configuration, the more your own results will differ from those given in the text. Although you can play an MP3 audio file on a lowly 486-class processor, encoding an MP3 on the same machine would take a long time—more time than most people are willing to wait. And if you're working with video streams, you'll need the fastest computer, memory, and hard disk you can afford. Basic hardware and software requirements to work with the examples given in this book are shown in the tables that follow.

Table I-1   Basic Hardware Requirements

CPU	Intel Celeron, Pentium III, or Pentium 4; AMD Duron or Athlon, running at 1 GHz or faster
RAM	256 MB or greater; 512 MB or greater for best performance
Hard disk	30 GB or greater, with at least 15 GB of free space
Video card	ATI Radeon 8500 All-In-Wonder (or equivalent card with broadcast TV tuner)
Sound card	Any DirectShow-supported sound card (most sound cards) with microphone and/or line inputs
Webcam	Logitech QuickCam Pro 3000 (This webcam has an integrated microphone; you'll need a separate microphone if your webcam doesn't have one built-in.)
Digital camcorder	Sony DRC-TRV900 or equivalent (Most digital camcorders will work, as long as they have FireWire/IEEE 1394 capabilities, but some older model Canon cameras don't perform well with DirectShow.)

Table I-2   **Basic Software Requirements**

Operating system	Windows XP with Service Pack 1 (Certain Direct-Show features for personal video recorders are implemented only in this version of Windows XP.)
Development tool	Microsoft Visual Studio .NET or Visual C++ .NET
DirectX SDK	Release 9 or later
Windows Media Format SDK	Release 9 or later
Windows Media Player	Version 9 or later
Windows Media Encoder	Version 9 or later

Before you begin to work through the examples in this book, you'll need to install all hardware and software as given in the previous tables. Very few configurations will exactly match what I've listed, especially on the hardware side of things; configurations vary widely in the PC world. However, it's important to try to get a software configuration that's as close as possible to the one I've given. This book was written for the latest version of DirectX SDK (version 9 as of this writing), Windows XP (Service Pack 1 is a must-have addition because it adds support for features covered in Chapter 7), the Windows Media Format 9 Series SDK, and Windows Media Player 9 Series. If any of these components are missing from your computer, some of the examples given in this book simply won't work, and you might go nuts looking for your own mistakes before you realize that the problem isn't with your code but is with your configuration.

The latest version of Windows Media Player can be downloaded from the Microsoft Web site, along with the Windows XP Service Pack. Before you go any further, install any software you need to ensure that your software configuration matches the one I've given.

A Roadmap to This Book

This book has been written for the complete DirectShow novice; you don't need to know anything about DirectShow—or even audio or video—to get started. If you're already familiar with DirectShow, chances are you'll be able to race through the first three chapters of this book very quickly. However, it's always a good idea to review the pages, just to see if there's anything covered that you might not be familiar with.

The basics covered in Part I of this book include a firm understanding of the DirectShow filter, which is the core component of all DirectShow applications. Filters come in three flavors, as mentioned earlier—capture filters, transform filters, and render filters—and they're connected together to process a media stream from source to renderer. To demonstrate this, we'll open up the DirectShow prototyping application, GraphEdit, which allows you to visually explore DirectShow filters, creating your own DirectShow applications with nothing more than a few clicks of the mouse. Next we'll dive headlong into some C++ programming with the Microsoft Component Object Model (COM), the interface "wrapper" for DirectShow filters, and create some very simple C++ programs (only a few tens of lines of code each) illustrating how Direct-Show can be used to play a range of media files. If you're planning to use DirectShow only to add some media playback to your application, this basic information might be all you'll ever need to read.

With the basics behind us, we'll dive headlong into DirectShow. The organization of Part II of the book echoes the three basic types of DirectShow filters: capture, transform and renders. We'll explore how to capture audio and video from a broad range of sources, including camcorders, broadcast TV capture cards, and webcams. Each of these devices has its own peculiar properties, so each chapter explores a different capture device. An example application is included with each chapter, which could be used in a "cookbook" formula for your own applications. (Go ahead; reuse this code.) Next, we'll explore the DirectShow editing services, which allow you to slice-and-dice video and audio streams and then "paste" them back together along a timeline. Finally, we'll focus on the Video Mixing Renderer (VMR), a powerful new addition to Direct-Show that allows you to mix multiple video streams into a single stream. By the end of Chapter 9, you'll have a thorough understanding of media capture, editing, and rendering within DirectShow.

In Part III you'll learn how to write your own DirectShow transform filters; when you're done with this section, you'll be able to extend DirectShow in any way you'd like, either with a custom DirectShow filter or by creating a DirectX Media Object (DMO), which is similar to a DirectShow filter but can also be used in other DirectX applications. Starting with a DirectShow filter that converts color video to black and white, we'll explore a framework that could form the basis of almost any transform filter of your own design. Using another DirectShow filter known as Sample Grabber, which grabs media samples as they pass through the filter, you'll see how to add your own application-level processing to DirectShow. That'll be followed by coverage of source filters, and you'll learn how to write your own source filters, producing media streams for DirectShow to process. Finally, we'll explore the world of DMOs, creating an audio delay effect that can be used within DirectShow or in DirectSound, the audio library for DirectX applications.

The two concluding chapters cover advanced topics that will interest dedicated DirectShow programmers: the AVI format and the Windows Media Format.

We'll get down and dirty into the bits and bytes of the AVI format, which will come in handy if you're ever creating the kind of code that manipulates or creates media streams—inside or outside of DirectShow. Windows Media Format is a brand-new architecture that provides unprecedented flexibility in the creation and management of a wide range of media formats, and we'll learn how to compose our own Windows Media streams programmatically.

A comprehensive reference for DirectShow could easily run to 1000 pages. The DirectX SDK has a complete set of documentation on DirectShow, and those pages are the final authority. This book is a complement to the SDK documentation to help you get your feet wet with DirectShow. Before you finish this book, you'll find that DirectShow is one of the hidden jewels of the Microsoft operating systems—a powerful platform for multimedia that's easy to use and performs well on a wide range of hardware. You'll have no trouble dreaming up your own DirectShow applications, and after you've read this book, you'll understand how to bring them to life.

Although this book has been reviewed and fact-checked, I alone am responsible for any factual errors you might find in the text. Please e-mail me at *mark@playfulworld.com* if you find one so that it can be corrected in subsequent editions.

Support Information

Every effort has been made to ensure the accuracy of this book and the companion content. Microsoft Press provides corrections for books through the World Wide Web at

http://www.microsoft.com/mspress/support/

To connect directly to the Microsoft Press Knowledge Base and enter a query regarding a question or an issue that you may have, go to

http://www.microsoft.com/mspress/support/search.asp

If you have comments, questions, or ideas regarding the book or its companion content, please send them to Microsoft Press via e-mail to

MSPInput@microsoft.com

or via postal mail to

Microsoft Press
Attn: *Programming Microsoft DirectShow*
   for Digital Video and Television Editor[1]
One Microsoft Way
Redmond, WA 98052-6399

Please note that product support is not offered through the preceding addresses.

Part I

The Basics

1

DirectShow Concepts

From the viewpoint of the application programmer, Microsoft DirectShow is composed of two types of classes of objects: *filters*, the atomic entities of Direct-Show; and *filter graphs*, collections of filters connected together to provide specific functionality. Just as atoms are composed of electrons, protons, and neutrons, filters are composed of *pins*, which can either receive an input stream or send an output stream to another filter. Conceptually, filters can be thought of as function calls in a DirectShow programming language, while a filter graph is the program composed of those function calls. Here is what it might look like, in pseudo C++ code:

```
FilterGraph() {
    SourceFilter();       // A source filter
    TranformFilter();     // Usually, a transform filter
    :                     // As many other filters as needed
    RendererFilter();     // A renderer filter
}
```

As is the case in most programming languages, the DirectShow filter graphs execute sequentially, from the first filter to the last. Data enters at the first filter in the filter graph, passes along to the second filter, and so on. What makes a DirectShow filter graph different from a common C++ program is that it also executes continuously. When a filter graph starts its execution, data begins to flow across the filters in a filter graph like a waterfall descending a series of stairs. This data flow is commonly known as a *stream*. This stream is operated on by all filters in a filter graph simultaneously. Chapter 10 contains a detailed exploration of exactly how data flows across a filter graph and how DirectShow adjusts its operation to keep the filter graph from running dry or being overwhelmed with a data stream.

One important point distinguishes a DirectShow filter graph from an ordinary computer program: a filter graph can have multiple streams flowing across it and multiple paths through the filter graph. For example, a DirectShow application can simultaneously capture video frames from a webcam and audio from a microphone. This data enters the filter graph through two independent *source* filters, which would likely later be multiplexed together into a single audio/video stream. In another case, you might want to split a stream into two identical streams. One stream could be sent to a video renderer filter, which would draw it upon the display, while the other stream could be written to disk. Both streams execute simultaneously; DirectShow sends the same bits to the display and to the disk.

DirectShow filters make computations and decisions internally—for instance, they can change the values of bits in a stream—but they cannot make decisions that affect the structure of the filter graph. A filter simply passes its data along to the next filter in the filter graph. It can't decide to pass its data to filter A if some condition is true or filter B if the condition is false. This means that the behavior of a filter graph is completely predictable; the way it behaves when it first begins to operate on a data stream is the way it will always operate.

Although filter graphs are entirely deterministic, it is possible to modify the elements within a filter graph programmatically. A C++ program could create filter graph A if some condition is true and filter graph B if it's false. Or both could be created during program initialization (so that the program could swap between filter graph A and filter graph B on the fly) as the requirements of the application change. Program code can also be used to modify the individual filters within a filter graph, an operation that can change the behavior of a filter graph either substantially or subtly. So, although filter graphs can't make decisions on how to process their data, program code can be used to simulate that capability.

For example, consider a DirectShow application that can capture video data from one of several different sources, say from a digital camcorder and a webcam. Once the video has been captured, it gets encoded into a compact Windows Media file, which could then be dropped into an e-mail message for video e-mail. Very different source and transform filters are used to capture and process a video stream from a digital camcorder than those used with a webcam, so the same filter graph won't work for both devices. In this case, program logic within the application could detect which input device is being used—perhaps based on a menu selection—and could then build the appropriate filter graph. If the user changes the selection from one device to another, program logic could rebuild the filter graph to suit the needs of the selected device.

Modular Design

The basic power and flexibility of DirectShow derives directly from its modular design. DirectShow defines a standard set of Component Object Model (COM) interfaces for filters and leaves it up to the programmer to arrange these components in some meaningful way. Filters hide their internal operations; the programmer doesn't need to understand or appreciate the internal complexities of the Audio Video Interleaved (AVI) file format, for example, to create an AVI file from a video stream. All that's required is the appropriate sequence of filters in a filter graph. Filters are atomic objects within DirectShow, meaning they reveal only as much of themselves as required to perform their functions.

Because they are atomic objects, filters can be thought of and treated just like puzzle pieces. The qualities that each filter possesses determine the shape of its puzzle piece, and that, in turn, determines which other filters it can be connected to. As long as the pieces match up, they can be fitted together into a larger scheme, the filter graph.

All DirectShow filters have some basic properties that define the essence of their modularity. Each filter can establish connections with other filters and can negotiate the types of connections it's willing to accept from other filters. A filter designed to process MP3 audio doesn't have to accept a connection from a filter that produces AVI video—and probably shouldn't. Each filter can receive some basic messages—run, stop, and pause—that control the execution of the filter graph. That's about it; there's not much more a filter needs to be ready to go. As long as the filter defines these properties publicly through COM, Direct-Show will treat it as a valid element in a filter graph.

This modularity makes designing custom DirectShow filters a straightforward process. The programmer's job is to design a COM object with the common interfaces for a DirectShow filter, plus whatever custom processing the filter requires. A custom DirectShow filter might sound like a complex affair, but it's really a routine job, one that will be covered extensively in the examples in Part III.

The modularity of DirectShow extends to the filter graph. Just as the internals of a filter can be hidden from the programmer, the internals of a filter graph can be hidden from view. When the filter graph is treated as a module, it can assume responsibility for connecting filters together in a meaningful way. It's possible to create a complete, complex filter graph by adding a source filter and a renderer filter to the filter graph. These filters are then connected with a technique known as *Intelligent Connect*. Intelligent Connect examines the filters in the filter graph, determines the right way to connect them, adds any necessary conversion filters, and makes the connections—all without any intervention from the programmer. Intelligent Connect can save you an enormous amount of programming time because DirectShow does the tedious work of filter connection for you.

There is a price to be paid for this level of automation: the programmer won't know exactly which filters have been placed into the filter graph or how they're connected. Some users will have installed multiple MPEG decoders—such as one for a DVD player and another for a video editing application. Therefore, these systems will have multiple filters to perform a particular function. With Intelligent Connect, you won't know which filter DirectShow has chosen to use (at least, when a choice is available). It's possible to write code that will make inquiries to the filter graph and map out the connections between all the filters in the filter graph, but it's more work to do that than to build the filter graph from scratch. So, modularity has its upsides—ease of use and extensibility—and its downsides—hidden code.

Hiding complexity isn't always the best thing to do, and you might choose to build DirectShow filter graphs step by step, with complete control over the construction process. Overall, the modular nature of DirectShow is a huge boon for the programmer, hiding gory details behind clean interfaces. This modularity makes DirectShow one of the very best examples of object-oriented programming (OOP), which promises reusable code and clean module design, ideals that are rarely achieved in practice. DirectShow achieves this goal admirably, as you'll see.

Filters

Filters are the basic units of DirectShow programs, the essential components of the filter graph. A filter is an entity complete unto itself. Although a filter can have many different functions, it must have some method to receive or transmit a stream of data. Each filter has at least one *pin*, which provides a connection point from that filter to other filters in the filter graph. Pins come in two varieties: *input* pins can receive a stream, while *output* pins produce a stream that can be sent along to another filter.

Filter Types

There are three basic classes of DirectShow filters, which span the path from input, through processing, to output (or, as it's often referred to, *rendering*). All DirectShow filters fall into one of these broad categories. A filter produces a stream of data, operates on that stream, or renders it to some output device.

Source Filters

Any DirectShow filter that produces a stream is known as a *source filter*. The stream might originate in a file on the hard disk, or it might come from a live device, such as a microphone, webcam, or digital camcorder. If the stream comes from disk, it could be a pre-recorded WAV (sound), AVI (movie), or Windows Media file. Alternately, if the source is a live device, it could be any of the many thousands of Windows-compatible peripherals. DirectShow is closely tied in to the Windows Driver Model (WDM), and all WDM drivers for installed multimedia devices are automatically available to DirectShow as source filters. So, for example, webcams with properly installed Windows drivers become immediately available for use as DirectShow source filters. Source filters that translate live devices into DirectShow streams are known as *capture source filter*s. Chapter 12 covers the software design of a source filter in detail.

Transform Filters

Transform filters are where the interesting work gets done in DirectShow. A *transform filter* receives an input stream from some other filter (possibly a source filter), performs some operation on the stream, and then passes the stream along to another filter. Nearly any imaginable operation on an audio or video stream is possible within a transform filter. A transform filter can parse (interpret) a stream of data, encode it (perhaps converting WAV data to MP3 format) or decode it, or add a text overlay to a video sequence. DirectShow includes a broad set of transform filters, such as filters for encoding and decoding various types of video and audio formats.

Transform filters can also create a *tee* in the stream, which means that the input stream is duplicated and placed on two (or more) output pins. Other transform filters take multiple streams as input and multiplex them into a single stream. Using a transform filter multiplexer, separate audio and video streams can be combined into a video stream with a soundtrack.

Renderer Filters

A *renderer filter* translates a DirectShow stream into some form of output. One basic renderer filter can write a stream to a file on the disk. Other renderer filters can send audio streams to the speakers or video streams to a window on the desktop. The *Direct* in *DirectShow* reflects the fact that DirectShow renderer filters use DirectDraw and DirectSound, supporting technologies that allow DirectShow to efficiently pass its renderer filter streams along to graphics and sound cards. This ability means that DirectShow's renderer filters are very fast and don't get tied up in a lot of user-to-kernel mode transitions. (In operating system parlance, this process means moving the data from an unprivileged level in an operating system to a privileged one where it has access to the various output devices.)

A filter graph can have multiple renderer filters. It is possible to put a video stream through a tee, sending half of it to a renderer filter that writes it to a file, and sending the other half to another renderer filter that puts it up on the display. Therefore, it is possible to monitor video operations while they're happening, even if they're being recorded to disk—an important feature we'll be using later on.

The Complete Picture

All DirectShow filter graphs consist of combinations of these three types of filters, and every DirectShow filter graph will have at least one source filter, one renderer filter, and (possibly) several transform filters. In each filter graph, a source filter creates a stream that is then operated on by any number of transform filters and is finally output through a renderer filter. These filters are connected together through their pins, which provide a well-defined interface point for transfer of stream data between filters.

Connections Between Filters

Although every DirectShow filter has pins, it isn't always possible to connect an input pin to an output pin. When two filters are connecting to each other, they have to reach an agreement about what kind of stream data they'll pass between them. For example, there are many video formats in wide use, such as DV (digital video), MPEG-1, MPEG-2, QuickTime, and so on. A transform filter that can handle DV might not be able handle any other video format. Therefore, a source filter that creates an MPEG-2 stream (perhaps read from a DVD) should not be connected to that transform filter because the stream data would be unusable.

The pins on a DirectShow filter handle the negotiation between filters and ensure that the pin types are compatible before a connection is made between any two filters. Every filter is required to publish the list of media types it can send or receive and a set of transport mechanisms describing how each filter wants the stream to travel from output pin to input pin. (Both media types and transport mechanisms will be covered in detail in Part III.)

When a DirectShow filter graph attempts to connect the output pin of one filter to the input pin of another, the negotiation process begins. The filter graph examines the media types that the output pin can transmit and compares these with the media types that the input pin can receive. If there aren't any matches, the pins can't be connected and the connection operation fails.

Next the pins have to agree on a transport mechanism. Once again, if they can't agree, the connection operation fails. Finally one of the pins has to create an *allocator*, an object that creates and manages the buffers of stream data that the output pin uses to pass data along to the input pin. The allocator can be owned by either the output pin or the input pin; it doesn't matter, so long as they're in agreement.

If all these conditions have been satisfied, the pins are connected. This connection operation must be repeated for each filter in the graph until there's a complete, uninterrupted stream from source filter, through any transform filters, to a renderer filter. When the filter graph is started, a data stream will flow from the output pin of one filter to the input pin of the other through the entire span of the filter graph.

Intelligent Connect

One of the greatest strengths of DirectShow is its ability to handle the hard work of supporting multiple media formats. Most of the time it's not necessary for the programmer to be concerned with what kinds of streams run through a filter graph. Yet to connect two pins, DirectShow filters must have clear agreement on the media types they're handling. How can both statements be true simultaneously? Intelligent Connect automates the connection process between two pins. You can connect two pins directly, so long as their media types agree. In a situation in which the media types are not compatible, you'll often need one (or several) transform filters between the two pins so that they can be connected together. Intelligent Connect does the work of adding and connecting the intermediate transform filters to the filter graph.

For example, a filter graph might have a source filter that produces a stream of DV data—perhaps it's connected to a camcorder. This filter graph has a renderer filter that writes a file to disk. These two filters have nothing in common. They don't share any common media types because the DV data is encoded and interleaved and must be decoded and de-interleaved before it can be written to a file. With Intelligent Connect, the filter graph can try combinations of intermediate transform filters to determine whether there's a way to translate the output requirements of the pin on the source filter into the input requirements of the render filter. The filter graph can do this because it has access to all possible DirectShow filters. It can make inquiries to each filter to determine whether a transform filter can transform one media type to another—which might be an intermediate type—transform that type into still another, and so on, until the input requirements of the renderer filter have been met. A DirectShow filter graph can look very Rube Goldberg–esque by the time the filter graph succeeds in connecting two pins, but from the programmer's point of view, it's a far easier operation. And if an Intelligent Connect operation fails, it's fairly certain there's no possible way to connect two filters. The Intelligent Connect capability of DirectShow is one of the ways that DirectShow hides the hard work of media processing from the programmer.

Filter Graphs

The DirectShow filter graph organizes a group of filters into a functional unit. When connected, the filters present a path for a stream from source filters, through any transform filters, to renderer filters. However, it isn't enough to connect the filters; the filter graph has to tell the filters when to start their operation, when to stop, and when to pause. In addition, the filters need to be synchronized because they're all dealing with media samples that must be kept in sync. (Imagine the frustration if the audio and video kept going out of sync in a movie.)

For this reason, the filter graph generates a software-based clock that is available to all the filters in the filter graph. This clock is used to maintain synchronization and allows filters to keep their stream data in order as it passes from filter to filter. Available to the programmer, the filter graph clock has increments of 100 nanoseconds. (The accuracy of the clock on your system might be less precise than 100 nanoseconds because accuracy is often determined by the sound card or chip set on your system.)

When the programmer issues one of the three basic DirectShow commands—run, stop, or pause—the filter graph sends the messages to each filter in the filter graph. Every DirectShow filter must be able to process these messages. For example, sending a run message to a source filter controlling a webcam will initiate a stream of data coming into the filter graph from that filter, while sending a stop command will halt that stream. The pause command behaves superficially like the stop command, but the stream data isn't cleared out like it would be if the filter graph had received a stop command. Instead, the stream is frozen in place until the filter graph receives either a run or stop command. If the run command is issued, filter graph execution continues with the stream data already present in the filter graph when the pause command was issued.

The Life Cycle of a Sample

To gain a more complete understanding of DirectShow, let's follow a sample of video data gathered from a DV camcorder as it passes through the a filter graph on its way to the display. Figure 1-1 illustrates the path.

Figure 1-1   Path of video data gathered from a camcorder

The video sample is generated in a source filter—in this case, a capture source filter because the filter is capturing from a live device, a camera, rather than reading from a disk. Video camcorders in the United States, Canada, and Japan (and some other regions and countries) generate 30 frames of video data per second; it's reasonably safe to assume that one DirectShow sample will be equivalent to one frame of video captured by the camcorder. In this case, the source capture filter is a WDM object that speaks directly to the computer's hardware (which, in turn, is communicating directly with the camcorder, probably over a FireWire interface). The capture source filter issues commands to the driver for the camcorder, and in return, the filter receives data. Each packet of data is equivalent to one frame of video.

In this example, the capture source filter's primary role is to convert the packets of data arriving from the camcorder into series of samples. When considered as a whole, these discrete samples compose a stream of video data formatted for DirectShow. Once the camcorder data has been converted into a stream, it can be presented on the source filter's output pin so that it can be passed along to a downstream filter. Additonally, the capture source filter provides a timestamp for each sample in the stream so that DirectShow can maintain sample processing in the correct order; that is, samples captured first will be processed first.

The next filter in the graph is a transform filter, a DV video decoder. This filter takes the raw video data presented by the source capture filter and processes it in two significant ways. First it will likely convert the color model of the video stream from the YUV model common in camcorders and other digital imaging devices to the RGB model commonly used on computer displays. Many different color models are used by imaging and display devices, and you'll find that many of the DirectShow transform filters convert from one color model to another to perform their tasks.

Next the DV video decoder might convert the interlaced video fields presented by the camcorder into non-interlaced video images. Using interlacing, a single frame of video imagery is actually broken down into two fields. The first field contains all the odd-numbered lines of video information, while the second field contains all the even-numbered lines. The two fields must be combined—that is, de-interlaced—to produce the non-interlaced (also known as *progressive scan*) image used on nearly all computer displays. These two transformations, first of the color model and then de-interlacing, have created a video stream that can now be rendered on the display. After processing, these samples are presented at the output pin of the DV video decoder, which maintains the per-sample timestamp, ensuring that the images stay correctly synchronized as they move from filter to filter.

Finally the stream arrives at its destination, the video renderer. The renderer filter accepts a properly formatted video stream from the DV video decoder and draws it onto the display. As each sample comes into the renderer filter, it is displayed within the DirectShow output window. Samples will be displayed in the correct order, from first to last, because the video renderer filter examines the timestamp of each sample to make sure that the samples are played sequentially. Now that the sample has reached a renderer filter, DirectShow is done with it, and the sample is discarded once it has been drawn on the display. The buffer that the filter allocated to store the sample is returned to a pool of free buffers, ready to receive another sample.

This flow of samples continues until the filter graph stops or pauses its execution. If the filter graph is stopped, all of its samples are discarded; if paused, the samples are held within their respective filters until the filter graph returns to the running state.

Summary

At this point, you should have a basic understanding of how DirectShow works. DirectShow applications create filter graphs; these filter graphs are composed of filters connected to form a path from stream capture to the display or storage of a stream. Filters are independent, object-oriented modules that handle one specific function in the processing of a media stream: capture or display of a video image, playing a sound, and so on. Now that we've covered these basic points, we'll begin to explore GraphEdit, a useful DirectShow application that allows you to create your own, fully functional filter graphs with just a few mouse clicks so that you can put these abstract concepts into practice.

2

GraphEdit

As you read Chapter 1, you might have visualized DirectShow filters as being boxes with input and output pins, connected with "wires," one filter to another, across a filter graph. The DirectX SDK has a tool, GraphEdit, that makes these DirectShow visualizations explicit, executable filter graphs. GraphEdit is Direct-Show's visual filter graph editor, and this chapter covers the features and uses of this tool.

Introducing GraphEdit

The basic elements of DirectShow applications—filters, connections, and filter graphs—can be easily represented visually, and drawing a diagram of a Direct-Show filter graph can be an important aid in the design process. GraphEdit can be thought of as a whiteboard on which prototype DirectShow filter graphs can be sketched. However, because GraphEdit is built using DirectShow components, these whiteboard designs are fully functional, executable DirectShow programs. More than just a design tool, GraphEdit is a rapid prototyping environment for DirectShow. Any DirectShow application, regardless of complexity, can be built and tested in GraphEdit before you write a single line of application code.

To launch GraphEdit, select Programs from the Start menu, select Microsoft DirectX 9.0 SDK, select DirectX Utilities, and then select GraphEdit. When the program launches, you'll be presented with a large blank area, representative of an empty filter graph with no component filters, as shown in Figure 2-1.

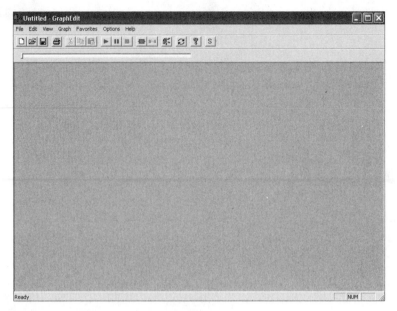

Figure 2-1   GraphEdit's startup state

Rendering Media Files

GraphEdit makes it easy to render a wide range of media files. From the File menu, select Render Media File. You'll be presented with an Open File dialog box asking you to select a file to be rendered. Select the file John Boy 9 – Foggy Day.wav (included on the CD-ROM). If your DirectX installation is correct, you should see the the filter graph shown in Figure 2-2.

GraphEdit has created a complete filter graph, with three components. From left to right, the filter graphs are

- A source filter that points to the WAV file

- A transform filter that parses the file into a series of samples

- A renderer filter that passes the stream along to the default Direct-Sound device

As explained in Chapter 1, these three types of filters—source, transform, and renderer—can be found in nearly every filter graph. The filter graph created by GraphEdit to render the WAV file is minimal but complete. To hear the WAV file being rendered to the speakers (or whichever DirectSound device has been selected as the default), click the Play button on the toolbar, immediately below the menu bar, as shown in Figure 2-3.

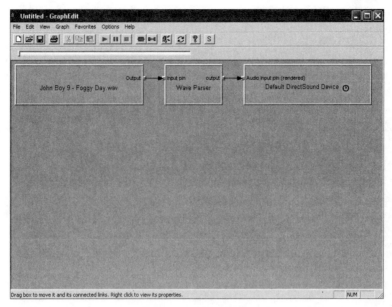

Figure 2-2   Filter graph to render a WAV file

When you click the Play button, the WAV file begins to render and the control below the toolbar begins to fill with color, corresponding to how much of the WAV file has been read into the filter graph. You can pause the filter graph by clicking Pause or stop it by clicking Stop. (As you might expect, the Play, Pause, and Stop buttons send the run, pause, and stop messages to the filter graph.) After the entire stream has rendered to the DirectSound device, GraphEdit stops the filter graph.

Using the Render Media File option, a broad range of media files—all the types understood by DirectShow—can be rendered. In fact, trying to render these files is a good test of the DirectShow capabilities of your system. If you open a media file and DirectShow can't render it, it's likely that you don't have the appropriate collection of DirectShow filters (which might encourage you to write a DirectShow filter that could render the media type you're interested in).

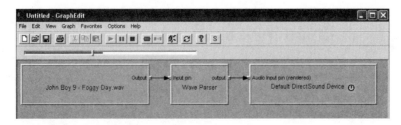

Figure 2-3   Rendering the WAV file

Enumerating Filter Types

To understand what kinds of filter graphs you can create in GraphEdit, you have to enumerate (list) all the possible filters available for DirectShow's use. From GraphEdit's Graph menu, select the first item, Insert Filters, and you'll see the dialog box shown in Figure 2-4.

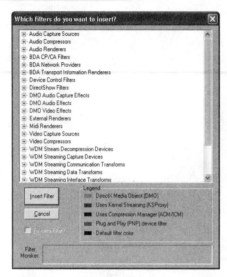

Figure 2-4 GraphEdit's Insert Filters dialog box enumerating all available DirectShow filters

This dialog box uses the Windows convention of expandable lists of items. To the left of each list entry in the dialog box is a plus sign, which hides a list of DirectShow filters underneath. Clicking on the DirectShow Filters entry will present the entire list of DirectShow filters available to GraphEdit. The other filters enumerated in the Insert Filters dialog box are Windows Driver Model (WDM) devices (all valid WDM devices are available to Direct-Show as filters), DirectX Media Objects (DMOs), Video for Windows devices, and so forth.

Building a Filter Graph from Scratch

Now that you've enumerated the filters available to DirectShow, it's possible to build up a filter graph—say, one that will render an AVI movie—from scratch.

Begin by selecting New from the File menu, which will clear out any existing filter graph. Next you'll need a source filter that points to the AVI file. From the list of DirectShow filters, select the entry labeled File Source (Async) and click the button marked Insert Filter. You'll immediately be presented with a file selection dialog box with the message "Select an input file for this filter to use." Select the AVI file Sunset.avi from the CD-ROM, and you should see the filter within GraphEdit, as shown in Figure 2-5.

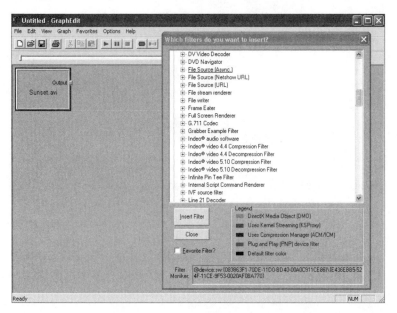

Figure 2-5   A source filter—the beginning of every DirectShow filter graph

The AVI file in the source filter needs to be divided into two streams, one with video data and one with audio data. The DirectShow transform filter AVI Splitter makes the division; insert it into the filter graph.

The source filter and the transform filter need to be connected, from the output pin of the source filter to the input pin of the transform filter. To make this connection, click the output pin of the source filter, drag the mouse pointer over the input pin of the transform filter, and release the mouse button, as shown in Figure 2-6.

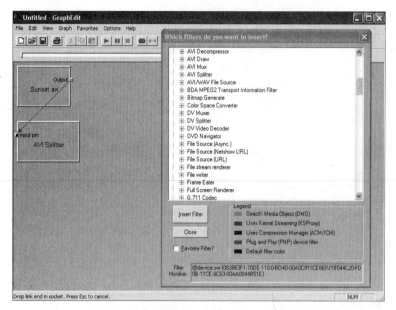

Figure 2-6 Creating a connection between an output pin and an input pin

GraphEdit automatically rearranges the filters so that they fit together smoothly, as Figure 2-7 shows.

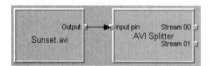

Figure 2-7 GraphEdit adjusting the position of the filter

The AVI Splitter transform filter produces two streams, which are available on output pins Stream 00 and Stream 01. Although it's less than clear from these labels, Stream 00 is a video stream and Stream 01 is an audio stream. (This confusing nomenclature is a result of the fact that an AVI file can have a wide variety of media types stored within, which means you couldn't appropriately name a pin VideoOut or AudioOut because there might be no video or audio in any given AVI file.) To render the audio stream, you need to insert the renderer filter Default DirectSound Device from the list of Audio Renderers in the Insert Filters dialog box. Connect output pin Stream 01 to the Audio Input pin of the renderer filter. Now your filter graph should look like the one shown in Figure 2-8.

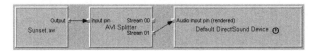

Figure 2-8   A DirectSound renderer filter added

Rendering the video is a two-step process. Because this AVI file contains digital video (DV) and audio data, a transform filter known as the DV Video Decoder must be added to the filter graph. Add the filter, and connect pin Stream 00 from the AVI Splitter filter to the XForm In pin of the DV Video Decoder. Finally a video renderer can be selected from the list of DirectShow filters. Although several types of video renderers are available—including full-screen and off-screen renderers—we'll use the generic Video Renderer, which sends the video to a window on the display that will be opened when the filter graph begins to run. Add the filter, and connect the output pin XForm Out from the DV Video Decoder to the Input pin of the Video Renderer. When it's all done, the filter graph will look like Figure 2-9.

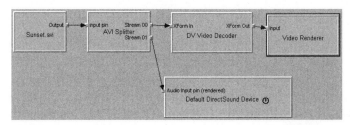

Figure 2-9   A complete filter graph rendering both audio and video streams of the AVI file

At this point, click Play. A new window titled ActiveMovie Window will open on the screen and display the AVI file as it plays, as shown in Figure 2-10. The window's title bar is a holdover from the time, a few years back, when DirectShow was known as ActiveMovie. (The movie has a silent soundtrack, so don't expect to hear anything from the speakers as the movie is playing.)

That's what it takes to create a filter graph from scratch; filters have to be inserted into the filter graph manually and connected appropriately. However, GraphEdit provides two alternative techniques to speed the creation of filter graphs: rendering pins and Intelligent Connect.

Figure 2-10   The AVI file in mid-playback

Creating Filter Graphs with Rendering Pins

Another technique that quickly renders media files from within GraphEdit uses rendering pins. Starting from an empty filter graph, add a File Source (Async) source filter to the filter graph and select Sunset.avi as the input file. Right-click the output pin of the filter. You'll see the menu shown in Figure 2-11.

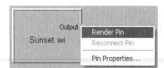

Figure 2-11   The pin menu with per-pin options on each filter

Select Render Pin. The resulting filter graph should be identical to the filter graph you built from scratch—without the additional steps of finding the correct DirectShow filters, inserting them into the filter graph, and connecting them appropriately. You can "Render Pin" from any output pin in the filter graph, not just a source filter. You can use this feature to finish a partially complete filter graph or, as in this case, to build the entire filter graph.

Simplifying Design Tasks with Intelligent Connect

In Chapter 1, you used the filter graph to connect output pins that accepted different media types by stringing a set of intermediate transform filters between the pins. This feature, known as Intelligent Connect, allows the filter graph to assume most of the heavy lifting involved in graph building. This same feature can be put to work in your DirectShow programs to simplify coding tasks in many situations. Intelligent Connect is turned on in GraphEdit by default. (To turn it off, clear the Connect Intelligent menu option in the Graph menu.)

To use Intelligent Connect, begin by creating a filter graph with two filters: first a File Source (Async) filter, pointing to the file Sunset.avi, and next a Video Renderer filter. You've now got a filter graph with a source filter and a renderer filter, but no transform filters. However, GraphEdit will let you create a connection from the output pin of the source filter to the input pin of the renderer filter, as shown in Figure 2-12.

Figure 2-12   A source filter can't be connected directly to a renderer filter, unless…

This connection won't work on its own. The media type of the output pin of the source filter does not agree with the media type required by the input pin of the video renderer. That's when Intelligent Connect steps in and adds the intermediate filters needed to transform AVI file data into video that can be rendered to the display, as shown in Figure 2-13.

Figure 2-13   …Intelligent Connect is used, in which case intermediate transform filters are added.

The filter graph has added AVI Splitter and DV Video Decoder transform filters, both of which are needed to translate the output of the source filter into video data that can be rendered to the display. Note that the audio stream hasn't been rendered. Rather than rendering the media file, Intelligent Connect simply found a path to connect a source filter to a renderer filter. If the renderer filter had been a Default DirectSound Device rather than a Video Renderer, the resulting filter graph would have looked like Figure 2-14.

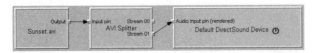

Figure 2-14   A source filter connected to an audio renderer requiring one transform filter

Capturing Video from a Digital Camcorder to Disk

One of the most important capabilities of DirectShow is its ability to make quick work of the various audio and video capture devices, such as DV camcorders, which have become increasingly popular in the last few years. Many PCs have IEEE 1394 (FireWire) connectors so that DV camcorders can be plugged directly into a PC for digital capture, editing, and production of video material. In particular, Microsoft Windows XP makes it very easy to work with digital camcorders, and the inclusion of Windows Movie Maker provides a level of software support for the digital camcorder that hasn't been seen before in Windows systems. For the rest of this chapter, we'll assume that there's a DV camcorder attached to your computer system, most probably through a high-speed IEEE 1394 interface.

You'll now use GraphEdit to create a filter graph that will take the input from the capture source filter representing the DV camcorder and write that data out to disk as a high-resolution AVI movie file. To begin, clear the filter graph with the New item from the File menu. Now open the Insert Filters dialog box, and open the list of Video Capture Sources. Depending on how many video capture devices are attached to your system, this list could be quite long or could contain just one entry.

> **Note**   If you don't see anything on the list, make sure your camera is on and plugged in to your computer correctly. If you still don't see anything on the list, you might be having a problem with the drivers associated with your DV camcorder. Windows XP includes a standard driver for camcorders connected with IEEE 1394, but your camcorder won't necessarily work correctly with that driver.

Somewhere in the list you'll see the entry Microsoft DV Camera And VCR. This is the standard DirectShow filter that acts as a capture source filter for both digital camcorders and VCRs. Add the filter to the filter graph. Next add the DV Splitter from the list of DirectShow filters and connect the DV A/V Out pin from the source filter to the Input pin of the DV Splitter filter. The DV Splitter, as the name suggests, splits the audio/video (A/V) stream coming from the source filter into two streams, an audio stream identified on an output pin as AudOut00 and a video stream identified as DVVidOut0.

You would like to be able to monitor the video stream so that you can see what's coming out of the camera as the video stream is being written to disk. For you to do so, the video stream must be split into two components, which can be done using a DirectShow transform filter known as the Smart Tee. When this transform filter is inserted into the filter graph, the DV Splitter output pin DVVidOut0 should be connected to its input pin. The Smart Tee has two output pins, appropriately labeled Capture and Preview. If you use the Render Pin function on the Preview pin of the Smart Tee, you get a filter graph that can monitor the output of the camcorder. The filter graph should now look like Figure 2-15.

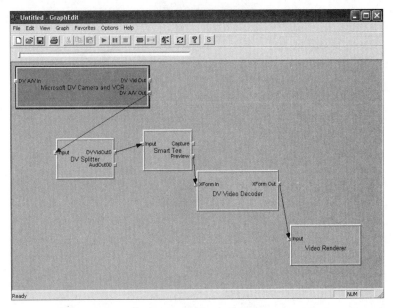

Figure 2-15   An incomplete filter graph for DV camcorder capture and monitoring

At this point, the separate audio and video streams have to be recombined (or *multiplexed*) into a single stream so that they can be written to a file. Add the AVI Mux DirectShow transform filter to the graph. The AVI Mux has one input pin, Input 01. Connect the output pin Capture from the Smart Tee to this input pin, and a second input pin, Input 02, appears on the AVI Mux. (This process will keep going indefinitely; as you add inputs, the AVI Mux adds pins.) Connect the AudOut00 pin from the DV splitter to the Input 02 pin on the AVI Mux. Now the AVI Mux is mixing the video and audio streams from the camcorder into a single AVI-formatted stream. Finally add a File Writer renderer filter from the Insert Filters dialog box. Doing so will open a file-selection dialog box that asks for an output file name. Call this file *DVCAM.AVI*. Once the filter has been added to the filter graph, connect the AVI Out pin of the AVI Mux to the In pin of the DVCAM.AVI File Writer. The completed filter graph should look like Figure 2-16.

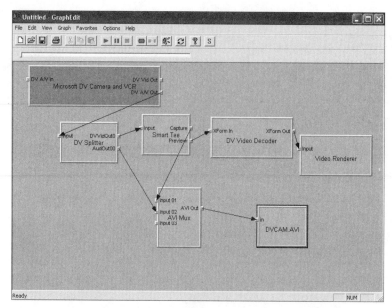

Figure 2-16   The complete filter graph for DV camcorder capture and monitoring

When you click Play, a monitor window will open on the display, showing the live output from the camcorder, as shown in Figure 2-17.

Figure 2-17   The DV capture filter graph displaying the live output from the camcorder

AVI files get big very quickly, at the rate of about 250 MB per minute, so make sure you have plenty of disk space available when you run this filter graph. After you click the Stop button, an AVI file named DVCAM.AVI is on the disk. This file can be played in the Windows Media Player, or you can use the Render Media File menu item in GraphEdit to play it. You'll see that the filter graph faithfully captured the camera's output to disk.

Filter graphs created by GraphEdit can be saved to disk or opened from disk. If you choose Save Graph from the application's File menu, you can save the filter graph to a file with a .GRF extension. GraphEdit will open .GRF files and other GraphEdit files, so if you're tinkering with a filter graph design, you can save work in progress and return to it later.

Using Windows Media for File Storage

For a final example using GraphEdit, we'll adopt a more streamlined approach to file storage. Although the high resolution of AVI files is attractive, AVI files quickly fill up an entire disk with video data. Windows Media is an alternative solution for video storage; it's as much as several hundred times more efficient for the storage of A/V streams in disk files.

To convert your existing AVI-creating filter graph into one that creates Windows Media files, remove the AVI Mux and File Writer filters from the filter graph. Now you need to add a renderer filter that will create a Windows Media Advanced Streaming Format (ASF) stream. You'll find the WM ASF Writer in the list of DirectShow filters. When you insert the filter, it will ask you to select an output file name. Use the name *DVCAM.ASF* for the output file. Now connect AudOut00 from the DV Splitter to the Audio Input 01 pin of the WM ASF Writer filter, and connect the Capture pin of the Smart Tee to the Video Input 01 pin of the WM ASF Writer. Intelligent Connect will automatically add a DV Video Decoder as an intermediate step between the Smart Tee and the WM ASF Writer. You should get a filter graph that looks like Figure 2-18.

When you click Play, the monitor window will once again show the live feed from the camcorder. After you click Stop, look for the file DVCAM.ASF. It should be much smaller. For example, a 10-second AVI file comes in at around 40 MB. A 10-second ASF file should be about 250 KB. These ASF files can be played in the Windows Media Player, or you can use the Render Media File capability inside GraphEdit.

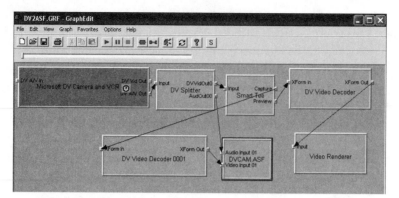

Figure 2-18 DV capture filter graph that produces smaller ASF files

Setting Filter Properties

The WM ASF Writer offers a wide range of options for the degree of file compression in its output files. These options are accessible to the DirectShow programmer through COM, but they're also available to the GraphEdit user. Right-click the WM ASF Writer and select Filter Properties. You'll see the properties dialog box shown in Figure 2-19.

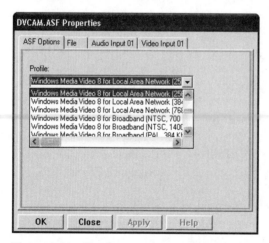

Figure 2-19 The filter properties dialog box for the WM ASF Writer renderer filter

In the Profile drop-down list, you can select from a broad array of compression techniques. The WM ASF Writer filter will create a 256-Kbps stream by default, but streams from 28.8 Kbps (suitable for modem users) all the way up to 1500 Kbps (for use on LANs) can be created. The greater the bandwidth, the better the image quality—and the larger the files.

Most DirectShow filters have properties that can be examined from GraphEdit, and each pin on a filter has its own pin properties, also accessible through a right-click of the mouse. The pin properties are interesting to look at because you can see which media types an output pin can transmit and which media types an input pin can receive. It's an easy way to determine whether two filters are compatible. You can also examine the pin properties of connected pins, which will show you the actual media type of a pin-to-pin connection.

Summary

At this point, we've covered all the basics with GraphEdit, and you've created a number of DirectShow filter graphs useful for both media playback and media capture. Now it's time to move into the realm of C++ programming where we can create some real-world DirectShow applications.

3

Programming DirectShow Applications

Although sample DirectShow filter graphs can be constructed and tested in GraphEdit, application programmers want to use standard programming languages—either C or C++—to construct DirectShow applications. Although Visual Basic is an easy-to-learn and fully functional programming environment, the Visual Basic support for DirectShow programming interfaces is minimal. If you're a Visual Basic programmer, don't despair: nearly everything that follows is useful information, even if it can't be directly applied to your programming needs. For the purposes of this text, we'll be using the Microsoft Visual C++ integrated development environment, which provides a robust platform for the design and testing of DirectShow applications.

The design of a DirectShow application is straightforward and generally has three logical parts: initialization, where the application environment is established, followed by the construction of the DirectShow filter graph; execution, when the filter graph enters the running state and processes a stream of data; and cleanup, when data structures are deallocated and system resources released. This isn't significantly different from the model used by any other Windows application, and as a result, DirectShow applications can be combined with existing Windows applications very easily.

Before we can dive in and create a simple "media player" using Direct-Show, a player that can be used to play any media types for which there are corresponding DirectShow filters (at the very least, these will include AVI, WAV, and Windows Media files), we need to cover some ground for programmers unfamiliar with the Microsoft Component Object Model (COM) programming interfaces. The DirectShow programming interfaces to filters and filter graphs present themselves as COM objects, so most DirectShow applications are COM-intensive. Although this might sound daunting, you don't need to know very much about COM to write fully functional DirectShow programs.

COM Basics

During the 1990s, as operating systems and application programs grew progressively more complex, software architects struggled with the need to produce reusable code objects that could, through clearly defined interfaces, be reused throughout an operating system or application program. Such objects could simplify the design of programs dramatically. Rather than rely on native functionality, which could dramatically increase the complexity of a program, the programmer could call on these reusable code objects as needed.

For example, a word processor and an e-mail client both need access to a spelling checker—so why write two spelling checkers when a reusable code object could be invoked by both programs when needed? In the ideal case, nothing would need to be known about the reusable code object other than its name. Once the programmer included this ideal object, the program would be able to query it to determine its properties. Like a normal object, this object would have data and methods, both of which would be accessible (if public) to the invoking program. In short, the ideal reusable code object would act just like code written by the programmer.

By the mid-1990s, Microsoft had introduced COM, its version of the reusable code object. Although the first generations of COM were somewhat rough in their design, nearly a decade of refinement has produced a level of functionality that begins to approach the ideal of the reusable code object. A COM object, like a C++ object, has properties that can be inspected, methods to be invoked, and interfaces that illustrate characteristics inherited from base classes. The creator of a COM object can choose to hide or reveal any of these qualities, producing an object that is both easy to manage and easy to use.

Naming and GUIDs

As in the case of the ideal reusable code object, the only thing you need to know about a COM object is its name. However, this name isn't a string of Roman characters; it's a globally unique identifier (GUID), a string of hexadecimal numbers, in the format of 32 bits–16 bits–16 bits–16 bits–44 bits. The GUID is guaranteed to be unique, so each COM object has a unique name. (This is true only for COM objects you've created yourself if you follow Microsoft's rules for the creation of new GUIDs. Those details are available through the developer support section of Microsoft's Web site.) Fortunately, you don't have to remember these meaningless strings of numbers; each COM object used by DirectShow has been given a C++ defined name, also known as a *class ID*. The class ID is English-readable and easy to understand. For example, the COM object that represents a filter graph has the class ID *CLSID_FilterGraph*, which represents the GUID *e436ebb8-542f-11ce-9f53-0020af0ba770* (and thank goodness for that). The class ID provides the symbolic name that you'll use to instantiate a COM object.

Initializing and Releasing COM

Before COM can be used within a DirectShow application, the COM facilities must be initialized. (If you have multiple execution threads in your application, each thread must be initialized separately.) To initialize COM, add the following line of source code to the initialization routine of the application:

```
CoInitializeEx(NULL, COINIT_APARTMENTTHREADED) //Initializes COM
```

After COM has been initialized, calls to the COM libraries can be made in any desired fashion. Before the application terminates its execution, COM must be shut down again. (Failure to shut down COM could result in execution errors when another program attempts to use COM services .) To release COM services, add this line of code to the application's cleanup code:

```
CoUninitialize();      // Releases COM
```

No calls to the COM services can be made after COM has been uninitialized.

Creating an Instance of a COM Object

Once COM services have been initialized in DirectShow, you will likely make a number of COM invocations to create instances of COM objects. These calls will create various objects needed by the application, such as filters. One of the first COM invocations in any DirectShow application will generally be a call to create the Filter Graph Manager, an object that handles the internal details of the filter graph. (The filter graph isn't an object per se, but a logical construction consisting of several COM objects working closely together.)

The COM routine *CoCreateInstance* is used to create COM objects. In the case of the Filter Graph Manager, the code to create it might look like this:

```
IGraphBuilder *graphBuilder = NULL;    // Pointer to created object
HRESULT hr = CoCreateInstance(CLSID_FilterGraph,
                    NULL,
                    CLSCTX_INPROC_SERVER,
```

```
                IID_IGraphBuilder,
                (void **)&pGraphBuilder);
```

The *CoCreateInstance* call takes five arguments, beginning with a class ID—in this case *CLSID_FilterGraph*—which requests that a COM object representative of a filter graph (really, a Filter Graph Manager) be created. The *NULL* parameter indicates that this is not an aggregate object, which will be the case in any DirectShow application. The value *CLSCTX_INPROC_SERVER* indicates the that the COM object is being loaded from an in-process (local to your application) DLL. This value is always present in this parameter.

The next argument is an interface ID, which informs COM of the unique interface being requested by the caller. In this case, the value is *IID_IGraphBuilder*, which means that you will be retrieving the object's *IGraphBuilder* interface, which has methods for building filter graphs. Later, you'll need to use another interface on the same object, *IMediaControl*, which provides methods to start, stop, and pause the graph. The pointer address is returned in the last parameter. This pointer is cast as *void***, a generic pointer to a pointer, because the function could return a pointer to any number of objects.

Nearly every COM invocation returns a status code of some sort or another; this code should always be examined for error values, using the macros SUCCEEDED and FAILED to test for success or failure. A COM call that generates an error indicates either a logical error in the program or some failure of the operating system to fulfill a request, perhaps because resources already in use or as yet uninitialized have been requested by the program.

When you're through with a COM interface, you need to invoke its *Release* method so that the object will know how to delete itself at the appropriate time. For the preceding code fragment, this method might look like this:

```
pGraphBuilder->Release();  // Release the object
pGraphBuilder = NULL;      // And set it to NULL
```

If you fail to release COM interfaces, objects will not get deleted and you'll clutter up your memory, suffer a performance hit, and possibly confuse the operating system into thinking that resources are being used after you've finished with them. So make sure you clean up after your COM invocations.

Querying Interfaces in COM Objects

After an object has been instantiated through a COM call, a DirectShow application will often need access to additional interfaces on the object. For example, if an application programmer wants to have control over the execution of the filter graph, a pointer to the Filter Graph Manager's *IMediaControl* interface will have to be acquired. It's the same object being manipulated in either case, but each interface presents unique methods and properties suited for a particular task.

To acquire this interface, you need to send a query (request) to the object using any of its interfaces that you have already obtained. In this case, we already have its *IGraphBuilder* interface, so we'll use that interface. If we assume that the code fragment in the previous section has already executed successfully, that call might look like this:

```
IMediaControl *pMediaControl = NULL;    // Store pointer to interface
hr = pGraphBuilder->QueryInterface(IID_MediaControl,
                                   (void**)&pMediaControl);
```

The *QueryInterface* method takes two parameters. The first parameter is the interface ID (a GUID) for the requested interface. In this case, the interface ID references the *IMediaControl* interface. The second parameter is a pointer to a storage location for the returned interface. Once again, an error code will be returned if the query fails.

Using COM Objects

For the most part, objects instantiated through calls to *CoCreateInstance* behave just as a standard, well-designed C++ object would. Once it's been instantiated, a COM object can be treated much like any other C++ object that has been created on the heap. It must be released when it's no longer needed, and it provides a portable container for properties and methods that will work across any application in the operating system's environment. Every interface on a COM object inherits from the *IUnknown* interface, which, in addition to *QueryInterface*, has two other methods that control the object's lifetime. Each time a COM object returns any of its interfaces to a client (such as your application) through the initial call to *CoCreateInstance* or later calls to *QueryInterface*, it calls its own *AddRef* method to increment its reference count. When a client is finished with an interface, it must call *Release*, and the COM object decrements its reference count by one. When the count reaches zero, meaning there are no outstanding interface pointers, the object deletes itself. That is why failure to call *Release* after you finish with an interface results in memory leaks.

All DirectShow filters are COM objects—including those you create for yourself—so when we get into the subject of writing your own filters, we'll cover the internal construction of COM objects in much greater detail.

Configuration of Visual Studio .NET for DirectShow Programming

The development environment used in this book for DirectShow applications is the Microsoft Visual Studio .NET integrated development environment. The Visual C++ and Visual Basic programming languages are included in Visual Studio .NET, and they provide the raw platform for the creation of Windows applications.

Beyond Visual Studio .NET, the DirectX 9.0 Software Development Kit (SDK) is an essential element in the creation of DirectShow applications. The DirectX 9.0 SDK contains all the source files, headers, and libraries (along with a lot of helpful documentation) that will need to be linked with your own source code to create a functional DirectShow application.

If you already have Visual Studio .NET installed on the computer you'll be using for DirectShow application development, you might need to check whether the correct DirectX 9.0 SDK directories are in the include paths for the Visual C++ compiler and linker. (You'll know pretty quickly if your environment hasn't been set up correctly because your applications will generate errors during the compile or linking phases of program generation.)

To inspect the settings for your projects, open the Property Pages dialog box for your Visual C++ project. In the C/C++ folder, examine the value of the field labeled Additional Include Directories. The file path for the DirectX 9.0 SDK include files should be the first value in that field.

After you've ensured that the DirectX 9.0 SDK include files are available to the compiler, click on the folder labeled Linker and examine the value of the field Additional Dependencies. Here you should find a file path that points to the DirectX 9.0 SDK object libraries. If you don't, add the file path to the list of other file paths (if any) in the field.

At this point, Visual Studio .NET is ready for your programming projects. To test it, open the project DSRender (on the CD-ROM) and try to build it. If it compiles and executes without errors, everything has been set up correctly. If you have problems, ensure that the DirectX 9.0 SDK has been installed correctly.

Now, with all these important essentials out of the way, let's take a look at DSRender, our first peek at a DirectShow application program. Like many of the other projects presented in this book, it's designed for console-mode operation. This means that many of the Windows API calls that deal with the particulars of the graphical user interface—windows, menus, dialog boxes, and the like— have been left out of the project, leaving only the meat of the DirectShow application. The code samples provided with this book are designed to become the kernels of your own DirectShow applications, so the code is "clean" and uncluttered by the requirements of a fully loaded Windows application.

DSRender: A DirectShow Media Player in C++

DSRender, one of the simplest DirectShow applications to write, would be among the most difficult to engineer without DirectShow. The application's action is straightforward: it displays an Open File dialog box, allows the user to select a file, and then attempts to render that file on the user's computer. The media type doesn't matter—it could be an AVI movie, a WAV sound, Windows Media, an MP3 song, or an MPEG movie. As long as there are DirectShow filters to handle the specifics of the file format, the file will be rendered.

Examining *main*

The source code file DSRender.cpp has only three functions, including the standard C/C++ function *main*, the entry point for the program. It's the only function of interest to us, so here it is in all its (brief) glory:

```
// DSRender.cpp
// A very simple program to render media files using DirectShow
//
int main(int argc, char* argv[])
{
    IGraphBuilder *pGraph = NULL;    // Graph builder interface
    IMediaControl *pControl = NULL;  // Media control interface
    IMediaEvent   *pEvent = NULL;    // Media event interface

    if (!GetMediaFileName()) {  // Local function to get a file name
        return(0);              // If we didn't get it, exit
    }

    // Initialize the COM library.
    HRESULT hr = CoInitializeEx(NULL, COINIT_APARTMENTTHREADED);
    if (FAILED(hr))
    {
        // We'll send our error messages to the console.
        printf("ERROR - Could not initialize COM library");
        return hr;
    }

    // Create the Filter Graph Manager and query for interfaces.
    hr = CoCreateInstance(CLSID_FilterGraph, NULL, CLSCTX_INPROC_SERVER,
                          IID_IGraphBuilder, (void **)&pGraph);
    if (FAILED(hr))    // FAILED is a macro that tests the return value
    {
```

```
            printf("ERROR - Could not create the Filter Graph Manager.");
            return hr;
    }


    // Use IGraphBuilder::QueryInterface (inherited from IUnknown)
    // to get the IMediaControl interface.
    hr = pGraph->QueryInterface(IID_IMediaControl, (void **)&pControl);
    if (FAILED(hr))
    {
        printf("ERROR - Could not obtain the Media Control interface.");
        pGraph->Release();// Clean up after ourselves
        pGraph = NULL;
        CoUninitialize();   // And uninitialize COM
        return hr;
    }


    // And get the Media Event interface, too.
    hr = pGraph->QueryInterface(IID_IMediaEvent, (void **)&pEvent);
    if (FAILED(hr))
    {
        printf("ERROR - Could not obtain the Media Event interface.");
        pGraph->Release();     // Clean up after ourselves
        pControl->Release();
        CoUninitialize();  // And uninitialize COM
        return hr;
    }


    // To build the filter graph, only one call is required.
    // We make the RenderFile call to the Filter Graph Manager
    // to which we pass the name of the media file.
#ifndef UNICODE
    WCHAR wFileName[MAX_PATH];
    MultiByteToWideChar(CP_ACP, 0, g_PathFileName, -1, wFileName,
                        MAX_PATH);
    // This is all that's required to create a filter graph
    // that will render a media file!
    hr = pGraph->RenderFile((LPCWSTR)wFileName, NULL);
#else
    hr = pGraph->RenderFile((LPCWSTR)g_PathFileName, NULL);
#endif

    if (SUCCEEDED(hr))
    {
        // Run the graph.
        hr = pControl->Run();
        if (SUCCEEDED(hr))
        {
            // Wait for completion.
```

```
        long evCode;
        pEvent->WaitForCompletion(INFINITE, &evCode);

        // Note: Do not use INFINITE in a real application
        // because it can block indefinitely.
    }

    // And stop the filter graph.
    hr = pControl->Stop();

    // Before we finish, save the filter graph to a file.
    SaveGraphFile(pGraph, L"C:\\MyGraph.GRF");
    }

    // Now release everything and clean up.
    pControl->Release();
    pEvent->Release();
    pGraph->Release();
    CoUninitialize();

    return 0;
}
```

Understanding DSRender Line by Line

We've walked through much of the code in the section "COM Basics" earlier in this chapter. The application enters at *main*, sets up storage for a few variables (pointers to COM objects), and gets a file name with a call to the local function *GetMediaFileName* (peek at the source code if you need to see the details of that basic Windows function), and then initializes COM with a call to *CoInitialize*.

If all of this has proceeded successfully (and it should), the application next instantiates a Filter Graph Manager object with a call to *CoCreateInstance*, and obtains in that same call the *IGraphBuilder* interface on that object, which provides methods that allow you to build a filter graph. Once the *IGraph-Builder* interface has been obtained (if this fails, this might indicate problems with DirectX or the operating system), two *QueryInterface* method calls are made to retrieve additional interfaces that are exposed by the Filter Graph Manager. The first of these calls returns an *IMediaControl* interface, which has methods for changing the execution state of the filter graph, as explained previously. The second of these calls requests an *IMediaEvent* object. The *IMedia-Event* interface provides a way for the filter graph to signal its own state changes to the DirectShow application. In this case, *IMediaEvent* will be used to track the progress of media playback, and it will pause execution of the application until playback is done. (For operating system geeks: this is possible because the DirectShow filters execute in a different thread from the Direct-Show application.)

Now some magic happens. With just a single line of code, the entire filter graph is built. When the *IGraphBuilder* method *RenderFile* is invoked (with the name of the media file), the Filter Graph Manager object examines the media file's type and determines the appropriate set of filters—source, transform, and renderer—that need to be added to the filter graph. These filters are added to the filter graph and then connected together. If *RenderFile* returns without errors, DirectShow found a path from source to renderer. If the call to *Render-File* fails, DirectShow lacked the filters to play the media file—or perhaps the file was corrupted.

With the filter graph built, a one-line call to the *IMediaControl* interface invoking its *Run* method begins execution of the filter graph. Although the filter graph begins executing, the *Run* method returns immediately because the data streaming code is running in a separate thread that has been started by the source filter. Media file playback commences. If the media file is a movie, a playback window will open on the display; if it's a sound file, there won't be any visible sign of playback, but sounds should start coming from the computer's speakers. Figure 3-1 shows an AVI file being played.

Figure 3-1   DSRender playing the AVI file Sunset.avi

This application, as written, needs to pause during playback of the media file. If it didn't, the application would terminate just after the filter graph had started playback, and that wouldn't be very useful. This is where the *IMedia-*

Event interface comes into play. Invoking its *WaitForCompletion* method with a value of *INFINITE* causes the application to wait until the Filter Graph Manager learns that the media file has completed its playback. In a real-world application, you wouldn't use a value of *INFINITE* in the call to *WaitForCompletion*; if something happened to stall or halt the playback of the media file, the application would wait—forever. This is fine for a first DirectShow example, but other programming examples in this book will show you how to exploit the *IMedia-Event* interface more effectively.

After playback is complete, a call to the *Stop* method of the *IMediaControl* object halts the execution of the filter graph. This stop call is necessary because a filter graph doesn't stop by itself when a media file has been fully rendered.

Saving a Filter Graph to a .GRF File

Immediately after the filter graph is stopped, you'll see a call to a local function, *SaveFilterGraph*, which takes two arguments: a pointer to the *IGraphBuilder* interface and a file name. *SaveFilterGraph* saves a GraphEdit-viewable copy of the filter graph, so you can see the filter graph that's been built by DSRender. Here's the code for *SaveFilterGraph*:

```
// Pass it a file name in wszPath, and it will save the filter graph
// to that file.
HRESULT SaveGraphFile(IGraphBuilder *pGraph, WCHAR *wszPath)
{
    const WCHAR wszStreamName[] = L"ActiveMovieGraph";
    HRESULT hr;
    IStorage *pStorage = NULL;

    // First, create a document file that will hold the GRF file
    hr = StgCreateDocfile(
        wszPath,
        STGM_CREATE | STGM_TRANSACTED | STGM_READWRITE |
            STGM_SHARE_EXCLUSIVE,
        0, &pStorage);
    if(FAILED(hr))
    {
        return hr;
    }

    // Next, create a stream to store.
    IStream *pStream;
    hr = pStorage->CreateStream(
        wszStreamName,
        STGM_WRITE | STGM_CREATE | STGM_SHARE_EXCLUSIVE,
        0, 0, &pStream);
```

```
if (FAILED(hr))
{
    pStorage->Release();
    return hr;
}

// The IpersistStream::Save method converts a stream
// into a persistent object.
IPersistStream *pPersist = NULL;
pGraph->QueryInterface(IID_IPersistStream,
                    reinterpret_cast<void**>(&pPersist));
hr = pPersist->Save(pStream, TRUE);
pStream->Release();
pPersist->Release();
if (SUCCEEDED(hr))
{
    hr = pStorage->Commit(STGC_DEFAULT);
}
pStorage->Release();
return hr;
}
```

This function is straightforward, although it uses a few components we haven't yet encountered. Beginning with a call to the Windows function *Stg-CreateDocfile*, an output file is opened, creating an *IStorage* object (in other words, an object that exposes the *IStorage* interface) that represents the file. (Note that this is an example of a COM object that is not created directly through *CoCreateInstance* but rather through a helper function.) Next an *IStream* stream object is created; this stream is used to provide a data path to the output file. The magic in this function happens when the Filter Graph Manager's *IPersistStream* interface is obtained by a call to the *QueryInterface* method of *IGraphBuilder*. The *IPersistStream* interface contains methods that create *persistent* stream objects, which can be written to a storage medium such as a file and retrieved later. When the *Save* method of *IPersistStream* is invoked—with a parameter that points to the *IStream* object—the filter graph data structure is written to the stream.

If all of this goes as planned, a call to the *Commit* method of the *IStorage* interface writes the data to disk. At this point, a "snapshot" of the filter graph has been written out. This program uses the hard-coded string C:\MyGraph.GRF as the file name, but this name can be modified by you to any system-legal file path and name. After you run DSRender you'll find the file MyGraph.GRF on your hard disk. Double-click it and GraphEdit will launch; you'll see the filter graph created by DSRender. This filter graph will vary, depending on the media type of the file being rendered. Figure 3-2 shows the MyGraph.GRF filter graph.

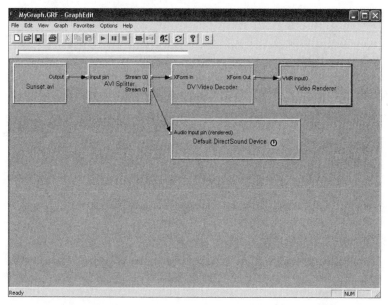

Figure 3-2   GraphEdit showing the filter graph MyGraph.GRF created by DSRender

DSRender is a very slapdash example of a DirectShow application—no frills, no extra UI details, just media playback. Yet a very broad set of media can be played with this simple application because the DirectShow *IGraphBuilder* object handles the hard work of selecting and connecting the appropriate filters together to create a functional filter graph. Now we need to move on and learn how to do the heavy lifting for ourselves, building a filter graph in C++ code line by line. Well, mostly....

DSBuild: Building a Filter Graph (Mostly) Manually

The DSBuild application does most of the heavy lifting involved in creating an audio player for a wide variety of audio formats—essentially any audio format supported by DirectShow, including the audio tracks of AVI and Windows Media movies. The application code creates a Filter Graph Manager object and then creates two filters: a source filter (which points to a disk file) and an audio renderer filter. Then, using the Intelligent Connect capability of the Filter Graph Manager, the application connects the output pin of the source filter to the input pin of the audio renderer, adding the necessary intermediate transform filters to provide a path between source and renderer. Once that path has been created, the filter graph begins execution, plays the media file until completion, and then stops.

Examining *main*, Again

The source code in file DSBuild.cpp has four functions, and three of these are nearly identical to their counterparts in DSRender.cpp. The extra function, *Get-Pin*, will be examined in detail in the section "Locating Pins and *GetPin*" a bit further along. We need to begin with a detailed examination of *main*, which initially looks a lot like the version in DSRender.cpp.

```
// DSBuild implements a very simple program to render audio files
// or the audio portion of movies.
//
int main(int argc, char* argv[])
{
    IGraphBuilder *pGraph = NULL;
    IMediaControl *pControl = NULL;
    IMediaEvent   *pEvent = NULL;
    IBaseFilter   *pInputFileFilter = NULL;
    IBaseFilter   *pDSoundRenderer = NULL;
    IPin          *pFileOut = NULL, *pWAVIn = NULL;

    // Get the name of an audio or movie file to play.
    if (!GetMediaFileName()) {
        return(0);
    }

    // Initialize the COM library.
    HRESULT hr = CoInitializeEx(NULL, COINIT_APARTMENTTHREADED);
    if (FAILED(hr))
    {
        printf("ERROR - Could not initialize COM library");
        return hr;
    }

    // Create the Filter Graph Manager object and retrieve its
    // IGraphBuilder interface.
    hr = CoCreateInstance(CLSID_FilterGraph, NULL, CLSCTX_INPROC_SERVER,
                        IID_IGraphBuilder, (void **)&pGraph);
    if (FAILED(hr))
    {
        printf("ERROR - Could not create the Filter Graph Manager.");
        CoUninitialize();
```

```
        return hr;
    }


    // Now get the media control interface...
    hr = pGraph->QueryInterface(IID_IMediaControl, (void **)&pControl);
    if (FAILED(hr)) {
        pGraph->Release();
        CoUninitialize();
        return hr;
    }


    // And the media event interface.
    hr = pGraph->QueryInterface(IID_IMediaEvent, (void **)&pEvent);
    if (FAILED(hr)) {
        pControl->Release();
        pGraph->Release();
        CoUninitialize();
        return hr;
    }


    // Build the graph.
    // Step one is to invoke AddSourceFilter
    // with the file name we picked out earlier.
    // Should be an audio file (or a movie file with an audio track).
    // AddSourceFilter instantiates the source filter,
    // adds it to the graph, and returns a pointer to the filter's
    // IBaseFilter interface.
#ifndef UNICODE
    WCHAR wFileName[MAX_PATH];
    MultiByteToWideChar(CP_ACP, 0, g_PathFileName, -1, wFileName, MAX_PATH);
    hr = pGraph->AddSourceFilter(wFileName, wFileName, &pInputFileFilter);
#else
    hr = pGraph->AddSourceFilter(wFileName, wFileName, &pInputFileFilter);
#endif


    if (SUCCEEDED(hr)) {

        // Now create an instance of the audio renderer
        // and obtain a pointer to its IBaseFilter interface.
        hr = CoCreateInstance(CLSID_DSoundRender, NULL,
                         CLSCTX_INPROC_SERVER, IID_IBaseFilter,
                         (void **)&pDSoundRenderer);

        if (SUCCEEDED(hr)) {

            // And add the filter to the filter graph
            // using the member function AddFilter.
            hr = pGraph->AddFilter(pDSoundRenderer, L"Audio Renderer");
```

```
    if (SUCCEEDED(hr)) {

            // Now we need to connect the output pin of the source
            // to the input pin of the renderer.
            // Obtain the output pin of the source filter.
            // The local function GetPin does this.
            pFileOut = GetPin(pInputFileFilter, PINDIR_OUTPUT);

            if (pFileOut != NULL) {   // Is the pin good?

                // Obtain the input pin of the WAV renderer.
                pWAVIn = GetPin(pDSoundRenderer, PINDIR_INPUT);

                if (pWAVIn != NULL) {   // Is the pin good?

                    // Connect the pins together:
                    // We use the Filter Graph Manager's
                    // member function Connect,
                    // which uses Intelligent Connect.
                    // If this fails, DirectShow couldn't
                    // render the media file.
                    hr = pGraph->Connect(pFileOut, pWAVIn);
                }
            }
        }
    }


    if (SUCCEEDED(hr))
    {
        // Run the graph.
        hr = pControl->Run();
        if (SUCCEEDED(hr))
        {
            // Wait for completion.
            long evCode;
            pEvent->WaitForCompletion(INFINITE, &evCode);

            // Note: Do not use INFINITE in a real application
            // because it can block indefinitely.
        }
        hr = pControl->Stop();
    }

    // Before we finish, save the filter graph to a file.
    SaveGraphFile(pGraph, L"C:\\MyGraph.GRF");

    // Now release everything we instantiated--
    // that is, if it got instantiated.
```

```
    if(pFileOut) {                // If it exists, non-NULL
        pFileOut->Release();      // Then release it
    }
    if (pWAVIn) {
        pWAVIn->Release();
    }
    if (pInputFileFilter) {
        pInputFileFilter->Release();
    }
    if (pDSoundRenderer) {
        pDSoundRenderer->Release();
    }
    pControl->Release();
    pEvent->Release();
    pGraph->Release();
    CoUninitialize();

    return 0;
}
```

The opening lines of the function are essentially the same as those from DSRender. A Filter Graph Manager object is instantiated through a COM call, and subsequent *QueryInterface* calls return pointers to its *IMediaControl* and *IMediaEvent* interfaces. That's everything needed to begin building the filter graph. At this point, we use a new method of *IGraphBuilder*, *AddSourceFilter*, which takes a file name as a parameter and returns a pointer to an *IBaseFilter* interface on the filter that was chosen and instantiated. The *IBaseFilter* interface is exposed by all DirectShow filters.

Next the audio renderer filter is created using *CoCreateInstance*, with a class ID value of *CLSID_DSoundRender*, which returns the *IBaseFilter* interface for that object. Once that filter has been created successfully, it is added to the filter graph with the ingeniously named *IGraphBuilder* method *AddFilter*. The *AddFilter* method takes two parameters. The first parameter is a pointer to the *IBaseFilter* interface on the filter to be added, while the second parameter is an application-defined string used to identify the filter. (You can use this string to name the filter whatever you like. This feature is particularly worthwhile when examining a filter graph in GraphEdit.)

Now we have two filters in the filter graph: a source filter pointing to the file and an audio output filter. They need to be connected together, probably through a path of transform filters. The transform filters required to connect source to renderer will vary by media type of the source file. Rather than examining the source file ourselves to determine what intermediate filters are needed (which would be a long and involved process), we'll use the DirectShow Intelligent Connect feature to do the work for us.

To begin, we'll need to obtain *IPin* interfaces—which, as the name suggests, are exposed by the pins on a filter—for both the output of the source filter and the input of the renderer. We use the local function *GetPin* (explained in detail in the next section) to obtain these interfaces on the pins we want to connect. Once we have both of these, we can invoke the *IGraphBuilder* method *Connect*. (*Connect* takes as parameters two pins; if successful, the method connects the two pins through some set of intermediate filters.) If the call to *Connect* fails, DirectShow wasn't able to build a path between source and renderer, possibly because the media type of the source file isn't supported by DirectShow or because the file didn't contain any audio.

As in DSRender, the application uses the *IMediaControl* interface's *Run* method to begin execution of the filter graph, and the *IMediaEvent* method *WaitForCompletion* pauses execution of the application until the media file has been completely rendered. At this point, the *Stop* method is called and the filter graph halts its execution. The filter graph is written to a file with a call to *SaveGraphFile*, the allocated interfaces are released, and the application terminates.

Even when created by hand, a filter graph isn't a difficult object to build or maintain. However, this application would have been significantly more difficult to write without Intelligent Connect, which allowed us to ignore the specifics of the media in the source file.

Locating Pins and *GetPin*

The local function *GetPin* allows us to locate input and output pins on a filter and retrieve the *IPin* interface that allows us to control the pins. The code for the function is concise, as shown here:

```
// This code allows us to find a pin (input or output) on a filter.
IPin *GetPin(IBaseFilter *pFilter, PIN_DIRECTION PinDir)
{
    BOOL        bFound = FALSE;
    IEnumPins   *pEnum;
    IPin        *pPin;

    // Begin by enumerating all the pins on a filter
    HRESULT hr = pFilter->EnumPins(&pEnum);
    if (FAILED(hr))
    {
        return NULL;
    }

    // Now look for a pin that matches the direction characteristic.
    // When we've found it, we'll return with it.
    while(pEnum->Next(1, &pPin, 0) == S_OK)
```

```
{
    PIN_DIRECTION PinDirThis;
    pPin->QueryDirection(&PinDirThis);
    if (bFound = (PinDir == PinDirThis))
        break;
    pPin->Release();
}
pEnum->Release();
return (bFound ? pPin : NULL);
}
```

The *IBaseFilter* interface has a member function, *EnumPins*, which returns an *IEnumPins* interface. This interface enables you to iterate through a list of all the pins on a filter. Each element in the *IEnumPins* list contains an *IPin* object. As the code walks through this list of pins, each pin is queried through an invocation of its *IPin::QueryDirection* method. If the direction matches the requirements, that *IPin* interface pointer becomes the function's return value—with one caveat: some filters have multiple input and output pins, and these pins can have different media types, so you can't know that a returned *IPin* will be useful in every situation. You could call *GetPin* on a digital video filter, expecting to get an output pin for digital video, only to find that it won't connect to a video renderer because the output pin is for the audio track that accompanies the video. This function doesn't discriminate.

Summary

As you can see from DSRender and DSBuild, it's not difficult to construct Direct-Show applications with lots of functionality. The definitions and interfaces for the DirectShow objects are straightforward and easy to use. It's this ease of use that makes DirectShow so powerful. In just a little more than 20 lines of code, you can build a fully functioning media player. All you need after that is user interface. That said, application programming for graphical user interfaces is time-consuming and generally takes more effort than the core of the application itself. Either of these examples can be dropped right into an existing Windows application pretty much as they are to provide broad media capabilities, although you would probably want to change the function names. Now, with the programming basics out of the way, we can move on to specific topics of interest, starting with the foundations of audio recording and playback.

Part II

Capture and Editing

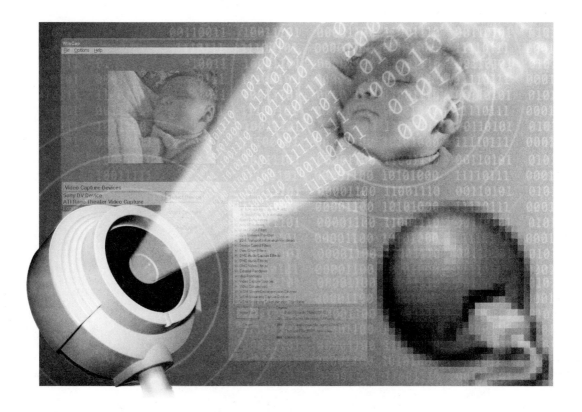

4

Capturing Audio with DirectShow

The next four chapters of this book deal with Microsoft DirectShow applications that capture media streams for manipulation by DirectShow. In most of the examples to follow, the streams will simply be written to disk for later playback or manipulation by another DirectShow application. The filter graphs we'll build will be relatively simple, consisting of a capture source filter (a special class of source filter that talks directly to capture hardware on the computer), one or two transform filters, and a renderer filter, which will write the stream to a file.

Although building filter graphs to capture streams is a straightforward affair, at the code level a number of issues need to be addressed to successfully create a filter graph. Starting with a very simple filter graph, which captures an incoming audio source as an AVI file (containing sound but no video), we'll progress through all the programming tricks you'll need to employ to successfully build DirectShow applications capable of capturing any media stream coming into your computer.

Capturing Audio with DSAudioCap

DSAudioCap is a console-based application that will record audio to a file (MyAVIFile.AVI) for as long as it runs. As a console application, it sends diagnostic information to the text-mode window it opens on the display, which is useful for debugging. This window also prompts the user to press the Enter key to stop recording, at which point the filter graph is stopped and the application terminates.

Examining the *main* Function

Let's begin our analysis of DSAudioCap by taking a look at the *main* function. As in the earlier examples of DSBuild and DSRender, *main* opens with the instantiating of the Filter Graph Manager object. This object is followed by the acquisition of the *IMediaControl* interface to the Filter Graph Manager, which controls execution of the filter graph.

```
// A very simple program to capture audio to a file using DirectShow
//
int main(int argc, char* argv[])
{
    IGraphBuilder *pGraph = NULL;          // Filter graph builder object
    IMediaControl *pControl = NULL;        // Media control object
    IFileSinkFilter *pSink = NULL;         // Interface on file writer
    IBaseFilter *pAudioInputFilter = NULL; // Audio capture filter
    IBaseFilter *pFileWriter = NULL;       // File writer filter

    // Initialize the COM library.
    HRESULT hr = CoInitialize(NULL);
    if (FAILED(hr))
    {
        // We'll send our error messages to the console.
        printf("ERROR - Could not initialize COM library");
        return hr;
    }

    // Create the Filter Graph Manager and query for interfaces.
    hr = CoCreateInstance(CLSID_FilterGraph, NULL, CLSCTX_INPROC_SERVER,
                        IID_IGraphBuilder, (void **)&pGraph);
    if (FAILED(hr))  // FAILED is a macro that tests the return value
    {
        printf("ERROR - Could not create the Filter Graph Manager.");
        return hr;
    }

    // Using QueryInterface on the graph builder object,
    // get the IMediaControl object.
    hr = pGraph->QueryInterface(IID_IMediaControl, (void **)&pControl);
    if (FAILED(hr))
    {
        printf("ERROR - Could not create the Media Control object.");
        pGraph->Release();  // Clean up after ourselves
        CoUninitialize();  // And uninitalize COM
        return hr;
    }
```

```
// OK, so now we want to build the filter graph
// using an AudioCapture filter.
// But there are several to choose from,
// so we need to enumerate them and then pick one.
hr = EnumerateAudioInputFilters((void**) &pAudioInputFilter);
hr = EnumerateAudioInputPins(pAudioInputFilter);

// Add the audio capture filter to the filter graph.
hr = pGraph->AddFilter(pAudioInputFilter, L"Capture");

// Next add the AVIMux. (You'll see why.)
IBaseFilter *pAVIMux = NULL;
hr = AddFilterByCLSID(pGraph, CLSID_AviDest, L"AVI Mux", &pAVIMux);

// Connect the filters.
hr = ConnectFilters(pGraph, pAudioInputFilter, pAVIMux);

// And now we instance a file writer filter.
hr = AddFilterByCLSID(pGraph, CLSID_FileWriter,
                      L"File Writer", &pFileWriter);

// Set the file name.
hr = pFileWriter->QueryInterface(IID_IFileSinkFilter, (void**)&pSink);
pSink->SetFileName(L"C:\\MyWAVFile.AVI", NULL);

// Connect the filters.
hr = ConnectFilters(pGraph, pAVIMux, pFileWriter);

if (SUCCEEDED(hr))
{
    // Run the graph.
    hr = pControl->Run();
    if (SUCCEEDED(hr))
    {
        // Wait patiently for completion of the recording.
        wprintf(L"Started recording...press Enter to stop recording.\n");

        // Wait for completion.
        char ch;
        ch = getchar();  // We wait for keyboard input
    }

    // And stop the filter graph.
    hr = pControl->Stop();

    wprintf(L"Stopped recording.\n");  // To the console
```

```
            // Before we finish, save the filter graph to a file.
            SaveGraphFile(pGraph, L"C:\\MyGraph.GRF");
        }

        // Now release everything and clean up.
        pSink->Release();
        pAVIMux->Release();
        pFileWriter->Release();
        pAudioInputFilter->Release();
        pControl->Release();
        pGraph->Release();
        CoUninitialize();

        return 0;
    }
```

Enumerating System Devices in DirectShow

At this point in the function, a call is made to *EnumerateAudioInputFilters*, which is local to the application. This function is required because before a capture source filter can be added to the filter graph, it must be identified and selected. Unlike other DirectShow filters (which can be identified by a GUID), capture source filters and other filters that are tied to hardware devices are identified as a class of device. Using DirectShow calls, you can walk through the list of all filters in this class and select the one you want to use for your capture application.

Being able to enumerate capture filters gives you ultimate flexibility in the design of your DirectShow application because all capture resources are available to the application, not just those that have been designated as default devices by the user or the system. This functionality also means that DirectShow remains open to new hardware devices as they're introduced by manufacturers—you won't need a revision of DirectShow to deal with every new card or interface that comes down the path. Some WDM drivers installed in conjunction with the installation of multimedia devices are recognized by DirectShow and added to its enumerated lists of available filters. Figure 4-1 shows the Insert Filters dialog box listing audio capture devices.

On the other hand, now is a good time to ask yourself an important question: are you relying on specific hardware components in your DirectShow application? You could specify which capture source filter will be used in your application, but if that source filter isn't on the user's system (because it relies on hardware the user hasn't installed), your application will fail. It's best to design a DirectShow application for the widest possible range of devices to ensure that a user won't encounter any unexpected failures when he or she runs your code.

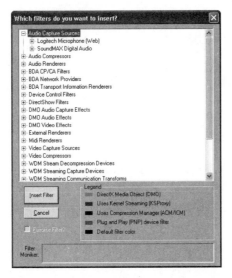

Figure 4-1   GraphEdit enumerating audio capture devices in the Insert Filters dialog box

Here's the source code for *EnumerateAudioInputFilters*:

```
// Enumerate all of the audio input devices
// Return the _first_ of these to the caller
// That should be the one chosen in the control panel.
HRESULT EnumerateAudioInputFilters(void** gottaFilter)
{
    // Once again, code stolen from the DX9 SDK.
    // Create the System Device Enumerator.
    ICreateDevEnum *pSysDevEnum = NULL;
    HRESULT hr = CoCreateInstance(CLSID_SystemDeviceEnum, NULL,
                        CLSCTX_INPROC_SERVER, IID_ICreateDevEnum,
                        (void **)&pSysDevEnum);

    if (FAILED(hr))
    {
        return hr;
    }

    // Obtain a class enumerator for the audio input category.
    IEnumMoniker *pEnumCat = NULL;
    hr = pSysDevEnum->CreateClassEnumerator(CLSID_AudioInputDeviceCategory,
                            &pEnumCat, 0);
```

```
    if (hr == S_OK)
    {
        // Enumerate the monikers.
        IMoniker *pMoniker = NULL;
        ULONG cFetched;
        if (pEnumCat->Next(1, &pMoniker, &cFetched) == S_OK)
        {
            // Bind the first moniker to an object.
            IPropertyBag *pPropBag;
            hr = pMoniker->BindToStorage(0, 0, IID_IPropertyBag,
                (void **)&pPropBag);
            if (SUCCEEDED(hr))
            {
                // To retrieve the filter's friendly name,
                // do the following:
                VARIANT varName;
                VariantInit(&varName);
                hr = pPropBag->Read(L"FriendlyName", &varName, 0);
                if (SUCCEEDED(hr))
                {
                    wprintf(L"Selecting Audio Input Device: %s\n",
                            varName.bstrVal);
                }
                VariantClear(&varName);

                // To create an instance of the filter,
                // do the following:
                // Remember to release gottaFilter later.
                hr = pMoniker->BindToObject(NULL, NULL, IID_IBaseFilter,
                                            gottaFilter);
                pPropBag->Release();
            }
            pMoniker->Release();
        }
        pEnumCat->Release();
    }
    pSysDevEnum->Release();
    return hr;
}
```

This function begins by creating an instance of a COM object known as the System Device Enumerator. This object will enumerate all the hardware devices of a specified type once its *CreateClassEnumerator* method is invoked with a GUID indicating the class of devices to be enumerated. In this case, the GUID *CLSID_AudioInputDeviceCategory* is requesting an enumeration of all the audio capture source filters on the system, but it could also be *CLSID_VideoInputDeviceCategory* for video capture source filters, or even *CLSID_AudioCompressorCategory* for all audio compression filters. (Although audio compression isn't generally performed in hardware, each compressor is considered a system device and is treated as if it were hardware rather than software.) The resulting list of devices is placed into an object of the *IEnum-Moniker* class. An enumerated class (which generally includes the letters *Enum* in its class name) can be examined, element by element, by invoking its *Next* method. In this case, invoking *Next* will return an *IMoniker* object, which is a lightweight COM object used to obtain information about other objects without having to instantiate them. The *IMoniker* object returns references to a "bag" of data related to the enumerated DirectShow filter, which is then placed into an *IPropertyBag* object with an invocation of the *IMoniker* method *BindToStorage*.

Once the *IPropertyBag* object has been instantiated, it can be queried using its *Read* method for string data labeled as its *FriendlyName*, which is to say the English-readable name (rather than the GUID) for the filter. That string is then printed to the console. The string identifies the first filter in the enumerated list, which is also the default audio capture device, established by the user through his or her preferences in the Sound control panel. (It's a bad idea to count on any particular device showing up first on the list of audio capture devices because, at any point, the user might go into the Sound control panel and muck things up.)

Once the name of the device has been printed to the console, another method call to the *IMoniker* object *BindToObject* creates an instance of the filter object, and this object is returned to the calling function. It will later need to be destroyed with a call to its *Release* method.

Although this function returns an object representing the first filter in the enumerated list—the default selection as specified in the control panel—with a few modifications, the function could return a list of objects and names. These objects and names could then be used to build menus or other GUI features that would allow the user to have complete control over which of possibly several audio capture sources would be used within a DirectShow application.

Enumerating Input Pins on an Audio Capture Device

Immediately upon return to the *main* function, another call is made to a different local function, *EnumerateAudioInputPins*. This function examines all the input pins on the selected audio input filter object; we'll need to do this to determine which input pin is active. If you examine of the Volume control panel (generally accessible through the system tray), you can see that several different sources of audio input usually exist on a PC. Most PCs have some sort of CD audio, line audio, microphone, and auxiliary inputs. Other sources will capture the sound data passing through the system, as though the PC had an internal microphone, capturing its own sound-making capabilities in real-time. Figure 4-2 shows various audio input pins on an audio capture filter.

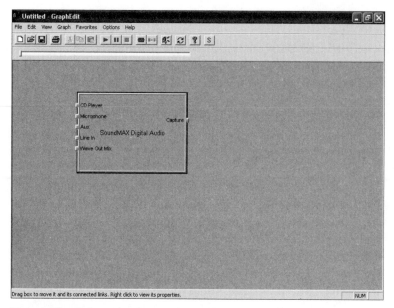

Figure 4-2   GraphEdit showing the various audio input pins on an audio capture filter

The local function *EnumerateAudioInputPins* allows us to examine the audio input filter's pins, as shown here:

```
// Code adopted from example in the DX9 SDK.
// This code allows us to find the input pins an audio input filter.
// We'll print out a list of them, indicating the enabled one.
HRESULT EnumerateAudioInputPins(IBaseFilter *pFilter)
{
    IEnumPins    *pEnum = NULL;
    IPin         *pPin = NULL;
    PIN_DIRECTION PinDirThis;
    PIN_INFO      pInfo;
    IAMAudioInputMixer *pAMAIM = NULL;
    BOOL pfEnable = FALSE;

    // Begin by enumerating all the pins on a filter.
    HRESULT hr = pFilter->EnumPins(&pEnum);
    if (FAILED(hr))
    {
        return NULL;
    }

    // Now, look for a pin that matches the direction characteristic.
    // When we've found it, we'll examine it.
```

```
while(pEnum->Next(1, &pPin, 0) == S_OK)
{
    // Get the pin direction.
    pPin->QueryDirection(&PinDirThis);
    if (PinDirThis == PINDIR_INPUT) {

        // OK, we've found an input pin on the filter.
        // Now let's get the information on that pin
        // so we can print the name of the pin to the console.
        hr = pPin->QueryPinInfo(&pInfo);
        if (SUCCEEDED(hr)) {
            wprintf(L"Input pin: %s\n", pInfo.achName);

            // Now let's get the correct interface.
            hr = pPin->QueryInterface(IID_IAMAudioInputMixer,
                                (void**) &pAMAIM);
            if (SUCCEEDED(hr)) {

                // Find out whether the pin is enabled.
                // Is it the active input pin on the filter?
                hr = pAMAIM->get_Enable(&pfEnable);
                if (SUCCEEDED(hr)) {
                    if (pfEnable) {
                        wprintf(L"\tENABLED\n");
                    }
                }
                pAMAIM->Release();
            }
            pInfo.bFilter->Release();  // from QueryPinInfo
        }
    }
    pPin->Release();
}
pEnum->Release();
return hr;
}
```

The *EnumerateAudioInputPins* function was adapted from the *GetPin* function used in the previous chapter. A pointer to a DirectShow *IBaseFilter* object is passed by the caller, and its pins are enumerated within an *IEnumPins* object by a call to the *IBaseFilter* method *EnumPins*. Using the *Next* method on the *IEnumPins* object, an *IPin* object is instantiated for every pin within the enumerated list. The *IPin* object is then tested with a call to the *QueryDirection* method: is the pin an input pin? If it is, the *QueryPinInfo* method of *IPin* is invoked. This method returns a *PIN_INFO* data structure, containing (in English) the name of the pin, which is then printed on the console.

Now comes a bit of DirectShow magic. Each pin on an audio input filter is an object in its own right and presents an *IAMAudioInputMixer* interface as one of its properties. This interface allows you to control various parameters of the pin, such as its volume level. The *IAMAudioInputMixer* interface for each *IPin* object is retrieved with a *QueryInterface* call. (This call will fail if you're not acting on an *IPin* that is part of an audio input filter.) Once this object is instanced, one of its properties is examined with a call to *get_Enable*. If *TRUE* is returned, the pin is enabled—that pin is the active input pin for the filter, and the corresponding audio input is enabled. (The default active input pin is set through the Volume control panel; it's the enabled item in the list of recording inputs.) Figure 4-3 shows pin properties of the audio input pins.

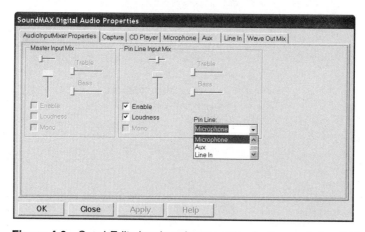

Figure 4-3 GraphEdit showing pin properties for the audio input pins

Although this routine only reads whether a pin is enabled, it is possible, through a corresponding call to the *put_Enable* method, to change the value on the pin, thereby selecting or removing an audio input. (You should be very careful that you have only one input enabled at a time, unless you know that your audio hardware can handle mixing multiple inputs.) This function indicates only the currently enabled input, but it's very easy to modify it so that it selects an alternative input. And, once again, this function could easily be rewritten to return an array of *IPin* objects to the caller. This list could then be used to build a GUI so that users could easily pick the audio pin themselves.

Connecting DirectShow Filters

DSAudioCap adds a convenience function, *ConnectFilters*, which can be used by the programmer to handle all the nitty-gritty of connecting two filters together. It's actually three separate functions, as shown here:

```
// Find an unconnected pin on a filter.
// This too is stolen from the DX9 SDK.
HRESULT GetUnconnectedPin(
    IBaseFilter *pFilter,    // Pointer to the filter.
    PIN_DIRECTION PinDir,    // Direction of the pin to find.
    IPin **ppPin)            // Receives a pointer to the pin.
{
    *ppPin = 0;
    IEnumPins *pEnum = 0;
    IPin *pPin = 0;
    HRESULT hr = pFilter->EnumPins(&pEnum);
    if (FAILED(hr))
    {
        return hr;
    }
    while (pEnum->Next(1, &pPin, NULL) == S_OK)
    {
        PIN_DIRECTION ThisPinDir;
        pPin->QueryDirection(&ThisPinDir);
        if (ThisPinDir == PinDir)
        {
            IPin *pTmp = 0;
            hr = pPin->ConnectedTo(&pTmp);
            if (SUCCEEDED(hr))  // Already connected--not the pin we want
            {
                pTmp->Release();
            }
            else  // Unconnected--this is the pin we want
            {
                pEnum->Release();
                *ppPin = pPin;
                return S_OK;
            }
        }
        pPin->Release();
    }
    pEnum->Release();
    // Did not find a matching pin.
    return E_FAIL;
}


// Connect two filters together with the Filter Graph Manager,
// Stolen from the DX9 SDK.
// This is the base version.
HRESULT ConnectFilters(
    IGraphBuilder *pGraph, // Filter Graph Manager.
    IPin *pOut,            // Output pin on the upstream filter.
    IBaseFilter *pDest)    // Downstream filter.
{
```

```
    if ((pGraph == NULL) || (pOut == NULL) || (pDest == NULL))
    {
        return E_POINTER;
    }

    // Find an input pin on the downstream filter.
    IPin *pIn = 0;
    HRESULT hr = GetUnconnectedPin(pDest, PINDIR_INPUT, &pIn);
    if (FAILED(hr))
    {
        return hr;
    }
    // Try to connect them.
    hr = pGraph->Connect(pOut, pIn);
    pIn->Release();
    return hr;
}


// Connect two filters together with the Filter Graph Manager.
// Again, stolen from the DX9 SDK.
// This is an overloaded version.
HRESULT ConnectFilters(
    IGraphBuilder *pGraph,
    IBaseFilter *pSrc,
    IBaseFilter *pDest)
{
    if ((pGraph == NULL) || (pSrc == NULL) || (pDest == NULL))
    {
        return E_POINTER;
    }

    // Find an output pin on the first filter.
    IPin *pOut = 0;
    HRESULT hr = GetUnconnectedPin(pSrc, PINDIR_OUTPUT, &pOut);
    if (FAILED(hr))
    {
        return hr;
    }
    hr = ConnectFilters(pGraph, pOut, pDest);
    pOut->Release();
    return hr;
}
```

Two versions of *ConnectFilters* are included as local functions in
DSAudioCap, which is possible because the two have different calling parameters and C++ can handle them differently through its capability with overloaded
functions. The bottom version of *ConnectFilters* is the one invoked by *main*,
and it calls *GetUnconnectedPin*, which is a function very much like *GetPin*,

except that it returns the first unconnected output pin on the source filter. The results are passed along to the other version of *ConnectFilters*, which calls *GetUnconnectedPin* again, this time searching for an input pin on the destination filter. Once everything's been discovered, a call is made to the Filter Graph Manager method *Connect*, which connects the two pins.

Adding a Filter by Its Class ID

One more convenience function exists in DSAudioCap, *AddFilterByCLSID*, which adds a filter to the graph by its unique class ID. It will be used frequently in future examples.

```
// A very useful bit of code
// stolen from the DX9 SDK.
HRESULT AddFilterByCLSID(
    IGraphBuilder *pGraph,    // Pointer to the Filter Graph Manager
    const GUID& clsid,        // CLSID of the filter to create
    LPCWSTR wszName,          // A name for the filter
    IBaseFilter **ppF)        // Receives a pointer to the filter
{
    if (!pGraph || ! ppF) return E_POINTER;
    *ppF = 0;
    IBaseFilter *pF = 0;
    HRESULT hr = CoCreateInstance(clsid, 0, CLSCTX_INPROC_SERVER,
                            IID_IBaseFilter,
                            reinterpret_cast<void**>(&pF));
    if (SUCCEEDED(hr))
    {
        hr = pGraph->AddFilter(pF, wszName);
        if (SUCCEEDED(hr))
            *ppF = pF;
        else
            pF->Release();
    }
    return hr;
}
```

Although *AddFilterByCLSID* doesn't do anything spectacular, it does save some time in coding because it encapsulates the object creation and filter addition actions into a single function call. You'll probably want to use it in your own DirectShow applications.

Using the Audio Capture Filter Graph

The filter graph for DSAudioCap is composed of three filters. First is an audio input filter, as explored earlier. Next comes an AVI multiplexer (or AVI mux). This filter takes a number of media streams and multiplexes them into a single stream formatted as an AVI file. These streams can be video, audio, or a combination of the two. An AVI mux is one of the ways to create a movie with synchronized video and audio portions; as streams arrive at the multiplexer, they're combined into a single, synchronized stream. The final component in the filter graph is a File Writer filter, which writes the AVI stream to disk.

Adding a File Writer Filter

Nearly all capture applications write their captured streams to a disk file. Several objects can serve as file "sinks," meaning that they write stream data. The most common of these is the DirectShow File Writer filter object. In DSAudio-Cap, the File Writer filter is instantiated and added to the filter graph, and then its *IFileSink* interface is instantiated through a call to *QueryInterface*. This object exposes methods that allow you to programmatically set the name and path of the file to be written to disk, through a call to its *SetFileName* method. Figure 4-4 shows the filter graph created by DSAudioCap.

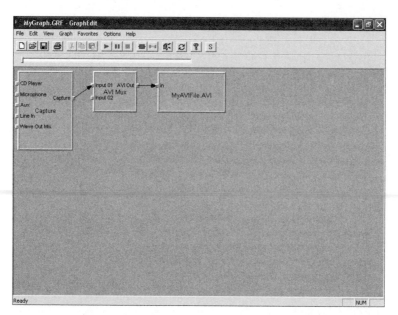

Figure 4-4   Filter graph MyGraph.GRF, as created by DSAudioCap

Executing the DSAudioCap Filter Graph

Once the file name has been set and all the filters have been connected together, the *Run* method is sent to the filter graph's control object. From this point, the filter graph captures audio and writes it to an ever-growing AVI file until the Enter key is pressed. Watch out: this file can get very big very quickly. (We're using an old but venerable call to *getchar* to watch for keyboard input.) Once the Enter key has been pressed, the filter graph control object makes a call to its *Stop* method, which terminates execution of the filter graph. Figure 4-5 shows DSAudioCap running.

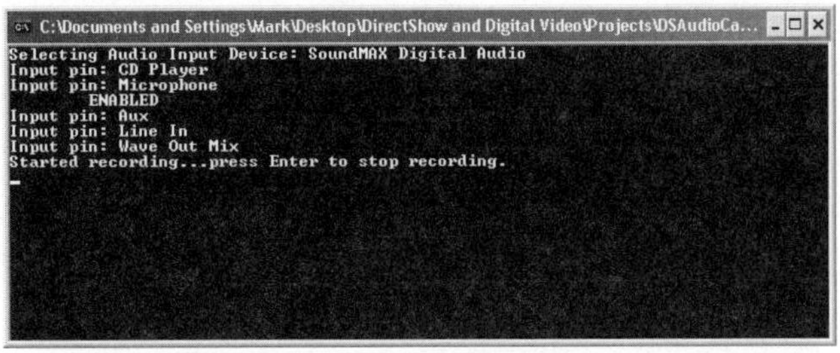

Figure 4-5   DSAudioCap executing from the command line

We've kept the call to *SaveGraphFile* in this program (and will continue to do so), which means that after the program terminates its execution, you can use GraphEdit to examine the filter graph created by DSAudioCap.

After you execute this application, there should be a file named MyAVI-File.AVI on disk. Double-clicking the file (or opening it from Windows Media Player) will allow you to hear the sound that was captured by DSAudioCap.

Adding Audio Compression with DSAudioCapCom

The sound that's captured by DSAudioCap is uncompressed, so file sizes build very quickly, at just about the same rate they do on a standard audio CD—about 700 MB per hour. However, numerous transform filters are available to DirectShow that can compress audio to a fraction of its uncompressed size. We've already covered everything you need to know to add a compressor filter to the filter graph. Like audio input devices, audio compressor filters must be enumerated and selected from a list.

The only major difference between DSAudioCap and DSAudioCapCom (the version with compression) is the addition of one function, *Enumerate-AudioCompressorFilters*, as shown in the following code:

```
// Enumerate all of the audio compressors.
// Return the one with the matching name to the caller.
HRESULT EnumerateAudioCompressorFilters(void** gottaCompressor,
                                        wchar_t* matchName)
{
    // Once again, code stolen from the DX9 SDK.
```

```
// Create the System Device Enumerator.
ICreateDevEnum *pSysDevEnum = NULL;
HRESULT hr = CoCreateInstance(CLSID_SystemDeviceEnum, NULL,
                              CLSCTX_INPROC_SERVER,
                              IID_ICreateDevEnum,
                              (void **)&pSysDevEnum);
if (FAILED(hr))
{
    return hr;
}


// Obtain a class enumerator for the audio input category.
IEnumMoniker *pEnumCat = NULL;
hr = pSysDevEnum->CreateClassEnumerator(CLSID_AudioCompressorCategory,
                                        &pEnumCat, 0);

if (hr == S_OK)
{
    // Enumerate the monikers.
    IMoniker *pMoniker = NULL;
    ULONG cFetched;
    BOOL done = false;
    while ((pEnumCat->Next(1, &pMoniker, &cFetched) == S_OK) && (!done))
    {
        // Bind the first moniker to an object.
        IPropertyBag *pPropBag;
        hr = pMoniker->BindToStorage(0, 0, IID_IPropertyBag,
                                     (void **)&pPropBag);
        if (SUCCEEDED(hr))
        {
            // Retrieve the filter's friendly name.
            VARIANT varName;
            VariantInit(&varName);
            hr = pPropBag->Read(L"FriendlyName", &varName, 0);
            if (SUCCEEDED(hr))
            {
                wprintf(L"Testing Audio Compressor: %s\n",
                    varName.bstrVal);

                // Is it the right one?
                if (wcsncmp(varName.bstrVal, matchName,
                        wcslen(matchName)) == 0)
                {
                    // We found it; send it back to the caller
                    hr = pMoniker->BindToObject(NULL, NULL,
                                                IID_IBaseFilter,
                                                gottaCompressor);
                    done = true;
```

```
                }
            }
            VariantClear(&varName);
            pPropBag->Release();
        }
        pMoniker->Release();
    }
    pEnumCat->Release();
}
pSysDevEnum->Release();
return hr;
}
```

To add an audio compressor to this filter graph, begin by enumerating all of the *CLSID_AudioCompressorCategory* filters in a method call to *CreateClass-Enumerator*. You do this because DirectShow treats the audio compressors as individual objects with their own class IDs. However, we have no way of knowing the class ID of a given audio compressor—something we'll need to instantiate a DirectShow filter. In this case, we use the call to *CreateClassEnumerator* as a way of learning the class IDs of all audio compressors available to DirectShow.

Once we have the enumerated list, we step through it using the *Next* method, until we find an audio compressor whose *FriendlyName* property matches the name we're looking for. In this program, we're matching the name Windows Media Audio V2, a codec that should be included on your system. (If it's not, use GraphEdit to list the audio compressors installed on your system— see Figure 4-6—and change the string to match one of those entries.)

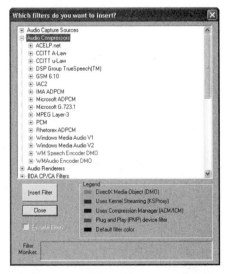

Figure 4-6   Locating the *FriendlyName* property for an audio compressor in GraphEdit's Insert Filters dialog box

When the matching object is found, it's instantiated and returned to the caller. This function is nearly identical to *EnumerateAudioInputFilters*, so you can begin to see how these functions can easily be repurposed for your own application needs.

The only major difference in this version of the *main* function is that the returned audio compressor filter is added to the filter graph using *AddFilter* and *ConnectFilter*, as shown here:

```
// Now, enumerate the audio compressors.
// Look for a match, which we'll return.
hr = EnumerateAudioCompressorFilters((void**) &pAudioCompressor,
                                    L"Windows Media Audio V2");

// Then add it to the filter graph.
hr = pGraph->AddFilter(pAudioCompressor, L"Windows Media Audio V2");

// Connect it to the audio input filter.
hr = ConnectFilters(pGraph, (IBaseFilter*) pAudioInputFilter,
                pAudioCompressor);
```

We've also added a bit of substance to the File Writer filter. The File Writer filter exposes a number of interfaces, including *IFileSink*, which can be used to set the name of the file, and *IFileSink2*, which can be used to set the mode parameter for the File Writer filter. If the mode is *AM_FILE_OVERWRITE*, the file will be deleted and re-created every time the filter graph begins execution. That's the behavior we want, so we've included a few extra lines of code:

```
// And we'll also destroy any existing file.
hr = pFileWriter->QueryInterface(IID_IFileSinkFilter2, (void**)&pSink2);
pSink2->SetMode(AM_FILE_OVERWRITE);
```

After you've run DSAudioCapCom, you'll see that its file sizes increase much more slowly than DSAudioCap because the files are compressed. As you become familiar with the different types of audio compression—some are better for voice, others for music—you might consider modifying the compression filters used in your DirectShow programs on a task-dependent basis: different compression for different sounds.

Summary

In this chapter, we've covered how to discover and enumerate the various audio capture devices connected to a PC. Once we've learned the list of audio capture devices available to DirectShow, we've been able to build capture filter graphs and write these audio streams to disk files. DirectShow can be used as the basis of a powerful audio capture and editing application. (Editing is covered in Chapter 8.) Alternatively, you can use DirectShow for audio playback—although there are easier ways to do that, using DirectSound.

Now we'll move along to video capture with webcams. Here compression isn't just an option; it's a necessity because video files can easily fill your entire hard disk in just a few minutes.

5

Capturing Audio and Video from a Webcam

Webcams have become nearly ubiquitous peripherals for today's PCs. They're inexpensive and produce video imagery of varying quality—often dependent on how much the webcam cost or how fast your computer runs. Furthermore, you don't have to do much to set up a webcam: just plug it into an available port, and you're ready to go. Windows XP provides desktop-level access to webcams (and all digital cameras attached to the computer) through Windows Explorer; here you can take single frames of video and save them to disk as photographs.

A webcam appears as a video input source filter in DirectShow. Like the audio input source filters we covered in the last chapter, the webcam produces a stream of data that can then be put through a DirectShow filter graph. Some webcams—particularly older models—capture only video, relying on a separate microphone to capture audio input. Many recent versions of webcams, including the Logitech webcam I have on my own system, bundle an onboard microphone into the webcam, and this microphone constitutes its own audio capture source filter.

For this reason, DirectShow applications will frequently treat webcams as if they are two independent devices with entirely separate video and audio capture components. That treatment is significantly different from a digital camcorder, which provides a single stream of multiplexed audio and video data; that single stream of digicam data is demultiplexed into separate streams by DirectShow filters. Although this treatment makes webcams a tiny bit more complicated to work with, their ubiquity more than makes up for any programming hoops you'll have to jump through.

Introducing DSWebcamCap

The DirectShow application DSWebcamCap captures separate video and audio inputs from a Logitech webcam to a file. Although a specific brand of webcam is explicitly specified in the code of DSWebcamCap, it is very easy to modify a few string constants and have the program work with any version of webcam. The application takes the combined streams and puts them into a filter known as the WM ASF Writer. This filter compresses audio and video streams using the powerful Windows Media Video codecs. The encoded content is put into an ASF file, which, according to the Microsoft guidelines, should have either a .WMA or .WMV file extension. (In this case, we're creating a file with the .ASF extension, which stands for Advanced Systems Format. This file will be functionally identical to a file with a .WMV extension. ASF is a *container* format, a file type that can contain any of a number of stream formats, including both WMV and WMA, so it's well suited to this task.) The WM ASF Writer allows you to select a variety of compression levels for the output file, so you can create very small files from a rich video source.

Examining *main*

As in our earlier examples, nearly all the application's work is performed inside its *main* function, as the following code shows:

```
int main(int argc, char* argv[])
{
    ICaptureGraphBuilder2 *pCaptureGraph = NULL; // Capture graph builder
    IGraphBuilder *pGraph = NULL; // Graph builder object
    IMediaControl *pControl = NULL; // Media control object
    IFileSinkFilter *pSink = NULL; // File sink object
    IBaseFilter *pAudioInputFilter = NULL; // Audio Capture filter
    IBaseFilter *pVideoInputFilter = NULL; // Video Capture filter
    IBaseFilter *pASFWriter = NULL; // WM ASF File filter

    // Initialize the COM library.
    HRESULT hr = CoInitialize(NULL);
    if (FAILED(hr))
    {
        // We'll send our error messages to the console.
        printf("ERROR - Could not initialize COM library");
        return hr;
    }

    // Create the Capture Graph Builder and query for interfaces.
    hr = CoCreateInstance(CLSID_CaptureGraphBuilder2, NULL,
                    CLSCTX_INPROC_SERVER, IID_ICaptureGraphBuilder2,
```

```
                            (void **)&pCaptureGraph);
if (FAILED(hr))  // FAILED is a macro that tests the return value
{
    printf("ERROR - Could not create the Filter Graph Manager.");
    return hr;
}


// Use a method of the Capture Graph Builder
// to create an output path for the stream.
hr = pCaptureGraph->SetOutputFileName(&MEDIASUBTYPE_Asf,
    L"C:\\MyWebcam.ASF", &pASFWriter, &pSink);

// Now configure the ASF Writer.
// Present the property pages for this filter.
hr = ShowFilterPropertyPages(pASFWriter);

// Now get the Filter Graph Manager
// that was created by the Capture Graph Builder.
hr = pCaptureGraph->GetFiltergraph(&pGraph);

// Using QueryInterface on the graph builder,
// get the Media Control object.
hr = pGraph->QueryInterface(IID_IMediaControl, (void **)&pControl);
if (FAILED(hr))
{
    printf("ERROR - Could not create the Media Control object.");
    pGraph->Release();  // Clean up after ourselves
    CoUninitialize();  // And uninitalize COM
    return hr;
}


// Get an audio capture filter.
// There are several to choose from,
// so we need to enumerate them, pick one, and
// then add the audio capture filter to the filter graph.
hr = GetAudioInputFilter(&pAudioInputFilter, L"Logitech");
if (SUCCEEDED(hr)) {
    hr = pGraph->AddFilter(pAudioInputFilter, L"Webcam Audio Capture");
}

// Now create the video input filter from the webcam.
hr = GetVideoInputFilter(&pVideoInputFilter, L"Logitech");
if (SUCCEEDED(hr)) {
    hr = pGraph->AddFilter(pVideoInputFilter, L"Webcam Video Capture");
}


// Use another method of the Capture Graph Builder
// to provide a render path for video preview.
```

```
IBaseFilter *pIntermediate = NULL;
hr = pCaptureGraph->RenderStream(&PIN_CATEGORY_PREVIEW,
    &MEDIATYPE_Video, pVideoInputFilter, NULL, NULL);

// Now add the video capture to the output file.
hr = pCaptureGraph->RenderStream(&PIN_CATEGORY_CAPTURE,
    &MEDIATYPE_Video, pVideoInputFilter, NULL, pASFWriter);

// And do the same for the audio.
hr = pCaptureGraph->RenderStream(&PIN_CATEGORY_CAPTURE,
    &MEDIATYPE_Audio, pAudioInputFilter, NULL, pASFWriter);

if (SUCCEEDED(hr))
{
    // Run the graph.
    hr = pControl->Run();
    if (SUCCEEDED(hr))
    {
        // Wait patiently for completion of the recording.
        wprintf(L"Started recording...press Enter to stop recording.\n");

        // Wait for completion.
        char ch;
        ch = getchar();  // We wait for keyboard input
    }

    // And stop the filter graph.
    hr = pControl->Stop();

    wprintf(L"Stopped recording.\n");  // To the console

    // Before we finish, save the filter graph to a file.
    SaveGraphFile(pGraph, L"C:\\MyGraph.GRF");
}

// Now release everything and clean up.
pSink->Release();
pASFWriter->Release();
pVideoRenderer->Release();
pVideoInputFilter->Release();
pAudioInputFilter->Release();
pControl->Release();
pGraph->Release();
pCaptureGraph->Release();
CoUninitialize();

return 0;
}
```

After COM has been initialized, we find ourselves in unfamiliar territory. Instead of instantiating a Filter Graph Manager object, we use *CoCreateInstance* to create an instance of the Capture Graph Builder object. This object is specifically designed to assist in the construction of filter graphs that capture audio and video input to files, but it can also be used to construct other types of graphs. As soon as the object has been created, we invoke its *ICaptureGraphBuilder2::SetOutputFileName* method. This method takes a pointer to a media type—in this case, *MEDIASUBTYPE_Asf*, indicating an ASF file—and creates an output file with the name passed as the next parameter.

The call to *SetOutputFileName* creates an instance of a WM ASF Writer filter. A pointer to the filter's *IBaseFilter* interface is returned in *pASFWriter*, and a pointer to the filter's *IFileSinkFilter* interface is returned in *pSink*. We'll need a pointer to the WM ASF Writer filter, and you might need the *IFileSinkFilter* interface. For example, if you want to change the name of the output file to some value other than that passed in the call to *SetOutputFileName*, you need *IFileSinkFilter*.

If we'd wanted to create an AVI file—as we will in the next chapter when we're dealing with digital video from a camcorder—we would have passed a pointer to *MEDIASUBTYPE_Avi* as the first parameter. In that case, instead of returning a pointer to a WM ASF Writer filter, the call would have returned a pointer to an AVI Mux filter, which combines the audio and video streams into an AVI-formatted stream. You'd still need to write that stream to a file by using the File Writer renderer filter, whereas the WM AVI Writer combines both multiplexing and file writing features in a single renderer filter.

When Should You Compress?

When capturing video, in some scenarios it is preferable to simply save the data without compressing it. Most webcams output some sort of YUV video, although some output RGB, which requires significantly more bandwidth and hard drive space. Depending on the type of video, the size of the video frames, and the speed of your CPU, a compressor might not be able to keep up with the incoming video stream. If you save the uncompressed data in an AVI file by using the AVI Mux and the File Writer, you can come back and compress it later. When the graph's source data is coming from a file, the compressor (in this case the WM ASF Writer) controls the speed at which the data is processed. In some cases, this might be faster than real time, and in some cases, it might be slower. Either way, no frames will be dropped because the source filter is reading from a local file.

Examining and Changing a Filter's Property Pages

The WM ASF Writer created by the call to *SetOutputFileName* has a wide range of options that control how it uses the Windows Media compression algorithms. A file can be highly compressed, which saves space but sacrifices quality, or it can be relatively expansive, consuming valuable hard disk resources but requiring fewer CPU cycles to process. These values can be set internally (which we'll cover in Chapter 15), or they can be presented to the user in a property page. Many DirectShow filters implement property pages, which are dialog boxes that expose the inner settings of a filter. The *ShowFilterPropertyPages* function presents the property pages of a filter.

```
// Show the property pages for a filter.
// This is stolen from the DX9 SDK.
HRESULT ShowFilterPropertyPages(IBaseFilter *pFilter) {

    /* Obtain the filter's IBaseFilter interface. (Not shown) */
    ISpecifyPropertyPages *pProp;
    HRESULT hr = pFilter->QueryInterface(IID_ISpecifyPropertyPages,
                                         (void **)&pProp);
    if (SUCCEEDED(hr))
    {
        // Get the filter's name and IUnknown pointer.
        FILTER_INFO FilterInfo;
        hr = pFilter->QueryFilterInfo(&FilterInfo);
        IUnknown *pFilterUnk;
        pFilter->QueryInterface(IID_IUnknown, (void **)&pFilterUnk);

        // Show the page.
        CAUUID caGUID;
        pProp->GetPages(&caGUID);
        pProp->Release();
        OleCreatePropertyFrame(
            NULL,                  // Parent window
            0, 0,                  // Reserved
            FilterInfo.achName,    // Caption for the dialog box
            1,                     // # of objects (just the filter)
            &pFilterUnk,           // Array of object pointers.
            caGUID.cElems,         // Number of property pages
            caGUID.pElems,         // Array of property page CLSIDs
            0,                     // Locale identifier
            0, NULL                // Reserved
        );

        // Clean up.
        pFilterUnk->Release();
```

```
        FilterInfo.pGraph->Release();
        CoTaskMemFree(caGUID.pElems);
    }
    return hr;
}
```

The *ShowFilterPropertyPages* function exposes the *ISpecificPropertyPages* interface of the *IBaseFilter* passed by the caller and then gets the name of the filter. It also creates an interface to an *IUnknown* object, which exposes all the interfaces of a given object. That information is passed in a call to *OleCreatePropertyFrame*, which manages the property pages dialog box for user input. When this function is executed, you should see a property page dialog box that looks something like the one shown in Figure 5-1.

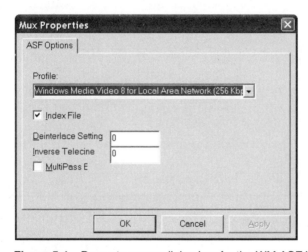

Figure 5-1   Property pages dialog box for the WM ASF Writer

The operating system handles the details of user input, and when the user closes the dialog box, control returns to the function, which cleans itself up and exits.

Some, but not all, DirectShow filters have a property page associated with them, but it's not a good idea to show the property page to the user. These property pages are designed for testing by the programmer, so they don't meet Microsoft's user interface guidelines or accessibility requirements; they could potentially confuse the user. In this case, however, the property page serves a useful purpose for testing: it allows you to adjust file compression parameters to suit your needs.

It's not necessary to use property pages to change the settings on the WM ASF Writer, and, in fact, you cannot use the filter's default property page to enable the latest Windows Media 9 Series Audio and Video codecs. But there is a set of COM interfaces that allow you to adjust all the features available to the Windows Media encoder and to make your own property page for end users; these interfaces will be covered in detail in Chapter 15.

Working with the Filter Graph Manager of a Capture Graph

After using the Capture Graph Builder to create the filter graph, we must obtain the *IMediaControl* interface on the Filter Graph Manager to run, stop, and pause the graph. By calling *ICaptureGraphBuilder2::GetFilterGraph*, we obtain a pointer to the Filter Graph Manager's *IGraphBuilder* interface. We can then use that interface to obtain the *IMediaControl* interface.

The *EnumerateAudioInputFilters* function used in DSAudioCap has been reworked slightly to create *GetAudioInputFilter*, which returns an audio input filter with a specific *FriendlyName*, if it exists. The function is invoked with a request for a filter with the "Logitech" label—a microphone built into the webcam. Changing the value of this string returns a different audio input filter if a match can be found. You'd change this string if you were using another brand of webcam in your own DirectShow programs. (Ideally, you'd write a program that wouldn't be tied to any particular brand of hardware, allowing the user to select from a list of hardware that had been recognized by DirectShow as being attached to the computer.) Once the appropriate filter is located, it's added to the filter graph using the *IGraphBuilder* method *AddFilter*.

Next we do much the same thing with video input devices. We've created the *GetVideoInputFilter* routine, which is nearly a carbon copy of *GetAudio-InputFilter*, except that the GUID for the class enumerator provided in the call to *CreateClassEnumerator* is *CLSID_VideoInputDeviceCategory* rather than *CLSID_AudioInputDeviceCategory*. Once again, the function walks through the list of available capture devices, looking for one that has a *FriendlyName* that will match the one I'm looking for, which is labeled "Logitech." An instance of the matching video input filter is returned to the caller, and it's then added to the filter graph. (Monikers are a fast, cheap way to find a particular filter because DirectShow doesn't need to create instances of each filter object to determine its *FriendlyName* or other properties.)

Building the DSWebcamCap Filter Graph

Next we need to add a video renderer to the filter graph so that we can watch the video at the same time we are saving it to disk. To do so, invoke the *ICaptureGraphBuilder2* method *RenderStream* to connect the video renderer to the appropriate pins in the filter graph. *RenderStream* handles all the filter creation and connection necessary to produce a path from an input stream to a particular renderer. In this case, we want to render a preview (monitor) to the display, so we pass a pointer to *PIN_CATEGORY_PREVIEW* as the first value, followed by *MEDIATYPE_Video*, indicating that we're interested in a video stream. Then we pass two *NULL* values. The first *NULL* value tells *RenderStream* that no intermediate filter needs to be connected in the filter graph. If there is a filter you want to place into the path of the renderer (such as the Smart Tee filter, an encoder, or some other transform filter), supply a pointer to that filter as this argument. The second *NULL* value allows the *RenderStream* method to create a monitor window for the video stream, so we can see the video capture on screen while it is being written to file. *RenderStream* will determine the best path between the input filter and the renderer filter.

Frequently, calls to *RenderStream* will result in the addition of transform filters known as Smart Tees to the filter graph. A Smart Tee takes a single stream and converts it into two identical, synchronized streams. One of these streams is designated as the capture stream and presented on the filter's Capture pin, and the other stream is designated as a preview stream and presented on the filter's Preview pin.

What makes the Smart Tee so smart? The Smart Tee understands priorities, and it will never cause the capture stream to lose frames. If the CPU starts getting overloaded with video processing, the Smart Tee will detect the overloading and drop frames from the preview display, sacrificing the preview in favor of capture quality. Using the Smart Tee, you might see a jerky preview, but the captured file should be perfect.

To complete the construction of the filter graph, we make two more calls to *RenderStream*. The first call connects the video capture filter to the WM ASF Writer that's been created by the *ICaptureGraphBuilder2* object. In this case, *PIN_CATEGORY_CAPTURE* is passed as the first parameter of *RenderStream*; this parameter tells *RenderStream* that it should connect the capture stream rather than the preview stream. The Smart Tee filter will be added if needed. After the first call to *RenderStream* is completed, another call is made to *RenderStream*, with parameters to specify that the audio stream should be connected to the WM ASF Writer.

That concludes the construction of the filter graph. Because we've used the Capture Graph Builder to handle the details of wiring the filters together, it's taken only a few lines of code to create a functional filter graph. This filter graph will capture camcorder video and audio streams to a file while providing a video monitor window on the display. When the application invokes the Filter Graph Manager's *Run* method, a small preview window will open on the display, showing the real-time output of the webcam, even as the webcam's video stream is written to a disk file.

Summary

In this chapter, we covered video capture with webcams—inexpensive, low-resolution video cameras, which have become nearly ubiquitous PC peripherals. Despite their low-quality imagery, webcams provide an important portal between the real world and the PC. They can turn any PC into a moviemaking workstation and they can send your image around the world in just a few clicks—or a few lines of DirectShow code.

Although DSWebcamCap seems very simple, it is the foundation of everything you'd need to add video capture and video e-mail capability to any Internet-based application. All the essentials—video and audio capture, video monitoring, and data compression—are included in this demonstration program. Although the program lacks the nicety of a user interface, line for line it's an incredibly powerful multimedia authoring application, and it could easily be integrated within any application, including e-mail, a Web browser, a peer-to-peer file sharing program, and so on. DSWebcamCap is a good example of the power that DirectShow brings to the application programmer; many tens of thousands of lines of code are "under the hood," hidden away in DirectShow filters that we need know nothing about to use them.

Webcams are the low-tech end in the world of digital video. They're commonplace but not very powerful. Digital video cameras are the high-end hardware of this world, and it's now time to examine how to use DirectShow to control these increasingly popular devices.

6

Capture and Output Using DV Camcorders

Since their introduction in the late 1990s, DV camcorders have become the favored choice for millions of home video enthusiasts. These camcorders have become inexpensive—the low-end models retail for about $300—and are more reliable than their analog counterparts. They also have some features that leave analog camcorders far behind. First among these is that they are entirely digital devices. A digital camcorder is essentially a custom computer, designed to capture video imagery and audio, which it converts to a digital data stream. This stream is then written to a high-density storage medium, such as miniDV, DVCAM, Digital8, DVCPRO, and MicroMV tape formats. Some digital cameras will encode their media streams as MPEG data and write it to a removable disk drive or a recordable DVD in real-time. Because a DV camcorder creates digital data rather than an analog broadcast TV signal, these devices are uniquely compatible with personal computers, and since their introduction, many software packages have been developed to allow consumers to create their own movies, using nothing more than a DV camcorder, a PC, and some software.

The capability to produce broadcast-quality television (or even feature films) at home is a big deal. Mainstream theatrical films have been created using DV camcorders, saving millions of dollars in production costs versus comparable films made using "wet process" movie cameras and film. One of the biggest expenses in filmmaking (other than paying for big-name stars and scores of fancy special effects) is the cost of developing film. This cost vanishes with digital video, and a new generation of filmmakers have eagerly adopted DV as their medium of choice. It's cheap, it looks great, and the filmmaker can do all the post-production on a typical computer. What's more, for folks lucky enough to be using a "prosumer" model digital video camera—such as Sony's $1800 DCR-TRV950—the quality of the images will be almost indistinguishable from a $35,000 high-end digital camera. Both CNN and ABC's *Nightline* now equip their field correspondents with these cheap, high-quality digital cameras, which give them the ability to shoot footage easily, nearly anywhere.

Microsoft DirectShow provides the operating system resources to handle these camcorders, both the high-end models and the more consumer-oriented devices. Furthermore, DirectShow is well-engineered to deal with DV streams, either presented through a hardware device (a camcorder) or through a disk-based file. A nice collection of source capture and transform filters makes working with DV a straightforward affair—easier, in many ways, than working with a webcam.

Examining the DV Format

Before going any further into the details of DV camcorders and DirectShow, it's important to cover the basics of the digital video or DV format. DV is a specification for video and audio, just as JPEG and GIF are standards for images and WAV is a standard for audio. DV is markedly different from other video formats you might be familiar with, such as MPEG-2 (used on DVDs) or Windows Media, because the DV format was designed with an eye toward capture and editing of high-quality images. DV has been optimized for production, not distribution. DV files are huge—a minute of DV runs to about 230 megabytes! Why is it so fat? Many video compression formats, such as MPEG-2, employ the technology of keyframes. A keyframe can be thought of as a snapshot of the video stream, which can be used by successive video frames to help construct their contents without specifying everything in the frame because those frames can refer back to the keyframe. This functionality saves lots of data storage, but it also means that editing the file is much harder because the entire image isn't encoded in every frame.

In DV format, there is no keyframing, or rather, every frame is its own keyframe. The entire image is available in every frame of DV file—that's one reason they're such disk-hoggers. However, there is a big benefit to this richness of detail: you can pop a DV file into Adobe Premiere or Windows Movie Maker and work on it quite easily. To do the same with an MPEG-2 file, on the other hand, requires lots of computation on the computer's part because it reconstructs frames from keyframe data. This difference means that editing a DV file is faster than editing an equivalent MPEG-2 file.

Although the video fields (30 frames per second, 2 fields per frame, 60 fields per second) captured by the camcorder and output to the DV stream are complete, without any need of keyframe data to reconstruct fields, each field is internally compressed using a technique called discrete cosine transform (DCT). DCT is mathematically analogous to a similar compression technique used to make JPEG images small in size, yet highly detailed. This intrafield compression keeps DV files from being even bigger than they otherwise would be, but it comes at a price: a DV stream doesn't have all the detailed resolution that a fatter stream would, but it represents a good tradeoff between file size and image quality.

Another tradeoff between file size and image quality in DV format is apparent from the way that brightness and color information (*luma* and *chroma* in the parlance of DV) are stored. Rather than storing an RGB bitmap, which is what you might expect from a digital imaging device, DV streams express luma and chroma in YUV format. (A detailed explanation of YUV format can be found in Chapter 10.) The specifics of the YUV format used in consumer-level DV devices tend to favor red hues over blue ones, so DV devices tends to be more sensitive to reds than blues. Additionally, there are encoding differences between PAL-format DV (used in Europe and much of the rest of the world) and NTSC-format DV (used in the Americas and Japan). This encoding difference means that PAL-format DV loses some of its chroma information if converted to NTSC-format DV, and vice-versa.

Finally, the DV format should not be confused with the AVI file format frequently used as a container for DV data. Although Microsoft Windows operating systems prefer to store DV data in AVI files (other operating systems store them differently), there ultimately isn't any necessary connection between DV format and AVI. AVI format provides a convenient package for a DV-format video stream and a DV-format audio stream, but the specifics of the AVI file format are stripped out of the data when it's streamed to a DV device, such as a camcorder. (There's a wealth of information about the AVI file format in Chapter 14.) If you wanted to, you could write your own capture, transform, and render filters for a different DV-format–compatible file type so that you wouldn't need the AVI format at all. That's entirely permissible—but it's extremely unlikely that other packages, such as Premiere, would work with your newly created file type.

Using IEEE 1394, FireWire, iLink, and USB 2.0

Nearly all digital camcorders can be connected directly to a computer through a high-speed network interface. Here's where it gets a bit confusing because the same network interface is known by a multitude of names. In the world of Microsoft and its associates, the network interface is identified as IEEE 1394. This is the network specification approved by the Institute of Electrical and Electronics Engineers, a professional organization that has an internationally recognized standards body. For those familiar with Apple's Macintosh, the interface is known as FireWire—a trademark owned by Apple and, until recently, available only to Apple's licensees. Finally, Sony, who codeveloped FireWire with Apple, calls the interface iLink. Whether it's called IEEE 1394, FireWire, or iLink, it's all exactly the same thing—a high-speed network protocol designed specifically to facilitate communication between digital cameras and computers. (The protocol can be used with other devices, such as external disk drives, but its genesis was in the world of digital camcorders.) For the sake of clarity and because it's the term preferred in the Microsoft universe, it'll be identified hereafter as IEEE 1394.

One of the most useful features of IEEE 1394 is that it configures itself; you don't need to set up any addresses or switches or configure any software to use an IEEE 1394 device with your computer. (You do need to have the appropriate drivers installed on your computer, but those drivers are installed as part of the Windows operating system and should already be on the computer.) From the user's perspective, all that needs to be done is to connect an IEEE 1394 cable from the camcorder to the computer. When the camcorder powers up, the computer assigns it a network address and the computer and camcorder begin to communicate. That communication happens at very high speeds; the IEEE 1394 network runs at 400 megabits per second (Mbps), or roughly 4 times faster than fast Ethernet. That gives IEEE 1394 plenty of bandwidth to deal with the stream of video coming from a camcorder. In 2002, a new specification known as IEEE 1394b bumped the network speed up to at least 800 Mbps and up to 1600 Mbps with the right type of cabling. (The original IEEE 1394 specification was renamed IEEE 1394a.)

Like a computer connected to a network, an IEEE 1394 camcorder can read data from the network; this data can either be an audio-video stream or commands. Unlike computers, camcorders are custom-purpose objects with a few well-defined functions, such as play, record, pause, rewind, and fast-forward. All these commands can be transmitted to a camera through its IEEE 1394 interface, which gives the computer complete control over the camcorder without any intervention from the user. No buttons need to be pressed on the camcorder to get it to rewind a tape or record a segment of video. When connected, the camcorder becomes a computer peripheral.

Although IEEE 1394 reigns as the standard du jour for digital camcorders, a new protocol, Universal Serial Bus version 2 (USB 2), offers even greater speed (480 Mbps) and will be even more widely available on PCs than IEEE 1394, which isn't standard equipment on many PCs. Today, some camcorders have both USB 1 and IEEE 1394 network connections. The USB connection is most often used to transfer webcam video and still images to the host computer, while the IEEE 1394 connection is used to transfer video streams. USB 1 has a top speed of 10 Mbps, which is not really enough to handle a data stream from a digital camcorder. However, with the introduction of USB 2, we can expect to see a battle between the two standards for the title of unquestioned champion for connectivity to DV camcorders. From the point of view of the DirectShow programmer, it's unlikely that a switch from IEEE 1394 to USB 2 will require a change in a single line of code, but this situation is still unfolding, and a programmer with an eye to the future would be well advised to test any digital video software with both standards, just to be sure. As of this writing, the audio/video (A/V) specifications for USB 2 have not yet been finalized, so no one yet knows how USB 2 will play in the DirectShow environment.

Understanding DV Stream Types

DV describes a number of specific stream formats. The two you're most likely to encounter are known as SDL-DVCR and SD-DVCR. SDL-DVCR is the format used by consumer-level camcorders in their "LP" mode, and it delivers a stream bandwidth of 12.5 Mbps. Although the Windows driver for IEEE 1394 devices will acquire data from a device in SDL-DVCR mode, none of the supplied codecs will decode it. (There are third-party solutions that you can use if you find you need this capability.)

SD-DVCR is sent by camcorders in "SP" mode (or doing a live image capture). This format delivers a stream at 25 Mbps. That's the standard data rate for DV streams. Both SD-DVCR and SDL-DVCR are supported on miniDV and Digital8 tapes, and both stream formats are fully supported in DirectShow. The DVCAM tape format also records a 25-Mbps stream, but the timecode information recorded on DVCAM tape is more robust. (Timecode will be explained in the "Timecode" sidebar later in this chapter.)

For the video professional, HD-DVCR is the high definition version of the DV standard, and it carries a stream bandwidth of 50 Mbps. With this format, you get 1125 lines of screen resolution, whereas SDL-DVCR delivers 480 lines of resolution. HD-DVCR is generally reserved for video productions that will be shown theatrically, after a transfer to film (film has a much higher resolution than SDL-DVCR), or for programming that's being shot for high-definition television (HDTV) broadcast.

Although the HD-DVCR stream can be transmitted over an IEEE 1394 link, that doesn't imply that an HD-DVCR stream can simply be brought into and manipulated by a DirectShow filter graph. The standard capture source filter for DV devices will not work correctly with an HD-DVCR stream, nor will any of the other DV-specific filters. They're designed for SD-DVCR streams. A third-party DirectShow filter would be able to handle HD-DVCR decoding, but you don't get that filter as part of any Microsoft operating system.

Issuing Commands

One important consideration to keep in mind when working with electromechanical devices such as camcorders is that although they can respond to a command immediately, it takes some period of time before the command is actually executed by the device. For example, when a digital camcorder transitions from stop mode to record mode, it takes a number of seconds (generally, no more than three seconds, but the time varies from camcorder to camcorder) before the tape has threaded its way around the various heads and capstans inside the camcorder, and recording can't begin until that process has been completed. This delay will affect your DirectShow programs because issuing a command to a digital camcorder doesn't mean that the device immediately enters the requested state. Ten seconds is an eternity on a processor that executes a billion instructions per second.

For this reason, it's important to query the state of electromechanical devices after a command has been issued to them so that you can track the device as it enters the requested state—or fails to do so. (For example, a miniDV tape could be record-protected, and therefore the camcorder would be unable to enter record mode.) Furthermore, it's possible that a device might say it has entered a particular mode before it actually has. Digital camcorders are notorious for reporting that they've entered record mode before they can actually begin recording a data stream. This functionality isn't an issue for a human being hand-operating a camcorder because a person can tolerate a delay between pushing the record button and seeing "REC" show up on the camcorder's viewfinder. However, this situation could be disastrous for a DirectShow programmer, who might be writing out just a few seconds of video—video that would be dropped by the camcorder as it entered record mode.

Although the specifications vary from model to model, in general, the more expensive the camcorder, the more quickly it will respond to electromechanical commands. Even so, it's a good idea to build some "play" into your DirectShow applications where electromechanical features are concerned. Listen to the device before you begin to use it, and design your programs with the knowledge that sometimes these devices tell fibs.

There are some things you can do to minimize these kinds of issues. Most camcorders have a pause mode, which will cue the tape around the play and record heads and leave it there. (You can't leave a device in pause mode forever, however, because these devices will automatically exit pause mode after a few minutes to prevent damage to those heads.) When playing video from a digital camcorder, a good practice is to put the device into play mode and then immediately issue the pause command. The camcorder will cue the tape but won't move it through the playback mechanism. When you issue the play command again, the playback will begin almost immediately. This same technique can be used for record mode, which generally takes a bit longer to enter than play mode. First enter record mode, then pause—and wait a bit—and then enter record mode again. Although it won't make for an immediate response from an inherently slow device, this technique speeds things up quite a bit and makes for better, more robust application design.

Processing Video and Audio Streams

Devices such as DV camcorders present a single stream through the IEEE 1394 interface. This stream is an interleaved mixture of video data and audio data. Although the specifics of this stream structure are complex, in general, the stream will consist of alternating fields of video information followed by a sample of audio data. Television is composed of fields of information, two of which make each frame of the picture. In the USA, television signals are composed of 30 frames per second (fps), transmitted as 60 fields, with each field holding half of the image. The fields are interlaced in alternating lines, as if they were two combs pressed into each other. For DV camcorders, each field is an image of 720×480 pixels; this 3:2 aspect ratio is a little wider than the 4:3 ratio that gives television screens their characteristic rectangular shape. The digital camcorder image is much higher quality than the standard analog television image, which is generally given as 460×350 pixels, but that's an approximation at best. Cheaper television sets overscan, so some of those pixels are lost on the top, bottom, right side, and left side of the screen.

Consumer DV camcorders generally record live audio in stereo at 32,000 samples per second with 12 bits of resolution per sample, which isn't quite the same fidelity as a compact disc but is more than enough for many applications. However, all camcorders can record audio streams of 48,000 samples per second with 16 bits of resolution per sample. That's better than CD quality. So it's possible, and even easy, to create digital video presentations that are far sharper and better sounding than any TV broadcast. Although they'll never look as good as 35-millimeter movies (which have a resolution of approximately 2000×2000 pixels), they'll easily surpass anything you'll see on a television—unless you already have an HDTV!

Although the recording medium—miniDV, DVCAM, or Digital8—contains both the video and audio tracks, DirectShow will demultiplex these streams into separate components, so DirectShow applications can process video while leaving the audio untouched, or vice versa. In any case, when dealing with DV camcorders, the filter graph will have to work with multiple streams, just as was necessary when working with webcams in Chapter 5. The difference with DV camcorders is that both streams will be produced by the same capture source filter, whereas a webcam generally requires separate capture source filters for the video and audio streams.

An entirely different filter graph must be built to handle recording of a DV stream to a digital camcorder. In that case, the filter graph will take a source (perhaps from an AVI file) and convert it into a multiplexed video and audio DV-format stream. Two DirectShow filters, the DV Video Encoder and DV Mux, will do this conversion for you. Once the combined DV-format stream has been created, it's sent along to the device to be recorded.

Building Filter Graphs

DirectShow includes a number of filters that are specifically designed for processing of DV streams. The most important of these are the Microsoft DV Camera and VCR (MSDV) capture source filter and the DV Splitter, DV Mux, DV Video Encoder, and DV Video Decoder transform filters. Most filter graphs built to handle DV streams will have at least one (and probably several) of these filters.

In the previous chapter, we noted that the enumerated list of video capture filters included a filter specific to my Logitech webcam. If I had a variety of webcams from a variety of manufacturers attached to my system, these too would show up as separate entries on the list. DirectShow works with DV devices a bit differently because Windows already has a full set of drivers used to communicate with IEEE 1394 devices. All this functionality has been gathered into a single DirectShow filter, the MSDV capture source filter. The filter has one input pin, which can receive a multiplexed A/V stream. It's unusual for a capture source filter to have an input pin, but in this case, it makes perfect sense: we will want to be able to write streams to this device—that is, to write to the tape inside the camcorder. The filter also has two output pins; one of them presents a video-only stream to the filter graph, while the other presents a multiplexed A/V stream.

In most cases, you'll want to route the multiplexed A/V stream through your filter graph, which is where the DV Splitter transform filter becomes useful. The DV Splitter takes the multiplexed A/V stream of DV data on its input pin and "splits" the stream into separate video and audio streams, on two output pins. On the other hand, if you have separate DV video and audio streams and you need to multiplex them—perhaps so that they can be written to a camcorder—you'll want to use the DV Mux transform filter, which takes the video and audio streams on separate input pins and produces a multiplexed stream on its output pin.

If you have a video stream that you want to send to a camcorder, it needs to be in DV format before it can be accepted as an input by the DV Mux filter. To put the stream into DV format, pass the video stream through the DV Video

Encoder. (In GraphEdit, it's not listed among the DirectShow filters; it's enumerated separately in the Video Compressors category.) The filter has two pins: the input pin receives a video stream, while the output pin issues a DV-encoded video stream. Intelligent Connect will not add the DV Video Encoder for you automatically. If you need it, you'll need to instantiate it in the filter graph and identify it within *RenderStream* calls as an intermediate filter.

Finally the inverse of the DV Video Encoder filter is the DV Video Decoder, which takes a DV-encoded video stream and converts it to another stream format. The exact output format from the DV Video Decoder is negotiated by the DV Video Decoder and the filter downstream from it. There are several possible output stream formats, and the DV Video Decoder will try to match its output to the needs of the downstream filter.

Working with WinCap

Mike Wasson on the DirectShow Documentation Team created a very useful application that presents all the basic principles involved in capture from and recording to a digital camcorder. (It does a lot more than that, but you'll have to wait until Chapter 7 before we cover the rest of its features.) This program, known as WinCap, uses the Windows GUI to present an interface to all the video capture devices on a user's system, and it gives you a wide range of control over these devices. (At this point, you should use Microsoft Visual Studio .NET to build an executable version of the WinCap sample program included on the companion CD.) When you launch WinCap, you should see a window on your display that looks something like Figure 6-1.

In the lower left corner of the WinCap window, WinCap presents a list of all video capture devices detected on your computer. (If you don't see your digital camcorder in this list, check to see that it's powered on. When powered on, it should show up in the list of available devices.) On my computer, I have three video capture devices installed: the webcam (which we covered in Chapter 5), an ATI TV tuner card (which we'll cover in Chapter 7), and a "Sony DV Device," which is a generic name for my Sony TRV900 digital camcorder.

To select a video capture device, click its entry in the list of video capture devices and then click Select Device. When I select the Logitech QuickCam Web entry, which corresponds to my webcam, and then click Select Device, the upper portion of the WinCap window displays a live video stream captured from the webcam, as shown in Figure 6-2.

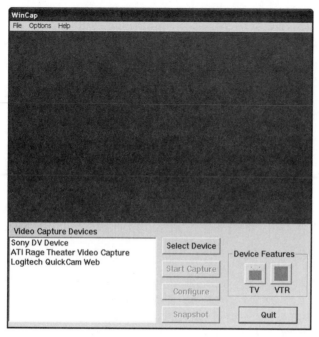

Figure 6-1   On startup, WinCap showing all available video capture devices

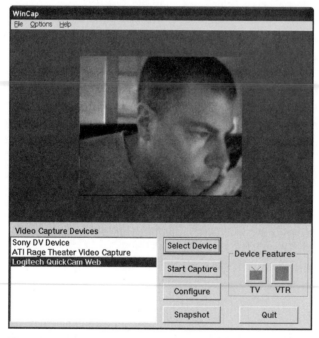

Figure 6-2   A live video stream in the WinCap window

We've already covered webcams in some detail, so we'll move along to the digital camcorder. When I select the Sony DV Device entry from the list of video capture devices and then click Select Device, I don't immediately get a video image. Instead, a new window opens on the screen, as shown in Figure 6-3.

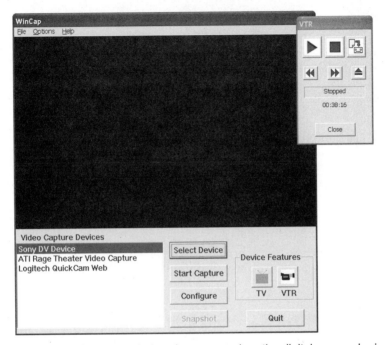

Figure 6-3   The new window that opens when the digital camcorder is selected for video capture

This new window, labeled VTR, has a number of familiar buttons, with the industry-standard icons for play, stop, rewind, fast forward, and eject. (There's a sixth icon, which we'll come to shortly.) Why did this window open? Why can't I see a live image from the camcorder? The reason is a function of how camcorders are designed. Camcorders generally have at least two operating modes: camera mode, in which images are recorded to tape, and VTR (video tape recorder) mode, in which images stored on tape can be played back through the camera. At the time I clicked the Select Device button, my camera was in VTR mode, so I got a window with VTR controls on the display. If I were to switch modes from VTR to camera and then select the device, I'd see what we had been expecting to see initially, a live picture from the device, as shown in Figure 6-4.

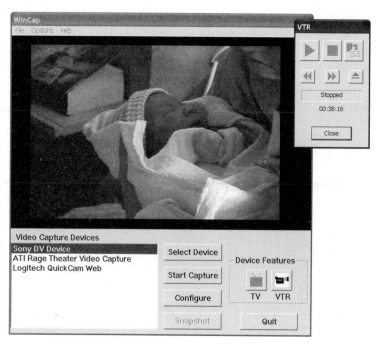

Figure 6-4   A live picture from the camcorder with the VTR controls disabled

The WinCap window displays a live image from the camcorder. Although the VTR window is open, all its controls are disabled. When a camcorder is in camera mode, it won't respond to commands such as play, record, or fast-forward. This functionality won't matter for our purposes because it's possible to record a live image from a camera in VTR mode—all you need to do is send the appropriate commands to it.

WinCap allows you to capture video and audio streams to an AVI file; you can select the file name for the capture file with the Set Capture File command on the File menu. (If you don't set a name, it will default to C:\CapFile.avi.) To begin capture, click Start Capture; to stop the capture, click Stop Capture (the same button). The AVI file created from the captured video stream can be played in Windows Media Player or any other compatible application, such as Adobe Premiere.

Finally, when the camcorder is in VTR mode, WinCap can write a properly formatted AVI file to the camcorder, making a video recording of the movie in the AVI file. (This AVI file must contain DV-encoded video; if the video is in any other format, it won't be written to the camcorder and the application will fail.) That's the sixth button in the VTR window, which shows a file icon pointing to a tape icon. When you click the icon, you'll be presented with a file selection dialog box that filters out everything except AVI files. Select an appropriate AVI file (such as Sunset.AVI, included on the companion CD), and it will be written out to the camcorder. Now that we've covered some of the basic features of WinCap, let's begin a detailed exploration of how it works.

Modular C++ Programming and WinCap

All the DirectShow programming examples presented thus far in this book have been very simply structured. They barely qualify as C++ programs. Objects are instantiated, and method calls are made on those objects, but that's about as far as we've gotten into the subtleties of C++ programming. WinCap is a formally structured C++ program with separate code modules for each of the user interface elements (such as the main window, the VTR controls, and so on) as well as a separate module for program initialization, device control, and so forth.

This modularity makes the code somewhat more difficult to follow; you'll need to noodle through the various modules—there are 13 of them—as we go through the portions of the code relevant to understanding how to manipulate a digital camcorder in DirectShow. To make this an easier process, program listings in this portion of the book will be modified slightly. The object that contains a method will be presented in the method's implementation, and any time a method is referenced in the text, it will be referenced through its containing object. For example, the method that processes UI messages for the main WinCap window will be identified as *CMainDialog::OnReceiveMsg*. This notation should help you find the source code definitions and implementation of any method under discussion. Table 6-1 describes the function of the 13 WinCap C++ modules.

Table 6-1   The WinCap C++ Modules

Module Name	Description
AudioCapDlg.cpp	Dialog box handling code for the Select An Audio Capture Device dialog box; populates list with audio capture devices
CDVProp.cpp	Dialog box and device handling code for the VTR dialog box that appears when a DV device is selected
CTunerProp.cpp	Dialog box and device handling code for the TV dialog box that appears when a TV tuner is selected (discussed in Chapter 7)
ConfigDlg.cpp	Handles display of property pages associated with a capture device
Device.cpp	Code to populate list with video capture devices, selection of video capture devices

Table 6-1   The WinCap C++ Modules   *(continued)*

Module Name	Description
Dialog.cpp	Basic C++ class infrastructure for WinCap dialog boxes
ExtDevice.cpp	Handles the *IAMExtDevice*, *IAMExtTransport*, and *IAMExtTimecode* interfaces for a video capture device
MainDialog.cpp	Event handling for the WinCap main dialog box window
SampleGrabber.cpp	Code for taking a snapshot from the video stream, placing it into the C:\Test.bmp file on disk
WinCap.cpp	Program entry point
graph.cpp	Code to instantiate and handle the filter graph manager and capture graph builder interfaces
stdafx.cpp	Standard C++ file to handle all includes for the prebuilt header files
utils.cpp	Various convenience and utility functions

Initializing WinCap

WinCap begins with some basic Microsoft Foundation Classes (MFC) initialization sequences and calls *CoInitialize*, which sets up the Component Object Model (COM) for use by the application. Shortly after that, the main dialog box window—the WinCap window—is instantiated, which results in a call to *CMainDialog::OnInitDialog*. This method does a bit more initialization to the user interface elements in the dialog box, such as enabling and disabling buttons, and so on, and calls *CMainDialog::RefreshDeviceList*. This function creates the video capture device list with a call to *CDeviceList::Init*, which is passed with the value *CLSID_VideoInputDeviceCategory*. *CDeviceList::Init* should look a bit familiar by now, as it enumerates all the video input devices known to DirectShow, a technique we've already covered.

```
HRESULT CDeviceList::Init(const GUID& category)
{
    m_MonList.clear();

    // Create the System Device Enumerator.
    HRESULT hr;
    CComPtr<ICreateDevEnum> pDevEnum;
    hr = pDevEnum.CoCreateInstance(CLSID_SystemDeviceEnum, NULL,
        CLSCTX_INPROC_SERVER);
    if (FAILED(hr))
    {
        return hr;
    }
```

```
    // Obtain a class enumerator for the video capture category.
    CComPtr<IEnumMoniker> pEnum;
    hr = pDevEnum->CreateClassEnumerator(category, &pEnum, 0);

    if (hr == S_OK)
    {
        // Enumerate the monikers.
        CComPtr<IMoniker> pMoniker;
        while(pEnum->Next(1, &pMoniker, 0) == S_OK)
        {
            m_MonList.push_back(pMoniker);
            pMoniker.Release();
        }
    }
    return hr;
}
```

The monikers for each enumerated video input device are placed into a list object managed by *CDeviceList*. When control returns to *CMainDialog::RefreshDeviceList*, it issues a call to *CDeviceList::PopulateList*, which queries for the description of the device (supported by some DV camcorders). If the description is found for the device, the description is returned. Otherwise, the routine retrieves the friendly name for the item, and each entry is added to the list box in the lower left corner of the WinCap window. This technique, in just a few lines of code, is exactly what you'll need in your own DirectShow applications if you want to present the user with a list of possible DirectShow devices or filters—video, audio, compressors, and so on.

Using the Active Template Library (ATL)

In the preceding code sample, some variable type declarations probably look unfamiliar, such as *CComPtr<ICreateDevEnum>*. This is our first encounter with the Microsoft Active Template Library (ATL), a set of template-based C++ classes that handle much of the housekeeping associated with object allocation. ATL itself is vast, and the smart pointer classes it offers (as given in the preceding code) are just the tip of the iceberg.

What is this *CComPtr*? In COM, the lifetime of an object is managed by the reference count. The object deletes itself whenever its reference count goes to zero (which means it is no longer being used in the application). Conversely, if the reference count never goes to zero, the object is

(continued)

Using the Active Template Library (ATL)   *(continued)*

never deleted—at least, not until the application terminates its execution. If you discard a COM reference pointer without releasing it, you have created a *ref count leak*, which means your application's memory space will become polluted with objects that are unused but still allocated.

One of the hardest things in COM client programming is avoiding ref count leaks. (The only thing harder is tracking them down!) This is especially true when functions have multiple exit points. When you leave a function, you must release every valid interface pointer (but not release any that are still *NULL*). Traditionally, you'd design functions with a single exit point, which is good programming practice (it's what we all learned in school) but hard to carry out in many real-world situations.

Smart pointers—supported by ATL—are an elegant solution to the reference count problem, and if used correctly, smart pointers can save you a lot of debugging time. For example, *CComPtr* is an ATL template that manages a COM interface pointer. For example, consider this line of code from the snippet given earlier:

```
CComPtr<ICreateDevEnum> pDevEnum;
```

This declaration creates a pointer to an object of class *ICreateDevEnum* and initializes its value to *NULL*. Now the *CoCreateInstance* call can be made as a method of the COM smart pointer. That's one big difference between user-declared pointers and ATL smart pointers. Additionally, ATL smart pointers will delete themselves when they go out of scope, which means that if you've defined an ATL smart pointer nested deep in several pairs of braces (or parentheses), it will delete and dereference itself automatically the next time you hit a closing brace or closing parenthesis. If it's defined within the main body of a function, the pointer will be deleted when the function exits.

In true C++ style, ATL smart pointers overload two basic C++ operators, *&* and ->. You can take *&pDevNum*, and it will work correctly, even though you're not pointing to an *ICreateDevEnum* object but to an ATL wrapper around it. The pointer operation *pDevEnum*-> also works as it should, allowing you to make method calls and variable references on an ATL smart pointer as if it were a real pointer.

These ATL pointers are used liberally throughout WinCap; most of the time, you won't have any trouble understanding their operation. If you do have more questions, there's extensive documentation on ATL within Visual Studio.

Selecting a Digital Camcorder

Once the list of video capture devices has been created and populated with entries known to DirectShow, it is possible to select a device and control it. Although any valid video capture device can be selected, in this section, we'll consider only what happens when a digital camcorder is selected.

When a video capture device is selected and the Select Device button is clicked, the *CMainDialog::OnSelectDevice* method is invoked, which immediately invokes the *CMainDialog::InitGraph* method. This is where the DirectShow Filter Graph Manager directly interacts with WinCap. The application maintains communication with the DirectShow Filter Graph Manager through a *CGraph* object. The *CMainDialog* object has a private variable named *m_pGraph* that is a *CCaptureGraph* object derived from the *CGraph* class but specifically used to build a capture filter graph. These classes are application defined, created by WinCap, and shouldn't be confused with either the *IGraphBuilder* or *ICaptureGraphBuilder2* interfaces offered by DirectShow. *CMainDialog::InitGraph* creates a new *CCaptureGraph* object, which in turn creates a new Filter Graph Manager object.

Next *CMainDialog::OnSelectDevice* calls *CCaptureGraph::AddCaptureDevice*, passing it the moniker for the video capture device. *CCaptureGraph::AddCaptureDevice* creates the DirectShow filter that manages the capture device and then adds it to the filter graph after clearing the filter graph of any other filters with a call to *CCaptureGraph::TearDownGraph*. At this point, *CMainDialog::OnSelectDevice* calls its *CMainDialog::StartPreview* method. This method builds a fully functional filter graph that will display a preview from the selected video capture device (in this case, a DV camcorder) in the WinCap window. *CMainDialog::StartPreview* calls *CCaptureGraph::RenderPreview*. Here's the implementation of that method:

```
HRESULT CCaptureGraph::RenderPreview(BOOL bRenderCC)
{
    HRESULT hr;

    OutputDebugString(TEXT("RenderPreview()\n"));

    if (!m_pCap) return E_FAIL;

    // First try to render an interleaved stream (DV).
    hr = m_pBuild->RenderStream(&PIN_CATEGORY_PREVIEW,
        &MEDIATYPE_Interleaved, m_pCap, 0, 0);
    if (FAILED(hr))
    {
```

```
    // Next try a video stream.
    hr = m_pBuild->RenderStream(&PIN_CATEGORY_PREVIEW,
        &MEDIATYPE_Video, m_pCap, 0, 0);
}

// Try to render CC. If it fails, we still count preview as successful.
if (SUCCEEDED(hr) && bRenderCC)
{
    // Try VBI pin category, then CC pin category.
    HRESULT hrCC = m_pBuild->RenderStream(&PIN_CATEGORY_VBI, 0,
        m_pCap, 0, 0);
    if (FAILED(hrCC))
    {
        hrCC = m_pBuild->RenderStream(&PIN_CATEGORY_CC, 0,
            m_pCap, 0, 0);
    }
}

if (SUCCEEDED(hr))
{
    InitVideoWindow();       // Set up the video window
    ConfigureTVAudio(TRUE);  // Try to get TV audio going
}

return hr;
}
```

This method is straightforward. It repeatedly calls the *RenderStream* method on *m_pBuild*, an *ICaptureGraphBuilder2* COM object. In the first *RenderStream* call, the stream is specified as *MEDIATYPE_Interleaved*; that is, DV video, where the video and audio signals are woven together into a single stream. Specifying this stream is a bit of a trick to test whether the video capture device is a digital camcorder or something else altogether, because a webcam or a TV tuner will not produce interleaved video but a camcorder will. So, if the first call to *RenderStream* is successful, we know we're dealing with interleaved video, which indicates a digital camcorder. There's a bit of code to deal with TV tuners and closed-captioning, which we'll cover extensively in a later chapter. Finally a call to *CGraph::InitVideoWindow* sends the video preview to a specific region in the WinCap window. This is done by the DirectShow Video Renderer filter, which we've used several times before.

Once again, back in *CMainDialog::OnSelectDevice*, we determine whether we were successful in producing a preview of the video stream. If so, we call *CMainDialog::SaveGraphFile*. This method, which I added to WinCap, is identical to the function we've used in our previous DirectShow applications, and it's been incorporated here so that you can see the kinds of filter graphs generated by WinCap. Once the filter graph has been written out, we call the filter graph manager's *Run* method, and the filter graph begins its execution.

Although we've begun execution of the filter graph, we're not quite done yet. We want to do more than just get a preview from the digital camcorder; we want to be able to control it. We need to display a control panel appropriate to the device we're controlling, so we'll need to determine the type of the device and then open the appropriate dialog box. Two public variables of *CMainDialog*—*DVProp* and *TVProp*—manage the interface to the video capture device. *DVProp* is designed to work with DV camcorders, and *TVProp* is designed to interface with TV tuners. Which one do we use? How can we tell whether we have a camcorder or a TV tuner? *DVProp* is an instance of the *CDVProp* class, which is derived from the *CExtDevice* class, which furnishes the implementation of the *InitDevice* method, as follows:

```
void CExtDevice::InitDevice(IBaseFilter *pFilter)
{

    m_pDevice.Release();
    m_pTransport.Release();
    m_pTimecode.Release();

    // Query for the external transport interfaces.

    CComPtr<IBaseFilter> pF = pFilter;
    pF.QueryInterface(&m_pDevice);

    if (m_pDevice)
    {
        // Don't query for these unless there is an external device.
        pF.QueryInterface(&m_pTransport);
        pF.QueryInterface(&m_pTimecode);

        LONG lDeviceType = 0;
        HRESULT hr = m_pDevice->GetCapability(ED_DEVCAP_DEVICE_TYPE,
            &lDeviceType, 0);
        if (SUCCEEDED(hr) && (lDeviceType == ED_DEVTYPE_VCR) &&
            (m_pTransport != 0))
        {
            m_bVTR = true;
            StartNotificationThread();
        }
    }
}
```

In this method, a *QueryInterface* call is made, requesting the *IAMExtDevice* interface to the capture graph filter object—if it exists. If it does exist, DirectShow has determined that this device is an external device. That's good, but it's not quite all that's needed. Two more calls to *QueryInterface* are made. The first call requests the *IAMExtTransport* interface. If this result is good, the device has VTR-like controls and is a digital camcorder in VTR mode. The second call requests the *IAMTimecodeReader* interface, which, if good, means that you can read the timecode on the tape inside the camcorder.

Timecode

DV camcorders leave a timestamp of information embedded in every frame captured by the device. This data is encoded in HH:MM:SS:FF format, where FF is the frame number (0–29 for standard 30-fps video). It's very useful information because with timecode you can, for example, know when to stop rewinding a tape if you're searching for a specific position within it. While it hardly qualifies as random access—stopping a tape takes time, and in general, you won't be able to stop it at precisely the location you want—timecode is very useful and provides a guide to the medium.

Through the three *QueryInterface* calls, we've learned enough to know what kind of device is attached to the computer and what its capabilities are. If the device is external and has VTR-like characteristics, it must be a digital camcorder in VTR mode. If the device does not have VTR-like characteristics, it must be a digital camcorder in camera mode. In either case, the device should be able to provide timecode; if it doesn't, that might mean there's a problem with the device—or that there's no tape in it! To be entirely sure that we have a VTR-capable device, a call is made to the *GetCapability* method of *IAMExtDevice*, and this result is compared to *ED_DEVTYPE_VCR*. If the result is *true*, the device has VCR capabilities.

CExtDevice::InitDevice creates a separate program thread that tracks all state changes in the external device. The *CExtDevice::DoNotifyLoop* method is called repeatedly whenever a DV-type device is selected. *CExtDevice::DoNotify-Loop* issues a call to the *GetStatus* method on the *IAMExtTransport* interface with *ED_MODE_CHANGE_NOTIFY* passed as a parameter. When a change in state occurs, a private message is sent to the message queue of WinCap's main window. If the device doesn't support notification, the *PollDevice* method is executed, which will poll the device repeatedly, looking for changes in the device's status. These state changes will be passed along to WinCap.

Finally, back in *CMainDialog::OnSelectDevice*, if *CExtDevice::HasDevice* returns *true*, meaning there is a digital camcorder connected, *CMainDialog::OnSelectDevice* calls the *DVProp::ShowDialog*, and the VTR window is drawn on the display. The status of the buttons in the VTR window is dependent on whether the device is in VTR mode; that is, if *CExtDevice::HasTransport* is *true*. If it is, the buttons are enabled with a call to *CDVProp::EnableVtrButtons*; if not, they're disabled with the same call.

Issuing Transport Commands

Now that WinCap has acquired all the interfaces needed both to control and monitor a digital camcorder, there's a straightforward mapping between user interface events (button presses) and commands issued to the device. In the case of either rewind or fast forward, a method call is made to *CExtDevice::Rewind* and *CExtDevice::FastForward*, respectively, which translates into a call to *CExtDevice::SetTransportState* with one of two values, either *ED_MODE_REW* or *ED_MODE_FF*. *CExtDevice::SetTransportState* has a little bit of overhead, but its essence is a single line of code that calls the *put_Mode* method of the *IAMExtTransport* interface, with either *ED_MODE_REW* or *ED_MODE_FF*, depending on the user request. That single command is all that's required to put the camcorder into either mode.

It's not much more complicated to put the device into play, stop, or record mode. In these cases, however, there's a bit of overhead inside the *CDVProp* methods in case the device is in another mode—for example, if the play button is pressed after a recording has been made to tape. In the case of the play button, it's all quite simple, as shown here:

```
void CDVProp::OnVtrPlay()
{
    if (m_pGraph)
    {
        // If previously we were transmitting from file to tape,
        // it's time to rebuild the graph.
        if (m_bTransmit)
        {
            m_pGraph->TearDownGraph();
            m_pGraph->RenderPreview();
            m_bTransmit = false;
        }
        m_pGraph->Run();
    }
    Play();
}
```

The structure of a DirectShow filter graph for tape playback is different from a filter graph used to write an AVI file to tape, so if the filter graph exists—that is, if *m_pGraph* is non-*NULL*—a test is made of *m_bTransmit*. If this is *true*, the filter graph is destroyed with a call to *CGraphBuilder::TearDownGraph* and rebuilt with a call to the *CGraphBuilder::RenderPreview* method. Once that process is complete, the *CExtDevice::Play* method is invoked, which, as is in the case of rewind and fast forward, results in a call to *CExtDevice::SetTransportState* with a passed value of *ED_MODE_PLAY*. Stopping tape playback is performed in a nearly identical way; in that case, the value sent to *CExtDevice::SetTransportState* is *ED_MODE_STOP*.

Recording an AVI File

Now that we've gone through the more basic controls for a camcorder, we'll move on to the more involved procedure of writing an AVI file to a digital camcorder. As discussed earlier in this chapter, AVI isn't the same thing as DV format, but DV data can be stored inside an AVI file format. DV-formatted AVI files come in two varieties, known as Type 1 and Type 2. Type 1 AVI files store the DV audio and video together as chunks, while Type 2 AVI files store the DV audio in a separate stream from the DV video. Most modern AVI tools and programs produce Type 2 AVI files, so those will be the ones we'll cover here, but both types are discussed in detail in Chapter 14.

When the user clicks the File Transmit icon, the *CDVProp::OnTransmit* method is invoked. Here the user selects an AVI file for transfer to camcorder. Once the selection is made, a call is made to *CCaptureGraph::RenderTransmit*. That method calls *CCaptureGraph::TearDownGraph*, destroying any existing filter graph, and then calls *CCaptureGraph::RenderType2Transmit* (assuming a Type 2 AVI file for clarity's sake), which builds a new filter graph. Here's the source code for that method:

```
HRESULT CCaptureGraph::RenderType2Transmit(const WCHAR* wszFileName)
{

    HRESULT hr;

    // Target graph looks like this:

    // File Src -> AVI Split -> DV Mux -> Inf Pin Tee -> MSDV (transmit)
    //                                             -> renderers

    CComPtr<IBaseFilter> pDVMux;
    CComPtr<IBaseFilter> pFileSource;

    // Add the DV Mux filter.
```

```
hr = AddFilter(m_pGraph, CLSID_DVMux, L"DV Mux", &pDVMux);
if (FAILED(hr))
{
    return hr;
}

// Add the File Source.
hr = m_pGraph->AddSourceFilter(wszFileName, L"Source", &pFileSource);
if (FAILED(hr))
{
    return hr;
}

// Connect the File Source to the DV Mux. This will add the splitter
// and connect one pin.
hr = ConnectFilters(m_pGraph, pFileSource, pDVMux);
if (SUCCEEDED(hr))
{
    // Find the AVI Splitter, which should be the filter downstream
    // from the File Source.
    CComPtr<IBaseFilter> pSplit;
    hr = FindConnectedFilter(pFileSource, PINDIR_OUTPUT, &pSplit);
    if (SUCCEEDED(hr))
    {
        // Connect the second pin from the AVI Splitter to the DV Mux.
        hr = ConnectFilters(m_pGraph, pSplit, pDVMux);
    }
}

if (FAILED(hr))
{
    return hr;
}

// Add the Infinite Pin Tee.
CComPtr<IBaseFilter> pTee;
hr = AddFilter(m_pGraph, CLSID_InfTee, L"Tee", &pTee);

if (FAILED(hr))
{
    return hr;
}

// Connect the DV Mux to the Tee.
hr = ConnectFilters(m_pGraph, pDVMux, pTee);
if (FAILED(hr))
{
```

```
        return hr;
    }

    // Connect the Tee to MSDV.
    hr = ConnectFilters(m_pGraph, pTee, m_pCap);
    if (FAILED(hr))
    {
        return hr;
    }

    // Render the other pin on the Tee, for preview.
    hr = m_pBuild->RenderStream(0, &MEDIATYPE_Interleaved, pTee, 0, 0);

    return hr;
}
```

This function should look very familiar to you because here a filter graph is built up, step by step, using available DirectShow filters. Figure 6-5 shows the filter graph created by WinCap to record the AVI file to the camera.

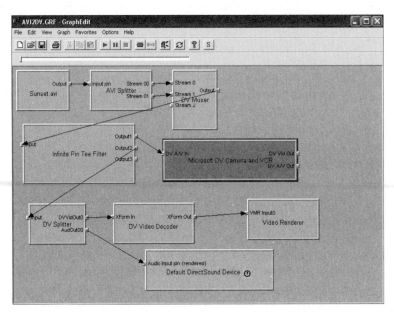

Figure 6-5   The filter graph created by WinCap

First a DV Mux filter is added to the filter graph with a call to *AddFilter*; this filter takes separate audio and video streams and multiplexes them into a single DV stream. These filters are intelligently connected using the *ConnectFilters* function (a function global to the application). This function adds an AVI Splitter filter between the two filters. Next the *FindConnectedFilter* function (another global function) locates the AVI Splitter filter and once located, connects the second pin from the AVI Splitter to the DV Mux. This splitting and recombining keeps the video and audio channels together as they pass from the file into the digital camcorder. If you don't split and recombine the stream, you'll end up with a video image but no audio. That's because we're dealing with a Type 2 AVI file here: the DV video and DV audio reside in separate streams and must be manipulated separately by DirectShow.

Next the method instantiates an Infinite Pin Tee filter. This filter is like a Smart Tee (which could have been used in its place), except that it has an unlimited number of output pins. (Also, we don't need the Smart Tee's ability to drop frames to conserve processor time.) In other words, the incoming stream can be replicated any number of times—limited by computer horsepower, of course—and every time another output pin on the Infinite Pin Tee receives a connection from another filter, another output pin is added to the Infinite Pin Tee. It truly has infinite pins—or at least one more than you'll use! The DV Mux is then connected to the Infinite Pin Tee.

At this point, the filter graph is nearly complete. The Infinite Pin Tee is connected to the filter representing the renderer filter, which in the case the Microsoft DV Camcorder and VCR filter, has an input stream to receive a stream. In addition, the Infinite Pin Tee is passed along in a call to the *RenderStream* method of the *ICaptureGraphBuilder2* interface on the filter graph builder. This call will add another output pin on the Infinite Pin Tee and send that along to the WinCap window so that the recording process can be monitored by the user as it happens.

As the last step in *CDVProp::OnTransmit*, the *CExtDevice::Record* method is invoked, which results in the invocation of *CExtDevice::SetTransportMode* with a value of *ED_MODE_RECORD*. Notice that the filter graph has not been started and data is not being transmitted across the filter graph. This is why it was important to set up a monitoring thread when we initialized the *CDVProp* object that manages the digital camcorder. As stated in the "Issuing Commands" section earlier in this chapter, a camcorder does not enter record mode for some time after the record command has been issued. However, once the device has entered record mode, the *CDVProp::OnDeviceNotify* method receives a message from the thread, and the Filter Graph Manager executes the *Run* method, beginning execution of the filter graph.

Capturing Video to an AVI File

WinCap makes capture to an AVI file very easy; the user only needs to click on the Start Capture button to begin the capture process. (AVI is a generic container format, like ASF; just because a file has an AVI extension doesn't imply that there's DV video information contained within it.) This action produces a call to the *CMainDialog::OnCapture* method. If capturing has already begun, the button reads Stop Capture, so the first thing the method does is determine whether capturing has already been going on. If so, capture ceases. If not, a call is made to *CCaptureGraph::RenderAviCapture*. This function builds a simple filter graph with a call to the *ICaptureGraphBuilder2* method *SetOutputFileName*, followed by a call to *RenderStream*. Once the filter graph has been built, a call to *CCaptureGraph::StopCapture*, which translates into a method call on the *ICaptureGraphBuilder2* method *ControlStream*. *ControlStream* allows you to set the capture parameters of a filter graph so that you can get frame-accurate capture from a stream. In this case, the parameters force any capture in progress to cease immediately. Once the filter graph has been set up, the Filter Graph Manager invokes the *Run* method and filter graph execution begins.

Back again in *CMainDialog::OnCapture*, *CCaptureGraph::StartCapture* is invoked, which translates into another call to *ControlStream*, this time with parameters that force capture to begin. With that step complete, WinCap begins to write an AVI file to disk, translating the video frames from the digital camcorder into a disk file.

When the user clicks the Stop Capture button, *CCaptureGraph::StopCapture* is invoked a final time, stopping the capture process. At this point, there should be an AVI file on the user's hard disk containing the entire content of the captured video stream. This file is likely to be very large because DV-based AVI files grow at something close to 240 MB per minute!

DirectShow doesn't sense any difference between capture from a live camcorder and capture from a miniDV tape being played through a camcorder in VTR mode. As far as DirectShow is concerned, it's a DV stream and that's it. However, for the programmer, the difference is significant because in VTR mode, the programmer has to start the filter graph, start the tape, play the tape (sending the DV stream through the filter graph), stop the tape, and—after a second or two has passed to allow for device latency in responding to commands—stop the filter graph.

Clocks and the Filter Graph

Every filter graph has to find some way to synchronize the media streams as they pass through the filter graph. Synchronization is particularly important if multiple streams are passing through a filter graph. If they become desynchronized, the results will very likely be unacceptable. For this reason, the Filter Graph Manager chooses a clock source that it uses to synchronize its operations across the entire filter graph.

Clocks and the Filter Graph

Selection of a clock source is based on the available sources. The Filter Graph Manager first looks for live capture sources, such as the Microsoft DV Camera and VCR capture source filter. That filter is connected to the IEEE 1394 bus and its associated drivers, which have their own clock. Because the stream flowing across the filter graph is being generated by the capture source filter, using that filter as the clock source will help keep all streams in the filter graph properly synchronized.

If there isn't a usable capture source filter, the Filter Graph Manager will try to use a time source from the Microsoft DirectSound Renderer filter, which is generally an interface to some hardware on the computer's sound card. The filter graph must be using the DirectSound Renderer filter if it is to become the clock source for the filter graph. The Filter Graph Manager will not add the DirectSound Renderer filter to the filter graph just to acquire a clock source. Using a DirectSound-generated clock is more than convenient; the clocking circuitry on a PC's sound card is highly accurate, and providing a clocking source through the audio hardware keeps the video synchronized with the audio. If the DirectSound Renderer isn't the clock for the filter graph, the audio renderer works through DirectSound to synchronize the clock generated by the sound card with the DirectShow system clock.

As a last resort, if the Filter Graph Manager can't acquire a clock source from a capture source filter or the DirectSound Renderer filter, it uses the system time as its clock source. The system time is the least optimal clock source because the stream passing through the graph isn't being synchronized to any clock involved in capturing the stream, which could lead to a situation where two streams passing through different portions of the graph could progressively desynchronize with respect to one another.

One way to explore clock assignments within the filter graph is to create a few capture and rendering filter graphs in GraphEdit. If a filter can act as the clock source for the filter graph, its filter is "branded" with a small icon of a clock. You'll also see the Select Clock menu item enabled when you right-click a filter that can be used as the clock source for a filter graph. Selecting that menu item sets the filter graph's clock source to the selected filter.

From the programmer's perspective, any filter object that exposes the *IReferenceClock* interface can be used as the reference clock for a filter graph. To change the reference clock on a filter graph, use the *IMediaFilter* interface, exposed by the Filter Graph Manager object. The interface has a method, *SetSyncSource*, which is passed a pointer to the new *IReferenceClock* to be used as the reference clock.

Monitoring Timecode

In the "Timecode" sidebar earlier in this chapter, we learned that digital video-tape has a timestamp, known as timecode, that tracks the tape's position. The VTR window displays the tape's timecode in an inset area underneath the VTR buttons. Whenever the VTR window needs to be updated—and that's driven by a simple timer set up when the window initializes—it makes a call to *CDVProp::DisplayTimecode*, which in turn calls *CExtDevice::GetTimecode*. Here's the implementation of that method:

```
HRESULT CExtDevice::GetTimecode(DWORD *pdwHour, DWORD *pdwMin, DWORD *pdwSec, D
WORD *pdwFrame)
{
    if (!HasTimecode())
    {
        return E_FAIL;
    }

    if (!(pdwHour && pdwMin && pdwSec && pdwFrame))
    {
        return E_POINTER;
    }

    // Initialize the struct that receives the timecode.
    TIMECODE_SAMPLE TimecodeSample;
    ZeroMemory(&TimecodeSample, sizeof(TIMECODE_SAMPLE));
    TimecodeSample.dwFlags = ED_DEVCAP_TIMECODE_READ;

    HRESULT hr;
    if (hr = m_pTimecode->GetTimecode(&TimecodeSample),  SUCCEEDED(hr))
    {
        // Coerce the BCD value to our own timecode struct,
        // in order to unpack the value.

        DV_TIMECODE *pTimecode =
            (DV_TIMECODE*)(&(TimecodeSample.timecode.dwFrames));

        *pdwHour = pTimecode->Hours10 * 10 + pTimecode->Hours1;
        *pdwMin = pTimecode->Minutes10 * 10 + pTimecode->Minutes1;
        *pdwSec = pTimecode->Seconds10 * 10 + pTimecode->Seconds1;
        *pdwFrame = pTimecode->Frames10 * 10 + pTimecode->Frames1;
    }
    return hr;
}
```

If the device has timecode capabilities—that is, if *CExtDevice::HasTime-code* returns a non-*NULL* result, a structure defined as *TIMECODE_SAMPLE* is initialized and then passed along as a parameter to the *IAMTimecodeReader* method *GetTimecode*. *GetTimecode* returns the tape's current timecode format, not in decimal notation, but in binary-coded decimal, an antique notation that's rarely used anymore. Because of this notation, there's a bit of arithmetic to convert the binary-coded decimal to decimal, and that value is returned in four parts: hours, minutes, seconds, and frames. Don't attempt to use the raw, unconverted values returned by *GetTimecode*; they're not proper decimal numbers and will lead to all sorts of errors.

DV Devices, Timecode, Synchronization, and Dropped Frames

Some DV devices—in particular, Sony camcorders—will create non-sequential timecodes, which means that as your tape advances through the play heads, the timecode value could actually return to 00:00:00:00. This is a convenience feature (as Sony sees it) because the camera decides (based on its own internal calculations) that an entirely new sequence of video has begun, at which point the timecode is zeroed and the count begins again.

This situation is a possible gotcha for programmers searching for a particular timecode on a tape. For example, you might find more than one point on a tape that has a 00:00:00:00 timecode. If you're looking for the start of the tape, it's probably best to rewind the tape to its beginning instead of search for a particular timecode. (To get around this problem, some DV filmmakers take a blank tape and simply record onto it with no source video to establish a continuous timecode from beginning to end of tape.) This timecode problem is one reason that professionals working with digital video often opt for a DVCAM-capable camcorder. Although DVCAM records the same 25 Mbps stream as miniDV and Digital8 camcorders, the timecode is maintained continuously from the start of the tape through to its end.

Another issue that a DirectShow programmer might encounter when working with DV timecode is that the timestamps on DV media samples do not match the computer clock. DirectShow uses the IEEE 1394 bus clock contained within the IEEE 1394 data packets to create a timestamp value that's added to the media sample data as it passes through the filter graph. This clock isn't the same as the computer's clock (the *REFERENCE_TIME* value given in 100-nanosecond increments), so over a long enough time period, the system time and the DV timestamp will drift

(continued)

DV Devices, Timecode, Synchronization, and Dropped Frames   *(continued)*

---

apart. Is this a problem? It might be if you're relying on perfect synchronization between the system clock and media sample timestamps.

DirectShow provides an interface on every video capture source filter known as *IAMDroppedFrames*. This interface provides a way for the filter graph to report frames dropped by the capture filter. Frames can get dropped if the computer gets too busy performing some other task to service the capture source filter or if the computer's hard disk isn't fast enough to write the entire DV stream to disk. The *IAMDroppedFrames* interface presents the GetNumDropped and GetDroppedInfo methods so that the DirectShow application can detect dropped frames and, perhaps, recover any lost data. (An application could detect dropped frames and in the case of a VTR source, rewind the input DV stream to a position before the lost frames and capture the source stream once again.) Dropped frames can also be the fault of the camcorder; errors on a DV tape playing through a camcorder can produce dropped frames.

Getting Device Information

It's often important to know specific parameters about an external device connected to a computer. In the case of a digital camcorder, for example, it might be very important to know whether there's a tape in the unit. If there isn't, you might need to alert users before they attempt to record to a nonexistent tape! Although it's not a part of WinCap, the following function can be integrated into your own DirectShow applications to give you the ability to detect a tape-not-present situation, as well as tell you something about the capabilities of the device attached to the user's computer:

```
HRESULT DV_GetTapeInfo(void)
{
    HRESULT hr;
    LONG    lMediaType = 0;
    LONG    lInSignalMode = 0;

    // Query Media Type of the transport.
    hr = MyDevCap.pTransport->GetStatus(ED_MEDIA_TYPE, &lMediaType);
    if (SUCCEEDED(hr))
    {
        if (ED_MEDIA_NOT_PRESENT == lMediaType)
        {
```

```
        // We want to return failure if no tape is installed.
        hr = S_FALSE;
}
else
{

        // Now let's query for the signal mode of the tape.
        MyDevCap.pTransport->GetTransportBasicParameters
          (ED_TRANSBASIC_INPUT_SIGNAL, &lInSignalMode, NULL);
        Sleep(_MAX_SLEEP);
        if (SUCCEEDED(hr))
        {   // Determine whether the camcorder supports NTSC or PAL.
            switch (lInSignalMode)
            {
                case ED_TRANSBASIC_SIGNAL_525_60_SD :
                g_AvgTimePerFrame = 33;  // 33 ms (29.97 FPS)
                printf("VCR Mode - NTSC\n");
                break;

            case ED_TRANSBASIC_SIGNAL_525_60_SDL :
                g_AvgTimePerFrame = 33;  // 33 ms (29.97 FPS)
                printf("VCR Mode - NTSC\n");
                break;

            case ED_TRANSBASIC_SIGNAL_625_50_SD :
                g_AvgTimePerFrame = 40;  // 40 ms (25 FPS)
                printf("VCR Mode - PAL\n");
                break;

            case ED_TRANSBASIC_SIGNAL_625_50_SDL :
                g_AvgTimePerFrame = 40;  // 40 ms (25 FPS)
                printf("VCR Mode - PAL\n");
                break;

            default :
                printf("Unsupported or unrecognized tape format type\n.");
                g_AvgTimePerFrame = 33;  // 33 ms (29.97 FPS); default
                break;
            }

            printf("Avg time per frame is %d FPS\n",
                g_AvgTimePerFrame);
        }
        else
        {
            printf("GetTransportBasicParameters Failed (0x%x)\n", hr);
        }
```

```
        }
    }
    else
    {
        printf("GetStatus Failed (0x%x)\n", hr);
    }
    return hr;
}
```

The *DV_GetTapeInfo* function—from the sample program DVApp, an excellent sample program that covers many DV features not explored in Win-Cap—begins with a call to the *IAMExtTransport* method *GetStatus*, passed with a parameter of *ED_MEDIA_TYPE*. This call translates into a request for the media type inserted into the external device, which in this case is a digital camcorder. If the method returns a value of *ED_MEDIA_NOT_PRESENT*, there's no tape in the device.

Next a call to the *IAMExtTransport* method *GetTransportBasicParameters*, passed with a parameter of *ED_TRANSBASIC_INPUT_SIGNAL*, will return a value that indicates the format of the video signal encoded on the tape. A value of *ED_TRANSBASIC_SIGNAL_525_60_SD* or *ED_TRANSBASIC_SIGNAL_525_60_SDL* indicates a video format of 30 fps, the NTSC standard used in the USA and Japan. A value of *ED_TRANSBASIC_SIGNAL_625_50_SD* or *ED_TRANS-BASIC_SIGNAL_625_50_SDL* indicates a video format of 25 fps, the PAL standard used widely across Europe, Africa, and Asia.

Several other properties can be queried with the *GetTransportBasic-Parameters* method call. Information on these properties can be found in the DirectShow SDK documentation.

Issuing Raw AV/C Commands

In some situations, the hardware control options offered by DirectShow filters are not enough to handle the particulars of your digital camcorder–based application. DirectShow provides a clean and concise interface to the camcorder for such basic operations as play, record, fast forward, and rewind. But what if you want to eject the tape from the camcorder? As you see in the VTR dialog box, there's a button featuring the eject glyph, which attempts to eject the tape from the selected camcorder. Ejection can't be done with any of the basic functionality offered by the *IAMExtTransport* interface. Instead, it has to be done through a raw Audio Video Control (AV/C) command sent directly to the device.

DirectShow does offer a mechanism to issue raw AV/C commands to attached IEEE 1394 devices. The *IAMExtTransport* interface's *GetTransportBasic-Parameters* method can be used to issue these raw commands. Here's the implementation of the *CDVProp::Eject* method, which sends a raw AV/C command to the camcorder:

```
void CDVProp::Eject()
{
    BYTE AvcCmd[512]; // Big enough for the command
    ZeroMemory(AvcCmd, sizeof(AvcCmd));

    BYTE EjectCommand[] = { 0x00, 0x20, 0xC1, 0x60 };
    memcpy(AvcCmd, EjectCommand, sizeof(EjectCommand));

    long cbCmd = sizeof(EjectCommand);
    HRESULT hr =
        GetTransport()->GetTransportBasicParameters(ED_RAW_EXT_DEV_CMD,
        &cbCmd, (LPOLESTR*)AvcCmd);

    return;
}
```

To issue a raw AV/C command, a buffer is created, cleared, and then loaded with the command to be sent to the device. This buffer has to be big enough to handle any return message sent from the device, so here we've created a buffer of 512 bytes, the maximum message length. The buffer is passed in a call to the *GetTransportBasicParameters* method with a value of *ED_RAW_EXT_DEV_CMD* passed as the first parameter, indicating that this is a raw AV/C command. The call is processed synchronously; control will not return until the command has been completed. At this point, the returned buffer should have whatever response codes were issued by the device, and the method's return value should be examined for any Windows error code.

The topic of raw AV/C commands is a big one, too rich to be covered in detail in this book. The relevant documentation on AV/C commands can be found on the Web site of the IEEE 1394 Trade Association, *www.1394ta.org*, under Specifications. Here you'll find links to documentation describing the format and definition of the call and return values of each of the AV/C commands implemented by IEEE 1394 devices.

A final warning: you should use a raw AV/C command only when you have no other choice. The eject function is not offered by Windows and it isn't implemented in all camcorders, so we need to use raw AV/C functionality to implement it. Raw AV/C commands are not managed by Windows, and the program will wait for a response to the command before continuing program execution. Therefore, if the device fails to respond for some reason, your program could be waiting a long, long time.

Multiple DV Camcorders on a Computer

IEEE 1394 allows multiple camcorders to be connected to a host computer. Although you might be tempted to think that this would allow you to work with multiple DV video streams simultaneously in your filter graph, the truth of the matter is that it is at best unreliable. Here are some technical comments explaining why from the DirectShow engineering group at Microsoft.

CMP (Connection Management Procedure) issues   IEEE 1394 devices need to establish peer-to-peer connection for streaming. This is different from USB, where the host is always in control. To start streaming, the device and the PC establish a connection, which is an agreement for the data producer and consumer to transmit and listen to the same isochronous channel. (Isochronous channels allow the transmitter to reserve a portion of bandwidth on a network.) This is done via the CMP protocol. IEEE 1394 uses 64 channels (0 through 63), with channel 63 reserved for broadcast. Many DV camcorders are not CMP compliant, so the PC does not initiate the connection. It relies on the camcorder to make a broadcast connection on channel 63. Because there is only one broadcast channel, DirectShow can work with only one such non-compliant DV device on a 1394 bus.

Bandwidth   Although IEEE 1394a supports up to 400 Mbps networking, most consumer DV camcorders use the 100 Mbps rate. Bandwidth is measured in "bandwidth units" of 20.3 nanoseconds (ns). There are 6144 units per 125 millisecond (ms) cycle. For isochronous (streaming) transfer, 25 ms (20 percent) is reserved for asynchronous control data, leaving 80 percent for the isochronous transfer (4915 units). A typical consumer DV camcorder has a 25-Mbps video stream, but there is additional overhead for audio and things like 1394 packet headers. The calculation for one DV stream according to IEC 61883-1 is 2512 units, which is more than half of the 4915 available. If the DV device is the isochronous resource manager (IRM), it will make the available bandwidth value slightly higher (greater than 5024 units or 82 percent) to allow two DV streams, although this does not comply with the IEEE 1394 specification. If the PC is the IRM, it reserves exactly 80 percent of bandwidth, following the specification, with the result that only one camcorder will be visible to the DirectShow application—the one that's turned on first.

Camera mode   If two legacy (non-CMP) camcorders are connected to the computer, the PC does not establish the connection. The devices

Multiple DV Camcorders on a Computer

will compete to use the broadcast channel (63) for streaming, and probably the first one to stream will get the broadcast channel. If you have a mix of one legacy and one CMP-compliant device, the situation gets even more complicated, so it's not a reliable scenario.

VTR mode   If both cameras are in VTR mode and the application plays a tape on only one device, then it should work.

If you do have multiple cameras of the same type (same manufacturer, make, and model) on your system, you're going to need some way to distinguish them. Their monikers will have the same *Description* and *FriendlyName* values, so they can't be used for this purpose. Instead, you'll need to get the *DevicePath* property from the property bag. (We covered how to use the property bag when enumerating devices in Chapter 4.) This isn't a human-readable string (it's not text), but it is unique to each camcorder. That string can be used to differentiate between multiple camcorders of the same type on a single system. How you chose to represent these camcorders to the user ("Sony Camcorder 1," "Sony Camcorder 2," etc.) is up to you.

Summary

As can be seen from WinCap, DirectShow provides a very flexible framework for on-the-fly creation of filter graphs that can both record streams from DV camcorders and write streams to them. Once the proper interfaces have been created, sending control signals to these external devices is as easy as a single line of code. Using timecode, it's possible to queue a tape to a particular point, either for capture or recording purposes. Everything in this chapter can be repurposed for your own uses in your own projects and could form the foundation for a powerful video editing tool, such as Microsoft Windows Movie Maker 2 or Adobe Premiere.

Now we'll move on to the other half of WinCap, which provides a platform for working with TV tuners. They're more complicated but also more rewarding. In the next chapter, you'll learn what makes a personal video recorder tick.

7

Working with TV Tuners and Pausing Live Video Streams

Ever since the emergence of the World Wide Web in the middle of the 1990s, pundits and futurists have predicted the dawn of *convergence*, an almost mystical state of communion wherein the television, home computer, and entertainment center would become as one, a single device that could carry broadcast media, Internet, video games, movies-on-demand, and so on. Although convergence sounded like a great idea—particularly to other pundits and futurists—media companies weren't too happy to share the spotlight (and advertising revenues) with the upstart "new media" companies and did all they could to frustrate the seemingly inevitable combination of old and new media. When AOL purchased Time Warner in early 2000, it seemed as though the age of convergence had finally come; now, some years later, AOL Time Warner seems more of a misconception than a business ideal, and convergence has entered the living room through a Trojan horse—the personal video recorder.

The idea behind the personal video recorder, or PVR, is a simple one: take a live analog TV signal, convert it to digital, and then write its data to a high-capacity storage medium, such as a hard disk. Unlike a VCR, there'd be no temperamental tapes to fuss with or to jam in the mechanical innards of a machine that few people even know how to program. (Think of all those VCRs in the world that still blink 12:00, and you can grasp the problem.) With a PVR you'd get high-quality digital copies of your favorite TV programs, which you'd be able to record by scrolling through a schedule of available channels and programming, selecting only those shows you'd be interested in watching. For the user interface alone, the PVR represents a quantum leap over the VCR.

In March 1999, the first PVR, TiVo, came to market—and it was an immediate success. Including TiVo along with the ReplayTV PVR from SONICblue, Inc., more than a million PVRs have been sold in just the first three years since their introduction, making them among the most successful consumer electronics devices of all time. Both products provide on-demand recording of analog TV signals, which can be played back at any time. Their most interesting feature, however, is the live pause capability they add to TV viewing. With the press of a button, TV programming can be stopped in the middle of a broadcast (which comes in handy if, for example, the phone rings during your favorite episode of "The Simpsons") and resumed with the press of another button. What kind of magic is this?

Basically, the PVR is always digitizing the TV signal and writing it to the hard disk. In normal operation, this stream of digital data is also immediately sent to the TV set. When the unit pauses live TV, the stream of video data continues to be written to the hard disk, while the stream to the TV pauses. Once the PVR re-enters play mode, the stream playback continues from the pause point, while the incoming stream continues to be rewritten to the PVR's disk. This gap between record and playback also makes it possible to "skip over" commercials (which is why SONICblue was sued by several major TV production companies), and it allows you to "rewind" a live broadcast, to watch a scene again and again, before resuming your normal viewing. This concept of buffered TV viewing has made the PVR a must-have item for anyone who has had the opportunity to "time-shift" a TV program.

As you've already learned, Microsoft DirectShow provides a lot of functionality similar to that provided by a PVR. For example, you can capture a video stream in the filter graph and then write it to disk, while also previewing it to the display. In addition to the features we've already covered, DirectShow has a number of filters that specifically provide features designed to work with PC-based TV tuner cards. These cards—which can be purchased for less than $100—connect to an antenna or a cable TV signal and provide all the hardware needed to decode an analog TV signal, converting it to a digital format that can be manipulated by the PC. These peripherals generally come with software that provides basic PVR features. For example, many of them allow you to record a TV program to an MPEG movie file for later viewing through an associated application, such as Windows Media Player.

Noting the success of the PVR, Microsoft partnered with Hewlett-Packard and Samsung (at the time of this writing), introducing its own Windows XP Media Center Edition product in the autumn of 2002. The Hewlett-Packard product is a PC containing an on-board TV tuner with an integrated MPEG-2 encoder. The MPEG-2 encoder keeps the files nice and small and allows hundreds of hours of video programming to be stored on the system's hard disk.

The computer also comes equipped with Windows XP Service Pack 1. This service pack is necessary because it provides a few new DirectShow filters, known as the Stream Buffer components. These components provide the basis for buffered viewing of video signals, just like TiVo.

Now that the Microsoft operating systems have become PVR friendly, we can expect to see an explosion in the use of TV tuner cards in the PC over the next few years, as the convergence promised nearly a decade ago begins to take shape. Windows programmers (and hopefully, more than a few readers of this book) will be able to use these new operating system features to build applications that make TV viewing an integral part of the PC experience; we might even see the day when a Windows-based PVR is just another desktop icon, like Internet Explorer. That's when TV viewing, Internet access, and electronic entertainment converge in an easy-to-use device. That's real convergence.

Working with TV Tuners in DirectShow

Although the DirectShow filters that provide TV tuner functionality are as easy to use as any other DirectShow filters—because their internal operations are effectively hidden from view—the filter graphs created can be enormously complex. For example, the WinCap application creates the filter graph shown in Figure 7-1 when my ATI Rage Theatre Video Capture device is selected.

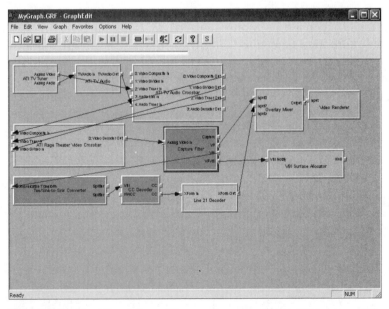

Figure 7-1   The DirectShow filter graph created for a TV tuner, which contains 11 filters

No fewer than 11 filters are required to fully implement a TV tuner in DirectShow—and that's without any capture or buffering capabilities that we might want in a PVR. However, this number of filters is a pretty common state of affairs for TV tuners, and although your own filter graphs might be less complex—depending on the TV tuner hardware and its associated drivers—your filter graphs are likely to be at least this crowded with filters. We'll walk through this filter graph step-by-step to get a sense of how the TV data stream passes from capture to display. Again, your own filter graphs might look a bit different.

To begin with, the ATI TV Tuner filter acts as a control node where the programmer can set the tuner channel and adjust other hardware features of the tuner card. Although the filter graph shows streams for Analog Video and Analog Audio, these streams are just abstractions and are not flowing through the filter graph. Nonetheless, a lot of processing can be done on these abstract signals before they enter the filter graph, so the Analog Audio output pin is connected to the TV Audio In input pin on the ATI TV Audio filter. This filter controls the audio capabilities of the stream. Broadcast television can be received in either monaural or stereo sound, and this filter can switch between these two modes. In addition, many broadcasts also have a Secondary Audio Program (SAP), often in a foreign language (in the United States, generally Spanish), and the ATI TV Audio filter can also be used to choose between audio channels. Within the filter, these audio channels are identified as Language A and Language B.

The TV Audio Out pin of the ATI TV Audio filter and the Analog Video output pin of the ATI TV Tuner are connected, respectively, to the Audio Tuner In pin and Video Tuner In pin of the ATI TV Audio Crossbar. A *crossbar*, a hardware feature found on many TV tuner cards, routes various analog inputs across the hardware (in this case, the ATI Rage 8500 TV Tuner card) to determine which of several inputs will be sent to the hardware that translates the analog signal into a digital data stream. These signals are then passed to another crossbar, the ATI Rage Video Theatre Crossbar filter; the Video Tuner Out pin is connected to the Video Tuner In pin, the Video SVideo Out pin is connected to the Video SVideo In pin, and the Video Composite Out pin (which contains both audio and video signals) is passed to the Video Composite In pin. This filter passes the signal through to a single output pin on the ATI Rage Video Theatre Crossbar filter, Video Decoder Out. After everything has been correctly routed by the crossbar circuitry of the TV tuner, the hardware begins the process of analog-to-digital conversion.

The Capture Filter has four output pins. The VBI pin (named after the vertical blanking interval) is used for closed captioning (CC), the text description and narration that's carried within most broadcast TV signals for people who are hard of hearing, which can be decoded by nearly all televisions manufactured after 1995. (If you've never seen how closed captioning works, launch

WinCap and select a TV tuner device. You'll see closed captioning in action because it's enabled by default in WinCap. If you don't see any text overlaid across the video image, try changing channels—the program you're viewing might not have closed captioning.)

The output of the VBI pin is passed along to the Communication Transform input pin of the Tee/Sink-to-Sink Converter filter. Like the Smart Tee and Infinite Tee, this filter creates multiple output streams from a single input stream. The signal is divided into two streams, each presented on a Splitter output pin. One of these outputs is passed along to the CC Decoder filter, which translates the VBI signal into closed-captioning data. (If you're working with international TV signals, DirectShow supports World Standard Teletext level 1.5, but you'll have to consult the Microsoft DirectX SDK documentation for details on how to decode that signal.) The closed-captioning data (pairs of bytes) is passed along through the CC output pin to the input pin of the Line 21 Decoder filter, a standard DirectShow filter that translates the closed-captioning data into a bitmap with the closed-captioned text drawn onto it. That stream is presented on the filter's output pin.

The VPVBI output pin is directly connected to a specialized DirectShow filter, the VBI Surface Allocator. The VBI Surface Allocator filter reserves some space within the dedicated graphics memory of the TV tuner card (which, in this case, is also a video display card) so that the decoded VBI signal can be written directly to a hardware buffer on the graphics card. Although it's not a renderer filter, the VBI Surface Allocator has no downstream connections to other filters—although it does have an output pin, Null, that connects to nothing else.

Now that the closed-captioning data has been successfully decoded, it's brought into Input 2 of the Overlay Mixer filter, which mixes text captioning data with a video stream. There are two situations in which you're likely to encounter a mix of video and text streams: closed-captioned TV broadcasts, as explored here, and DVD playback when the subtitling feature has been turned on. The third output pin on the Capture filter, VP (for video port), which provides the digitized video stream from the TV tuner, is connected to Input 1 on the Overlay Mixer filter.

The video port connection between the Capture filter and the Overlay Mixer filter is performed using kernel streaming to pass the bits very quickly from one filter to the other. Kernel streaming has always been a core feature of DirectX because it allows slow computers (such as those of just a few years ago) to handle high bit-rate devices, such as video digitizers. The downside of kernel streaming through a video port is that it's not possible to add filters into the stream between the Capture filter and the Overlay Mixer. The video port connection is dedicated and can't be interfered with in any way. Now that computers have gotten much faster, video ports are being deemphasized by

Microsoft and will soon be a thing of the past, but as of this writing, many TV tuners support capture through a video port.

The connection of video and closed-captioning streams to the Overlay Mixer creates a text overlay (closed captioning) on the broadcast video image. Finally the Output pin of the Overlay Mixer filter is connected to the Input pin on the Video Renderer (which we've seen many times before), and the filter graph is complete. The TV signal has been received, processed, digitized, broken into separate streams for video and closed captioning, and then recombined into a single video image. In this case, the Overlay Mixer is doing the actual on-screen rendering of the digitized TV signal, while the Video Renderer is managing only the on-screen window in which the video appears.

Although there's no explicit path for audio rendering in this filter graph, when the filter graph is run, audio does come through the speakers. How does this happen? There's a bit of magic in the ATI TV Audio Crossbar—hidden from view—that connects the audio output to the appropriate sound hardware and keeps it all properly synchronized.

Now that we've walked through a filter graph for a TV tuner, let's turn back to WinCap to gain an understanding of the DirectShow programming that creates these complex filter graphs. It's easier to do than you might think. Note that what follows applies only to analog TV signals. DirectShow has a set of filters designed for digital television and high-definition television (HDTV), but they're well beyond the scope of this book. If you'd like more information on those filters, you can find it in the DirectX SDK documentation.

Video Control

When creating TV applications, an alternative approach is to use the Video Control, an ActiveX control that supports analog TV tuners, DVD, file playback, and also a new generation of digital TV tuners based on the Microsoft Broadcast Driver Architecture (BDA). The Video Control is used in Windows XP Media Center Edition, and in many ways, it greatly simplifies the creation of TV filter graphs. In this chapter, we build a TV application the old-fashioned way to demonstrate the underlying concepts that the Video Control hides from view. Also, this chapter doesn't cover digital TV support. At the time of writing, digital TV tuners are not yet widely available. That situation is expected to change in the near future, however, so if you're looking to create a digital TV application, or even an analog TV application using Microsoft Visual Basic or a scripting language, check out the DirectShow SDK documentation under "Microsoft TV Technologies."

Using WinCap for TV Capture

As discussed in Chapter 6, when launched, WinCap presents a list of all available video capture devices connected to the system, including webcams, digital camcorders, digital VCRs, and TV tuners. When you select a TV tuner device from the list and then click the Select Device button, you'll see a second window open, as shown in Figure 7-2.

Figure 7-2   The Television dialog window that opens alongside the Win-Cap window when a TV tuner is selected

In addition to the broadcast TV image, in the upper portion of the WinCap window, a second window, named Television, opens alongside it. This window is the equivalent of a TV remote control. You can punch numbers onto the keypad, hit the Enter button, and change channels. The Scan area of the dialog box has up and down arrows that allow you to scan through the channels, respectively incrementing and decrementing the channel number. In addition, you can turn closed captioning on or off by clicking in the CC check box, or you can mute the audio by selecting the Mute check box. Now let's take a look at how WinCap implements these features using DirectShow.

Selecting a TV Tuner Device

After WinCap is launched, the list of video capture devices is created with calls to *CMainDialog::Init* and *CDeviceList::Populate*, which fills it with all video capture devices known to DirectShow. Although any valid video capture device can be selected, in this chapter, we'll consider only what happens when a TV tuner is selected.

When a TV tuner device is selected and the Select Device button is clicked, the *CMainDialog::OnSelectDevice* method is invoked. This method immediately invokes the *CMainDialog::InitGraph* method, which is where the DirectShow Filter Graph Manager directly interacts with WinCap. The application maintains communication with the DirectShow Filter Graph Manager through a *CGraph* object. The *CMainDialog* object has a private variable, named *m_pGraph*, which is a *CCaptureGraph* object derived from the *CGraph* class, but it's specifically used to build a capture filter graph. *CMainDialog::Init-Graph* creates a new *CCaptureGraph* object that in turn creates a new Filter Graph Manager object.

Next *CMainDialog::OnSelectDevice* calls *CCaptureGraph::AddCapture-Device*, passing it the moniker for the video capture device. This method instantiates an object to manage the DirectShow filter and then adds it to the filter graph—after clearing the filter graph of any other filters with a call to *CCapture-Graph::TearDownGraph*. At this point, *CMainDialog::OnSelectDevice* calls the *CMainDialog::StartPreview* method. This method builds a fully functional filter graph that will display a preview from the selected video capture device (in this case, the TV tuner) in the WinCap window. *CMainDialog::StartPreview* calls *CCaptureGraph::RenderPreview*. In Chapter 6, we covered the implementation of that method, but because we're going to trace a different path through the method, it is presented here again:

```
HRESULT CCaptureGraph::RenderPreview(BOOL bRenderCC)
{
    HRESULT hr;

    OutputDebugString(TEXT("RenderPreview()\n"));

    if (!m_pCap) return E_FAIL;


    // First try to render an interleaved stream (DV).
    hr = m_pBuild->RenderStream(&PIN_CATEGORY_PREVIEW,
        &MEDIATYPE_Interleaved, m_pCap, 0, 0);
    if (FAILED(hr))
    {
        // Next try a video stream.
        hr = m_pBuild->RenderStream(&PIN_CATEGORY_PREVIEW,
            &MEDIATYPE_Video, m_pCap, 0, 0);
    }

    // Try to render CC. If it fails, we still count preview as successful.
```

```
if (SUCCEEDED(hr) && bRenderCC)
{
    // Try VBI pin category, then CC pin category.
    HRESULT hrCC = m_pBuild->RenderStream(&PIN_CATEGORY_VBI, 0,
        m_pCap, 0, 0);
    if (FAILED(hrCC))
    {
        hrCC = m_pBuild->RenderStream(&PIN_CATEGORY_CC, 0,
            m_pCap, 0, 0);
    }
}

if (SUCCEEDED(hr))
{
    InitVideoWindow();        // Set up the video window
    ConfigureTVAudio(TRUE);   // Try to get TV audio going
}

return hr;
}
```

In this case, when a TV tuner device has been selected, the first call to the *ICaptureGraphBuilder2* method *RenderStream* will fail because the parameter *MEDIATYPE_Interleaved* won't match the stream type. The method then makes another call to *RenderStream*, this time with *MEDIATYPE_Video*, the type appropriate to TV tuners. This call should succeed (if things are working correctly), and a filter graph will be built, looking very much like the filter graph that we've already examined, with the exception of the closed-captioning portion of the filter graph. That portion of the filter graph is created with a second call to *RenderStream*; this call is passed with *PIN_CATEGORY_VBI* as the first parameter, requesting that the VBI signal be used as the source for closed-captioning text. If this call fails (and it might, depending on the filters added to the filter graph by the initial call to *RenderStream*), a second *RenderStream* call is made, this time with *PIN_CATEGORY_CC*, which will attempt to use a filter pin with closed-captioning data as the source for the text to be rendered into the video stream. If either of these calls succeeds—and there's a chance that neither will—the components necessary to handle closed-captioned decoding and overlay into the video image are added to the filter graph.

Finally, after the capture graph has been built, a call is made to *CCapture-Graph::ConfigureTVAudio*. In this method, the TV audio stream is rendered, as shown here:

```
HRESULT CCaptureGraph::ConfigureTVAudio(BOOL bActivate)
{
    if (!m_pCap) return S_FALSE;
```

```
// Basically we have to grovel the filter graph for a crossbar filter,
// then try to connect the Audio Decoder Out pin to the Audio Tuner In
// pin. Some cards have two crossbar filters.

// Search upstream for a crossbar.
IAMCrossbar *pXBar1 = NULL;
HRESULT hr = m_pBuild->FindInterface(&LOOK_UPSTREAM_ONLY, NULL, m_pCap,
    IID_IAMCrossbar, (void**)&pXBar1);
if (SUCCEEDED(hr))
{
    // Try to connect the audio pins.
    hr = ConnectAudio(pXBar1, bActivate);
    if (FAILED(hr))
    {
        // Search upstream for another crossbar.
        IBaseFilter *pF = NULL;
        hr = pXBar1->QueryInterface(IID_IBaseFilter, (void**)&pF);
        if (SUCCEEDED(hr))
        {
            IAMCrossbar *pXBar2 = NULL;
            hr = m_pBuild->FindInterface(&LOOK_UPSTREAM_ONLY, NULL, pF,
                IID_IAMCrossbar, (void**)&pXBar2);
            pF->Release();
            if (SUCCEEDED(hr))
            {
                // Try to connect the audio pins.
                hr = ConnectAudio(pXBar2, bActivate);
                pXBar2->Release();
            }
        }
    }
    pXBar1->Release();
}

return hr;
}
```

The *CCaptureGraph::ConfigureTVAudio* method searches the filter graph constructed by the *RenderStream* calls. It begins with a call to the *ICaptureGraphBuilder2* method *FindInterface*. This method searches a filter graph, starting with a pointer to a filter in the graph, and searches either upstream or downstream from it for a filter with a matching interface identifier—in this case, *IID_IAMCrossbar*. (Use *LOOK_DOWNSTREAM_ONLY* to search downstream.) That interface identifier should (in the case of the ATI Rage Video 8500 TV Tuner) return a pointer to the ATI TV Audio Crossbar filter within the filter graph. If that call succeeds, a call to the global function *ConnectAudio* is made.

```
HRESULT ConnectAudio(IAMCrossbar *pXBar, BOOL bActivate)
{
    // Look for the Audio Decoder output pin.
    long i = 0;
    HRESULT hr = FindCrossbarPin(pXBar, PhysConn_Audio_AudioDecoder,
        FALSE, &i);
    if (SUCCEEDED(hr))
    {
        if (bActive)  // Activate the audio
        {
            // Look for the Audio Tuner input pin.
            long j = 0;
            hr = FindCrossbarPin(pXBar, PhysConn_Audio_Tuner, TRUE, &j);
            if (SUCCEEDED(hr))
            {
                return pXBar->Route(i, j);
            }
        }
        else  // Mute the audio
        {
            return pXBar->Route(i, -1);
        }
    }
    return E_FAIL;
}
```

ConnectAudio uses the local function *FindCrossbarPin* to locate a pin of type *PhysConn_Audio_AudioDecoder*, that is, a physically connected audio decoder (which is visible in the filter graph). It then finds another pin on the crossbar *PhysConn_Audio_Tuner*, which represents the audio tuner portion of the crossbar, and then calls the *Route* method to connect the two pins. In a sense, the *Route* method virtually "wires" connections in the crossbar. When this connection is made, audio is rendered to the PC's speakers. To mute the audio, all that needs to be done is to break the connection with another call to *Route*.

Although it might seems as though the audio is being passed through DirectShow, the TV tuner card generally sends the audio directly to the computer's sound card (often with the help of a cross-connecting cable that takes an output on the TV Tuner and connects it to an input of the sound card), usually through Line In or CD Audio In pins. So while the crossbar filter is sending commands to the TV tuner card, the filter is not processing the audio data in any way.

Back in *CCaptureGraph::ConfigureTVAudio*, if the call to *ConnectAudio* fails for any reason, the method attempts to locate another audio crossbar in the filter graph and again calls *ConnectAudio*. This call is made to cover cases where there might be multiple audio crossbars in the filter graph, which could potentially happen. At that point, control returns to *CCaptureGraph::Render-Preview*, which returns to *CMainDialog::SelectDevice*, and we're all done. Video imagery will be sent to the upper portion of the WinCap window, and sound will come through the designated audio output device.

Selecting a TV Channel

When the TV tuner device is selected from the list of available video capture devices, the control interface, *IAMTVTuner*, which maintains communication with the TV tuner, is created with a call to *CTunerProp::InitDevice* and then stored in the local variable *m_pTuner*. At the same time, the Line 21 Decoder filter is also located, and a pointer to its control interface, *IAMLine21Decoder*, is placed in *m_pLine21*. These interfaces receive the messages that control various parameters, such as the decoding of closed captioning and the selection of a TV channel.

The keypad on the Television dialog box accepts clicks on the number pad as input, but it doesn't process them until the Enter button has been pressed. When that happens, this bit of code, inside *CTunerProp::OnReceiveMsg*, is executed:

```
case IDC_CHAN_ENTER:            // Submit new channel to the tuner
    if (m_pTuner)
    {
        HRESULT hr = m_pTuner->put_Channel(m_lNewChannel, -1, -1);
            if (SUCCEEDED(hr))
            {
                m_lChannel = m_lNewChannel;
            }
            else
            {
                // Failed.  Restore old channel.
                m_lNewChannel = m_lChannel;
                hr = m_pTuner->put_Channel(m_lNewChannel, -1, -1);
            }
    }
    m_bStartNewChannel = false;
    RedrawControl(IDC_CHANNEL_DRAW);
    return TRUE;
```

To change the channel on a TV tuner, you need to invoke only the *put_Channel* method on the *IAMTVTuner* interface. The first parameter passed in *put_Channel* is the channel number, and the second and third parameters, which are both set to –1 in this case, handle the video and audio subchannel information, which are useful only if you're adjusting the tuning on a satellite broadcast receiver.

Conversely, if you want to determine what channel the TV tuner is receiving, you can make a call to the *IAMTVTuner* interface method *get_Channel*, which will return the channel number (and subchannels, if they're relevant). Additionally, if you need to know the range of possible channels—to ensure that you can reject any illegal channel request—use *get_ChannelMinMax*, which will return the minimum and maximum legal channel numbers. Although the call returns a range of valid channel numbers, there's no guarantee that every channel in the range will contain a signal; some of the channels could be blank or just static.

(The idea of a "channel number" doesn't have a fixed meaning in some countries. Although "Channel 5" has a distinct frequency associated with it in the United States, this isn't true around the world. Consult the DirectX SDK documentation topic on "International Analog TV Tuning" for more information on channel selection around the world.)

Finally, there's another *IAMTVTuner* interface method that can help you discover the capabilities of your tuner card. Some TV tuner cards cover only the range of normal TV channels, while others can also tune in radio stations in the AM and/or FM bands. If these capabilities are present, you'll want to present the appropriate interface controls to the user. When you make a call to *GetAvailableModes*, a bit field is returned, which can be logically compared against the following values: *AMTUNER_MODE_TV* indicates that a TV tuner is present, *AMTUNER_MODE_FM_RADIO* indicates that an FM radio tuner is present, and *AMTUNER_MODE_AM_RADIO* indicates that an AM radio tuner is present. Finally, *AMTUNER_MODE_DSS* indicates that a Digital Satellite Service (DSS) receiver is connected. These values are not mutually exclusive. A call to *GetAvailableModes* could indicate that several (or all) of these capabilities are present. As you can see in Figure 7-2, the Television dialog box offers radio buttons for TV, FM, and AM modes. The buttons are enabled if the matching capabilities are present on the tuner.

That brings to a close our exploration of the basic capabilities of the TV tuner. Capture to an AVI file, which we covered in Chapter 6 with respect to digital camcorders and digital VCRs, works in precisely the same way with a TV tuner, with one exception: audio capture. Because the TV tuner audio crossbar sends the audio signal directly to the computer's sound card, audio capture to an AVI file will require the addition of an audio capture filter and might require some user input (as is provided in WinCap) to select the appropriate capture device. Now we need to move along to explore the stream buffering capabilities offered by DirectShow (if you have Windows XP Service Pack 1 installed), which allow you to pause a live video or TV broadcast in mid-stream.

Buffering DirectShow Media Streams

With the release of Windows XP Service Pack 1, two new filters were added to DirectShow to handle buffered playback of media streams. These filters replace the renderer and capture filters that you'd expect to find in a filter graph. The media stream (or streams, if you consider that audio and video might be on different streams as they pass through a filter graph) passes through the filter graph and is sent to the Stream Buffer Engine Sink filter. This filter takes the stream and writes it to a series of disk files. Another filter, the Stream Buffer Engine Source filter, reads the streams from the files created by the Stream Buffer Engine Sink filter and passes them downstream to a renderer.

Although it might seem that you'd create a single filter graph with separate streams for the Sink and Source filters, DirectShow requires that you create two completely separate filter graphs. Although we haven't explored this form of DirectShow programming, it's entirely safe to create multiple filter graphs within a single application. To create a buffering DirectShow application, create one filter graph that takes the capture stream—which might be coming from a camcorder, TV tuner, webcam, and so on—and write it out through the Stream Buffer Engine Sink. Then create a second filter graph that uses a Stream Buffer Engine Source as the capture filter, passing those streams (remember, multiple streams can be buffered with the Stream Buffer Engine) along to a renderer. Figure 7-3 will help you understand data flow in a buffering Direct-Show application.

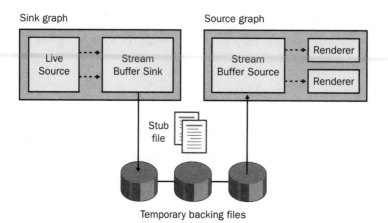

Figure 7-3 The two filter graphs required in a buffering DirectShow application

Once the filter graphs have been created and begin executing, streams are written to disk by the Stream Buffer Engine Sink in the first filter graph. At the same time, this data is received by the Stream Buffer Engine Source in the second filter graph. Because these filter graphs are entirely separate, it's possible to pause the second filter graph without affecting the execution of the first filter graph. This means that, for example, a TV broadcast can be paused at the Stream Buffer Engine Source, while the broadcast continues to be written to disk through the Stream Buffer Engine Sink. From the user's perspective, the TV broadcast will pause at the user's command until the filter graph receives the run command, which causes it to resume playback. None of the TV broadcast will be lost because the Stream Buffer Engine Source will write the content to disk, where it will stay, safe and secure, until the Stream Buffer Engine Sink reads it in. Conversely, if the first graph, containing the Stream Buffer Engine Sink, is paused, playback will pause when the Stream Buffer Engine Source runs out of buffered stream to render.

Now you can see why DirectShow requires two entirely separate filter graphs when using the stream buffering capabilities. Because these filter graphs are independent, control messages sent to one filter graph (pause, run, and stop) don't affect the other in any way. In addition, you can send commands to the Stream Buffer Engine Source that will "rewind" or "fast-forward" the stream, which gives you the capability to provide the user with VCR-like controls over the stream. Those commands have no effect on the Stream Buffer Engine Sink filter, which keeps writing its streams to disk, oblivious to any playback commands issued to the Stream Buffer Engine Source filter.

Building a Buffering TV Application

Now that we've explored the theory of the Stream Buffer Engine, we need to put it into practice and "roll our own" TiVo equivalent. Although using the Stream Buffer Engine might seem complex, its requirements are only a little greater than those for a more prosaic DirectShow application.

Although any stream can be buffered using DirectShow—the Stream Buffer Engine doesn't care what kind of data is being spooled out to disk—the Stream Buffer Engine has some preferences when it comes to video streams. As of the first release of the Stream Buffer Engine, video streams should be passed to the Stream Buffer Engine Sink in one of two formats: either DV Video, which you'll receive from a digital camcorder or digital VCR, or MPEG-2, which is the video encoding format used on DVDs. MPEG-2 is the preferred format for the Stream Buffer Engine, and it is used by the first generation of Media Center PCs because some TV tuner cards perform on-the-fly MPEG-2 encoding of their video signals. One important consideration is that an MPEG-2 video stream must be passed through the MPEG-2 Video Stream Analysis filter before going on to the Stream Buffer Engine Sink. This filter is used to detect frame boundaries and other video characteristics that are important for handling "trick play" effects such as rewind and fast-forward. You can pass other video streams to the Stream Buffer Engine Sink, but the Source won't be able to render them for you, making them, in essence, useless. Audio streams don't have the same constraints; you can pass any kind of recognizable audio stream or closed-captioning data, and the Stream Buffer Engine will handle it.

All this means that you might need to convert a given video stream to a specific format (either MPEG-2 or DV Video) if it isn't already in one of the two supported formats. For example, if you build a buffering application for a webcam (which would be a little weird, but you could do it), you'll have to convert its video stream from its native format to DV Video before passing it into the Stream Buffer Engine Sink. You do so by routing the stream through a DV Video Encoder filter (a built-in DirectShow filter) before it enters the Stream Buffer Engine Sink.

Although you might think that you could just pass a stream directly from a DV camcorder into the Stream Buffer Engine Sink, given that it's already in a legal format, this isn't actually so. The stream from a DV camcorder is a multiplexed signal of combined video and audio streams. These streams need to be demultiplexed, using the DV Splitter filter, before the separated video and audio streams can be passed along to the Stream Buffer Engine Sink. If you don't do this, you'll see nothing but a black video image when the Source renders the multiplexed stream.

Finally, when dealing with TV tuners, you must remember that the digitized output might not be provided in either MPEG-2 or DV format, which means a conversion is often necessary when putting a broadcast TV signal through the Stream Buffer Engine. (Digital TV signals are already in MPEG-2 format and won't need to be converted at all.) In addition to the video stream, an audio stream also has to be sent to the Stream Buffer Engine Sink. This process is not as straightforward as it might sound because TV tuners do very strange things to the audio portion of a TV broadcast. On my own computer (equipped with an ATI Rage 8500), I had to wire the audio output from the TV tuner card into one of the inputs on my sound card (Line In). If I don't do that, I don't have any audio signal from my TV tuner.

The reasons for such a strange configuration of hardware are murky. It might seem more appropriate to create a DirectShow-compatible audio capture filter for the TV tuner so that the TV audio stream can be directly captured by the filter graph. However, in most cases, you'll need to create an audio capture filter for your computer's sound card and then use that filter as the audio source for the TV signal, passing that stream along to the Stream Buffer Engine Sink.

The preceding are the basic cautions that need to be observed when creating a buffering DirectShow application. Now let's look at the main function of a simple DirectShow program, TVBuff, which takes a live TV signal and provides TiVo-like functionality using the Stream Buffer Engine. Here's how things begin:

```
// A basic program to buffer playback from a TV Tuner using DirectShow.
int main(int argc, char* argv[])
{
    ICaptureGraphBuilder2 *pCaptureGraph = NULL;    // Capture graph
                                                    // builder object
    IGraphBuilder *pGraph = NULL;   // Graph builder object for sink
    IMediaControl *pControl = NULL; // Media control interface for sink

    IGraphBuilder *pGraphSource = NULL; // Graph builder object for source
    IMediaControl *pControlSource = NULL; // Filter control interface

    IBaseFilter *pVideoInputFilter = NULL; // Video Capture filter
    IBaseFilter *pDVEncoder = NULL;         // DV Encoder Filter
    IBaseFilter *pAudioInputFilter = NULL;  // Audio Capture filter

    IStreamBufferSink *pBufferSink = NULL;

    // Initialize the COM library.
    HRESULT hr = CoInitialize(NULL);
    if (FAILED(hr))
    {
        // We'll send our error messages to the console.
        printf("ERROR - Could not initialize COM library");
        return hr;
    }

    // Create the capture graph builder and query for interfaces.
    hr = CoCreateInstance(CLSID_CaptureGraphBuilder2, NULL,
        CLSCTX_INPROC_SERVER, IID_ICaptureGraphBuilder2,
        (void **)&pCaptureGraph);

    if (FAILED(hr)) // FAILED is a macro that tests the return value
    {
        printf("ERROR - Could not create the capture graph builder.");
        return hr;
    }

    // Create the Filter Graph Manager and query for interfaces.
    hr = CoCreateInstance(CLSID_FilterGraph, NULL, CLSCTX_INPROC_SERVER,
                        IID_IGraphBuilder, (void **)&pGraph);
```

```
// Now tell the capture graph builder about the Filter Graph Manager.
hr = pCaptureGraph->SetFiltergraph(pGraph);

// Using QueryInterface on the graph builder,
// get the Media Control object.
hr = pGraph->QueryInterface(IID_IMediaControl, (void **)&pControl);
if (FAILED(hr))
{
    printf("ERROR - Could not create the Media Control object.");
    pCaptureGraph->Release();
    pGraph->Release();  // Clean up after ourselves
    CoUninitialize();  // And uninitialize COM
    return hr;
}
```

There's nothing here we haven't seen before. This code is all standard DirectShow initialization code that creates a capture graph builder and then instantiates a Filter Graph Manager associated with it. This filter graph will handle the Stream Buffer Engine Sink. That's why it's associated with a capture Filter Graph Manager—this is where the streams will originate. Now we need to build the filter graph and fill it with appropriate capture and transform filters.

```
// Now create the video input filter from the TV Tuner.
hr = GetVideoInputFilter(&pVideoInputFilter, L"ATI");
if (SUCCEEDED(hr)) {
    hr = pGraph->AddFilter(pVideoInputFilter, L"TV Tuner");
}

// Now, let's add a DV Encoder, to get a format the SBE can use.
hr = AddFilterByCLSID(pGraph, CLSID_DVVideoEnc, L"DV Encoder",
    &pDVEncoder);

// Now that the capture sources have been added to the filter graph
// we need to add the Stream Buffer Engine Sink filter to the graph.
// Add the Stream Buffer Source filter to the graph.
CComPtr<IStreamBufferSink> bufferSink;
hr = bufferSink.CoCreateInstance(CLSID_StreamBufferSink);
CComQIPtr<IBaseFilter> pSinkF(bufferSink);
hr = pGraph->AddFilter(pSinkF, L"SBESink");

// Now add the video capture to the output file.
hr = pCaptureGraph->RenderStream(&PIN_CATEGORY_CAPTURE, &MEDIATYPE_Video,
    pVideoInputFilter, pDVEncoder, pSinkF);

// Now we've got to wire the Audio Crossbar for the TV signal.
hr = ConfigureTVAudio(pCaptureGraph, pVideoInputFilter);

// Now we instantiate an audio capture filter,
// which should be picking up the audio from the TV tuner...
```

```
hr = GetAudioInputFilter(&pAudioInputFilter, L"SoundMAX Digital Audio");
if (SUCCEEDED(hr)) {
    hr = pGraph->AddFilter(pAudioInputFilter, L"TV Tuner Audio");
}

// And now we add the audio capture to the sink.
hr = pCaptureGraph->RenderStream(&PIN_CATEGORY_CAPTURE, &MEDIATYPE_Audio,
    pAudioInputFilter, NULL, pSinkF);

// And now lock the Sink filter, like we're supposed to.
hr = bufferSink->QueryInterface(&pBufferSink);
hr = pBufferSink->LockProfile(NULL);

// Before we finish, save the filter graph to a file.
SaveGraphFile(pGraph, L"C:\\MyGraph_Sink.GRF");
```

We make a call to *GetVideoInputFilter* (you might remember this function from Chapter 4), which returns a pointer to an instanced filter with a name that matches the string *ATI*. Note that these hard-coded strings specify hardware that might not be on your system, and it's not the right way to do things, except by way of example. The appropriate mechanism—enumerating a list of devices and then letting the user select from it—has already been covered in Chapter 6 as part of WinCap, so we don't need to discuss it here. The TV tuner's video capture filter is added to the filter graph, along with a DV Encoder filter. This filter will handle the translation between the format of the digital video stream from the TV tuner and the Stream Buffer Engine Sink filter.

Once those filters have been added, we need to instantiate an *IStream-BufferSink* filter, which is added to the filter graph. Because we're using the capture graph builder to help us build the filter graph, we can use the *Render-Stream* method to create a render path between the capture filter (that is, the TV tuner) and the Stream Buffer Engine Sink filter, requesting that it pass the stream through the DV Encoder filter on the way to the Sink filter.

Next we deal with the peculiar nature of TV tuner audio (as discussed previously) by making a call to *ConfigureTVAudio*. This function is a slightly modified version of the method *CCaptureGraph::ConfigureTVAudio* in WinCap, which was fully covered in Chapter 6. The function connects the audio input and output pins of the crossbar using the *Route* method in the *ConnectAudio* function, which is itself taken from WinCap. (At this point, audio might begin to play on some computers with some combinations of TV tuner cards and sound hardware. That's because the audio crossbar routing is sending the signal from the TV tuner to the sound card.)

Now that we have a path for the broadcast audio signal into the filter graph, we call *GetAudioInputFilter*. (Once again, I've passed it the *Friendly-Name* of the sound card on my computer, SoundMAX, but your sound card probably has a different *FriendlyName*.) That filter is added to the graph, and another call to *RenderStream* creates a connection between it and the Stream Buffer Engine Sink. Because this is an audio stream, we don't need any intermediate conversion and the stream is passed directly to the Sink filter.

Now we need to issue a command to the Sink filter through its *IStreamBufferSink* interface. This call, *LockProfile*, initializes the file system requirements for stream buffering, creating a stub file, which is basically a pointer to other files where the stream data is being stored. This stub file is needed for the Stream Buffer Engine Source filter because it provides all the information the Source filter will need when it starts reading streams through the Stream Buffer Engine. Although the DirectShow SDK documentation states that *LockStream* is called automatically when the Filter Graph Manager executes its *Run* call, it's better to do it explicitly. You can use an explicit call to *LockProfile* to specify a file name for the stub file. The Stream Buffer Engine Source, which reads the stub file information and translates it into DirectShow streams, can be located in an entirely separate application, as long as the file name is known to both programs. (Alternately, the processes could be running at different privilege levels within the same application. The security IDs provided for in the *IStreamBufferInitialize* interface method *SetSIDs* allow you to control access to the buffer files.)

Finally we make a call to *SaveFilterGraph* so that we can take a snapshot of the filter graph with all capture and Stream Buffer Engine Sink elements, as shown in Figure 7-4.

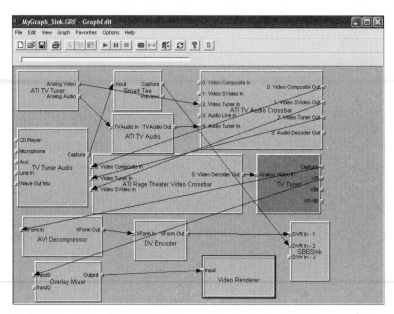

Figure 7-4   One of the TVBuff filter graphs, which feeds streams into the Stream Buffer Engine Sink filter

The capture filter, labeled "TV Tuner," sends its output through an AVI Decompressor filter, converting the TV tuner's output to match the input requirements of the DV Encoder. From the DV Encoder, the video stream passes into the Sink filter, while the SoundMAX card, labeled "TV Tuner Audio," sends its output through a Smart Tee filter and then into the Sink filter. We can have as many streams as we need going into the Sink filter. For example, closed-captioning information could be sent to the Sink filter to be decoded after it passes out of the Stream Buffer Engine Source filter in a second filter graph. Now that we've built the first filter graph, we have to move on to the second.

```
// OK--now we're going to create an entirely independent filter graph.
// This will be handling the Stream Buffer Engine Source,
// which will be passed along to the appropriate renderers.
hr = CoCreateInstance(CLSID_FilterGraph, NULL, CLSCTX_INPROC_SERVER,
                      IID_IGraphBuilder, (void **)&pGraphSource);

// Using QueryInterface on the graph builder,
// get the Media Control object.
hr = pGraphSource->QueryInterface(IID_IMediaControl,
    (void **)&pControlSource);

// Now instantiate the StreamBufferEngine Source
// and add it to this filter graph.
// Add the Stream Buffer Source filter to the graph.
CComPtr<IStreamBufferSource> pSource;
hr = pSource.CoCreateInstance(CLSID_StreamBufferSource);
CComQIPtr<IBaseFilter> pSourceF(pSource);
hr = pGraphSource->AddFilter(pSourceF, L"SBESource");
hr = pSource->SetStreamSink(bufferSink);
CComQIPtr<IStreamBufferMediaSeeking> pSourceSeeking(pSource);
```

Once again, we build a filter graph; however, because this filter graph isn't very complicated, we don't need to create a capture graph builder. Instead, we create the standard *IGraphBuilder* interface. Once that interface has been instantiated and its media control interface has been queried, we move on to instance the Stream Buffer Engine Source filter, *IStreamBufferSource*, and its associated interfaces. The filter is added to the graph, and then a call is made to its *SetStreamSink* method. This method gets a pointer to the *IStreamBufferSink* object located in the first filter graph. This call is used identify the Stream Buffer Engine Sink associated with this Source filter. Once that's done, the Source filter has complete knowledge of the stream types that it can supply to the filter graph.

Finally we get a pointer to the *IStreamBufferMediaSeeking* interface. This interface will be used a bit further along, when we want to control our position in the stream, giving us the ability to rewind or fast-forward a stream. With all the setup work done in this second filter graph, rendering the streams available through the Stream Buffer Engine Source filter becomes a very simple affair.

```
// Now, all we need to do is enumerate the output pins on the source.
// These should match the streams that have been setup on the sink.
// These will need to be rendered.
// Render each output pin.
CComPtr<IPin> pSrcOut;
CComPtr<IEnumPins> pPinEnum;
hr = pSourceF->EnumPins(&pPinEnum);
while (hr = pPinEnum->Next(1, &pSrcOut, 0), hr == S_OK)
{
    hr = pGraphSource->Render(pSrcOut);
    pSrcOut.Release();
}
```

We've seen code fragments like this before, in Chapter 4. We use the enumeration features of the *IEnumPins* object to walk through all the output pins on the Stream Buffer Engine Source filter. Each pin corresponds to a media stream, and as each pin is detected, the filter graph's *Render* method is called for that pin. In the case of a TV tuner, there are two streams—video and audio—sent into the Sink filter, and there will be two corresponding output pins—again, video and audio—available on the Source filter. Each of these streams is rendered independently; the video output is rendered with a Video Renderer filter, and the audio output is rendered with a Default DirectSound Device filter.

That's all that's required to construct the second filter graph; there are no fancy capture filters to deal with and no stream conversions required. Every output pin from the Stream Buffer Engine Source filter has been rendered. For a final touch, we call *SaveGraphFile* to preserve a copy of the filter graph in a disk file. Now we can send the Run message to both filter graphs and then go into a loop waiting for keyboard input from the user.

```
if (SUCCEEDED(hr))
{
    // Run the graphs.  Both of them.
    hr = pControl->Run();
    hr = pControlSource->Run();

    if (SUCCEEDED(hr))
    {
        // Wait patiently for completion of the recording.
        wprintf(L"ENTER to stop, SPACE to pause, →
            BACKSPACE to rewind, F to fastforward.\n");
```

```
bool done = false;
bool paused = false;
while (!done) {

    // Wait for completion.
    int ch;
    ch = _getch();        // We wait for keyboard input
    switch (ch) {
        case 0x0d:        // ENTER
            done = true;
            break;

        case 0x20:        // SPACE
            if (paused) {
                wprintf(L"Playing...\n");
                pControlSource->Run();
                paused = false;
            } else {
                wprintf(L"Pausing...\n");
                pControlSource->Pause();
                paused = true;
            }
            break;

        case 0x08:        // BACKSPACE - Rewind one second,
                          // if possible

            // First, let's find out how much play we have.
            // We do this by finding the earliest, latest,
            // current, and stop positions.
            // These are in units of 100 nanoseconds.  Supposedly.
            LONGLONG earliest, latest, current, stop, rewind;
            hr = pSourceSeeking->GetAvailable(&earliest, &latest);
            hr = pSourceSeeking->GetPositions(&current, &stop);

            // We would like to rewind 1 second,
            // or 10000000 units
            if ((current - earliest) > 10000000) { // Can we?
                rewind = current - 10000000;       // Yes
            } else {
                rewind = earliest; // Back up as far as we can
            }

            // If we can, change the current position
            // without changing the stop position.
            hr = pSourceSeeking->SetPositions(&rewind,
                AM_SEEKING_AbsolutePositioning,
                NULL, AM_SEEKING_NoPositioning);
```

```
                          break;

              case 0x46:  // That's F
              case 0x66:  // And f - Fast-forward one second,
                          // if possible

                 // First, let's find out how much play we have.
                 // We do this by finding the earliest, latest,
                 // current, and stop positions.
                 // These are in units of 100 nanoseconds.  Supposedly.
                 LONGLONG fastforward;
                 hr = pSourceSeeking->GetAvailable(&earliest, &latest);
                 hr = pSourceSeeking->GetPositions(&current, &stop);

                 // We would like to fast-forward 1 second,
                 // or 10000000 units.
                 if ((latest - current) > 10000000) {  // Can we?
                     fastforward = current + 10000000; // Yes
                 } else {
                     fastforward = latest;// Just go forward
                 }

                 // If we can, change the current position
                 // without changing the stop position.
                 hr = pSourceSeeking->SetPositions(&fastforward,
                     AM_SEEKING_AbsolutePositioning,
                     NULL, AM_SEEKING_NoPositioning);

                 break;

              default:  // Ignore other keys
                 break;
         }
       }
   }
```

Here we encounter the real magic of the Stream Buffer Engine. We go into a loop driven by user keypresses (not very elegant, but effective). A tap on the space bar pauses or resumes the playback of the second Stream Buffer Engine Source filter graph, simply by calling the Filter Graph Manager's *Pause* and *Run* methods. That's all that's required to add TiVo-like pause/resume functionality! Because the filter graphs are entirely separate, a pause command issued to one filter graph has no effect on the other.

Things get only a little more complex when the user presses the back-space key (which rewinds the stream one second) or the F key (which fast-forwards it one second). Here we use the *IStreamBufferMediaSeeking* interface of the Source filter. (This interface is identical to the *IMediaSeeking* interface used throughout DirectShow to search through a stream. *IMediaSeeking* is acquired by querying the filter graph, while *IStreamBufferMediaSeeking* is acquired by querying a specific filter.) The *IStreamBufferMediaSeeking* interface knows the Source filter's position in the stream, the total duration of the stream, and the stream's start and stop points. We need to know that information before we can change the Source filter's position in the stream. When the Source filter changes its position to an earlier point in the stream, it will appear to the user as though the stream has rewound; if a later point in the stream is selected, it will appear as though the stream has been fast-forwarded.

Two calls need to be made before positional changes in the stream can be effected. These calls, to *IStreamBufferMediaSeeking* methods *GetAvailable* and *GetCurrent*, return values, in 100-nanosecond (100 billionths of a second) intervals, indicating the start and stop points of the stream, and the current and stop points of the stream, respectively. Why do we need this information? We have to ensure that we don't rewind to a point before the start of the stream or fast-forward past the end of the stream.

Some simple arithmetic ensures that there's enough room between the current position in the stream and some area either before it (in the case of rewind) or after it (for fast-forward). At this point, another call is made, this one to *IStreamBufferMediaSeeking* method *SetPositions*. This method takes four parameters. The first parameter is a value representing the new current stream position (in effect, it resets the stream position), along with a parameter that indicates it is an absolute value (which it is, in this case) or a value relative to the Source's current position in the stream. The third and fourth parameters allow you to change the stop position in the stream. we don't want to do this, so we pass *NULL* and *AM_Seeking_NoPositioning* as the values in these fields, which preserves the stream's stop position. Once the call is made, playback immediately proceeds from the new stream position, and the user sees either a 1-second rewind or a 1-second fast-forward. These changes in stream position can be repeated as many times as desired, but only when the filter graph is executing. If the filter graph is paused, the changes will have no effect.

Finally, after the user hits the Enter key, we stop both filter graphs, clean everything up, and exit.

```
// And let's stop the filter graph.
hr = pControlSource->Stop();
hr = pControl->Stop();

wprintf(L"Stopped.\n"); // To the console
}
```

```
// Now release everything, and clean up.
pSourceSeeking.Release();
pSinkF.Release();
bufferSink.Release();
pSourceF.Release();
pSource.Release();
pDVEncoder->Release();
pVideoInputFilter->Release();
pAudioInputFilter->Release();
pControlSource->Release();
pGraphSource->Release();
pControl->Release();
pGraph->Release();
pCaptureGraph->Release();
pBufferSink->Release();
CoUninitialize();

return 0;
}
```

As you've probably already realized, using the Stream Buffer Engine doesn't take a lot of code or a lot of work, but it can provide enormous functionality to your DirectShow applications—if you need it. Although TVBuff demonstrates the rudimentary capabilities of the Stream Buffer Engine, a lot more can be done with it than we've covered here. For example, a permanent, high-quality recording of a TV program can be recorded to a sink file for later playback, which is very similar to the kind of functionality that TiVo offers.

We haven't touched on the issue of stale content, which is created when a live broadcast is paused and then the channel is changed. Because the new channel's video stream hasn't been buffered, the stream buffer engine needs to clear the buffer of the previous channel's data or else rewinding the channel could result in a leap back to an earlier channel. (Holes can also be created when a buffer is deleted in the Stream Buffer Engine sink. The sink creates a series of five-minute files to hold stream data and then begins deleting them, from last to most recent, but because of the seeking features of the Stream Buffer Engine, you could be viewing the earliest buffer while a buffer following it has already been deleted.) You'll want to look at the Stream Buffer Engine event codes in the DirectX SDK documentation for more information on how to catch and prevent these situations from occurring.

Summary

TV tuner cards and peripherals are becoming ever-more-common features of the PC landscape; Microsoft, in conjunction with Hewlett-Packard, has been working to bring the Media Center to every home. With the advent of the PVR, people have different expectations for their TV viewing. They expect their programs to be recorded invisibly and available instantaneously, and they expect to time-shift their viewing at will, pausing, rewinding, or fast-forwarding TV programs.

What we've covered in this chapter are the essentials for working with TV tuners and buffered streams, the two core components in a PVR. Truthfully, it takes a lot more than this to create a TiVo-like device. Most of TiVo's magic is in its user interface design, which makes it easy to record and retrieve programming. However, TiVo requires a connection to your home telephone because it dials into its own information service every evening, downloading new program listings and uploading usage information. The home PC, connected to the Internet, has several advantages over TiVo. For example, many PCs are always connected to the Internet, and they have blazingly fast processors with huge supplies of memory. This gives the PC a kind of flexibility that TiVo can't begin to touch.

TiVo can record up to 40 hours of TV programming, which the Stream Buffer Engine could do as well—provided it had access to 500 GB of disk space! DV-encoded video files take up lots of disk space and will eat up a computer's capacity quite quickly. We've already covered how to take a DV-encoded stream and convert it into the much more compact Windows Media format. This is the kind of technique you'd need to employ if you were going to design a PC-based TiVo—because you could store thousands of hours of television on your computer's hard disk, instead of a few tens of hours. The Windows Media Center PC stores its captured TV programming in MPEG-2 format, which uses from 1 to 3 GB per hour, depending on the quality of the capture. That's one reason the Stream Buffer Engine has been optimized to work with MPEG-2 streams. Whether you choose to use MPEG-2 or Windows Media, you'll find that DirectShow is an incredible foundation for a new generation of TV applications that could make the promise of convergence real.

8

Editing Media Using DirectShow Editing Services

PC-based video editing is one of the most exciting developments to emerge in the field during the last half-dozen years. After Web browsing and e-mail, video editing might be the next most compelling reason to purchase a new, powerful PC. Now regularly equipped with IEEE 1394 connectors, ready for digital camcorders, most PCs ship with a copy of Microsoft Windows Movie Maker, a video capture and editing package written using Microsoft DirectShow. Although Windows Movie Maker isn't as full-featured as the professional-grade products such as Adobe Premiere or Avid Xpress DV (which can cost hundreds to thousands of dollars), it's an entry-level tool that allows a novice user to capture video from a camcorder, place it onto a timeline, add an audio track (if desired), and then render a new movie. Then the user can write the movie to a disk file in various Windows Media formats for easy streaming over the Internet or to be dropped into an e-mail. The movie can also be recorded back to a digital camcorder so that it can be viewed on a TV, transferred to a VHS tape, and so on.

Such capabilities are a big deal with proud new parents, for example, who shoot hours and hours of footage of baby's birth, first step, first birthday, and so on, and use Windows Movie Maker to make short films for the grandparents, siblings, friends, and anyone else who'll sit still long enough to watch them. The day after my own nephew, Alex, was born, I made a 3-minute movie/birth announcement that I sent out to friends and family around the world. Filmmaking is a fun hobby, and although most of us will never approach the artistry of professional filmmakers, with tools such as Windows Movie Maker, near-professional-quality films can be handcrafted at home on the family PC.

DirectShow includes a complete set of functionality known as the DirectShow Editing Services (DES), which can easily add powerful editing features to any DirectShow application. Although Windows Movie Maker uses these services, the application barely scratches the surface of what's possible with DirectShow. As the video-editing public becomes more sophisticated, there's a greater need for ever-more-powerful tools. To that end, Microsoft recently upgraded Windows Movie Maker and added features that allow the application to "analyze" video clips and even assemble these clips into short movies, without much user input. Soon, a homemade movie will be no more than a few mouse-clicks away.

Understanding DES Concepts

Before diving headlong into the programming for DES, we need to cover some of the concepts key to understanding how DES is organized. The basic unit of media manipulated by DES is known as the *clip*. A clip can be either an audio or a video segment, and it can be any length. A short clip could be a single frame of video footage, just one-thirtieth of a second, while a longer one could stretch for many minutes. In addition, there's no preferred format for either video or audio clips. DirectShow converts all clips to a common format—that is, if it can locate transform filters to handle the conversion from clip format to its common format. Clips are sometimes called *source objects* because they are the ultimate source material for any editing project.

The editing process consists of placing clips together into a timeline. The timeline is the key feature of a DES application. You can visualize a timeline as a line that extends horizontally from left to right, and as you move from left to right, you progress chronologically. Clips are arranged along the timeline with DES commands; you can set the start and stop time for any clip, relative to the timeline, placing each clip precisely where you want it.

A minimum of two independent timelines are available for your use: one works with video clips, and the second is for audio clips. Many video clips have their own audio soundtracks, and keeping the timelines separate allows you to "score" a video clip with a new audio soundtrack. Although the timelines are separate, they keep time together. A point on the video timeline will be rendered into the final movie at the same time as the corresponding point on the audio timeline.

Each timeline is composed of any number of tracks. You might be familiar with this term from audio recording. Most modern albums are recorded onto 48 separate tracks, each of which can be recorded independently. When recording is complete, these tracks are mixed together—by the album's producer—into a finished product. That's the way tracks work within DES; each timeline has as many tracks as required to accommodate the clips that are to be mixed into a movie. You can have multiple clips on a single track, but clips can't overlap on the same track. In other words, if you want to fade from one video clip into another (using a transition, which we'll discuss in a moment), you place the clips on two different tracks in timeline positions that would cause the end of one clip to overlap the beginning of the next. You can do the same thing with audio tracks and fade from one sound to another, or you can mix audio tracks together. A collection of tracks can be gathered into an object known as a *composition*. The composition is a convenient way to group tracks together and manipulate them as a unit. Finally the entire collection of compositions composes the timeline. Again, video and audio keep separate timelines, so they have separate collections of compositions, which are composed of separate tracks, each containing clips. Figure 8-1 shows the timeline model.

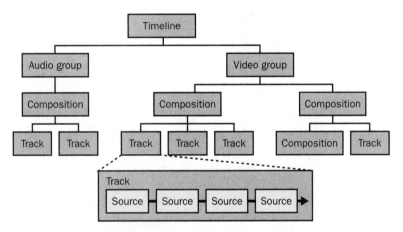

Figure 8-1   The timeline model, which gathers objects into tracks and tracks into compositions

Clips can be reused; just because you've put a clip on one track doesn't imply that you can't use it elsewhere. In fact, you can reuse clips as often as you like throughout a track, composition, or timeline. You can get some very interesting effects this way, including repetitive sounds, video patterns, and so on.

The final elements in the DES model are transitions. A transition is an effect—such as a fade from one video clip to another—that is added to a track and is applied to the rendered movie. Although transitions reside within a single track, they can affect other tracks. For example, you could use a fade effect in one video track to fade from the current clip within that track to a clip within another track, which means that transitions can and often must reference tracks outside themselves. Beyond transitions, which define how one track ends while another begins, there are track effects, which allow you to change the appearance of a source clip (for example, transform color to black and white) when it's rendered into a movie. A rich set of both transitions and effects is built into DES, for both audio and video. Nearly anything you might want is already available to you in DirectShow.

Source clips, transitions, tracks, compositions, and timelines are the basic elements manipulated by DES. Let's continue our exploration of DES with a simple console-based program that simply displays a list of the available audio and video effects and transitions. You can also create your own custom effects and transitions using the Microsoft DirectX Media 6.0 SDK, which can be downloaded at *http://www.microsoft.com/downloads/release.asp?ReleaseID=45808*.

Listing DES Effects

This short program, DESList, allows you to list all the video effects available on your computer:

```
// Enumerate all of the effects.
HRESULT EnumerateEffects(CLSID searchType)
{
    // Once again, code stolen from the DX9 SDK.

    // Create the System Device Enumerator.
    ICreateDevEnum *pSysDevEnum = NULL;
    HRESULT hr = CoCreateInstance(CLSID_SystemDeviceEnum, NULL,
        CLSCTX_INPROC_SERVER, IID_ICreateDevEnum, (void **)&pSysDevEnum);
    if (FAILED(hr))
    {
        return hr;
    }

    // Obtain a class enumerator for the effect category.
    IEnumMoniker *pEnumCat = NULL;
    hr = pSysDevEnum->CreateClassEnumerator(searchType, &pEnumCat, 0);

    if (hr == S_OK)
    {
        // Enumerate the monikers.
        IMoniker *pMoniker = NULL;
        ULONG cFetched;
        while (pEnumCat->Next(1, &pMoniker, &cFetched) == S_OK)
        {
            // Bind the first moniker to an object.
```

```
                IPropertyBag *pPropBag;
                hr = pMoniker->BindToStorage(0, 0, IID_IPropertyBag,
                    (void **)&pPropBag);
                if (SUCCEEDED(hr))
                {
                    // To retrieve the filter's friendly name, do the following:
                    VARIANT varName;
                    VariantInit(&varName);
                    hr = pPropBag->Read(L"FriendlyName", &varName, 0);
                    if (SUCCEEDED(hr))
                    {
                        wprintf(L"Effect: %s\n", varName.bstrVal);
                    }
                    VariantClear(&varName);
                    pPropBag->Release();
                }
                pMoniker->Release();
            }
            pEnumCat->Release();
        }
        pSysDevEnum->Release();
        return hr;
}

// A very simple program to list DES effects using DirectShow.
//
int main(int argc, char* argv[])
{

    // Initialize the COM library.
    HRESULT hr = CoInitialize(NULL);
    if (FAILED(hr))
    {
        // We'll send our error messages to the console.
        printf("ERROR - Could not initialize COM library");
        return hr;
    }

    // OK, so now we want to build the filter graph
    // using an AudioCapture filter.
    // But there are several to choose from,
    // so we need to enumerate them, then pick one.
    hr = EnumerateEffects(CLSID_VideoEffects1Category);
    hr = EnumerateEffects(CLSID_VideoEffects2Category);

    CoUninitialize();

    return 0;
}
```

This program bears a resemblance to DSAudioCap, which it's based on. The basic function is very straightforward: after COM is initialized, two calls are made to the *EnumerateEffects* function. Each time the function is called, a different CLSID is passed, indicating which set of effects should be enumerated. *CLSID_VideoEffects1Category* enumerates all the effects that can be applied to a single source clip, while *CLSID_VideoEffects2Category* enumerates all the transitions that can be used when going from one source clip to another.

EnumerateEffects is a direct adaptation of the DSAudioRender function *EnumerateAudioCaptureFilters*; it uses the system device enumerator to create a list of monikers corresponding to the CLSID. Then that list is walked through, and the *FriendlyName* for each entry is printed to the console. If your system is configured in a manner resembling my own, here's what you should see on that list (shown in two columns to save space):

```
Effect: Fade              Effect: Iris
Effect: BasicImage        Effect: RadialWipe
Effect: Chroma            Effect: Fade
Effect: Matrix            Effect: ZigZag
Effect: Pixelate          Effect: RandomBars
Effect: ICMFilter         Effect: Spiral
Effect: Scale             Effect: Pixelate
Effect: Blur              Effect: Wheel
Effect: Glow              Effect: Inset
Effect: Alpha             Effect: Compositor
Effect: DropShadow        Effect: Blinds
Effect: Wave              Effect: Wipe
Effect: Additive Surface  Effect: CheckerBoard
Effect: Shadow            Effect: GradientWipe
Effect: Emboss            Effect: Slide
Effect: Engrave           Effect: Barn
Effect: Light             Effect: Stretch
                          Effect: RandomDissolve
```

The entries up to *Light* on this list correspond to the effects available to DES, while the next entries, beginning with *Iris*, are the transitions DES can use. (Although you might think that we could add two more calls to *EnumerateEffects* with CLSIDs of *CLSID_AudioEffects1Category* and *CLSID_AudioEffects2Category*, these calls return empty lists. Audio effects have to be addressed individually by their CLSIDs.) Now that we know the effects and transitions available to use, we can put them to work in a simple DirectShow application that uses DES to create an automated editing program.

Programming DES

The following application, DESClip, displays a File dialog box asking the user to point to an AVI file. DESClip uses this clip as the foundation for a new movie, adding a five-second clip to the front of it, transitioning to the clip, which plays in its entirety, and then following with a five-second closing clip. The whole movie is scored with a soundtrack that replaces any native sounds that might be part of the source clips.

Creating a Timeline and Track Group

We'll take a look at the entire application, beginning with *main*.

```
int main(int argc, char* argv[])
{

    // Let's get a media file to render.
    if (!GetMediaFileName()) {
        return 0;
    }

    // Start by making an empty timeline.  Add a media detector as well.
    IAMTimeline *pTL = NULL;
    IMediaDet *pMD = NULL;
    CoInitialize(NULL);
    HRESULT hr = CoCreateInstance(CLSID_AMTimeline, NULL,
        CLSCTX_INPROC_SERVER, IID_IAMTimeline, (void**)&pTL);
    hr = CoCreateInstance(CLSID_MediaDet, NULL, CLSCTX_INPROC_SERVER,
        IID_IMediaDet, (void**)&pMD);

    // GROUP: Add a video group to the timeline.

    IAMTimelineGroup    *pGroup = NULL;
    IAMTimelineObj      *pGroupObj = NULL;
    hr = pTL->CreateEmptyNode(&pGroupObj, TIMELINE_MAJOR_TYPE_GROUP);
    hr = pGroupObj->QueryInterface(IID_IAMTimelineGroup, (void **)&pGroup);

    // Set the group media type. This example sets the type to "video" and
    // lets DES pick the default settings. For a more detailed example,
    // see "Setting the Group Media Type."
    AM_MEDIA_TYPE mtGroup;
    ZeroMemory(&mtGroup, sizeof(AM_MEDIA_TYPE));
    mtGroup.majortype = MEDIATYPE_Video;
    hr = pGroup->SetMediaType(&mtGroup);
    hr = pTL->AddGroup(pGroupObj);
    pGroupObj->Release();
```

First we make a call to get a valid AVI file name. COM is initialized, and instead of the normal *CoCreateInstance* call to create a Filter Graph Manager, we pass the GUID *CLSID_AMTimeline*, which returns an *IAMTimeline* object, the DES object that gives you overall control of the timeline. This call is immediately followed by another call to *CoCreateInstance* with the GUID *CLSID_MediaDet*, which returns an *IMediaDet* object. This object will be very useful later on when we're poking at our source clips, trying to learn their durations and what media types they contain.

Now that we've got an *IAMTimeline* object, we can start to create objects that drop into the timeline. The basic method for creating an object is *CreateEmptyNode*; the second parameter defines the object being created. In this case, *TIMELINE_MAJOR_TYPE_GROUP* is used to create a group, that is, the object that contains either the entire video timeline or the entire audio timeline. The next calls establish the media type for the timeline group. First a structure of type *AM_MEDIA_TYPE* is created, and its *majortype* field is initialized with the value *MEDIATYPE_Video*. In this case, DES picks the default output format, including the image size and the bit depth of the image. (Later we'll discuss how to establish our own media parameters using the *AM_MEDIA_TYPE* structure.) Once that's done, a call is made to the *IAMTimelineGroup* interface on the *IAMTimelineObj* object, the *SetMediaType* method. This call establishes that this timeline group is exclusively for video (we'll do the same for audio later), and then the timeline group is added to the master timeline with a call to the *IAMTimeline* method *AddGroup*.

Adding a Track to a Timeline

It takes only a few lines of code to add a track to the timeline, as shown here:

```
// TRACK: Add a track to the group.

IAMTimelineObj      *pTrackObj;
IAMTimelineTrack    *pTrack;
IAMTimelineComp     *pComp = NULL;

hr = pTL->CreateEmptyNode(&pTrackObj, TIMELINE_MAJOR_TYPE_TRACK);
hr = pGroup->QueryInterface(IID_IAMTimelineComp, (void **)&pComp);
hr = pComp->VTrackInsBefore(pTrackObj, 0);
hr = pTrackObj->QueryInterface(IID_IAMTimelineTrack, (void **)&pTrack);

pTrackObj->Release();
```

Once again, a call is made to the *IAMTimeline* method *CreateEmptyNode*, this time with *TIMELINE_MAJOR_TYPE_TRACK* as the passed parameter. This call returns an *IAMTimelineObj* object. Another query returns the *IAMTimelineComp* interface from the group object. (A group in DES is also considered a composition object because it contains one or more tracks.) The *IAMTimelineComp* interface is needed so that a call can be made to its *VTrackInsBefore* method. This method places the tracks together, front to back. There can be many tracks in a composition, so this call allows DES to assign an order to the tracks. A value of zero places the track in front of all other tracks, while higher values send the track "behind" tracks with lower priority values. After the track has been prioritized, we get the *IAMTimelineTrack* interface for it. This interface will be used as source clips are added to the track.

Adding a Source Clip

Adding a source clip—in this case, a video clip because we're working within the video track group—is a bit more complex than adding a track.

```
// SOURCE: Add a source clip to the track.

IAMTimelineSrc *pSource = NULL;
IAMTimelineObj *pSourceObj;

hr = pTL->CreateEmptyNode(&pSourceObj, TIMELINE_MAJOR_TYPE_SOURCE);
hr = pSourceObj->QueryInterface(IID_IAMTimelineSrc, (void **)&pSource);

// Set the times and the file name.
BSTR bstrFile = SysAllocString(OLESTR("C:\\DShow.avi"));
hr = pSource->SetMediaName(bstrFile);
SysFreeString(bstrFile);
hr = pSource->SetMediaTimes(0, 50000000);
hr = pSourceObj->SetStartStop(0, 50000000);
hr = pTrack->SrcAdd(pSourceObj);

pSourceObj->Release();
pSource->Release();
```

Once again, we begin with a call to the *IAMTimeline* method *CreateEmptyNode*; this time the passed parameter is *TIMELINE_MAJOR_TYPE_SOURCE*, which returns an *IAMTimelineObj* that we immediately query to get its *IAMTimelineSrc* interface. With this interface, we can set the parameters for this clip. First a call to the *IAMTimelineSrc* method *SetMediaName* sets the file name of the clip. (The file name can include full path information. In this case, we've hardcoded the path and required both DShow.avi and MSPress.avi to be in C:\. You wouldn't do this in a production program, of course!) The start and stop positions within the clip are set with a call to the *IAMTimelineSrc* method *SetMediaTimes*. These values are given in reference time—that is, units of 100 nanoseconds—so five seconds (the duration of this clip) has the outlandish reference time value of 50 million. This call ensures that the full five seconds of the clip are placed into the track. (We know how long the clip is because we created it earlier.) This call is followed by a call to the *IAMTimelineObj* method *SetStartStop*, which positions the clip within the track. These values, 0 and 50 million, set the clip so that it begins to play at the start of the track and continues for five seconds—just the length of the clip. If we had passed a range in *SetStartStop* of less than 50 million, the source clip would have been "sped up" so that the full length of it, set by the call to *SetMediaTimes*, would have been played in the allotted period. Finally the source clip's duration has been set, and its start and stop positions on the track have been established. The source clip is added to the track with a call to the *IAMTimelineTrack* method *SrcAdd*.

Adding a Transition

Because this is an opening clip, we want to add a nice video transition to the track, which will take us into the clip the user selected at application launch.

```
// TRANSITION:  Add a transition object to the track.
// Note that the GUID for the transition is hard-coded,
// but we'd probably want the user to select it.

IAMTimelineObj *pTransObj = NULL;
pTL->CreateEmptyNode(&pTransObj, TIMELINE_MAJOR_TYPE_TRANSITION);
hr = pTransObj->SetSubObjectGUID(CLSID_DxtJpeg);  // SMPTE Wipe
hr = pTransObj->SetStartStop(40000000, 50000000);  // The last second
IAMTimelineTransable *pTransable = NULL;
hr = pTrack->QueryInterface(IID_IAMTimelineTransable,
    (void **)&pTransable);
hr = pTransable->TransAdd(pTransObj);
IAMTimelineTrans *pTrans = NULL;
hr = pTransObj->QueryInterface(IID_IAMTimelineTrans, (void**)&pTrans);
hr = pTrans->SetSwapInputs(true);
```

Yet again, we begin with a call to *CreateEmptyNode*, passing *TIMELINE_MAJOR_TYPE_TRANSITION*, which returns an *IAMTimelineObj* that contains our transition element. The transition is selected with a call to the *IAMTimelineObj* method *SetSubObjectGUID*. This GUID is predefined as *CLSID_DxtJpeg*, which "wipes" the screen from this video source to a subsequent one (which we haven't yet put into a track). We want this transition to take one second, and we want it to be the last second of the clip; given this information, we can make a call to *SetStartStop* with the start value of 40 million, and a stop value of 50 million, which means that the transition will run between seconds 4 and 5 of the track. Next, to add the transition to the track, we get the *IAMTimelineTransable* interface from the track object and then call the *IAMTimelineTransable* method *TransAdd*. The transition has now been added to the track.

Finally we need to modify one of the parameters of the transition; we want to wipe from this track to another track, which is the inverse of the way this transition operates in its default state. To do this, we get the *IAMTimeline-Trans* interface from the *IAMTimelineObj* and then make a call to *SetSwapInputs*, which tells the transition to transition from this source clip to another, rather than from another source clip to this one.

Setting Transition Properties

The SMPTE Wipe transition is common, but it comes in many different flavors; you can wipe from the bottom of the screen to the top, right to left, and so on. DES provides about 100 different versions of the transition, and we're going to use one that features a triangle, point upward, coming out of the center of the screen. To do that, we're going to have to manipulate the transition's properties, as shown here:

```
// PROPERTY: Set a property on this transition.

IPropertySetter    *pProp;   // Property setter
hr = CoCreateInstance(CLSID_PropertySetter, NULL, CLSCTX_INPROC_SERVER,
    IID_IPropertySetter, (void**) &pProp);
DEXTER_PARAM param;
DEXTER_VALUE *pValue =
    (DEXTER_VALUE*)CoTaskMemAlloc(sizeof(DEXTER_VALUE));

// Initialize the parameter.
param.Name = SysAllocString(L"MaskNum");
param.dispID = 0;
param.nValues = 1;

// Initialize the value.
pValue->v.vt = VT_BSTR;
pValue->v.bstrVal = SysAllocString(L"103"); // Triangle, up
pValue->rt = 0;
pValue->dwInterp = DEXTERF_JUMP;

hr = pProp->AddProp(param, pValue);

// Free allocated resources.
SysFreeString(param.Name);
VariantClear(&(pValue->v));
CoTaskMemFree(pValue);
```

```
// Set the property on the transition.
hr = pTransObj->SetPropertySetter(pProp);
pProp->Release();
pTrans->Release();
pTransObj->Release();
pTransable->Release();
pTrack->Release();
```

To set the properties on our wipe transition, we need to call *CoCreate-Instance* to create an *IPropertySetter* object. Now we allocate and populate two structures, *DEXTER_PARAM* and *DEXTER_VALUE*. (*Dexter* was the internal name for DES at Microsoft, and it stuck around in these structure names.) The *DEXTER_PARAM* field *Name* contains a string that identifies the parameter we want to modify. (The content of this field varies enormously, depending on the transition you're using, and it can be found in the DirectX SDK documentation for the DirectShow transitions. Other transitions are installed with Microsoft Internet Explorer; information on those transitions can be found online). Because we're passing only one parameter, *nValues* is set to 1. The *DEXTER_VALUE* structure is now loaded with the specific values to be passed along with the parameter. In this case, the wipe we're using is number 103, which is placed into the structure. Once both data structures have been initialized, they're applied to the *IPropertySetter* object with a call to the *AddProp* method. After that, the *IAMTimelineObj* method *SetPropertySetter* is invoked and the property is applied to the transition. Now, when the movie is rendered, the transition will use the appropriate mask.

Determining the Media Type of a Source Clip

We're done with the first track, which contains only the opening clip and a transition. Now we need to create another track because a transition operates on source images contained in two separate tracks. The second track will contain the source clip selected by the user and our closing clip.

```
// TRACK:  Add another video track to the Timeline.

hr = pTL->CreateEmptyNode(&pTrackObj, TIMELINE_MAJOR_TYPE_TRACK);
hr = pComp->VTrackInsBefore(pTrackObj, 0);
hr = pTrackObj->QueryInterface(IID_IAMTimelineTrack, (void **)&pTrack);
pTrackObj->Release();

// SOURCE: Add a source to the track.

hr = pTL->CreateEmptyNode(&pSourceObj, TIMELINE_MAJOR_TYPE_SOURCE);
hr = pSourceObj->QueryInterface(IID_IAMTimelineSrc, (void **)&pSource);
```

```
    // Set file name.
#ifndef UNICODE
    WCHAR wFileName[MAX_PATH];
    MultiByteToWideChar(CP_ACP, 0, g_PathFileName, -1, wFileName, MAX_PATH);
    BSTR bstrFile = SysAllocString((const OLECHAR*) wFileName);
    // This is all that's required to create a filter graph
    // that will render a media file!
#else
    BSTR bstrFile = SysAllocString((const OLECHAR*) g_PathFileName);
#endif
    hr = pSource->SetMediaName(bstrFile);

    // Figure out how big the track is, and add it in at that length.
    // We'll use the IMediaDet interface to do this work.
    hr = pMD->put_Filename(bstrFile);
    double psl = 0;
    hr = pMD->get_StreamLength(&psl);
    REFERENCE_TIME pSourceLength = psl * 10000000; // Convert units
    hr = pSource->SetMediaTimes(0, pSourceLength);
    hr = pSourceObj->SetStartStop(40000000, 40000000+pSourceLength);
    hr = pTrack->SrcAdd(pSourceObj);

    SysFreeString(bstrFile);
    pSourceObj->Release();
    pSource->Release();

    // SOURCE: Add another source to the track, after that sample.

    hr = pTL->CreateEmptyNode(&pSourceObj, TIMELINE_MAJOR_TYPE_SOURCE);
    hr = pSourceObj->QueryInterface(IID_IAMTimelineSrc, (void **)&pSource);

    // Set the times and the file name.
    hr = pSourceObj->SetStartStop(40000000+pSourceLength,
        40000000+pSourceLength+50000000);
    bstrFile = SysAllocString(OLESTR("C:\\MSPress.avi"));
    hr = pSource->SetMediaName(bstrFile);
    SysFreeString(bstrFile);
    hr = pSource->SetMediaTimes(00000000, 50000000);
    hr = pTrack->SrcAdd(pSourceObj);

    pSourceObj->Release();
    pSource->Release();
    pComp->Release();

    pTrack->Release();
    pGroup->Release();
```

We add a track using a clone of the code that we used to add the original video track, and then we add a source clip to the track. This point is when we use the *IMediaDet* object that instantiated during program initialization. We call its *put_Filename* method, which now allows the object to query the media file for many of its properties. Of concern to us is the duration of the clip; we're going to need to know how long the clip is before we can know where to drop a follow-on clip on the timeline. We get this value (in seconds) returned with a call to *get_StreamLength*. This number has to be converted into reference time, so it's multiplied by 10 million. This value is then used in subsequent calls to *SetMediaTime* and *SetStartStop*, positioning the clip accurately on the track and starting the clip 4 seconds into the timeline, allowing the opening clip to roll on until it begins its transition to this clip. The clip is added with a call to *SrcAdd*.

The follow-on clip is added with a few more lines of code, and the values passed in *SetStartStop* reflect the length of the source clip which precedes it, which keeps the timeline clean and consistent. Multiple clips on the same track can't occupy the same time on the timeline.

That finishes up the video group of tracks; we now have two tracks. The first track has an opening clip and a transition, while the second track has the user-selected clip with a follow-on clip.

Adding Audio Tracks

To add audio tracks to this movie, we need to create a new track group, like this:

```
// GROUP: Add an audio group to the timeline.

IAMTimelineGroup    *pAudioGroup = NULL;
IAMTimelineObj      *pAudioGroupObj = NULL;
hr = pTL->CreateEmptyNode(&pAudioGroupObj, TIMELINE_MAJOR_TYPE_GROUP);
hr = pAudioGroupObj->QueryInterface(IID_IAMTimelineGroup,
    (void **)&pAudioGroup);

// Set the group media type.
// We'll use the IMediaDet object to make this painless.
AM_MEDIA_TYPE amtGroup;
// Soundtrack file to use.
bstrFile = SysAllocString(OLESTR("C:\\FoggyDay.wav"));
hr = pMD->put_Filename(bstrFile);
hr = pMD->get_StreamMediaType(&amtGroup);
hr = pAudioGroup->SetMediaType(&amtGroup);
hr = pTL->AddGroup(pAudioGroupObj);
pAudioGroupObj->Release();
```

```
// TRACK: Add an audio track to the group.

IAMTimelineObj      *pAudioTrackObj;
IAMTimelineTrack    *pAudioTrack;
IAMTimelineComp     *pAudioComp = NULL;

hr = pTL->CreateEmptyNode(&pAudioTrackObj, TIMELINE_MAJOR_TYPE_TRACK);
hr = pAudioGroup->QueryInterface(IID_IAMTimelineComp,
    (void **)&pAudioComp);
hr = pAudioComp->VTrackInsBefore(pAudioTrackObj, 0);
hr = pAudioTrackObj->QueryInterface(IID_IAMTimelineTrack,
    (void **)&pAudioTrack);

pAudioTrackObj->Release();
pAudioComp->Release();
pAudioGroup->Release();


// SOURCE: Add another source to the track.

hr = pTL->CreateEmptyNode(&pSourceObj, TIMELINE_MAJOR_TYPE_SOURCE);
hr = pSourceObj->QueryInterface(IID_IAMTimelineSrc, (void **)&pSource);

// Set the times and the file name.
hr =  pSourceObj->SetStartStop(0, 50000000+pSourceLength+50000000);

hr = pSource->SetMediaName(bstrFile);
SysFreeString(bstrFile);
hr = pSource->SetMediaTimes(00000000, 50000000+pSourceLength+50000000);
hr = pAudioTrack->SrcAdd(pSourceObj);

pSourceObj->Release();
pSource->Release();
pAudioTrack->Release();
```

We create a new track group using the *CreateEmptyNode* call with the parameter *TIMELINE_MAJOR_TYPE_GROUP*, just as we did when we created the video track group. The difference comes when we set the media type for the group, and here again we use the *IMediaDet* object. First we call *put_Filename* with the name of the soundtrack file. (Doing so is a bit of a cheat because we don't add this source clip until a bit further along, but it's perfectly legal DirectShow programming.) Now we call the *IMediaDet* method *get_StreamMediaType*, which returns an *AM_MEDIA_TYPE* data structure packed with data that describes the particulars of the media in the audio source clip. The group becomes the audio group with a call to the *IAMTimelineGroup* method *SetMediaType*, which gets passed the same *AM_MEDIA_TYPE* structure that was returned by the call to *get_StreamMediaType*. Note that this will work only if the audio is uncompressed (in other words, WAV files will work, but MP3s will not) and DES supports the audio type.

The track group type determines the output type of the movie created by DirectShow. If you provide only a major type, such as *MEDIATYPE_Video* (as we did in our video track group), DirectShow will make some assumptions about the kind of formats it will output—assumptions you might or might not be happy with. You'll get better results if you set the output media type by building it from scratch. DES won't generate every video type or audio type. Source samples can be in any supported audio or video type, and the filter graph will automatically convert them when the movie is rendered.

Once the audio track group has been added to the timeline, a track is created and added to the timeline, and the source clip is created, has its start and stop points set so that they match the duration of the overall video clip, and is added to the track. At this point, we're done with the audio source clips, audio tracks, and audio group. We're ready to render this movie.

Rendering a Preview Movie

In DirectShow, the timeline is rendered with an object known as the *IRender-Engine*. It's created with a COM call, as shown here:

```
// Preview the timeline.
IRenderEngine *pRenderEngine = NULL;
CoCreateInstance(CLSID_RenderEngine, NULL, CLSCTX_INPROC_SERVER,
    IID_IRenderEngine, (void**) &pRenderEngine);
PreviewTL(pTL, pRenderEngine);
```

Once the *IRenderEngine* object has been instantiated, we can send a preview of the movie (so that you can inspect your work) to the display with a call to the local function *PreviewTL*.

```
// Preview a timeline.
void PreviewTL(IAMTimeline *pTL, IRenderEngine *pRender)
{
    IGraphBuilder    *pGraph = NULL;
    IMediaControl    *pControl = NULL;
    IMediaEvent      *pEvent = NULL;

    // Build the graph.
    pRender->SetTimelineObject(pTL);
    pRender->ConnectFrontEnd( );
    pRender->RenderOutputPins( );
```

```
// Run the graph.
pRender->GetFilterGraph(&pGraph);
pGraph->QueryInterface(IID_IMediaControl, (void **)&pControl);
pGraph->QueryInterface(IID_IMediaEvent, (void **)&pEvent);
SaveGraphFile(pGraph, L"C:\\MyGraph_preview.GRF");  // Save the graph
                                                    // file to disk
pControl->Run();

long evCode;
pEvent->WaitForCompletion(INFINITE, &evCode);
pControl->Stop();

// Clean up.
pEvent->Release();
pControl->Release();
pGraph->Release();
}
```

The *IRenderEngine* object has three methods that speed the rendering of a movie preview, beginning with a call to *SetTimelineObject*, which binds the movie's timeline to the *IRenderEngine* object. This call is followed by a call to *ConnectFrontEnd*, which builds the front end of the filter graph, that is, everything except for the filters used to render the movie. That call is followed immediately by a call to *RenderOutputPins*, which completes the filter graph construction, building a filter graph that will preview the movie.

Next we use some code that should look very familiar: we acquire a pointer to the Filter Graph Manager, use it to query for interfaces to *IMediaControl* and *IMediaEvent*, and then execute the *IMediaControl* method *Run*. At this point, the Active Movie window will open on the display, and the movie will begin to render, as shown in Figure 8-2.

Figure 8-2   The timeline rendering to a preview window

When the filter graph finishes its execution, it receives a *Stop* message and the function exits. As you can see, most of the work required to render a timeline to the display is done in three method calls made to the *IRenderEngine* object.

Keep in mind that preview versions of movies can look choppy and their audio can get out of sync with the video portion of the movie. Neither will happen when the movie is written to a disk file, but they can possibly happen during preview—particularly on underpowered computers.

Rendering a Timeline to an AVI File

It's a little more complicated to render a timeline to a disk-based AVI file. Instead of rendering to a preview window, we must build a filter graph that creates an output file and sends the rendered movie to that file.

```
pRenderEngine->ScrapIt();
WriteTL(pTL, pRenderEngine, L"C:\\MyMovie.avi");

// Clean up.
pRenderEngine->ScrapIt();
pRenderEngine->Release();
pMD->Release();
pTL->Release();
CoUninitialize();

return 0;
}
```

First we need to destroy the filter graph we created on the call to *PreviewTL* by calling the *IRenderEngine* method *ScrapIt*. If you don't call *ScrapIt*, subsequent calls to the *IRenderEngine* object won't work correctly. With our cleanup complete, we can create the AVI file with a call to the local function *WriteTL*.

```
// Write a timeline to a disk file.
void WriteTL(IAMTimeline *pTL, IRenderEngine *pRender, WCHAR *fileName)
{
    IGraphBuilder     *pGraph = NULL;
    ICaptureGraphBuilder2 *pBuilder = NULL;
    IMediaControl     *pControl = NULL;
    IMediaEvent       *pEvent = NULL;

    // Build the graph.
    HRESULT hr = pRender->SetTimelineObject(pTL);
    hr = pRender->ConnectFrontEnd( );
```

```
hr = CoCreateInstance(CLSID_CaptureGraphBuilder2, NULL, CLSCTX_INPROC,
    IID_ICaptureGraphBuilder2, (void **)&pBuilder);

// Get a pointer to the graph front end.
hr = pRender->GetFilterGraph(&pGraph);
hr = pBuilder->SetFiltergraph(pGraph);

// Create the file-writing section.
IBaseFilter *pMux;
hr = pBuilder->SetOutputFileName(&MEDIASUBTYPE_Avi, fileName,
    &pMux, NULL);

long NumGroups;
hr = pTL->GetGroupCount(&NumGroups);

// Loop through the groups and get the output pins.
for (int i = 0; i < NumGroups; i++)
{
    IPin *pPin;
    if (pRender->GetGroupOutputPin(i, &pPin) == S_OK)
    {
        // Connect the pin.
        hr = pBuilder->RenderStream(NULL, NULL, pPin, NULL, pMux);
        pPin->Release();
    }
}

// Run the graph.
hr = pGraph->QueryInterface(IID_IMediaControl, (void **)&pControl);
hr = pGraph->QueryInterface(IID_IMediaEvent, (void **)&pEvent);
SaveGraphFile(pGraph, L"C:\\MyGraph_write.GRF");  // Save the graph
                                                  // file to disk

hr = pControl->Run();

long evCode;
hr = pEvent->WaitForCompletion(INFINITE, &evCode);
hr = pControl->Stop();

// Clean up.
if (pMux) {
    pMux->Release();
}
pEvent->Release();
pControl->Release();
pGraph->Release();
pBuilder->Release();
}
```

As in *PreviewTL*, we begin with calls to the *IRenderEngine* methods *Set-TimelineObject* and *ConnectFrontEnd*. However, because we want to render this file to disk, we need to take it step-by-step hereafter. We do so by creating an *ICaptureGraphBuilder2* object, which we'll use as the basis for a filter graph that will take the capture source (in this case, the portion of the filter graph created by the render engine) and send it out to a capture file. We need to give the *ICaptureGraphBuilder2* object a pointer to the Filter Graph Manager, so we retrieve it with a call to the *IRenderEngine* method *GetFilterGraph*. Next we call the *ICaptureGraphBuilder2* method *SetOutputFileName*, passing it our requested output media type (*MEDIATYPE_Avi*, which will produce an AVI file). That call will instantiate an AVI Mux filter and a file writer, and it will return a pointer to the AVI Mux filter in *pMux*.

Now we have to make an inquiry of the timeline, calling the *IAMTimeline* method *GetGroupCount*, which returns the number of track groups within the movie. We should have two track groups—one for video and one for audio—and each of these will need to be rendered separately. Inside of a loop, we call the *IRenderEngine* method *GetGroupOutputPin*, which returns an *IPin* corresponding to an output pin on a filter—created by the call to *ConnectFrontEnd*. As we find each output pin, we call *RenderStream* on each pin, connecting the *IRenderEngine*-created portion of the filter graph to the AVI file writer through the AVI Mux. Once that's done, we run the filter graph, which renders the movie to a disk file. And that's it—the movie is now on disk, ready to be viewed. When we return from the function, we do a little cleanup, close COM, and then exit the application.

The code in this example creates an uncompressed video file. You can encode the video to a compressed format (such as Windows Media) by inserting an encoder filter after the output pin. Specify the encoder filter in the fourth parameter to *RenderStream*.

```
IBaseFilter *pEncoder; // Pointer to the encoder filter
// Create the encoder filter (not shown).
hr = pBuilder->RenderStream(NULL, NULL, pPin, pEncoder, pMux);
```

Alternatively, you can use the Smart Render Engine instead of the Render Engine. The Smart Render Engine automatically compresses the video stream to the desired format. The section "Rendering a Project" in the DirectShow SDK documentation has more information on how this engine works.

Improving Video Output Quality

The example we've given here creates an output file that has only half the image width and height of the source AVI file because we used the default video parameters when we established the media type for the video track. Setting these parameters explicitly would have created a high-quality video output. To ensure high-quality output, which you might want if you're creating an AVI file that you'll want to write to a digital camcorder, the media subtype for the video group should be either *RGB24* or *RGB32*. Set the dimensions of the video group equal to the size of the largest video clip (in the case of DV, 720×480 pixels), and set the stretch mode on each clip to crop by calling *IAMTimelineSrc::GetStretchMode* with the *RESIZEF_CROP* flag. This flag prevents DES from stretching the source video to cover the entire area defined for the video group. Alternatively, you can write your own custom video resizer. (This feature is new in DirectX 9.) The default resizer in DES uses *StretchBlt* to resize the video, which is fast but does not produce the best quality. A number of better (but slower) algorithms exist for resizing video.

One final note: although we created an output file in AVI format, you could rewrite this application to create Windows Media files, which would lead to smaller file sizes. To do so, you'd pass *MEDIASUBTYPE_Asf* instead of *MEDIASUBTYPE_Avi* to *SetOutputFileName* in *WriteTL*. You'd also need to set the profile parameters for the output file, and you'll learn how to do that in Chapter 15.

Summary

There's obviously much more to DES than can be covered in a short piece of code. Nonetheless, DESClip covers all the basics of DES. It's possible—even desirable—to build a very rich editing program in DES, something along the lines of Adobe Premiere. The only difference between what you see in DESClip and what you see onscreen when you're using Adobe Premiere is user interface. Adobe Premiere makes all of this under-the-hood management of the timeline an intuitive process and allows you to easily change any of the source clips, transitions, effects, and groups that you'd use when making a movie. But all of those user interface bells and whistles aren't the magic that makes movie editing possible—that magic comes from DirectShow, and you now know how to construct your own sophisticated editing applications using DES.

9

Using the Video Mixing Renderer

Although most of the examples we've used in this book have a video component, we've employed only the Video Renderer filter for video output. This filter has proved entirely adequate thus far, but the Video Renderer is designed to render a single stream of video to a single rectangle on the screen. Microsoft DirectShow is capable of dealing with multiple video streams, all flowing through a filter graph in real time, with a range of transform filters capable of producing real-time video effects. With DirectShow and the latest generation of video hardware, we have enormously powerful video processing capabilities. DirectShow provides a video rendering filter to match those capabilities.

The Video Mixing Renderer (VMR) filter was first introduced with Microsoft Windows XP; today, as part of Microsoft DirectX 9, its capabilities are available across the entire range of Microsoft operating systems. In this chapter, we'll explore the capabilities of VMR 9, the Video Mixing Renderer released as part of DirectX 9. (VMR 7, which was part of the Windows XP release, is still available, but it will run only on Windows XP–based systems.) The VMR filter does exactly what the name says: it takes multiple video sources and allows you to mix them together in real time to produce spectacular results. The video mixer isn't a recent idea; hardware-based video mixers have been around for many years, costing anywhere from a few thousand to a few hundred thousand dollars. DirectShow offers a software-only solution for video mixing, which means you can have many of the same features of a TV studio right in your own computer, with the appropriate DirectShow application.

The basic function of the VMR is simple: it takes one or several video streams and mixes them into a single video stream, which is then rendered to the display. The VMR presents a series of interfaces to give the application programmer a very fine level of control over the display of each stream coming into the VMR. Not only can you control the mix of each video stream—by controlling the transparency, you can make streams fade in and out of each other—but you can also control the location of a stream in the output.

A video stream doesn't need to be spread across the entire output window; it could occupy a small corner, a thumbnail view that might be reminiscent of the picture-in-picture feature offered on high-end television sets. You can also use the VMR to mix static images into the video stream and produce an overlay of the video image, or you can take the VMR output and send it to a 3D model (rendered using Microsoft Direct3D, another component of DirectX) and paint the surface of a 3D model with a video image. With another VMR feature, reminiscent of the analog video, you can interactively change the hue, saturation, brightness, and contrast values of all video streams on a per-stream basis.

The VMR is very efficient, within the limits of the video card and processor you're using. That said, the VMR provides so much power that a DirectShow application mixing and blending a multitude of simultaneous video streams could harness nearly 100 percent of the CPU on all but the fastest computers. The features available to the VMR programmer are so comprehensive that we can do little more than cover its basic features and operations in this book. By itself, the VMR possesses more power and capability than any other single DirectShow filter. After you've read this chapter and studied the example code, you might be interested in reading the extensive documentation on the VMR in the DirectX documentation for C++, which covers the design and operation of the VMR in greater detail.

Video Renderers Available to DirectShow Programmers

Because video rendering depends so much on graphics hardware, it should not be surprising that as video hardware has improved over the past few years, DirectShow has added new Video Renderer filters capable of exploiting each new advance.

The (Plain Old Vanilla) Video Renderer

The initial video renderer was called, logically, the Video Renderer. It was designed using the 1.0 release of Microsoft DirectDraw back when the Intel 386 was the standard CPU and the high-end graphics cards had 4 MB of on-board memory, although many systems still had cards with only 512 KB or less. Because of the limited capabilities of the early hardware, the Video Renderer has no minimum hardware requirements. If it cannot allocate sufficient memory directly on the graphics card using DirectDraw, it will fall back to using the graphics device interface (GDI) and system memory to display the bitmaps. The Video Renderer filter was upgraded to use DirectDraw 3 if the hardware supported it. To maintain backward compatibility with existing DirectShow applications, this filter remains the default video renderer—except when an application is running on Windows XP.

The Overlay Mixer

A couple of years after the Video Renderer filter was created, when DVD drives were introduced, CPUs were still not fast enough to perform the MPEG-2 decoding in software. Hardware decoders were used, equipped with "video ports," which were cables that carried the decoded video signal directly from the decoder card to the video card, bypassing the host CPU and the system bus entirely. Many TV tuner cards, notably the popular ATI All-In-Wonder card, also use video port technology, although the tuner or decoder and graphics card are physically on the same board. To support video ports and a new feature on graphics cards called the *overlay surface*, Microsoft developed a new video renderer called the Overlay Mixer. Unlike the Video Renderer, the Overlay Mixer has a minimum hardware requirement, namely that the graphics card must have an overlay. The Overlay Mixer doesn't try to use GDI and system memory; if the graphics hardware offers no overlay surface, the filter will return an error and refuse to connect.

An overlay surface is a physical portion of memory on the graphics card distinct from the *primary surface*, which is the memory used to render the entire desktop. Overlay surfaces accept input in various YUV formats, which is conveniently the format in which decoders output their decoded video frames. The graphics hardware, which is significantly faster than the system CPU, converts the video into native RGB values for the display monitor inside the card's digital-to-analog converter.

For example, as a DVD is playing, the Overlay Mixer allocates sufficient memory on the overlay surface to contain the video rectangle of the specified size. It also notifies the graphics card of the size and position of that rectangle relative to the desktop. That rectangle is then filled with a color key (typically magenta) in the primary surface. Each time the card refreshes its frame buffer, it goes across each scan line, grabbing pixels from the primary surface memory and examining the color value. If the color value matches the color key, the graphics hardware discards that primary surface pixel and instead retrieves the corresponding pixel from the overlay surface memory.

Another new feature of the Overlay Mixer was its ability to handle secondary input streams containing bitmaps with closed captioning or DVD subpicture text or graphics. If such streams are present, the Overlay Mixer will write that data over the current video frame before delivering the frame to the overlay surface.

By the time of DirectX 8, around 1999, graphics hardware had continued to advance in both speed and the amount of memory available. These advances meant that even when displaying full-screen video at 30 frames per second (fps), the graphics card was spending much of its time waiting around doing nothing. It was like having a Ferrari but being able to use it only to go to the corner store. So, because software developers abhor a vacuum, they began to think of ways to put all that wasted horsepower to work, and the result was DirectX Video Acceleration, or DXVA.

DXVA is the 2D equivalent of 3D graphics accelerators, and it uses the same principles to speed up the rendering of graphics for games and other computer-generated graphics. If a graphics driver and a software decoder both support DXVA, the decoder is able to make use of the powerful graphics processing unit to perform, in its otherwise idle moments, some of the more computationally expensive decoding operations. By having the graphics processing unit (GPU) help it decode video, the decoder's demands on the CPU are significantly reduced, so that with DXVA on a typical modern system, it's possible to play back a full-screen DVD while putting only minimal demands on the CPU. The Overlay Mixer and both versions of the Video Mixing Renderer all support DXVA through API calls that enable the transfer of data between the decoder and the graphics hardware.

The Video Mixing Renderer 7

For all its advances over the Video Renderer, the Overlay Mixer still could not perform any true mixing of video images (also known as alpha blending), and it could not accept more than one video stream as input. Internally, it was still using older versions of DirectDraw. To address these limitations, the Video Mixing Renderer 7 (VMR 7) was introduced for the Windows XP operating system. The VMR 7 enables true blending of multiple incoming video streams, allowing for a whole range of new effects. It's also more resourceful than the Overlay Mixer in finding some video memory to use. It will first attempt to allocate memory on the overlay surface. If none is available, it will try the primary surface, then system video memory in the AGP address space, and finally, if all else fails, it will use system memory.

Another advance in the VMR 7 was its use of DirectDraw 7 rather than the mix of DirectDraw 3 and DirectDraw 1 used in the Overlay Mixer and Video Renderer. The VMR 7 didn't use Direct3D 8 to control the graphics hardware because this API didn't provide the required support for off-screen plain surfaces or DXVA decoding. But the most interesting innovation in the VMR 7 was its component architecture, which enables you to create your own custom allocator-presenter components (explained in the "Opening the Hood of the VMR" section later in this chapter) and take complete control over the rendering process. By writing your own allocator-presenter, you can render your video surfaces onto Direct3D geometries and create stunning video effects.

The Video Mixing Renderer 9

Adoption of the VMR 7 has been limited by the fact that it was available only for applications running on Windows XP. This situation has been rectified with the latest of the DirectShow video renderers, the Video Mixing Renderer 9 (VMR 9). This filter offers all the features of the VMR 7, simplifies the code required to insert your own allocator-presenter, and is available on all platforms supported by DirectX 9. The VMR 9 uses Direct3D 9 to control the graphics hardware. It offers support for hardware deinterlacing capabilities available on the latest graphics cards, and its support for Direct3D 9 pixel shaders means that you can control hue, saturation, and brightness on a per-stream basis. As you might expect, the VMR 9 hardware requirements are the most stringent of all the video renderers: the VMR 9 requires a fairly recent graphics card.

Almost as interesting as what the VMR 9 supports is what it doesn't support: video ports and overlay surfaces. Although these technologies were instrumental in making quality video possible on the PC, neither is necessary any longer given the sheer speed of modern CPUs and graphics hardware. Video ports are no longer needed because full-screen video can stream at 30 fps from a TV device or a DVD drive into system memory, where it's fully or partially decoded, and then back to the video graphics card through the AGP port.

Overlay surfaces are problematic because there's only one overlay surface per system, but users often want to display multiple video clips simultaneously. Also, the overlay requires a key color, which can interfere with any effects that the Windows shell is trying to do with windows that interest the video playback window. And because an RGB image of the video frame never actually exists in the overlay memory, pressing the Print Screen key copies only the color key, not the video image that the user expects. Therefore, it's much preferable, and now possible, to render video streams onto the device's primary surface—and this is what the VMR 9 does.

Opening the Hood of the VMR

Before we start to use the VMR in a DirectShow program, we need to examine the internal structure of the VMR. Unlike most other DirectShow filters, the VMR is not conceived of as a monolithic entity, but as a set of functional units, each with their own interfaces, as shown in Figure 9-1.

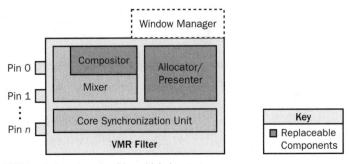

VMR in windowed mode with multiple input streams

Figure 9-1   The Video Mixing Renderer, which is composed of a number of functional units

The Mixer is a VMR COM component charged with managing multiple video streams as they enter the VMR. Each stream is assigned a Z value when it passes through the Mixer; the ordering of Z values determines the front-to-back order of the video streams. These streams can be thought of as a series of planes, the frontmost of which has the lowest Z value (closest to zero), while increasing Z values represent planes that are progressively "deeper" in the background and are rendered as being behind streams with lower Z values. Thus, a stream with a Z value of 1 would be rendered in front of a stream with a Z value of 2, 5, or 15.

The Compositor is another VMR COM component. It actually performs the task of blending the various video streams into a single stream. In the strictest sense, the Compositor is where the video mixing and rendering takes place, assisted by the other logical units within the VMR. The Compositor can apply a number of effects to the streams, such as making them transparent or mapping them to particular portions of a 3D object.

The allocator-presenter (yet another COM component) provides an interface between the graphics display hardware on the PC and the VMR. The default allocator-presenter is optimized for 2D video rendering, but by writing your own custom allocator-presenter, you can assume total control over how the composited video frame is rendered by the graphics hardware. With either version of the VMR, you can render video onto Direct3D objects and manipulate those objects using all the power of DirectX.

The Core Synchronization Unit (yes, a COM component) uses the *IReferenceClock* interface provided by the Filter Graph Manager to keep the operation of the VMR well synchronized, ensuring that video streams passing through the VMR remain synchronized with the rest of the filter graph. If the VMR gets overloaded, the Core Synchronization Unit can drop frames from the mix to prevent VMR desynchronization with the rest of the filter graph.

Finally, the Window Manager is used only if the VMR is operating in windowed mode; that is, if the VMR is in charge of maintaining its own display window for the VMR output stream. The VMR will create a window for output by default to maintain backward compatibility with existing applications—this is the way the old Video Renderer works. If a windowless mode is used, the VMR will draw its output into your application's window in a rectangle that you specify. Windowless mode is the recommended mode of operation for the VMR because you can handle all Windows messages directly in your application. VMR settings for windowless mode need to be established when the VMR is instantiated and initialized.

The VMR is configured by default with four input pins, each of which can receive its own video stream. One pin is created when the filter is instantiated, and three more are added when the first pin is connected. You can configure the filter for less than four pins, but it isn't necessary to use all available pins, and having extra unused pins on the VMR won't slow rendering. However, if you do have more than four input streams, you can create any additional pins that you might need (up to 16 inputs), but you need to do so before you start connecting any pins on the VMR.

Operating the VMR

The VMR is functionally similar to the DirectShow Video Renderer filter, except that it requires that the system have a fairly recent graphics card. The VMR requires full hardware acceleration, and Direct3D must be enabled. (You can check these capabilities on your system by using the DXDiag utility in the DirectX SDK.) The VMR sits at the downstream end of a filter graph and receives a number of video streams as input—anywhere from 1 to 16 streams. However, because of the unusual setup requirements of the VMR, a few instructions need to be followed to ensure error-free use of the VMR in your filter graphs.

The VMR must be added to the filter graph and fully configured before it's connected to any other filters. Connecting the VMR to other filters "freezes" the VMR configuration. The VMR can't be reconfigured—to change the number of input streams, go from windowed to windowless mode, and so on—once it has been connected to another filter. After the VMR has been instantiated, it must be programmed with the number of input streams it will receive, and then the VMR must be put into windowless mode, if it's to be used in that way. The VMR defaults to windowed mode, and you can't switch between windowless mode and windowed mode once the VMR has been connected to an upstream filter, so you need to set that up before any connections have been made. (The same is true for setting the number of input streams.)

One final adjustment, for the mixing preferences, must be set before the VMR is connected to any upstream filters. The mixing preferences are used to determine whether the output stream is to be decimated (lose resolution) and to set up any filtering used on the input streams. Changing the mixing preferences is recommended only for advanced applications. The VMR uses sensible default values, and it's rare that an application would need to change them.

Once this initialization work is complete, the VMR can receive connections from upstream filters. The VMR is capable of receiving a broad set of video formats, and it will convert them internally to an output format suitable for rendering. If the VMR can't negotiate a connection between an upstream video source and its input pin, either the conversion couldn't be performed inside the VMR or the VMR has run out of memory. (The VMR, unlike the old Video Renderer, doesn't use system memory, only video memory, either resident on the video card itself or AGP memory on the motherboard.)

When mixing different video sources, it becomes important to recognize the differences inherent in various video formats. Video designed to display on a computer is generated in a progressive-scan format, meaning that the entire image is drawn every frame. That's different from video designed for broadcast TV, where the two-fields-per-frame are interlaced together. For display on a computer monitor, the interlaced signal must be deinterlaced, that is, converted to progressive-scan format. That's something that will happen in the VMR before the video is displayed, using one of any number of possible techniques, each of which has its own quality vs. speed tradeoffs.

The VMR has an interface that allows you to adjust the deinterlacing techniques used on each video stream. These techniques are based inside the hardware on the graphics cards, so if your DirectShow program is running on a computer with very basic graphics hardware, there might not be a lot of options available. On the other hand, a top-of-the-line graphics card will be able to exploit the features of that card for deinterlacing. Full information on deinterlacing in the VMR can be found in the "Setting Deinterlace Preferences" page of the DirectX SDK documentation.

Working with the VMR: A Picture-in-Picture Application

Now that we've done some work with broadcast TV signals, we need to take a look at how DirectShow can be used to create one of the fancy special effects available on expensive TVs: picture-in-picture. This effect takes two separate video sources (in the case of a television, two separate TV tuners) and mixes them together into the same display window, placing the thumbnail of a video image over the lower-right corner of the primary image. Picture-in-picture TVs allow you to switch between the big picture and the thumbnail, so you can monitor one channel, even as you watch another. That's great for folks who want to watch one ball game while keeping an eye on another or are channel surfing while waiting for a commercial break to end.

We could build a full picture-in-picture TV application in DirectShow, but that would require that two TV tuners be connected to the user's computer. Although this is no big deal technically, it is very rare. Instead, the Pip9 application takes two video files (which you select from your hard disk) and streams them into the same application window, creating a picture-in-picture view, as shown in Figure 9-2.

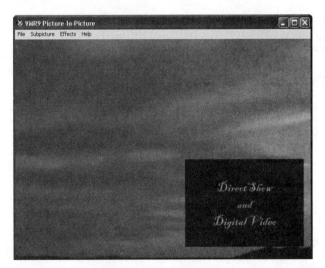

Figure 9-2   A demonstration of picture-in-picture using two AVI files

An Effects menu allows you to swap the two images, animate the swap, mirror either stream (flip it right-to-left), flip either stream up-to-down, and make ProcAmp (Process Amplification) adjustments to the brightness, hue, and saturation values on the primary stream. The Subpicture menu gives you rough control over the size and placement of the picture-in-picture thumbnail, allowing you to shrink or increase the size of the inset video, placing it into any of the four quadrants or the center of the video window. When both clips reach the end of their running time, they're rewound and begin to play again, endlessly.

Rather than a detailed line-by-line exploration of the Pip9 code, our examination will focus on four principle areas: the creation of the filter graph with the VMR, the code that creates the picture-in-picture effect, another piece of code that animates the swapping of the streams, and the dialog box that manages a virtual processing amplifier. In these examples (and the rest of the Pip9 application, which you can peruse at your leisure), you'll learn how to make the VMR work in your own DirectShow applications.

Initializing the VMR

Once the user has selected two valid movie files by selecting the Open Files menu item from the File menu, control is transferred to the *InitializeWindowlessVMR* function.

```
HRESULT InitializeWindowlessVMR(IBaseFilter **ppVmr9)
{
    IBaseFilter *pVmr=NULL;

    if (!ppVmr9)
        return E_POINTER;
    *ppVmr9 = NULL;

    // Create the VMR and add it to the filter graph.
    HRESULT hr = CoCreateInstance(CLSID_VideoMixingRenderer9, NULL,
        CLSCTX_INPROC, IID_IBaseFilter, (void**)&pVmr);

    if (SUCCEEDED(hr))
    {
        hr = pGB->AddFilter(pVmr, L"Video Mixing Renderer 9î);
        if (SUCCEEDED(hr))
        {
            // Set the rendering mode and number of streams.
            CComPtr <IVMRFilterConfig9> pConfig;

            JIF(pVmr->QueryInterface(IID_IVMRFilterConfig9,
                (void**)&pConfig));
            JIF(pConfig->SetRenderingMode(VMR9Mode_Windowless));
            JIF(pConfig->SetNumberOfStreams(2));

            // Set the bounding window and border for the video.
            JIF(pVmr->QueryInterface(IID_IVMRWindowlessControl9,
```

```
            (void**)&pWC));
        JIF(pWC->SetVideoClippingWindow(ghApp));
        JIF(pWC->SetBorderColor(RGB(0,0,0)));  // Black border

        // Get the mixer control interface for manipulation of video
        // stream output rectangles and alpha values.
        JIF(pVmr->QueryInterface(IID_IVMRMixerControl9,
            (void**)&pMix));
    }

    // Don't release the pVmr interface because we are copying it into
    // the caller's ppVmr9 pointer.
    *ppVmr9 = pVmr;
}


return hr;
}
```

This function is called once a Capture Graph Builder interface, *pGB*, exists to receive the instantiated VMR, which is created with a call to *CoCreateInstance*. The filter is immediately added to the filter graph. At this point, the VMR initialization occurs. A call to *QueryInterface* returns the *IVMRFilterConfig9* interface, which is put into windowless mode. The number of VMR input pins is set with a call to the *IVMRFilterConfig9* interface method *SetNumberOfStreams*.

The function then acquires the *IVMRWindowlessControl9* interface, which it uses to set the display characteristics of the VMR. The video clipping window—the target window for the rendered video stream—is set with a method call to *SetVideoClippingWindow*. In your own VMR applications, that call should be supplied with a handle to a window owned by your application. The border color of the rendered output (whatever might not be filled with the video imagery) is set to black with a call to *SetBorderColor*. Last the function acquires the *IVMRMixerControl9* interface, which will be used by other functions in Pip9 to manipulate the mixer in real time.

The video streams are brought into the filter graph in the utility function *RenderFileToVMR9*, which uses the *IFilterGraph2* method *RenderEx* to build the filter graph components that connect a disk-based movie file to the VMR. The *RenderEx* method allows you to specify that a renderer that already exists in the filter graph (in this case, the VMR) must be used to render the output pin of another filter—a File Source filter pointing to the movie. The value *AM_RENDEREX_RENDERTOEXISTINGRENDERERS* is passed as a parameter in the *RenderEx* call. (We need to be explicit about our choice of renderer because the VMR 9 is never the default renderer. In some cases, such as if the user's system has an old graphics card, the Filter Graph Manager might fall back to the old Video Renderer, which is not what you'd want at all.) Both movie files are added in successive calls to *RenderFileToVMR9* and connected to the first two available input pins on the VMR, which are now identifiable as stream 0 and stream 1.

Pip9 is not a very complex VMR application; only two streams are being mixed together. Even so, all the basics of VMR initialization and setup are presented in *InitializeWindowlessVMR*. A bit further along in application execution, the *InitVideoWindow* function is invoked. It uses the *IVMRWindowlessControl9* interface to tie the output from the VMR to the application's main window.

```
HRESULT InitVideoWindow(int nMultiplier, int nDivider)
{
    LONG lHeight, lWidth;
    HRESULT hr = S_OK;

    if (!pWC)
        return S_OK;

    // Read the default video size.
    hr = pWC->GetNativeVideoSize(&lWidth, &lHeight, NULL, NULL);
    if (hr == E_NOINTERFACE)
        return S_OK;

    // Account for requests of normal, half, or double size.
    lWidth = MulDiv(lWidth, nMultiplier, nDivider);
    lHeight = MulDiv(lHeight, nMultiplier, nDivider);

    int nTitleHeight = GetSystemMetrics(SM_CYCAPTION);
    int nBorderWidth = GetSystemMetrics(SM_CXBORDER);
    int nBorderHeight = GetSystemMetrics(SM_CYBORDER);

    // Account for size of title bar and borders for exact match
    // of window client area to default video size.
    SetWindowPos(ghApp, NULL, 0, 0, lWidth + 2*nBorderWidth,
        lHeight + nTitleHeight + 2*nBorderHeight,
        SWP_NOMOVE | SWP_NOOWNERZORDER);

    GetClientRect(ghApp, &g_rcDest);
    hr = pWC->SetVideoPosition(NULL, &g_rcDest);

    return hr;
}
```

The application learns the native width and height of the input streams through a call to *GetNativeVideoSize*. The output size is a function of the input streams. After *InitVideoWindow* performs some math to learn the true dimensions of the display rectangle, minus border and title bar dimensions, it assigns that value to the VMR through the *IVMRWindowlessControl9* method *SetVideo-Position*. Now when the Filter Graph Manager receives the *Run* command, VMR output will flow into the designated rectangle within the application's window.

When using the VMR in windowless mode, it's necessary to notify the VMR when your application receives certain Windows messages. When you receive a *WM_PAINT* message, call *IVMRWindowlessControl::RepaintVideo*. When you receive a *WM_DISPLAYCHANGE* message, call *IVMRWindowlessControl::DisplayModeChanged*. When you receive a *WM_SIZE* message, recalculate the position of the video and call *IVMRWindowlessControl::SetVideoPosition* if necessary.

Programming the VMR for Picture-in-Picture Display

To program picture-in-picture display using the VMR, all that's required is to set a display rectangle for the thumbnail picture, using a call to the *IVMRMixerControl9* method *SetOutputRect*. If the specified rectangle has a different dimension than the destination rectangle (which is covering the entire available area inside the window), the video output from the VMR will appear to be inset within the destination rectangle. The calculation generating the coordinates for an inset rectangle within a VMR window is performed with a normalized rectangle in a data structure known as *VMR9NormalizedRect*. The normalized rectangle spans the coordinates from (0, 0), the upper-left corner, through (1, 1), the lower-right corner. This area is known as the *composition space* (shown in Figure 9-3) for the VMR.

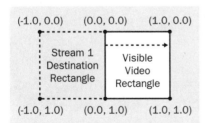

Figure 9-3   Composition space, which creates both on-screen and off-screen drawing areas

If desired, you can perform off-screen operations with the VMR by choosing coordinates that are not within the on-screen rectangle. For example, a VMR rectangle with an upper-left coordinate of (-1, 0) and a lower-right coordinate of (-0.01, 1) would not be visible because it's not within the on-screen area of the composition space. Clever use of the VMR's composition space could allow you to construct animations that cause off-screen elements (rendered in the VMR) to fly on screen or off screen programmatically.

Here's a very simple use of the *SetOutputRect* method in a function that's called repeatedly in the Pip9 application to set the visible areas of both video streams supplied to the VMR:

```
HRESULT UpdatePinPos(int nStreamID)
{
    HRESULT hr=S_OK;

    // Get a pointer to the selected stream's information.
    STRM_PARAM* p = &strParam[nStreamID];

    // Set the left, right, top, and bottom coordinates.
    VMR9NormalizedRect r = {p->xPos, p->yPos,
        p->xPos + p->xSize, p->yPos + p->ySize};

    // If mirrored, swap the left/right coordinates
    // in the destination rectangle.
    if (strParam[nStreamID].bMirrored)
    {
        float fLeft = strParam[nStreamID].xPos;
        float fRight = strParam[nStreamID].xPos +
            strParam[nStreamID].xSize;
        r.left = fRight;
        r.right = fLeft;
    }

    // If flipped, swap the top/bottom coordinates
    // in the destination rectangle.
    if (strParam[nStreamID].bFlipped)
    {
        float fTop = strParam[nStreamID].yPos;
        float fBottom = strParam[nStreamID].yPos +
            strParam[nStreamID].ySize;
        r.top = fBottom;
        r.bottom = fTop;
    }

    // Update the destination rectangle for the selected stream.
    if(pMix)
        hr = pMix->SetOutputRect(nStreamID, &r);

    return hr;
}
```

UpdatePinPos is called every time there's any change to the on-screen position of either video stream. Using a *VMR9NormalizedRect* structure (whose fields are manipulated elsewhere in the code), the VMR is configured with a *SetOutputRect* command to change the visible area of the stream. In the case where

Animated Stream Swap is selected from the Effects menu, a timer periodically changes the coordinates of both streams to different composition space values. *UpdatePinPos* is called after each coordinate change, and the stream output rectangles reflect that change in an animation that shows the streams swapping positions.

Two other, very simple functions keep the alpha (blending) and Z order of the streams updated appropriately.

```
HRESULT UpdatePinAlpha(int nStreamID)
{
    HRESULT hr=S_OK;

    // Get a pointer to the selected stream's information.
    STRM_PARAM* p = &strParam[nStreamID];

    // Update the alpha value for the selected stream.
    if(pMix)
        hr = pMix->SetAlpha(nStreamID, p->fAlpha);

    return hr;
}

HRESULT UpdatePinZOrder(int nStreamID, DWORD dwZOrder)
{
    HRESULT hr=S_OK;

    // Update the Z order for the selected stream.
    if(pMix)
        hr = pMix->SetZOrder(nStreamID, dwZOrder);

    return hr;
}
```

The function *UpdatePinAlpha* controls the alpha value, the transparency of the input stream when rendered into the output stream. The possible values range from 0 (completely transparent, hence invisible) to 1.0 (completely opaque). In the Pip9 application, the thumbnail stream is rendered with an alpha value of 0.6, or 60 percent opaque. This opacity means that you can see through the thumbnail stream to the stream behind it. The alpha value for a stream is set with a call to the *IVMRMixerControl9* method *SetAlpha*.

The function *UpdatePinZOrder* manipulates the Z value for a given stream. As stated previously, a Z value of 0 indicates the frontmost position, while higher Z values can be thought of as receding into the display. The lowest Z value is rendered in front of all other streams. For example, the thumbnail stream in Pip9 has a lower Z value than the full-screen stream and is rendered in the foreground. The Z value for a stream is set with a call to the *IVMRMixerControl9* method *SetZOrder*. Although it seems as though more programming should be required to create such a range of video effects—picture-in-picture, animation, and transparency—the VMR takes care of all these effects in just a few calls.

Programming the VMR ProcAmp

ProcAmp is a device that evolved out of necessity within the world of video hardware. In its physical manifestation, a ProcAmp is a black box that adjusts an incoming video signal so that its brightness, contrast, hue, and saturation values match those of a corresponding piece of downstream video gear. ProcAmps are often necessary when dealing with video signals because equipment produced by different manufacturers (and at different times) has differing requirements for signal strength, modulation, and so forth.

The DirectShow VMR has its own version of a ProcAmp. Rather than using an external analog device, the VMR ProcAmp manipulates the graphics hardware in the computer's display system to produce visually analogous effects—if the graphics card driver supports these kinds of effects. (As of this writing, only the very newest graphics cards supported ProcAmp effects.) Within the Effects menu of Pin, there's an item named ProcAmp Adjustments that brings up a dialog box with four sliders for control of brightness, hue, saturation, and contrast, as shown in Figure 9-4.

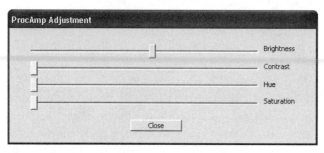

Figure 9-4   The Pip9 dialog box that allows you to adjust the VMR ProcAmp for each stream

Here's the Windows event-handler code that handles all events from the ProcAmp dialog box. Within it, you'll see the code that initializes the slider controls using VMR ProcAmp and code that changes those values as the sliders are moved.

```
LRESULT CALLBACK ProcAmpAdjustProc(HWND hWnd, UINT message, WPARAM wParam,
    LPARAM lParam)
{
    HRESULT hr;
    DWORD streamNum = 0;

    switch (message)
    {
        case WM_INITDIALOG:

        // Set up the slider ranges
        if (pMix)
        {
            DWORD streamNum = 0;
            VMR9ProcAmpControl myProcAmpControl;
            myProcAmpControl.dwSize = sizeof(VMR9ProcAmpControl);
            myProcAmpControl.dwFlags = 0;
            hr = pMix->GetProcAmpControl(streamNum, &myProcAmpControl);
            if (SUCCEEDED(hr))
            {
                // For each ProcAmp control, check if it's supported.
                // If so, get the range and set the slider value.
                // Otherwise, disable the control.

                DWORD prop;
                float *pVal;

                for (prop = ProcAmpControl9_Brightness,
                    pVal = &myProcAmpControl.Brightness;
                    prop < ProcAmpControl9_Mask;
                    prop <<= 1, pVal++)
                {
                    HWND hSlider = GetDlgItem(hWnd,
                        IDC_SLIDER_BASE + prop);

                    // Is this property supported?
                    if (myProcAmpControl.dwFlags & prop)
                    {
                        SendMessage(hSlider, TBM_SETRANGE, TRUE,
                            MAKELONG(0, 100));

                        // Let's get the range for this property
                        // to start with.

                        VMR9ProcAmpControlRange myProcAmpControlRange;
                        myProcAmpControlRange.dwSize =
                            sizeof(VMR9ProcAmpControlRange);
                        myProcAmpControlRange.dwProperty =
```

```
                        (VMR9ProcAmpControlFlags)prop;
            hr = pMix->GetProcAmpControlRange(streamNum,
                &myProcAmpControlRange);
            if SUCCEEDED(hr)
            {
                // We have value and ranges,
                // so let's normalize for a 1-100 scale.
                float totalRange =
                    myProcAmpControlRange.MaxValue -
                    myProcAmpControlRange.MinValue;
                float absoluteValue = *pVal -
                    myProcAmpControlRange.MinValue;
                double ratio = (absoluteValue/totalRange) *
                    100.0;
                long radical = (long)ratio;

                // Now we've got to set the slider to
                // reflect its value in the total range.
                SendMessage(hSlider, TBM_SETPOS, TRUE,
                    radical);
            }
        }
        else
        {
            // Graphics driver does not support this
            // property. Disable the slider.
            EnableWindow(hSlider, FALSE);
        }
    } // for
} else {

        // We failed the GetProcAmpControl call.
        // Disable all sliders.
        EnableWindow(GetDlgItem(hWnd,
            IDC_SLIDER_BRIGHTNESS), FALSE);
        EnableWindow(GetDlgItem(hWnd,
            IDC_SLIDER_CONTRAST), FALSE);
        EnableWindow(GetDlgItem(hWnd, IDC_SLIDER_HUE), FALSE);
        EnableWindow(GetDlgItem(hWnd,
            IDC_SLIDER_SATURATION), FALSE);
    }
}
return TRUE;

case WM_COMMAND:
    switch (wParam)
    {
        case IDC_PROCAMPCLOSE:
```

```
        EndDialog(hWnd, TRUE);
        break;


    }
    break;

case WM_HSCROLL:

    // Figure out which slider did the dirty work.
    HWND hCtl = (HWND)lParam;
    DWORD PropId = GetDlgCtrlID(hCtl) - IDC_SLIDER_BASE;
    DWORD dwPos = (DWORD)SendMessage(hCtl, TBM_GETPOS, 0, 0);

    // Now convert that to an absolute value.
    // Let's get the range for the property, to start with.
    VMR9ProcAmpControlRange myProcAmpControlRange;
    myProcAmpControlRange.dwSize = sizeof(VMR9ProcAmpControlRange);
    myProcAmpControlRange.dwProperty =
        (VMR9ProcAmpControlFlags)PropId;
    hr = pMix->GetProcAmpControlRange(streamNum,
        &myProcAmpControlRange);
    if SUCCEEDED(hr) {

        // OK, we have the value and the ranges for the property,
        // so let's normalize for a 1-100 scale.
        float totalRange = myProcAmpControlRange.MaxValue -
            myProcAmpControlRange.MinValue;
        float multiple = totalRange / 100.0f;
        float theValue = multiple * dwPos;
        // Add the offset back in.
        theValue = theValue + myProcAmpControlRange.MinValue;

        // And now, pass that set value back.
        VMR9ProcAmpControl myProcAmpControl;
        myProcAmpControl.dwSize = sizeof(VMR9ProcAmpControl);
        myProcAmpControl.dwFlags = PropId;
        myProcAmpControl.Brightness = theValue;
        hr = pMix->SetProcAmpControl(streamNum, &myProcAmpControl);

    } else {
        return FALSE;
    }
    return TRUE;
    break;


    }

    return FALSE;
}
```

ProcAmpAdjustProc is a standard Windows callback function that's invoked when events are generated and passed to the ProcAmp dialog box for processing. When the dialog box is first created, a *WM_INITDIALOG* message is generated. At this point, the Pip9 application needs to read the current brightness, hue, and saturation values for stream 0 (the large stream) so that it can set its slider values appropriately. Before any of the values can be read, a test is performed to ensure that the video hardware attached to the system supports the ProcAmp features of the VMR. We also test individually for each property because certain video cards might support some ProcAmp features while leaving others unimplemented. These tests are performed with a call to the *IVMRMixerControl9* method *GetProcAmpControl*, which is passed a pointer to a *VMR9ProcAmpControl* data structure. That structure is defined as follows:

```
typedef struct _VMR9ProcAmpControl
{
    DWORD dwSize;
    DWORD dwFlags;
    float Contrast;
    float Brightness;
    float Hue;
    float Saturation;
} VMR9ProcAmpControl;
```

When the call to *GetProcAmpControl* is made, the *dwSize* field of the *VMR9ProcAmpControl* structure must be set to the total size of the data structure, or the call will fail. On return, the *dwFlags* field will have flags set corresponding to the ProcAmp capabilities of the hardware.

```
typedef enum {
    ProcAmpControl9_Brightness = 0x00000001,
    ProcAmpControl9_Contrast   = 0x00000002,
    ProcAmpControl9_Hue     = 0x00000004,
    ProcAmpControl9_Saturation = 0x00000008,
    ProcAmpControl9_Mask    = 0x0000000F
} VMR9ProcAmpControlFlags;
```

Each of the four values (*ProcAmpControl9_Brightness*, *ProcAmp-Control9_Hue*, *ProcAmpControl9_Saturation*, and *ProcAmpControl9_Contrast*) is tested against the *dwFlags* field to determine whether ProcAmp control is supported for that feature. If ProcAmp control is supported, a call to the *IVMRMixerControl9* method *GetProcAmpControlRange* is made. The call receives a pointer to a *VRM9ProcAmpControlRange* data structure.

```
typedef struct _VMR9ProcAmpControlRange
{
    DWORD              dwSize;
    VMR9ProcAmpControlFlags dwProperty;
    float             MinValue;
    float             MaxValue;
    float             DefaultValue;
    float             StepSize;
} VMR9ProcAmpControlRange;
```

As before, the *dwSize* field must be set to the size of the *VMR9ProcAmpControlRange* structure, while the *dwProperty* field is passed a value corresponding to one of the *VMR9ProcAmpControlFlags*, which determines which value is returned by the call. On return, the *MinValue* and *MaxValue* fields hold the lower and upper permissible range values for the property. These values are used (in conjunction with a value returned in the appropriate field by the *GetProcAmpControl* call) to determine the slider's position at initialization. This operation is performed three times, once each for the brightness, hue, and saturation sliders.

When *ProcAmpAdjustProc* receives a *WM_HSCROLL* message indicating that one of the sliders is processing a user-interface event, the value of the slider is translated into a value appropriate to the range of the given property. This translation is done by getting the range of the property with a *GetProcAmpControlRange* call. Once the range is known, the new slider position is compared to it and a new value for the property is calculated. That value is applied to the property with a call to *SetProcAmpControl*, which is passed a pointer to a *VMR9ProcAmpControl* structure. Once again, the *dwSize* field must be set to the size of the *VMR9ProcAmpControl* structure, and the *dwFlags* field must have the appropriate bit or bits set to indicate which properties are being changed. (You can change multiple properties with a single *SetProcAmpControl* call.) The appropriate field of the *VMR9ProcAmpControl* structure must be set to the new value for the property. When the call is made, the new value is applied to the property. *ProcAmpAdjustProc* is concise because all of its processing is performed in just three calls on the *IVMRMixerControl9* interface: *GetProcAmpControl*, *GetProcAmpControlRange*, and *SetProcAmpControl*. These calls give you complete control over the VMR ProcAmp.

Using Direct3D with the VMR

Although well beyond the scope of this chapter (or this book), it's important to note that the render target of the VMR is completely under control of the programmer. You can write your own custom allocator-presenter module for the VMR, which can then be programmed to use a Direct3D object as the composition target, creating video texture maps. For this programming, you'll need to explore the *IVMRSurfaceAllocator9* and *IVMRImagePresenter9* interfaces, which allow access to the Direct3D data structures used by the VMR. (The DirectX SDK has a number of VMR 9 samples that also explore integration of the VMR with Direct3D.) In reality, the VMR is always drawing to a Direct3D surface, whether one is explicitly supplied to the VMR through the *IVMRSurfaceAllocator9* interface or created automatically by the VMR when it's initialized. This capability gives the VMR enormous power to create sophisticated skins for 3D objects—video texture maps, in the parlance of 3D—with very little additional VMR programming.

Summary

The VMR is one of the most powerful components within DirectShow. Using it, you can mix as many as 16 simultaneous video streams into a single output stream. That output stream can be sent to its own window, managed by the VMR, or sent to an application-specified window. The VMR can even use the output as a texture map applied to a Direct3D model. Although it's powerful, the VMR has elegant and simple interfaces that expose its functionality without unnecessary complications, which makes it the ideal filter for nearly any Direct-Show application that renders video to the display. If DirectShow is the hidden jewel within DirectX, the VMR is the hidden jewel within DirectShow.

Part III

DirectShow Filters for Video Processing

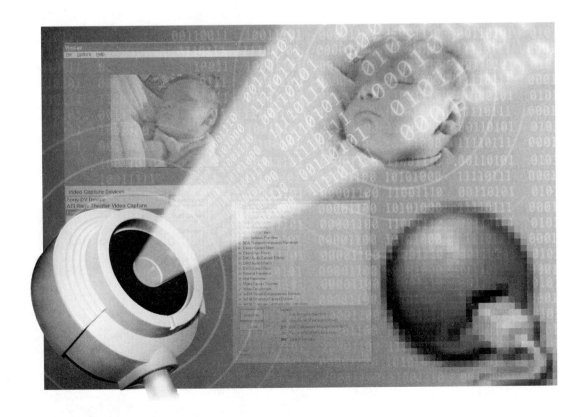

10

Writing a DirectShow Transform Filter

Now that we've covered Microsoft DirectShow application programming in some detail, using it to render and capture media streams, we can focus on the extensible architecture of DirectShow. DirectShow has been carefully designed to allow the programmer to create custom DirectShow filters—capture source filters, transform filters, and renderers. These hand-crafted filters can be instanced within and used by any filter graph within any DirectShow application.

This flexibility is an enormous strength of DirectShow and one that many applications already employ. For example, some video editing applications add their own suite of DirectShow filters when they install themselves and then employ these filters at application run time. It's possible—even desirable—to build a sophisticated media manipulation application out of a collection of DirectShow filters, each of which provides specific functionality within the application.

Although a few DirectShow programmers might be interested in the construction of a capture source filter or renderer filter, the vast majority of filters created for DirectShow are transform filters. Many Video for Windows and Windows Driver Model (WDM) drivers are already available to DirectShow as capture filters. Although a filter graph needs only one or two capture source filters and one or two renderer filters, it might have scores of transform filters between the capture and the renderer.

Transform filters handle tasks such as data compression and decompression, video encoding, file parsing, and stream splitting. And that's only a partial list of the kinds of tasks performed by transform filters. It's possible that you'll want to add your own features to a filter graph, processing an audio or a video stream in a very specific way to achieve a particular engineering goal. That's the role of the transform filter.

In this chapter, we'll explore a very simple transform filter, YUVGray, written by Mike Wasson of the DirectShow Documentation Group at Microsoft. This filter takes a video stream in one of two formats—either UYVY or YUY2 (we'll discuss these formats and their differences later in this chapter)—and removes all the color information from the stream, leaving the stream with only black and white data. This effect might be handy if you're trying to get a video image to look as though it were created in the 1950s, during the golden age of television. The filter's design is simple enough that it could be extended to a general filter that controls the saturation of the video image in real time.

Although YUVGray is not earth-shattering in its significance, it's quite easy to modify YUVGray to create your own DirectShow transform filter. For example, with just a change to a few lines of code, you could go from black and white to black and red, or black and green, or black and blue. You could even publish Component Object Model (COM) interfaces to your filter so that these color changes could be made in real time through a DirectShow application. So don't be fooled by the apparent simplicity of YUVGray; in these few lines of code are 'most everything you'll need to know to create your own DirectShow transform filters.

Examining Data Flow Across the Filter Graph

Although many DirectShow programmers won't need to know more about how streams flow across a filter graph than has already been explored, programmers who intend to implement their own DirectShow filters will need a more comprehensive explanation of how stream data travels from filter to filter across the filter graph. Fundamental to an understanding of data flow in the filter graph is the concept of transports. The term *transport* simply means the mechanism that two filters use to transfer data across their pin connections. Transports are defined by COM interfaces. Both an input pin on one filter and an output pin on another must agree on a transport mechanism before they can be connected; this process allows them to negotiate how they will exchange stream data as it passes from one filter to the other. The pins agree on the transport using *QueryInterface*—one pin queries the other pin for the interface that corresponds to the desired transport mechanism.

Two principle transport types are used in DirectShow filters: local memory transport and hardware transport. *Local memory transport* means that the memory is allocated in the computer's main memory or (for video renderers) in a DirectDraw surface or a Direct3D surface, which might be located in video memory. The term *hardware transport* refers to dedicated memory in hardware, such as video port connections. (A video port is a direct physical connection between a device and a portion of video memory.)

Most DirectShow filters negotiate local memory transport during the pin connection process, storing their stream data in the computer's main memory. Hardware transport is less common and is beyond the scope of this chapter. DirectShow filters utilizing local transport will allocate storage for transport during the connection process. This allocation is *always* done by the output pin, even if the buffers are being controlled by the input pin. The output pin has to inform the input pin of the downstream filter of the particulars of the buffers it has allocated for data transmission. When it's all working smoothly, local transport should look something like Figure 10-1.

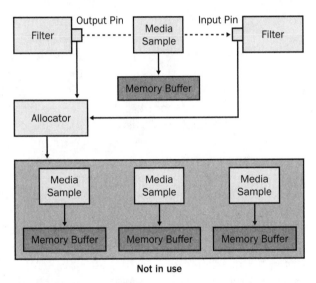

Figure 10-1   Local transport sends buffers of stream data through the filter graph

In this diagram, two filters, upstream and downstream, are connected through a pool of available buffers. Data is passed between the pools when a buffer is copied from the upstream pool into the downstream pool and then passed along to the downstream filter. It might seem as though some unnecessary copying is going on. Why can't one of the upstream buffers simply be passed along to the downstream filter? In some cases, such as transform-in-place filters, buffers are passed from filter to filter. In most situations, it actually makes a great deal of sense to keep the buffer pools isolated. Filters can do many different things, both simple and complex; consequently, the time it takes each filter to process a buffer's worth of stream data varies greatly. It could well be that the upstream filter can fill buffers several times faster than the downstream filter can accept them. By keeping the pools separate, the upstream filter can fill all its buffers at top speed and then wait until the downstream filter has emptied one or more of them before it begins operation again. This process leads to a clean execution model for the filter graph.

Local memory transport comes in two flavors, *push* and *pull*, defined by the *IMemInputPin* and *IAsyncReader* interfaces, respectively. In the push mechanism, using *IMemInputPin*, the upstream filter manages the flow of data between its output pin and a downstream input pin. When stream data is ready, the output pin calls a method on the downstream filter, pushing the data to it, which then accepts it and processes it, pushing it along to another filter downstream, and so on throughout the entire filter graph. The push transport mechanism is used through the *IMemInputPin* interface and employed most commonly if the source filter is a live device, such as a microphone or a digital camcorder, that is constantly generating a stream of data for the filter graph.

The other transport mechanism—pull—reverses the push model. In this case, the downstream filter pulls the data from the output pin of the upstream filter into the input pin of the downstream filter. If the source filter reads data from a file, the next filter in the filter graph is most often some kind of file parser, which converts the file's bits into a stream of video or audio data. In this case, the pull transport mechanism will be employed. The transform filter acting as a file parser makes requests of the upstream filter—basically, file read requests—and pulls that data into its input pin as it's presented on the output pin of the upstream filter.

The pull model uses the *IAsyncReader* interface. The upstream filter's operations are entirely under the control of the downstream filter. The pull model allows a parser, for example, to read in a stream of AVI video data. Because the parser knows the structure of an AVI file (which we'll cover in Chapter 14), the parser can request specific offsets into the file for specific data segments. Because the parser can read an AVI file into memory many times faster than it could stream across the filter graph, it can perform asynchronous file I/O, which is more efficient and consumes fewer operating system resources than synchronous I/O. Once past the file parser, the push model dominates the filter graph. The pull model is generally used only between the file source and the parser. After that, the rest of the pin connections in the filter graph use the push model.

An important point for the DirectShow application programmer to note is that quite often you can write data to video memory a great deal faster to than it can be read back into the computer's main memory. That's a natural function of the evolution of video display cards. Although it's very important for the computer to be able to write data to the display quickly, it's rarely necessary for the computer to read that data back into memory. So these devices have been optimized for writing data but not reading. For this reason, the DirectShow programmer should be aware that certain filters, such as filters that perform in-place transforms on buffers that might be in video memory, can potentially slow the execution of a filter graph significantly. (The crucial point to note is whether the memory is located in display hardware or local memory. Display hardware memory can be much slower to access.) Certain configurations of filter graphs cause streams to be pulled from filters supporting hardware that does not support high-speed read access. In these situations, the entire filter graph might grind to a halt while waiting for slow reads to execute. As a result, transform filters upstream from a video renderer filter should use copy transforms rather than in-place transforms.

When a filter graph is paused, it loads media sample buffers with stream data, which allows the filter graph to start operation immediately on receipt of the run command. (When the filter graph goes directly into run mode without pausing first, it pauses internally as its media sample buffers load.) Without this preloaded buffer, the filter graph would need to wait until the source filter had produced sufficient stream data to pass along to the next filter in the graph before execution could begin.

Finally, it's important to note how the three filter graph states—running, paused, and stopped—and their corresponding messages flow across the filter graph. When the filter graph receives a message to change state, the Filter Graph Manager sends the message to each filter in upstream order, that is, backward from any renderer filters, through any transform filters, and to the source filter. This process is necessary to prevent any samples from being dropped. If a source filter delivers data while the downstream filters are stopped, the downstream filters will reject the data, so the stop message propagates upstream. When a filter stops, it releases any allocated samples it holds, clearing its store of stream data.

Understanding Media Types

Media types are the key element in the negotiation process that connects an output pin to an input pin. Although this topic was introduced in a cursory way in Chapter 8—where we learned how to assign a media type for a DirectShow Editing Services (DES) track group—we need to explore fully the concept of the media type and its embodiment in the *AM_MEDIA_TYPE* data structure. Here's the C++ definition of that data structure:

```
typedef struct _MediaType {
    GUID      majortype;
    GUID      subtype;
    BOOL      bFixedSizeSamples;
    BOOL      bTemporalCompression;
    ULONG     lSampleSize;
    GUID      formattype;
    IUnknown *pUnk;
    ULONG     cbFormat;
    BYTE     *pbFormat;
} AM_MEDIA_TYPE;
```

For the purpose of connecting filters together—either manually or with Intelligent Connect—the first two fields in this structure, *majortype* and *subtype*, are the most significant. Both fields hold GUID values that correspond to a list of possible values. The *majortype* field refers to the general class of media, a broad-brush definition that provides a rough approximation of the media type. Table 10-1 shows a list of the possible values you'll see in the *majortype* field.

Table 10-1 GUID Values for the *majortype* Field

GUID	Description
MEDIATYPE_AnalogAudio	Analog audio
MEDIATYPE_AnalogVideo	Analog video
MEDIATYPE_Audio	Audio
MEDIATYPE_AUXLine21Data	Line 21 data; used by closed captions
MEDIATYPE_Interleaved	Interleaved; used by digital video (DV)
MEDIATYPE_Midi	MIDI format
MEDIATYPE_MPEG2_PES	MPEG-2 Packetized Elementary Stream (PES) packets
MEDIATYPE_ScriptCommand	Data is a script command; used by closed captions
MEDIATYPE_Stream	Byte stream with no timestamps
MEDIATYPE_Text	Text
MEDIATYPE_Timecode	Timecode data
MEDIATYPE_Video	Video

There are many different values that might be placed into the *subtype* field of the *AM_MEDIA_TYPE* structure. This field further refines the rough definition of the media type from a general class (audio, video, stream, and so on) into a specific format type. Table 10-2 shows just a few of the possible values that could go into the *subtype* field, which, in this case, are uncompressed RGB types associated with *MEDIATYPE_Video*.

Table 10-2   Selected GUID Values for the *subtype* Field

GUID	Description
MEDIASUBTYPE_RGB1	RGB, 1 bit per pixel (bpp), palettized
MEDIASUBTYPE_RGB4	RGB, 4 bpp, palettized
MEDIASUBTYPE_RGB8	RGB, 8 bpp
MEDIASUBTYPE_RGB555	RGB 555, 16 bpp
MEDIASUBTYPE_RGB565	RGB 565, 16 bpp
MEDIASUBTYPE_RGB24	RGB, 24 bpp
MEDIASUBTYPE_RGB32	RGB, 32 bpp, no alpha channel
MEDIASUBTYPE_ARGB32	RGB, 32 bpp, alpha channel

Each of these *subtype* GUIDs corresponds to a possible video stream format. There are many other possible video subformats and many possible audio subformats, such as MPEG-2 PES packet subformats.

The *lSampleSize* field of the *AM_MEDIA_TYPE* structure can be used to calculate the overall requirements to process a stream of that media type. This information is used during the connection process in calculations to allocate buffer pools of memory for the output pins on a filter. An audio sample contains an arbitrary length of audio data, while a video sample most often contains one complete frame. Because of stream compression techniques, the amount of memory needed to store a video frame or an audio sample can vary widely, so the value in *lSampleSize* gives the filter a useful hint when allocating memory.

The nitty-gritty information about a media stream is contained in two fields, *formattype* and *pbFormat*. The *formattype* field contains another GUID, which references one of the media formats understood by DirectShow, as shown in Table 10-3.

Table 10-3   GUID Values for the *formattype* Field

Format Type	Format Structure
FORMAT_None or *GUID_NULL*	None
FORMAT_DvInfo	*DVINFO*
FORMAT_MPEGVideo	*MPEG1VIDEOINFO*

Table 10-3 GUID Values for the *formattype* Field *(continued)*

Format Type	Format Structure
FORMAT_MPEG2Video	*MPEG2VIDEOINFO*
FORMAT_VideoInfo	*VIDEOINFOHEADER*
FORMAT_VideoInfo2	*VIDEOINFOHEADER2*
FORMAT_WaveFormatEx	*WAVEFORMATEX*

The *formattype* field works hand-in-hand with *pbFormat*, which holds a pointer to a dynamically allocated block of memory containing the appropriate format structure. For example, if the *formattype* field contains the GUID *FORMAT_WaveFormatEx* (implying WAV or similar audio data), the *pbFormat* field should hold a pointer to a *WAVFORMATEX* data structure. That data structure contains specific information about the WAV stream, including the sample rate, bits per sample, number of channels, and so on. Finally, the *cbFormat* field defines the size of the format block; that field must be initialized correctly before any call using the *AM_MEDIA_TYPE* structure is made.

Working with Media Samples

Filters pass data from output pin to input pin, from the origin to the end of the data stream. This stream data is passed as a series of media samples. Instead of passing pointers to memory buffers through the filter graph (which could get very dangerous very quickly because a dereferenced pointer could lead to a sudden crash), DirectShow encapsulates a media sample inside a COM object, *IMediaSample*. All DirectShow filters perform their stream data operations on instances of *IMediaSample*, which has the added advantage of allowing a filter to "own" a sample, making it less likely that the filter will hand out a sample that's already in use. (Each samples has a reference count to keep track of such things.) The use of the *IMediaSample* interface also prevents data from being overwritten accidentally.

When a filter receives a media sample, it can make a number of method queries on the *IMediaSample* interface to get the specifics it will need to operate on the data contained in the sample. The *GetPointer* method returns a pointer to the buffer of data managed by the media sample. To get the size of the buffer, call the *GetSize* method. The actual number of bytes of sample data can differ from the size of the sample buffer, so you'll use the *GetActualDataLength* method to find out how much of the buffer data is sample data. When there's been a change in the media type (see the next section for a full explanation of media types), the new type is returned by method *GetMediaType* (otherwise it returns *NULL*). The time the sample should start and finish (given in *REFERENCE_TIME* units of 100 nanoseconds) is returned by the *GetTime* method.

When there's a change from the media types negotiated during the connection process, the filter needs to redefine the properties of a media sample it presents on its output pin. For example, an audio source filter could change the audio sample rate, which means the output connection would need to signal a change in media type.

Each media sample has a timestamp, indicating the start and stop times of the sample, defined in stream time. Stream time begins when the filter graph enters the run state and increases in 100-nanosecond intervals until the filter graph is stopped. These timestamps are important for maintaining synchronization of a media stream and between media streams. Filters might need to examine the timestamps on several incoming samples to ensure that the appropriate portions of these samples are transformed together. For example, a filter that multiplexes audio and video streams into a single stream must use timestamp information to keep the streams properly synchronized with respect to each other.

Another COM interface, *IMemAllocator*, is responsible for creating and managing media samples. The allocator is a distinct COM object, with its own interfaces and methods. Although allocators aren't often overridden and implemented on a per-class basis, you'll see that the Sample Grabber in Chapter 11 does implement its own allocator object. DirectShow provides generic allocators and filter classes that use these allocators by default. One method of *CTransformFilter*, *DecideBufferSize* (a method that must be overridden in any filter implementation that descends from *CTransformFilter*), performs a calculation that determines how much memory is required for each media sample. That information is used during the pin connection negotiation process (discussed in the next section) so that media samples can be passed between two pins.

Connecting Pins Together

When two pins connect, they must agree on three things: a media type, which describes the format of the data; a transport mechanism, which defines how the pins will exchange data; and an allocator, which is an object, created and owned by one of the pins, that creates and manages the memory buffer pool that the pins use to exchange data. We'll now make a detailed examination of these steps.

When a connection is attempted between two filters, the filters must determine whether they can compatibly exchange a data stream. They use the *AM_MEDIA_TYPE* data structure, making queries to each other, until they establish that both can agree on the same media type for data transfer. Although the

Filter Graph Manager is responsible for adding filters to the graph and sending connection messages to pins on respective filters, the actual work of connecting pins together is performed by the pins themselves. This fact is one reason why an *IPin* object with its own methods is instantiated for every pin on a Direct-Show filter.

The connection process begins when the Filter Graph Manager calls the *IPin::Connect* method on the output pin. This method is passed a pointer to the downstream input *IPin* object and, optionally, a pointer to an *AM_MEDIA_TYPE* structure. The output pin can (and usually does) examine the *majortype* and *subtype* fields as a quick way to determine whether it should even bother continuing with the connection process. This way, filters don't waste time when they obviously don't deal with compatible media types, such as when a video transform filter might try to connect to an audio stream. The *Connect* method can fail immediately without wasting time going through an extensive connection process.

If the *AM_MEDIA_TYPE* provided to the output pin by the Filter Graph Manager is acceptable to the pin—that is, if there's some chance the filters can be connected together—the output pin immediately calls the input pin's *IPin::EnumMediaTypes* method. This method will return a list of the input pin's preferred media types. The output pin will walk through this list examining each media type returned, and if it sees anything it likes, it will specify a complete media type based on the list of preferred types and then signal the input pin that a connection should be made by invoking its *IPin::ReceiveConnection* method. If none of the media types are acceptable to the output pin, it will propose media types from its own list. If none of these succeed, the connection process fails.

Once the pins have agreed on a media type, they need to negotiate a transport, that is, whether a push or a pull model will be employed to transfer data between the pins. The most common transport is the push model, which is represented by the *IMemInputPin* interface on the *IPin* object. If the output pin determines through a query that the input pin supports this interface, the output pin will push the data downstream to the input pin.

Finally the two pins negotiate the number and size of memory buffers they will share when streaming begins. The upstream filter will write data into those buffers, while the downstream filter will read that data. Except in the case of hardware transport, the process of allocating and managing buffers is handled by a separate allocator object, which is owned by one of the pins. The pins negotiate which allocator will be used, together with the size and number of buffers that will be needed. In any case, the output pin is responsible for selecting the allocator, even if the output pin needs to make a request to the input pin to propose its own allocator. In both cases, the output pin is in control of the allocation process.

Most allocations are performed with regular memory allocation operations, but filters that represent hardware devices might create buffers on those devices. Such filters might insist on using their own allocators and reject allocation attempts from upstream output pins. For example, the DirectShow video renderers have their own allocators that create DirectDraw and Direct3D surfaces for display. The Video Renderer filter will use its own allocator, but if forced, it will use GDI (much slower) for rendering. The Video Mixing Renderer, covered in Chapter 9, will insist on using its own allocator. If the allocation negotiation succeeds, the *Connect* call returns successfully.

Selecting a Base Class for a DirectShow Filter

Transform filters, such as the Sample Grabber, are defined in C++ as individual classes, descendants of one of four different base classes from which they inherit their particular properties. The selection of a base class for your DirectShow filter is driven by the data-processing needs of the filter. If your intrafilter data processing needs are minimal, there's a base class that will do most of the work for you, but if you need a sophisticated filter, you'll find that another base class will give you the freedom to create a complex filter.

The *CTransInPlaceFilter* class is a base class designed for filters that pass along the upstream buffers they receive to downstream filters without any need to copy the data to new buffers. They transform the data in place, hence the name of the filter. The same buffer that's passed to a filter derived from *CTransInPlaceFilter* is passed to the next filter downstream. The Grabber Sample covered in the Chapter 11, which doesn't do much beyond ensuring that its input pin and output pin accept matching data types, is derived from *CTransInPlaceFilter*. Although this class doesn't provide a lot of flexibility in filter design, it does do most of the behind-the-scenes work involved in creating and managing the filter.

Most commonly, you'll be creating transform filter classes that are descendent from *CTransformFilter*, such as the YUVGray transform filter covered in this chapter. Filters based on *CTransformFilter* have separate input and output buffers, and they can manipulate the data in any desired way as the data passes between input and output. When an input buffer arrives, it's transformed by the filter—an operation that copies it into an output buffer so that it can be sent to the downstream filter. For filters that work with video signals, which are very sensitive to stream delays and synchronization issues, the *CVideoTransformFilter* class (designed primarily for use with video decoders) offers the same features as the *CTransformFilter* class, but it will automatically drop frames (that is, drop input samples) if the downstream renderer falls behind. Frame dropping can be very useful for transform filters that are placed on a preview render path of a filter graph, where video quality is being sacrificed to keep processor power available for an output rendering path.

Finally, for filters that have their own requirements above and beyond those provided for with these base classes, the *CBaseFilter* base class provides a shell of basic DirectShow filter functionality. *CBaseFilter* provides very little support for buffer management, connection negotiation, and so on, so if you do use *CBaseFilter* to create a DirectShow filter class, you'll be doing most of the work yourself. The upside of the extra effort required is that you can write a transform filter highly optimized to the kinds of tasks expected of it and produce a streamlined design that covers all the important implementation tasks without any extraneous code.

Exploring YUVGray

When creating any DirectShow filter—or any COM object that is intended to be made available across the entire operating system—the filter or object must be given a unique identifier for both its class and interface IDs. (You need an interface ID only if you're exposing a custom interface to the operating system.) These values are formatted as GUIDs and can be generated by the uuidgen.exe utility program, which should be installed on your system. (Alternatively, you can use the Create GUID command on the Tools menu of Visual Studio .NET.) To create the GUID you'll need for the YUVGray filter, you enter the following command line:

```
uuidgen -s >guids.txt
```

This command will generate a GUID and place it into the guids.txt file. This GUID can then be copied from guids.txt and pasted into your source code files as needed for class ID definitions. As you'll see shortly, this value will be the very first line in the YUVGray C++ file.

The YUVGray project contains two source files: YUVGray.cpp, the C++ source code; and YUVGray.def, the definitions file used to create a dynamic link library (DLL) from the compiled code. This DLL is then published to the operating system using the command-line program regsvr32.exe and becomes available to all DirectShow applications. The YUVGray filter needs to have its own class ID (GUID) defined so that it can be referenced by other COM applications, including DirectShow programs. Some of the first lines in YUVGray.cpp define the filter's class ID:

```
// Define the filter's CLSID
// {A6512C9F-A47B-45ba-A054-0DB0D4BB87F7}
static const GUID CLSID_YuvGray =
{ 0xa6512c9f, 0xa47b, 0x45ba, { 0xa0, 0x54, 0xd, 0xb0,
                                0xd4, 0xbb, 0x87, 0xf7 } };
```

This class ID definition could be included inside your own DirectShow applications, where you could use a function such as *AddFilterByCLSID* to add the YUVGray filter to your filter graph. There's one class method, *CYuvGray::CreateInstance*, and two functions, *DllRegisterServer* and *DllUnregisterServer*, that are required of any DLL. There are a few others, but their implementation is handled in the DirectShow base class library.

The *CYuvGray::CreateInstance* method is invoked by the DirectShow implementation of the class factory—when the COM call *CoCreateInstance* is passed with the class ID of the YUVGray filter. There's nothing exciting about this method and these functions; have a peek at the source code if you want to understand how they're implemented. Finally, COM objects must support the *IUnknown* interface; this interface is supported automatically by the class library.

Creating the Class Definition for YUVGray

The class definition for YUVGray is generic enough that it could easily form the basis for your own transform filters. YUVGray is declared as a descendant of *CTransformFilter*, which means that the filter has separate input and output buffers. The filter must copy data from an input buffer to an output buffer as part of its normal operation. Here's the complete class definition for YUVGray:

```
class CYuvGray : public CTransformFilter
{
public:

    // Constructor
    CYuvGray(LPUNKNOWN pUnk, HRESULT *phr) :
        CTransformFilter(NAME("YUV Transform Filter"), pUnk, CLSID_YuvGray)
        {}

    // Overridden CTransformFilter methods
    HRESULT CheckInputType(const CMediaType *mtIn);
    HRESULT CheckTransform(const CMediaType *mtIn, const CMediaType *mtOut);
    HRESULT DecideBufferSize(IMemAllocator *pAlloc,
        ALLOCATOR_PROPERTIES *pProp);
    HRESULT GetMediaType(int iPosition, CMediaType *pMediaType);
    HRESULT Transform(IMediaSample *pIn, IMediaSample *pOut);
```

```
    // Override this so we can grab the video format
    HRESULT SetMediaType(PIN_DIRECTION direction, const CMediaType *pmt);

    // Static object-creation method (for the class factory)
    static CUnknown * WINAPI CreateInstance(LPUNKNOWN pUnk, HRESULT *pHr);

private:
    HRESULT ProcessFrameUYVY(BYTE *pbInput, BYTE *pbOutput, long *pcbByte);
    HRESULT ProcessFrameYUY2(BYTE *pbInput, BYTE *pbOutput, long *pcbByte);

    VIDEOINFOHEADER m_VihIn;    // Holds the current video format (input)
    VIDEOINFOHEADER m_VihOut;   // Holds the current video format (output)

};
```

The class constructor *CYuvGray::CYuvGray* does nothing more than invoke the parent constructor for *CTransformFilter*, passing it the class ID for *CYuvGray*. Six methods, overridden from *CTransformFilter*, implement the guts of the YUVGray filter: *CheckInputType*, *CheckTransform*, *DecideBufferSize*, *GetMediaType*, *Transform*, and *SetMediaType*. The class definition also defines the *CreateInstance* method needed by the COM class factory and two private methods, *ProcessFrameUYVY* and *ProcessFrameYUY2*, which are invoked from within the *Transform* method and handle the actual bit-twiddling on each video frame.

Most of the implementation of *CYuvGray* is left in the hands of the parent class, *CTransformFilter*. The YUVGray filter doesn't depart too much from the standard model of how a transform filter behaves, so there isn't much to implement. The three major implementation areas are media type negotiation, buffer allocation, and data transformation.

Implementing Media Type Selection in a Transform Filter

Four methods must be implemented by a transform filter so that it can negotiate the media types it will receive on its input pin and provide on its output pin. If these methods are not implemented, the Filter Graph Manager will assume that the filter can receive any media type—something that's not likely ever to be true! Here's the implementation of these media type selection methods:

```
HRESULT CYuvGray::CheckInputType(const CMediaType *pmt)
{

    if (IsValidUYVY(pmt))
    {
        return S_OK;
    }
    else
```

```
        {
            if (IsValidYUY2(pmt)) {
                return S_OK;
            } else {
                return VFW_E_TYPE_NOT_ACCEPTED;
            }
        }
    }
}

HRESULT CYuvGray::CheckTransform(const CMediaType *mtIn,
                                 const CMediaType *mtOut)
{

    // Make sure the subtypes match
    if (mtIn->subtype != mtOut->subtype)
    {
        return VFW_E_TYPE_NOT_ACCEPTED;
    }

    if (!IsValidUYVY(mtOut))
    {
        if (!IsValidYUY2(mtOut)) {
            return VFW_E_TYPE_NOT_ACCEPTED;
        }
    }

    BITMAPINFOHEADER *pBmi = HEADER(mtIn);
    BITMAPINFOHEADER *pBmi2 = HEADER(mtOut);

    if ((pBmi->biWidth <= pBmi2->biWidth) &&
        (pBmi->biHeight == abs(pBmi2->biHeight)))
    {
        return S_OK;
    }
    return VFW_E_TYPE_NOT_ACCEPTED;

}

HRESULT CYuvGray::GetMediaType(int iPosition, CMediaType *pMediaType)
{
    // The output pin calls this method only if the input pin is connected.
    ASSERT(m_pInput->IsConnected());

    // There is only one output type that we want, which is the input type.

    if (iPosition < 0)
    {
        return E_INVALIDARG;
    }
```

```
        else if (iPosition == 0)
        {
            return m_pInput->ConnectionMediaType(pMediaType);
        }
        return VFW_S_NO_MORE_ITEMS;
}


HRESULT CYuvGray::SetMediaType(PIN_DIRECTION direction,
                              const CMediaType *pmt)
{
    if (direction == PINDIR_INPUT)
    {
        ASSERT(pmt->formattype == FORMAT_VideoInfo);
        VIDEOINFOHEADER *pVih = (VIDEOINFOHEADER*)pmt->pbFormat;

        // WARNING! In general you cannot just copy a VIDEOINFOHEADER
        // struct, because the BITMAPINFOHEADER member may be followed by
        // random amounts of palette entries or color masks. (See VIDEOINFO
        // structure in the DShow SDK docs.) Here it's OK because we just
        // want the information that's in the VIDEOINFOHEADER struct itself.

        CopyMemory(&m_VihIn, pVih, sizeof(VIDEOINFOHEADER));

        DbgLog((LOG_TRACE, 0,
            TEXT("CYuvGray: Input size: bmiWidth = %d, bmiHeight = %d,
                rcTarget width = %d"),
            m_VihIn.bmiHeader.biWidth,
            m_VihIn.bmiHeader.biHeight,
            m_VihIn.rcTarget.right));

    }
    else    // Output pin
    {
        ASSERT(direction == PINDIR_OUTPUT);
        ASSERT(pmt->formattype == FORMAT_VideoInfo);
        VIDEOINFOHEADER *pVih = (VIDEOINFOHEADER*)pmt->pbFormat;

        CopyMemory(&m_VihOut, pVih, sizeof(VIDEOINFOHEADER));

        DbgLog((LOG_TRACE, 0,
            TEXT("CYuvGray: Output size: bmiWidth = %d, bmiHeight = %d,
                rcTarget width = %d"),
            m_VihOut.bmiHeader.biWidth,
            m_VihOut.bmiHeader.biHeight,
            m_VihOut.rcTarget.right));
    }

    return S_OK;
}
```

All these methods manipulate an object of *CMediaType* class, defined in the DirectShow base classes. This class is a wrapper around the *AM_MEDIA_TYPE* structure. The first method, *CYuvGray::CheckInputType*, is passed a pointer to a *CMediaType* object, which is then passed to two local comparison functions, *IsValidUYVY* and *IsValidYUY2*. Both functions examine the *mediatype* and *subtype* fields of the *CMediaType* object. If the *mediatype* field is *MEDIATYPE_Video* and the *subtype* field is either *MEDIASUBTYPE_UYVY* or *MEDIASUBTYPE_YUY2*, *CYuvGray::CheckInputType* returns *S_OK* to the caller, indicating that the media type and format block are acceptable and defined properly (and presumably, a pin-to-pin connection will be made to the filter). Any other media types will cause the method to return *VFW_E_TYPE_NOT_ACCEPTED*, indicating that the requested media type is not acceptable to the filter.

The *CYuvGray::CheckTransform* method ensures that the filter can handle any data format transformation that might be required between its input and output pins. A filter can and often does issue an output stream in a different format than it receives on its input pin, and any transformation between stream formats has to be handled entirely within the filter. The *CYuvGray::CheckTransform* method receives pointers to two *CMediaType* objects, representing the input and output media types, respectively. The YUVGray filter does not perform any format translation on the stream passing through it. Although the filter can receive a video stream in either UYVY or YUY2 format, the output format is the same as the input format. This method compares the input and output media types and ensures that they're identical and valid. If that's the case, *S_OK* is returned to the caller. Otherwise, *VFW_E_TYPE_NOT_ACCEPTED* is returned as an error code.

The *CYuvGray::GetMediaType* method is used during media type negotiation on an attempt to connect the output pin of the filter to another filter. In classes derived from *CTransformFilter*, the input pin doesn't suggest any types. It's assumed that the upstream output pin has more information about what kind of data is being delivered than a downstream input pin. However, the output pin will suggest a type only if its associated input pin is connected. Because YUVGray doesn't modify the output format of the stream, the input pin connection on a filter establishes the acceptable media type for the filter (the media type is delivered from an upstream output pin), and that value is returned to the caller.

CYuvGray::SetMediaType copies the contents of the format information pointed to by the *pbFormat* field of the passed *CMediaType* object. This field points to a data structure with specific information about the media samples, including, in this case, the width and height of the video image. This information will be used in the *Transform* method. Of the four media type methods overridden in *CYuvGray*, only *SetMediaType* is implemented in the parent class.. The other three methods (*CheckInputType*, *CheckTransform*, *GetMediaType*) are virtual and must be implemented in any class derived from *CTransformFilter*.

These four methods provide all the implementation details for media negotiation within the filter. Small modifications to *CYuvGray::CheckInputType* will increase (or decrease) the number of media types supported by the filter, which would be very easy to do with the addition of an *IsValidXXXX* (where *XXXX* is a format type) function to the source code module. You can find lots of information on the internals of video formats supported by DirectShow in the DirectShow SDK documentation and online at the MSDN Library at *http://msdn.microsoft.com/library*.

Finally, a change to *CYuvGray::CheckTransform* will allow you to construct a filter that can perform a format translation internally, issuing a different format on its output pin than it was presented on its input pin. You'll need to code that format translation yourself, most likely within the *CYuvGray::Transform* method. The sample code useful for learning how to translate from one video format to another can be found in the MSDN Library pages.

Selecting Buffer Size in a Transform Filter

The *CYuvGray::DecideBufferSize* method is used during the output pin connection process. As explained earlier in this chapter, the output pin is responsible for negotiating the allocation of data stream buffers during the pin connection process, even if this allocation is actually done by the input pin of the downstream filter. In the case of a *CTransformFilter* object, this method is invoked with two parameters, a pointer to an *IMemAllocator* and a pointer to an *ALLOCATOR_PROPERTIES* structure—which was delivered to the filter by the downstream pin and which contains the downstream filter's buffer requests (if there are any). That structure has the following definition:

```
typedef struct _AllocatorProperties {
    long cBuffers;
    long cbBuffer;
    long cbAlign;
    long cbPrefix;
} ALLOCATOR_PROPERTIES;
```

The field *cBuffers* specifies the number of buffers to be created by the allocator, and *cbBuffer* specifies the size of each buffer in bytes. The *cbAlign* field specifies the byte alignment of each buffer, and *cbPrefix* allocates a prefix of a specific number of bytes before each buffer, which is useful for buffer header information. Here's the implementation of the method:

```cpp
HRESULT CYuvGray::DecideBufferSize(IMemAllocator *pAlloc,
    ALLOCATOR_PROPERTIES *pProp)
{
    // Make sure the input pin is connected.
    if (!m_pInput->IsConnected())
    {
        return E_UNEXPECTED;
    }

    // Our strategy here is to use the upstream allocator as the guideline,
    // but also defer to the downstream filter's request
    // when it's compatible with us.

    // First, find the upstream allocator...
    ALLOCATOR_PROPERTIES InputProps;

    IMemAllocator *pAllocInput = 0;
    HRESULT hr = m_pInput->GetAllocator(&pAllocInput);

    if (FAILED(hr))
    {
        return hr;
    }

    // ...now get the properties.

    hr = pAllocInput->GetProperties(&InputProps);
    pAllocInput->Release();

    if (FAILED(hr))
    {
        return hr;
    }

    // Buffer alignment should be non-zero [zero alignment makes no sense!].
    if (pProp->cbAlign == 0)
    {
        pProp->cbAlign = 1;
    }

    // Number of buffers must be non-zero.
    if (pProp->cbBuffer == 0)
    {
        pProp->cBuffers = 1;
    }

    // For buffer size, find the maximum of the upstream size and
    // the downstream filter's request.
```

```
    pProp->cbBuffer = max(InputProps.cbBuffer, pProp->cbBuffer);

    // Now set the properties on the allocator that was given to us.
    ALLOCATOR_PROPERTIES Actual;
    hr = pAlloc->SetProperties(pProp, &Actual);
    if (FAILED(hr))
    {
        return hr;
    }

    // Even if SetProperties succeeds, the actual properties might be
    // different than what we asked for. We check the result, but we look
    // at only the properties that we care about. The downstream filter
    // will look at them when NotifyAllocator is called.

    if (InputProps.cbBuffer > Actual.cbBuffer)
    {
        return E_FAIL;
    }

    return S_OK;
}
```

Although a connection can be made on the output pin of a transform filter before a connection is made to that filter's input pin, a filter might decide to renegotiate a pin connection. Once an input connection is made, it could force a reconnection on the output pin. For example, the media type for the YUVGray filter isn't established until a connection is made on the filter's input pin, so the output pin can't request a specific media type when connecting to downstream filters. The default behavior of the *CTransformFilter* class is to reject all connections on the output pin until the input pin has been connected.

You can see this happen in GraphEdit, for example, if you connect a filter graph downstream from a transform filter and then connect to its input pin. On those occasions when the media type can't be renegotiated successfully, GraphEdit will report that the graph is invalid and break the connections downstream from the filter.

The output pin allocates buffers when the pin connects, which shouldn't be allowed if the input pin isn't connected, so the method first calls the *CBasePin::IsConnected* method on the filter's input pin. If that call fails, *E_UNEXPECTED* signals an unusual error situation. If an input pin is found, the method attempts to use the input pin's allocator properties as guidelines when calculating the requirements of the output pin, ensuring that the allocation is equal on both input and output sides of the filter. Next the method examines the allocator properties requested by the upstream filter's input pin and does its best to satisfy both its own needs, as defined by the allocation requirements of the filter's input pin and the requests of the downstream input pin. (The thorough approach is to take the larger of the two allocation calculations and use that as the safest value.)

Once the desired allocator properties have been chosen, the output pin attempts to set these properties on the allocator by calling *IMemAllocator::SetProperties*. The *SetProperties* method might succeed even if the allocator cannot match the exact properties that you request. The results are returned in another *ALLOCATOR_PROPERTIES* structure (the *Actual* parameter). The filter should always check whether these values meet the filter's minimum requirements. If not, the filter should return a failure code from *DecideBufferSize*.

The implementation of the *DecideBufferSize* method will vary depending on the kind of transform being performed within the transform filter. For example, a format translation from one format to another format could produce a much larger output stream than input stream (or vice versa), and that would have to be dealt with inside the implementation of the *CYuvGray* class because that's the only place where the specifics of the translation are known. Such a situation would be commonplace in a transform filter that acted as a data compressor or decompressor. The output pin has nearly complete control over allocation of its output data stream buffers, and *DecideBufferSize* is the method where the class should perform all calculations needed to assess the storage requirements for the output stream.

Implementing the *Transform* Method

The *CYuvGray::Transform* method is the core of the YUVGray transform filter. It's invoked each time the filter receives a sample from the upstream filter. The method receives two pointers, each of which is an *IMediaSample* interface. These two pointers correspond to buffers containing the input (source) sample, which should already be filled with good data, and the output (destination) sample, which needs to be filled with good data by this method. The timestamps for the input sample have already been copied to the output sample by the *CTransformFilter* implementation of the *Receive* method. Here's the implementation of *CYuvGray::Transform*:

```
HRESULT CYuvGray::Transform(IMediaSample *pSource, IMediaSample *pDest)
{

    // Look for format changes from the video renderer.
    CMediaType *pmt = 0;
    if (S_OK == pDest->GetMediaType((AM_MEDIA_TYPE**)&pmt) && pmt)
```

```
    {
        DbgLog((LOG_TRACE, 0,
            TEXT("CYuvGray: Handling format change from the renderer...")));

        // Notify our own output pin about the new type.
        m_pOutput->SetMediaType(pmt);
        DeleteMediaType(pmt);
    }

    // Get the addresses of the actual buffers.
    BYTE *pBufferIn, *pBufferOut;

    pSource->GetPointer(&pBufferIn);
    pDest->GetPointer(&pBufferOut);

    long cbByte = 0;

    // Process the buffers.
    // Do it slightly differently for different video formats.
    HRESULT hr;

    ASSERT(m_VihOut.bmiHeader.biCompression == FCC('UYVY') ||
        m_VihOut.bmiHeader.biCompression == FCC('YUY2'));

    if (m_VihOut.bmiHeader.biCompression == FCC('UYVY'))
    {
        hr = ProcessFrameUYVY(pBufferIn, pBufferOut, &cbByte);
    }
    else if (m_VihOut.bmiHeader.biCompression == FCC('YUY2'))
    {
        hr = ProcessFrameYUY2(pBufferIn, pBufferOut, &cbByte);
    }
    else
    {
        return E_UNEXPECTED;
    }

    // Set the size of the destination image.

    ASSERT(pDest->GetSize() >= cbByte);

    pDest->SetActualDataLength(cbByte);

    return hr;
}
```

The method begins by looking at the media type for the downstream connection. The media type might have changed if the renderer downstream from this transform filter has requested a media type change, which can happen for two main reasons when the downstream filter is a video renderer. First, the legacy Video Renderer filter might switch between GDI and DirectDraw. Second, the Video Mixing Renderer (VMR) filter might update the format to reflect the surface stride required by the video driver. Before making a format change, the renderer calls *IPin::QueryAccept* to verify that the new format is OK. In the *CTransformFilter* class, this call is translated directly into a call to *Check-Transform*, which gets handled the usual way. The renderer then indicates the format change by attaching the media type to the next sample. The media type is retrieved by calling *GetMediaType* on the sample and passed along to the output pin's *SetMediaType* method.

Next pointers to both the input and output stream buffers are retrieved and the media subtype is examined, indirectly, by looking at the *biCompression* field of the *VIDEOINFOHEADER* structure. The contents of this structure are copied to local storage for both the input and output pins in the *CYuvGray::SetMediaType* method. If the video subtype (expressed in FOURCC format, that is, 4 bytes, each representing a single alphanumeric ASCII character) is either UYVY or YUY2, the transform can be performed.

YUV Format

Most programmers are familiar with the RGB color space. An RGB pixel is encoded using values for red, green, and blue. YUV is an alternate way to represent video images. In YUV, the grayscale information is separate from the color information. For each pixel, the grayscale value (called *luma*, abbreviated Y) is calculated as a weighted average of the gamma-corrected red, green, and blue components. The most common formula in use today is as follows:

$Y = 0.299R + 0.587G + 0.114B$

The color information (*chroma*) is represented as two *color difference* components, U and V, that are calculated from B - Y (blue minus luma) and R - Y (red minus luma). Various scaling factors can be applied to the result, depending on the video standard in use. Technically, *YUV* refers to one particular scaling factor, used in composite NTSC and PAL video. However, *YUV* is commonly used as a blanket term for a family of related formats that includes YCbCr, YPbPr, and others.

The human visual system is more sensitive to changes in brightness than it is to changes in color. Therefore, chroma values can be sampled

(continued)

YUV Format *(continued)*

less frequently than luma values without significantly degrading the perceived quality of the image. All the common consumer DV formats use some form of chroma downsampling. Chroma downsampling is described using the *a:b:c* notation, as shown in the following table:

Sampling	Description
4:2:2	2:1 horizontal downsampling, no vertical downsampling. Each scan line has two U and V samples for every four Y samples.
4:1:1	4:1 horizontal downsampling, no vertical downsampling. Each scan line has one U and V sample for every four Y samples.
4:2:0	2:1 horizontal downsampling and 2:1 vertical downsampling.

In addition, 4:4:4 means that the chroma is not downsampled—all the original U and V values are preserved. Some professional DV formats use 4:4:4 because there's no loss in color information. DVD video uses 4:2:0 sampling. Consumer DV formats are usually 4:2:0 or 4:1:1. By downsampling the chroma, the effective bit depth of the image is reduced. For example, 4:2:2 uses an average of 16 bits per pixel, rather than 24 bits per pixel for full 4:4:4 video.

UYVY and YUY2 are two different ways of representing a 4:2:2 YUV image in memory. The difference between these two formats is where they put their Y,U, and V values. In UYVY, the values are laid out as follows:

U0 Y0 V0 Y1U2 Y2 V2 Y3U4 Y4 V4 Y5

In YUY2, the values are laid out like this:

Y0 U0 Y1 V0Y2 U2 Y3 V2Y4 U4 Y5 V4

Each value is an 8-bit sample. As you can see, the same values are present; they're just arranged differently in memory.

The differences between UYVY and YUY2 format aren't enormous, but they're enough to guarantee that a piece of code that transforms one of them won't work at all on the other. That means that we need two entirely separate routines to handle the transform task, *CYuvGray::ProcessFrameUYVY* and *CYuvGray::ProcessFrameYUY2*. Here's the implementation of both methods:

```
HRESULT CYuvGray::ProcessFrameUYVY(BYTE *pbInput, BYTE *pbOutput,
                                   long *pcbByte)
{

    DWORD dwWidth, dwHeight;        // Width and height in pixels (input)
    DWORD dwWidthOut, dwHeightOut;  // Width and height in pixels (output)
    LONG  lStrideIn, lStrideOut;    // Stride in bytes
    BYTE  *pbSource, *pbTarget;     // First byte first row, source & target

    *pcbByte = m_VihOut.bmiHeader.biSizeImage;

    GetVideoInfoParameters(&m_VihIn, pbInput, &dwWidth, &dwHeight,
        &lStrideIn, &pbSource, true);
    GetVideoInfoParameters(&m_VihOut, pbOutput, &dwWidthOut, &dwHeightOut,
        &lStrideOut, &pbTarget, true);

    // Formats should match (except maybe stride).
    ASSERT(dwWidth == dwWidthOut);
    ASSERT(abs(dwHeight) == abs(dwHeightOut));

    // You could optimize this slightly by storing these values when the
    // media type is set, instead of recalculating them for each frame.

    for (DWORD y = 0; y < dwHeight; y++)
    {
        WORD *pwTarget = (WORD*)pbTarget;
        WORD *pwSource = (WORD*)pbSource;

        for (DWORD x = 0; x < dwWidth; x++)
        {

            // Each WORD is a 'UY' or 'VY' block.
            // Set the low byte (chroma) to 0x80
            // and leave the high byte (luma).

            WORD pixel = pwSource[x] & 0xFF00;
            pixel |= 0x0080;
            pwTarget[x] = pixel;
        }

        // Advance the stride on both buffers.

        pbTarget += lStrideOut;
        pbSource += lStrideIn;
    }

    return S_OK;

}
```

```
HRESULT CYuvGray::ProcessFrameYUY2(BYTE *pbInput, BYTE *pbOutput,
                                    long *pcbByte)
{

    DWORD dwWidth, dwHeight;         // Width and height in pixels (input)
    DWORD dwWidthOut, dwHeightOut;   // Width and height in pixels (output)
    LONG  lStrideIn, lStrideOut;     // Stride in bytes
    BYTE  *pbSource, *pbTarget;      // First byte first row, source & target

    *pcbByte = m_VihOut.bmiHeader.biSizeImage;

    GetVideoInfoParameters(&m_VihIn, pbInput, &dwWidth, &dwHeight,
        &lStrideIn, &pbSource, true);
    GetVideoInfoParameters(&m_VihOut, pbOutput, &dwWidthOut, &dwHeightOut,
        &lStrideOut, &pbTarget, true);

    // Formats should match (except maybe stride).
    ASSERT(dwWidth == dwWidthOut);
    ASSERT(abs(dwHeight) == abs(dwHeightOut));

    // You could optimize this slightly by storing these values when the
    // media type is set, instead of recalculating them for each frame.

    for (DWORD y = 0; y < dwHeight; y++)
    {
        WORD *pwTarget = (WORD*)pbTarget;
        WORD *pwSource = (WORD*)pbSource;

        for (DWORD x = 0; x < dwWidth; x++)
        {

            // Each WORD is a 'YU' or 'YV' block.
            // Set the high byte (chroma) to 0x80
            // and leave the low byte (luma).

            WORD pixel = pwSource[x] & 0x00FF;
            pixel |= 0x8000;
            pwTarget[x] = pixel;
        }

        // Advance the stride on both buffers.

        pbTarget += lStrideOut;
        pbSource += lStrideIn;
    }

    return S_OK;

}
```

Each function breaks each row of video data into a series of 16-bit chunks. In UYVY format, the lower 8 bits of each chunk has the luma data, while in YUY2 format, the upper 8 bits of each chunk holds the luma. In both cases, luma value is preserved and the U and V values are set to 128, effectively removing all the color information from the YUV format. But before any video processing takes place, the method has to learn some specifics of the video sample formats for both input and output so that it can correctly process the buffers.

Before any processing takes place, two calls are made to the local *GetVideoInfoParameters* function.

```
void GetVideoInfoParameters(
    const VIDEOINFOHEADER *pvih, // Pointer to the format header
    BYTE  * const pbData,        // Pointer to first address in buffer
    DWORD *pdwWidth,             // Returns the width in pixels
    DWORD *pdwHeight,            // Returns the height in pixels
    LONG  *plStrideInBytes,      // Add this to a row to get the new row down
    BYTE  **ppbTop,              // Pointer to first byte in top row of pixels
    bool bYuv
    )
{

    LONG lStride;

    //  For 'normal' formats, biWidth is in pixels.
    //  Expand to bytes and round up to a multiple of 4.
    if (pvih->bmiHeader.biBitCount != 0 &&
        0 == (7 & pvih->bmiHeader.biBitCount))
    {
        lStride = (pvih->bmiHeader.biWidth *
            (pvih->bmiHeader.biBitCount / 8) + 3) & ~3;
    }
    else  // Otherwise, biWidth is in bytes.
    {
        lStride = pvih->bmiHeader.biWidth;
    }

    //  If rcTarget is empty, use the whole image.
    if (IsRectEmpty(&pvih->rcTarget))
    {
        *pdwWidth = (DWORD)pvih->bmiHeader.biWidth;
        *pdwHeight = (DWORD)(abs(pvih->bmiHeader.biHeight));

        if (pvih->bmiHeader.biHeight < 0 || bYuv)   // Top-down bitmap
        {
            *plStrideInBytes = lStride; // Stride goes "down"
            *ppbTop          = pbData; // Top row is first
        }
```

```
        else  // Bottom-up bitmap
        {
            *plStrideInBytes = -lStride;     // Stride goes "up"
            *ppbTop = pbData + lStride *
                (*pdwHeight - 1);  // Bottom row is first
        }
    }
    else   // rcTarget is NOT empty. Use a sub-rectangle in the image.
    {
        *pdwWidth = (DWORD)(pvih->rcTarget.right - pvih->rcTarget.left);
        *pdwHeight = (DWORD)(pvih->rcTarget.bottom - pvih->rcTarget.top);

        if (pvih->bmiHeader.biHeight < 0 || bYuv)   // Top-down bitmap
        {
            // Same stride as above, but first pixel is modified down
            // and over by the target rectangle.
            *plStrideInBytes = lStride;
            *ppbTop = pbData +
                    lStride * pvih->rcTarget.top +
                    (pvih->bmiHeader.biBitCount * pvih->rcTarget.left) / 8;
        }
        else  // Bottom-up bitmap
        {
            *plStrideInBytes = -lStride;
            *ppbTop = pbData +
                    lStride * (pvih->bmiHeader.biHeight -
                    pvih->rcTarget.top - 1) +
                    (pvih->bmiHeader.biBitCount * pvih->rcTarget.left) / 8;
        }
    }
}
```

GetVideoInfoParameters returns the width and height of the video image (our sample filter is not prepared to deal with different values for the input and output samples), returns a pointer to the first pixel (upper-left corner) in the video image, and calculates the number of bytes—the *stride* (sometimes called *pitch* in the Direct3D documentation)—in each row of the image. It's important to understand that stride is a different value than image width. Although the image could be stored in 720 bytes per row, the stride for a row might be a figure in the range of 1024 bytes per row. So, simply incrementing a pointer by the image width value will not point you to the next row of image data. You need to use the stride value as your index increment. The stride information is used by both the transform routines to ensure that they stay within the bound of the video image and to ensure that they process only video data, leaving alone any other data padding that might be associated with how the video image is stored in computer memory. (For example, RGB video is always aligned on 32-bit boundaries in memory.)

In addition, *GetVideoInfoParameters* examines the format of the video image to determine if the image is expressed in top-down or bottom-up format. If the image is presented in top-down format, the first byte of video is the upper-left corner of the video image; if it's in bottom-up format, the first byte of video is the lower-left corner. The value returned for stride reflects the orientation, and given a pointer to a row of pixels, it allows you to write consistent loops, regardless of image orientation. Although this information wouldn't make a big difference for the YUV filter, if the transform operation involved a manipulation of pixel positions, the information would be absolutely essential. In your own video transform filters, you'll likely want to use the *GetVideoInfoParameters* function or something very much like it during the transform operation.

Top-Down vs. Bottom-Up Images

If you're new to graphics programming, you might expect that a bitmap would be arranged in memory so that the top row of the image appeared at the start of the buffer, followed by the next row, and so forth. However, this is not necessarily the case. In Windows, device-independent bitmaps (DIBs) can be placed in memory in two different orientations, bottom-up and top-down.

In a bottom-up DIB, the image buffer starts with the *bottom* row of pixels, followed by the next row up, and so forth. The top row of the image is the last row in the buffer. Therefore, the first byte in memory is the *lower-left* pixel of the image. In GDI, all DIBs are bottom-up. Figure 10-2 shows the physical layout of a bottom-up DIB.

(continued)

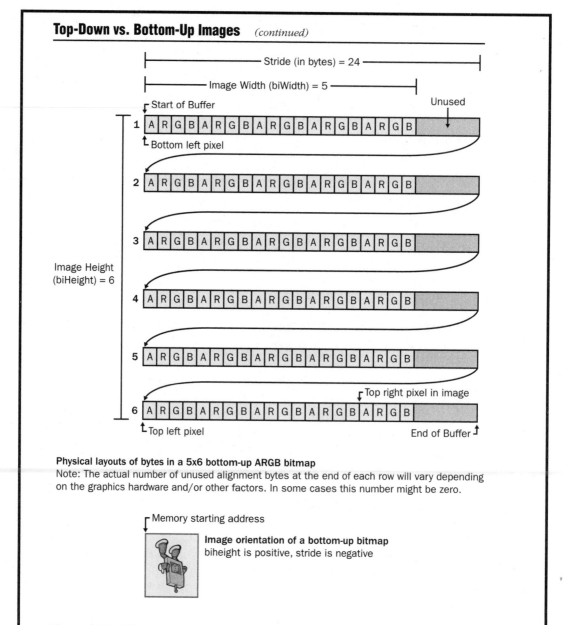

Top-Down vs. Bottom-Up Images   (continued)

Physical layouts of bytes in a 5x6 bottom-up ARGB bitmap
Note: The actual number of unused alignment bytes at the end of each row will vary depending on the graphics hardware and/or other factors. In some cases this number might be zero.

Image orientation of a bottom-up bitmap
biheight is positive, stride is negative

Figure 10-2   The physical layout of a bottom-up DIB

In a top-down DIB, the order of the rows is reversed. The *top* row of the image is the first row in memory, followed by the next row down. The bottom row of the image is the last row in the buffer. With a top-down

DIB, the first byte in memory is the *upper-left* pixel of the image. Direct-Draw uses top-down DIBs. Figure 10-3 shows the physical layout of a top-down DIB.

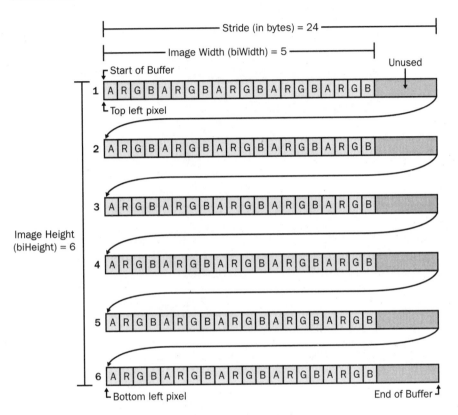

Physical layouts of bytes in a 5x6 top-down ARGB bitmap
Note: The actual number of unused alignment bytes at the end of each row will vary depending on the graphics hardware and/or other factors. In some cases this number might be zero.

Figure 10-3   The physical layout of a top-down DIB

(continued)

> **Top-Down vs. Bottom-Up Images** *(continued)*
>
> For RGB DIBs, the image orientation is indicated by the *biHeight* member of the *BITMAPINFOHEADER* structure. If *biHeight* is positive, the image is bottom-up. If *biHeight* is negative, the image is top-down.
>
> DIBs in YUV formats are always top-down, and the sign of the *biHeight* member is ignored. Decoders should offer YUV formats with positive *biHeight*, but they should also accept YUV formats with negative *biHeight* and ignore the sign.
>
> Also, any DIB type that uses a FOURCC value in the *biCompression* member should express its *biHeight* as a positive number no matter what its orientation is because the FOURCC format itself identifies a compression scheme whose image orientation should be understood by any compatible filter.

With the implementation of the *CYuvGray::Transform* method complete, the filter is now completely implemented. However, a few definitions still need to be declared for COM and DirectShow.

```
AMOVIESETUP_FILTER FilterInfo =
{
    &CLSID_YuvGray,        // CLSID
    g_wszName,             // Name
    MERIT_DO_NOT_USE,      // Merit
    0,                     // Number of AMOVIESETUP_PIN structs
    NULL                   // Pin registration information
};


CFactoryTemplate g_Templates[1] =
{
    {
        g_wszName,                  // Name
        &CLSID_YuvGray,             // CLSID
        CYuvGray::CreateInstance,   // Method to create an instance of MyComponent
        NULL,                       // Initialization function
        &FilterInfo                 // Set-up information (for filters)
    }
};
```

These two data structures are necessary to make the filter a COM-accessible entity. The *AMOVIESETUP_FILTER* data structure defines the information that gets written to the computer's registry file when the DLL is registered. We don't want this filter to be used by Intelligent Connect; the *MERIT_DO_NOT_USE* value in

AMOVIESETUP_FILTER means that Intelligent Connect won't attempt to use this filter as an intermediate connection between two other filters. Finally, the *CFactory-Template* data structure holds information that the DirectShow class factory uses when satisfying *CoCreateInstance* requests.

We also have a definitions file, YUVGray.def, which defines the published interfaces of the DLL.

```
LIBRARY YuvGray.DLL
DESCRIPTION 'YUV Gray Transform'
EXPORTS
    DllGetClassObject    PRIVATE
    DllCanUnloadNow      PRIVATE
    DllRegisterServer    PRIVATE
    DllUnregisterServer  PRIVATE
```

You might have noticed that the *DllGetClassObject* and *DllCanUnloadNow* methods aren't implemented in YUVGray.cpp. They're implemented in the base class library, so we don't have to do it ourselves.

Using the YUVGray Filter

Once you've compiled YUVGray.cpp and installed the DLL using regsvr32.exe, you should be able to find it in the enumerated list of DirectShow filters in GraphEdit, as shown in Figure 10-4.

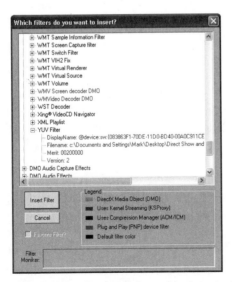

Figure 10-4   The YUV Filter visible in the list of DirectShow filters

On my own system, I built a small filter graph (shown in Figure 10-5) taking the output from my webcam—which produces a UYVY format video stream—through the YUV Filter and into the video renderer, so I get black and white output from a webcam. That might seem a bit bizarre given that an average webcam is already a low-resolution device, but it actually produces an image with the quality of an ancient television broadcast.

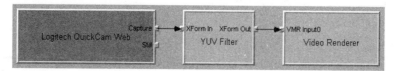

Figure 10-5   Three-element filter graph that uses the YUV filter to produce black and white output from my webcam

If you want to test YUY2 formats, try rendering an MPEG-1 file through your filter graph. The DirectShow MPEG-1 decoder prefers YUY2 format to UYVY format, and the YUV Filter will process a YUY2 format video stream if it's downstream from the MPEG-1 decoder.

Summary

The DirectShow transform filter is a primary building block in all DirectShow applications. The structure of a transform filter is easy to understand and has a straightforward implementation. The implementation of a transform filter consists principally of a few methods to negotiate the media types acceptable to the filter, the calculation of buffer allocations for the output pin, and the specific transform function.

The YUVGray transform filter clearly demonstrates the media negotiation, allocation, and transform features of a transform filter, and it provides an easy-to-modify code base for your own transform filters. It's easy to extend YUVGray to support other video stream types, such as RGB, and with some extra code, the filter could convert between stream types on the fly. In Chapter 13, we'll cover DirectX Media Objects (DMOs), which can be used to provide a way to create audio and video transforms for any application, not just those that use DirectShow. Together, DirectShow transform filters and DMOs can be used to create a wide range of real-time media effects.

11

Using the Sample Grabber Filter

Although many Microsoft DirectShow applications will benefit from the creation of a transform filter, transform filters can be difficult to test. Often, a programmer needs to construct a second filter just to test the output from his first one. The DirectShow Sample Grabber filter answers this need, although as we will see in this chapter, it can be used for much more than testing purposes.

The Sample Grabber is a standard transform filter that, in itself, does nothing to the media samples that pass through it. However, it exposes the *ISample-Grabber* interfaces to any DirectShow application that instantiates it. This interface allows you to "hook" your application into the media stream as it passes through the Sample Grabber. You can use the Sample Grabber to examine output from nearly any upstream filter because there are few restrictions on where the Sample Grabber is placed within the media stream. (It is neither a source nor a renderer filter, however, and any filter graph with the Sample Grabber must have both source and renderer filters.) The Sample Grabber allows a DirectShow application unrestricted access to the stream of media samples, in any media format that can be generated by a filter graph.

The Microsoft DirectX SDK actually contains two filters that expose the filter graph's media samples to an application: the Sample Grabber, a pre-built DirectShow filter; and the Grabber Sample, a sample Microsoft Visual C++ project. Although both perform essentially the same function, there are some interface differences between them, which would be reflected in the implementation of an application that used one or the other. In the first half of this chapter, we'll examine how you could use the Sample Grabber in a DirectShow application. In the second half, we'll explore the construction of the Grabber Sample and learn how a filter can connect to your applications.

The Sample Grabber delivers a powerful capability that can be employed in at least two ways. First, the Sample Grabber provides a mechanism with which on-the-fly analysis of a media stream can be performed. You can "peek" into a stream as it flows across the filter graph. For example, you might want to get audio levels from an audio track, so you could track the loudest sounds in a recording. Second, the Sample Grabber allows you to perform in-place transformations on the sample data. As long as the data that the Sample Grabber sends to you is returned in the same media sample, the Sample Grabber doesn't care what the application does with it. So, the application could "silence" audio data, replace a video stream with a test pattern, or, in the case of the Histogram application examined in this chapter, perform an analysis of each video frame, adjusting the visible qualities of the image. You can create an application with all the capabilities of a DirectShow filter (within the limits of an in-place transform) without having to create a filter.

When dropped into a filter graph, such as the one created by the Histogram application, the Sample Grabber looks just like any other transform filter, as shown in Figure 11-1.

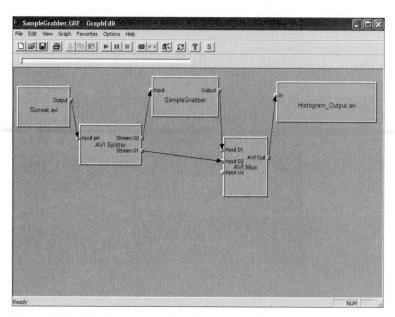

Figure 11-1 The Sample Grabber filter, which fits into the media stream as a normal transform filter

However, this filter graph doesn't tell the whole story because data is flowing from the Sample Grabber up to the Histogram application and back down again, as shown in Figure 11-2.

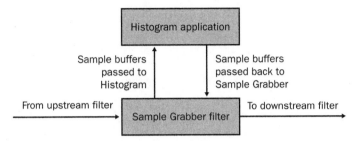

Figure 11-2   The Sample Grabber passing media samples to the Histogram application for processing

Every time the Sample Grabber receives a media sample to process, it signals to the Histogram (through a callback routine registered by the Histogram application when the Sample Grabber is instantiated) that a sample is ready. The Histogram processes the sample during the callback and returns control to the Sample Grabber when complete. The media sample is then presented on the output pin of the Sample Grabber and continues downstream.

Exploring the Histogram Application

The Histogram application transforms an incoming stream of video samples. The word *histogram* means that the application counts the frequency of every pixel value in each frame (or image) of the video stream. The application tracks how often a given pixel value occurs in a given frame. Once that information has been gathered, it's put to use in one of the following three specific ways, depending on which section of code is executed (which is determined by commenting/uncommenting code):

- A *histogram stretch* changes the values of each pixel in each frame so that the pixels utilize an entire range of possible values. A histogram stretch has the visible effect of changing the brightness of the image, and it's also known as *automatic gain control*. (The upper and lower range values can be set within the code.)

- A *histogram equalization* brings out details in an image that might otherwise be invisible because they're too dim or too bright.

■ A *logarithmic stretch* applies a logarithm operator to every pixel in the frame, which boosts the contrast in the darker regions of the image.

One of these three mathematical transformations is applied to every frame of the video. After it passes through the Sample Grabber, the video is DV (digital video) encoded and rendered to an output file. The resulting AVI file can be viewed with Windows Media Player. (The algorithms implemented in these histogram operations were found in *Handbook of Image and Video Processing*, Al Bovik, ed., Academic Press, 2000.)

Creating a Filter Graph Containing a Sample Grabber

The Histogram is a console-based application that has hard-coded file names inside it, and it produces an output AVI file at C:\Histogram_Output.AVI. (You'll need to have Sample.AVI in the root of drive C.) The application's simple filter graph is built, run, and torn down in one function, *RunFile*:

```
HRESULT RunFile(LPTSTR pszSrcFile, LPTSTR pszDestFile)
{
    HRESULT hr;

    USES_CONVERSION;  // For TCHAR -> WCHAR conversion macros

    CComPtr<IGraphBuilder> pGraph;    // Filter Graph Manager
    CComPtr<IBaseFilter> pGrabF;      // Sample grabber
    CComPtr<IBaseFilter> pMux;        // AVI Mux
    CComPtr<IBaseFilter> pSrc;        // Source filter
    CComPtr<IBaseFilter> pDVEnc;      // DV Encoder

    CComPtr<ICaptureGraphBuilder2> pBuild;

    // Create the Filter Graph Manager.
    hr = pGraph.CoCreateInstance(CLSID_FilterGraph);
    if (FAILED(hr))
    {
        printf("Could not create the Filter Graph Manager (hr = 0x%X.)\n",
            hr);
        return hr;
    }

    // Create the Capture Graph Builder.
    hr = pBuild.CoCreateInstance(CLSID_CaptureGraphBuilder2);
    if (FAILED(hr))
    {
        printf("Could not create the Capture Graph Builder (hr = 0x%X.)\n",
            hr);
```

```
        return hr;
    }
    pBuild->SetFiltergraph(pGraph);

    // Build the file-writing portion of the graph.
    hr = pBuild->SetOutputFileName(&MEDIASUBTYPE_Avi, T2W(pszDestFile),
        &pMux, NULL);
    if (FAILED(hr))
    {
        printf("Could not hook up the AVI Mux / File Writer (hr = 0x%X.)\n",
            hr);
        return hr;
    }


    // Add the source filter for the input file.
    hr = pGraph->AddSourceFilter(T2W(pszSrcFile), L"Source", &pSrc);
    if (FAILED(hr))
    {
        printf("Could not add the source filter (hr = 0x%X.)\n", hr);
        return hr;
    }


    // Create some filters and add them to the graph.

    // DV Video Encoder
    hr = AddFilterByCLSID(pGraph, CLSID_DVVideoEnc, L"DV Encoder", &pDVEnc);
    if (FAILED(hr))
    {
        printf("Could not add the DV video encoder filter (hr = 0x%X.)\n",
            hr);
        return hr;
    }
```

Although the Histogram source code uses the Active Template Library (ATL) features of Visual C++, this code should be very familiar by now. A Filter Graph Manager and a Capture Graph Builder are both instantiated and appropriately initialized. The Capture Graph Builder method *SetFileName* establishes the file name for the output AVI file, and *AddSourceFilter* is used to add the source file. Next a DV Encoder filter (the output stream is DV-encoded) is added. At this point, the Sample Grabber filter is instanced, added to the filter graph, and initialized before it's connected to any other filters.

```
    // Sample Grabber.
    hr = AddFilterByCLSID(pGraph, CLSID_SampleGrabber, L"Grabber", &pGrabF);
    if (FAILED(hr))
    {
```

```
        printf("Could not add the sample grabber filter (hr = 0x%X.)\n",
            hr);
        return hr;
    }
    CComQIPtr<ISampleGrabber> pGrabber(pGrabF);
    if (!pGrabF)
    {
        return E_NOINTERFACE;
    }

    // Configure the Sample Grabber.
    AM_MEDIA_TYPE mt;
    ZeroMemory(&mt, sizeof(AM_MEDIA_TYPE));
    mt.majortype = MEDIATYPE_Video;
    mt.subtype = MEDIASUBTYPE_UYVY;
    mt.formattype = FORMAT_VideoInfo;

    // Note: I don't expect the next few methods to fail...

    hr = pGrabber->SetMediaType(&mt);   // Set the media type
    _ASSERTE(SUCCEEDED(hr));

    hr = pGrabber->SetOneShot(FALSE);   // Disable "one-shot" mode
    _ASSERTE(SUCCEEDED(hr));

    hr = pGrabber->SetBufferSamples(FALSE); // Disable sample buffering
    _ASSERTE(SUCCEEDED(hr));

    hr = pGrabber->SetCallback(&grabberCallback, 0); // Set our callback
    // '0' means 'use the SampleCB callback'
    _ASSERTE(SUCCEEDED(hr));
```

Using the ATL smart pointers, a *QueryInterface* call is made to the Sample Grabber filter object requesting its *ISampleGrabber* interface. Once that interface has been acquired, the Sample Grabber can be configured. First the Sample Grabber has to be given a media type, so an *AM_MEDIA_TYPE* structure is instantiated and filled with a major type of *MEDIATYPE_Video* and a subtype of *MEDIASUBTYPE_UYVY*. (As covered in Chapter 10, this subtype means that the media samples in the stream are in YUV format, specifically UYVY.) A call to the *ISampleGrabber* method *SetMediaType* establishes the media type for the Sample Grabber. The Sample Grabber will accept any media type until a call is made to *SetMediaType*, at which point it will accept only matching media types. It's vital that the media type be set before the Sample Grabber is connected to other filters so that they can negotiate to meet the needs of the Sample Grabber.

A bit more initialization needs to be done to ensure the proper operation of the Sample Grabber. The Sample Grabber has the option of stopping the execution of the filter graph after it receives its first media sample, which comes in handy when grabbing still frames from a video file but would be a detriment to the operation of the histogram. To prevent this one-shot behavior from happening (we want continuous operation of the filter graph), we pass *FALSE* to the *ISampleGrabber* method *SetOneShot*. The Sample Grabber can also buffer samples internally as they pass through the filter; buffering is disabled by passing *FALSE* to *SetBufferSamples*. Finally the callback function within the Histogram application is initialized with a call to *SetCallback*. The Sample Grabber will call this function every time it receives a media sample. (The format of the object passed to *SetCallback* is discussed in the next section.) With the Sample Grabber filter fully initialized, construction of the filter graph can continue.

```
// Build the graph.
// First connect the source to the DV Encoder,
// through the Sample Grabber.
// This should connect the video stream.
hr = pBuild->RenderStream(0, 0, pSrc, pGrabF, pDVEnc);
if (SUCCEEDED(hr))
{
    // Next, connect the DV Encoder to the AVI Mux.
    hr = pBuild->RenderStream(0, 0, pDVEnc, 0, pMux);

    if (SUCCEEDED(hr))
    {
        // Maybe we have an audio stream.
        // If so, connect it the AVI Mux.
        // But don't fail if we don't...
        HRESULT hrTmp = pBuild->RenderStream(0, 0, pSrc, 0, pMux);

        SaveGraphFile(pGraph, L"C:\\Grabber.grf");
    }
}

if (FAILED(hr))
{
    printf("Error building the graph (hr = 0x%X.)\n", hr);
    return hr;
}

// Find out the exact video format.
hr = pGrabber->GetConnectedMediaType(&mt);
if (FAILED(hr))
{
    printf("Could not get the video format. (hr = 0x%X.)\n", hr);
    return hr;
}
```

```
VIDEOINFOHEADER *pVih;
if ((mt.subtype == MEDIASUBTYPE_UYVY) &&
    (mt.formattype == FORMAT_VideoInfo))
{
    pVih = reinterpret_cast<VIDEOINFOHEADER*>(mt.pbFormat);
}
else
{
    // This is not the format we expected!
    CoTaskMemFree(mt.pbFormat);
    return VFW_E_INVALIDMEDIATYPE;
}
```

Once the graph has been connected together with a few calls to *Render-Stream*, the Sample Grabber is queried for its media type using the *ISample-Grabber* method *GetConnectedMediaType*. If the returned subtype isn't *MEDIASUBTYPE_UYVY*, the function returns an error because the Histogram application can't process video frames in any format except UYVY. The function also checks that the format type is *FORMAT_VideoInfo*, which defines the format structure as a *VIDEOINFOHEADER* type. This check is performed because the Histogram application wasn't written to handle *VIDEOINFOHEADER2* format types. (The Sample Grabber filter doesn't accept *VIDEOINFOHEADER2* formats either.) The *VIDEOINFOHEADER2* structure is similar to *VIDEOINFOHEADER*, but it adds support for interlaced fields and image aspect ratios.

```
g_stretch.SetFormat(*pVih);
CoTaskMemFree(mt.pbFormat);

// Turn off the graph clock.
CComQIPtr<IMediaFilter> pMF(pGraph);
pMF->SetSyncSource(NULL);

// Run the graph to completion.
CComQIPtr<IMediaControl> pControl(pGraph);
CComQIPtr<IMediaEvent> pEvent(pGraph);
long evCode = 0;

printf("Processing the video file... ");

pControl->Run();
pEvent->WaitForCompletion(INFINITE, &evCode);
pControl->Stop();

printf("Done.\n");

return hr;
}
```

A global object, *g_stretch*, implements the methods that perform the mathematical transformation on the media sample. (One of three different instances of *g_stretch* can be created, depending on which line of code is uncommented. These three instances correspond to the three types of transforms implemented in the Histogram application.) A call to the *g_stretch SetFormat* method allows it to initialize with the appropriate height, width, and bit depth information needed for successful operation.

In a final step, a call is made to the *IMediaFilter* interface method *SetSyncSource*. This call sets the reference clock for the filter graph, which is used to preserve synchronization among all graph components and to define the presentation time for the filter graph. When passed *NULL*, as it is here, *SetSyncSource* turns off the filter graph's reference clock, allowing the filter graph components to run at their own rates, which is desirable because you will want the filter graph to process each sample as quickly as possible. If a reference clock was active, some filter graph components might choose to slow the graph down to maintain synchronization across the filter graph. With the reference clock turned off, this won't happen. (There aren't any filters in this particular filter graph that keep track of the reference clock, so we're being a bit overzealous here, for the sake of the example.)

Now that everything has been initialized, the *IMediaControl* and *IMediaEvent* interfaces are acquired from the Filter Graph Manager. Finally the filter graph is run to completion.

Defining the Sample Grabber Callback Object

The Sample Grabber was initialized with a callback object, which acts as a hook between the Sample Grabber and the Histogram application. Although instantiated by the Histogram application, the Sample Grabber doesn't know anything about the application; specifically, the Sample Grabber doesn't know how to pass media samples to the application. The interface between the application and the Sample Grabber is managed with the callback object *GrabberCB*, which is defined and implemented as follows:

```
class GrabberCB : public ISampleGrabberCB
{
private:
    BITMAPINFOHEADER m_bmi;  // Holds the bitmap format
    bool m_fFirstSample;     // True if the next sample is the first one

public:

    GrabberCB();
    ~GrabberCB();
```

```cpp
    // IUnknown methods
    STDMETHODIMP_(ULONG) AddRef() { return 1; }
    STDMETHODIMP_(ULONG) Release() { return 2; }
    STDMETHOD(QueryInterface)(REFIID iid, void** ppv);

    // ISampleGrabberCB methods
    STDMETHOD(SampleCB)(double SampleTime, IMediaSample *pSample);
    STDMETHODIMP BufferCB(double, BYTE *, long) { return E_NOTIMPL; }

};

GrabberCB::GrabberCB() : m_fFirstSample(true)
{
}

GrabberCB::~GrabberCB()
{
}

// Support querying for ISampleGrabberCB interface
HRESULT GrabberCB::QueryInterface(REFIID iid, void**ppv)
{
    if (!ppv) { return E_POINTER; }
    if (iid == IID_IUnknown)
    {
        *ppv = static_cast<IUnknown*>(this);
    }
    else if (iid == IID_ISampleGrabberCB)
    {
        *ppv = static_cast<ISampleGrabberCB*>(this);
    }
    else
    {
        return E_NOINTERFACE;
    }
    AddRef();  // We don't actually ref count,
               // but in case we change the implementation later.
    return S_OK;
}

// SampleCB: This is where we process each sample.
HRESULT GrabberCB::SampleCB(double SampleTime, IMediaSample *pSample)
{

    HRESULT hr;

    // Get the pointer to the buffer.
    BYTE *pBuffer;
    hr = pSample->GetPointer(&pBuffer);
```

```
    // Tell the image processing class about it.
    g_stretch.SetImage(pBuffer);

    if (FAILED(hr))
    {
        OutputDebugString(TEXT("SampleCB: GetPointer FAILED\n"));
        return hr;
    }

    // Scan the image on the first sample.
    // Re-scan if there is a discontinuity.
    // (This will produce horrible results
    // if there are big scene changes in the
    // video that are not associated with discontinuities.
    // Might be safer to re-scan
    // each image, at a higher perf cost.)

    if (m_fFirstSample)
    {
        hr = g_stretch.ScanImage();
        m_fFirstSample = false;
    }
    else if (S_OK == pSample->IsDiscontinuity())
    {
        hr = g_stretch.ScanImage();
    }

    // Convert the image.
    hr = g_stretch.ConvertImage();

    return S_OK;
}
```

The class declaration for *GrabberCB* inherits the methods of the *ISample-GrabberCB* interface. This interface defines two methods that must be implemented by the callback object, *GrabberCB::BufferCB* and *GrabberCB:: SampleCB*. However, the Sample Grabber filter can use only one of these callback methods at a time, so you can simply return *E_NOTIMPL* from the one you aren't going to use. The *GrabberCB::BufferCB* method would receive a sample buffer from the Sample Grabber, but because sample buffering was disabled when the Sample Grabber was instantiated, this method simply returns the error code *E_NOTIMPL*. The *GrabberCB::QueryInterface* implementation ensures that the appropriate interface is returned when handling *QueryInterface* calls made on the *GrabberCB* object.

The *GrabberCB::AddRef* and *GrabberCB::Release* methods implement fake reference counting. Normally, COM requires that an object keep a reference count and delete itself when the reference count goes to zero. In this case, we don't keep a reference count of this object, which means that the callback object must have a wider scope than the DirectShow filter graph so that the object doesn't accidentally get deleted while the Sample Grabber is still using it. That is why the *grabberCallback* object is implemented as a global variable. The variable stays in scope for the duration of the Histogram application's execution, and the object is automatically deleted when the application terminates execution.

Now we come to the heart of the *GrabberCB* object, the implementation of *GrabberCB::SampleCB*. This method is called every time the Sample Grabber filter has a sample to present to the Histogram application. The method communicates with *g_stretch*, the object that manages the histogram transformation, passing it a pointer to the media sample's memory buffer, which contains the raw sample data. On the first time through the method (that is, when the first media sample is ready for processing by the Histogram application), the *m_fFirstSample* flag is set *true* and the method calls *ScanImage*, which allows the histogram object to learn the particulars of the video frames that it will be processing. (This also happens if a discontinuity is detected, which happens when the filter graph pauses and restarts.) Finally the method calls the *ConvertImage* method of the histogram object, which performs the in-place transformation of the data in the buffer.

Although this might seem like a minimal implementation, this is all the implementation that's required to add the Sample Grabber filter to your DirectShow applications. The interesting part is what your application does with the media samples delivered to it by the Sample Grabber.

Processing Sample Grabber Media Samples

There are only a few major restrictions on the kind of processing that can take place on a sample presented by the Sample Grabber. The transformations must be performed in-place, within the same buffer presented by the Sample Grabber to the application. So, media format translations are not permissible, nor is any other operation that affects the media type or buffer size of the sample. If the Sample Grabber is upstream of a video renderer, performance of the filter graph will suffer because it will probably require hardware reads of the video graphics card, which can slow processing dramatically, as explained in Chapter 10.

In the Histogram application, the histogram image processing object *CImagePointOp* uses three methods for data translation: *SetFormat*, *ScanImage*, and *ConvertImage*. Because there are three possible implementations of *ScanImage* and *ConvertImage*, depending on which global histogram object is uncommented in the source code, we present the default case, *CEqualize* (which brings out detail across the image) as if it were the only implementation.

```
HRESULT CImageOp::SetFormat(const VIDEOINFOHEADER& vih)
{
    // Check if UYVY.
    if (vih.bmiHeader.biCompression != 'YVYU')
    {
        return E_INVALIDARG;
    }

    int BytesPerPixel = vih.bmiHeader.biBitCount / 8;

    // If the target rectangle (rcTarget) is empty,
    // the image width and the stride are both biWidth.
    // Otherwise, image width is given by rcTarget
    // and the stride is given by biWidth.

    if (IsRectEmpty(&vih.rcTarget))
    {
        m_dwWidth = vih.bmiHeader.biWidth;
        m_lStride = m_dwWidth;
    }
    else
    {
        m_dwWidth = vih.rcTarget.right;
        m_lStride = vih.bmiHeader.biWidth;
    }

    // Stride for UYVY is rounded to the nearest DWORD.
    m_lStride = (m_lStride * BytesPerPixel + 3) & ~3;

    // biHeight can be < 0, but YUV is always top-down.
    m_dwHeight = abs(vih.bmiHeader.biHeight);
    m_iBitDepth = vih.bmiHeader.biBitCount;

    return S_OK;
}

HRESULT CEqualize::_ScanImage()
{
    DWORD iRow, iPixel;  // looping variables
    BYTE *pRow = m_pImg; // pointer to the first row in the buffer

    DWORD  histogram[LUMA_RANGE];  // basic histogram
    double nrm_histogram[LUMA_RANGE]; // normalized histogram

    ZeroMemory(histogram, sizeof(histogram));
```

```
// Create a histogram.
// For each pixel, find the luma and increment the count for that
// pixel. Luma values are translated
// from the nominal 16-235 range to a 0-219 array.

for (iRow = 0; iRow < m_dwHeight; iRow++)
{
    UYVY_PIXEL *pPixel = reinterpret_cast<UYVY_PIXEL*>(pRow);

    for (iPixel = 0; iPixel < m_dwWidth; iPixel++, pPixel++)
    {
        BYTE luma = pPixel->y;
        luma = static_cast<BYTE>(clipYUV(luma)) - MIN_LUMA;
        histogram[luma]++;
    }
    pRow += m_lStride;
}

// Build the cumulative histogram.
for (int i = 1; i < LUMA_RANGE; i++)
{
    // The i'th entry is the sum of the previous entries.
    histogram[i] = histogram[i-1] + histogram[i];
}

// Normalize the histogram.
DWORD area = NumPixels();

for (int i = 0; i < LUMA_RANGE; i++)
{
    nrm_histogram[i] =
        static_cast<double>( LUMA_RANGE * histogram[i] ) / area;
}

// Create the LUT.
for (int i = 0; i < LUMA_RANGE; i++)
{
    // Clip the result to the nominal luma range.

    long rounded = static_cast<long>(nrm_histogram[i] + 0.5);
    long clipped = clip(rounded, 0, LUMA_RANGE - 1);

    m_LookUpTable[i] = static_cast<BYTE>(clipped) + MIN_LUMA;
}

return S_OK;
}
```

```
HRESULT CImagePointOp::_ConvertImage()
{
    DWORD iRow, iPixel;  // looping variables
    BYTE *pRow = m_pImg; // pointer to the first row in the buffer

    for (iRow = 0; iRow < m_dwHeight; iRow++)
    {
        UYVY_PIXEL *pPixel = reinterpret_cast<UYVY_PIXEL*>(pRow);

        for (iPixel = 0; iPixel < m_dwWidth; iPixel++, pPixel++)
        {
            // Translate luma back to 0-219 range.
            BYTE luma = (BYTE)clipYUV(pPixel->y) - MIN_LUMA;

            // Convert from LUT.
            // The result is already in the correct 16-239 range.
            pPixel->y = m_LookUpTable[luma];
        }
        pRow += m_lStride;
    }
    return S_OK;
}
```

The first method, *CImageOp::SetFormat*, is called from *RunFile* when all the connections have been made across the filter graph and the Sample Grabber is fully aware of the media type it will be presenting to the histogram object. (Although the Sample Grabber is initialized with a media type and subtype, the histogram object needs more detailed information to process each frame of video.) From the passed *VIDEOINFOHEADER* parameter, the method learns the width, height, stride, and bit depth of the image, information that the histogram object will need for processing.

When the Sample Grabber receives its first media sample from an upstream filter, it calls *CEqualize::ScanImage* from *GrabberCB::SampleCB*. This method walks through the image, pixel by pixel, creating a histogram, from which it extracts maximum and minimum luma values. (Luma is covered in the sidebar on YUV formats in Chapter 10.) This histogram is then normalized, and these values are placed into an array that is used by *CImageOp::ConvertImage*. When *CImageOp::ConvertImage* is called, the method extracts the old luma value of a pixel, looks it up in the array created by *CEqualize::ScanImage*, and inserts a new luma value for the pixel.

The differences between the three histogram techniques offered by this application are entirely based in the three implementations of the *ScanImage* method. Each method generates a unique array of luma values, which thereby changes the output of *CImageOp::ConvertImage*. You could easily write your own *ScanImage* implementations, adapting the code in this example program, to produce unique video effects.

This concludes the exploration of the Sample Grabber from the application designer's point of view. Now we'll examine the source code of the Grabber Sample, which is an alternate implementation of the Sample Grabber, with its own unique class ID and interface ID. The Grabber Sample source code is included in the DirectX SDK. It has a unique design that illuminates many internal features of DirectShow.

Exploring the Grabber Sample Source Code

The Grabber Sample begins with a class ID and an interface ID unique to the module, so it can be instantiated (with its class ID) and queried for its interfaces (with its interface ID). Next is a *typedef* that defines the callback format—that is, what data will be passed to the application through the Grabber Sample. This callback format is different from the one used by the Sample Grabber. The Grabber Sample callback is implemented as a function, not as a COM interface as it is in the Sample Grabber. Next comes the interface definition for the *IGrabberSample* interface. *IGrabberSample* implements methods that the application uses to communicate with the Grabber Sample. This interface can be located using *QueryInterface*.

```
//--------------------------------------------------------------------
// Define new GUID and IID for the grabber example so that they do NOT
// conflict with the official DirectX Grabber Sample filter
//--------------------------------------------------------------------
// {2FA4F053-6D60-4cb0-9503-8E89234F3F73}
DEFINE_GUID(CLSID_GrabberSample,
0x2fa4f053, 0x6d60, 0x4cb0, 0x95, 0x3, 0x8e, 0x89, 0x23, 0x4f, 0x3f, 0x73);

DEFINE_GUID(IID_IGrabberSample,
0x6b652fff, 0x11fe, 0x4fce, 0x92, 0xad, 0x02, 0x66, 0xb5, 0xd7, 0xc7, 0x8f);

// We define a callback typedef for this example.
// Normally, you would make the Grabber Sample support a COM interface,
// and in one of its methods you would pass in a pointer to a COM interface
// used for calling back.
typedef HRESULT (*SAMPLECALLBACK) (
    IMediaSample * pSample,
    REFERENCE_TIME * StartTime,
    REFERENCE_TIME * StopTime,
    BOOL TypeChanged );
```

```
// We define the interface the app can use to program us
MIDL_INTERFACE("6B652FFF-11FE-4FCE-92AD-0266B5D7C78F")
IGrabberSample : public IUnknown
{
    public:

        virtual HRESULT STDMETHODCALLTYPE SetAcceptedMediaType(
            const CMediaType *pType) = 0;

        virtual HRESULT STDMETHODCALLTYPE GetConnectedMediaType(
            CMediaType *pType) = 0;

        virtual HRESULT STDMETHODCALLTYPE SetCallback(
            SAMPLECALLBACK Callback) = 0;

        virtual HRESULT STDMETHODCALLTYPE SetDeliveryBuffer(
            ALLOCATOR_PROPERTIES props,
            BYTE *pBuffer) = 0;
};
```

Defining and Implementing the Filter Class

The definition of the filter class *CSampleGrabber* is closely based on the definition of the *IGrabberSample* interface. *CSampleGrabber* includes declarations for all the methods declared within *IGrabberSample*, but in this case, it actually includes the implementations of these methods. Here's the definition of the *CSampleGrabber* class:

```
class CSampleGrabber : public CTransInPlaceFilter,
                       public IGrabberSample
{
    friend class CSampleGrabberInPin;
    friend class CSampleGrabberAllocator;

protected:

    CMediaType m_mtAccept;
    SAMPLECALLBACK m_callback;
    CCritSec m_Lock; // serialize access to our data

    BOOL IsReadOnly( ) { return !m_bModifiesData; }

    // PURE, override this to ensure we get
    // connected with the right media type
    HRESULT CheckInputType( const CMediaType * pmt );
```

```
            // PURE, override this to callback
            // the user when a sample is received
            HRESULT Transform( IMediaSample * pms );

            // override this so we can return S_FALSE directly.
            // The base class CTransInPlace
            // Transform( ) method is called by its
            // Receive( ) method. There is no way
            // to get Transform( ) to return an S_FALSE value
            // (which means "stop giving me data"),
            // to Receive( ) and get Receive( ) to return S_FALSE as well.
            HRESULT Receive( IMediaSample * pms );

public:

            static CUnknown *WINAPI CreateInstance(LPUNKNOWN punk, HRESULT *phr);

            // Expose IGrabberSample
            STDMETHODIMP NonDelegatingQueryInterface(REFIID riid, void ** ppv);
            DECLARE_IUNKNOWN;

            CSampleGrabber( IUnknown * pOuter, HRESULT * pHr, BOOL ModifiesData );

            // IGrabberSample
            STDMETHODIMP SetAcceptedMediaType( const CMediaType * pmt );
            STDMETHODIMP GetConnectedMediaType( CMediaType * pmt );
            STDMETHODIMP SetCallback( SAMPLECALLBACK Callback );
            STDMETHODIMP SetDeliveryBuffer( ALLOCATOR_PROPERTIES props,
                                            BYTE * m_pBuffer );
};
```

CSampleGrabber uses the C++ feature of multiple inheritance, declaring both *CTransInPlaceFilter* and *ISampleGrabber* as ancestor classes and inheriting the variables and implementation of both classes. The only method implemented in the class definition is the *IsReadOnly* method, which checks the *m_bModifiesData* Boolean variable and returns its inverse. If *m_bModifiesData* is *true*, the filter is modifying data in its buffers.

Here's the implementation of the three protected methods of *CSampleGrabber—CheckInputType, Transform,* and *Receive*:

```
HRESULT CSampleGrabber::CheckInputType( const CMediaType * pmt )
{
    CheckPointer(pmt,E_POINTER);
    CAutoLock lock( &m_Lock );

    // if the major type is not set, then accept anything
```

```
    GUID g = *m_mtAccept.Type( );
    if( g == GUID_NULL )
    {
        return NOERROR;
    }

    // if the major type is set, don't accept anything else

    if( g != *pmt->Type( ) )
    {
        return VFW_E_INVALID_MEDIA_TYPE;
    }

    // subtypes must match, if set. if not set, accept anything

    g = *m_mtAccept.Subtype( );
    if( g == GUID_NULL )
    {
        return NOERROR;
    }
    if( g != *pmt->Subtype( ) )
    {
        return VFW_E_INVALID_MEDIA_TYPE;
    }

    // format types must match, if one is set

    g = *m_mtAccept.FormatType( );
    if( g == GUID_NULL )
    {
        return NOERROR;
    }
    if( g != *pmt->FormatType( ) )
    {
        return VFW_E_INVALID_MEDIA_TYPE;
    }

    // at this point, for this sample code, this is good enough,
    // but you may want to make it more strict

    return NOERROR;
}

HRESULT CSampleGrabber::Receive( IMediaSample * pms )
{
    CheckPointer(pms,E_POINTER);
```

```
HRESULT hr;
AM_SAMPLE2_PROPERTIES * const pProps = m_pInput->SampleProps();

if (pProps->dwStreamId != AM_STREAM_MEDIA)
{
    if( m_pOutput->IsConnected() )
        return m_pOutput->Deliver(pms);
    else
        return NOERROR;
}

if (UsingDifferentAllocators())
{
    // We have to copy the data.

    pms = Copy(pms);

    if (pms == NULL)
    {
        return E_UNEXPECTED;
    }
}

// have the derived class transform the data
hr = Transform(pms);

if (FAILED(hr))
{
    DbgLog((LOG_TRACE, 1, TEXT("Error from TransInPlace")));
    if (UsingDifferentAllocators())
    {
        pms->Release();
    }
    return hr;
}

if (hr == NOERROR)
{
    hr = m_pOutput->Deliver(pms);
}

// release the output buffer. If the connected pin still needs it,
// it will have addrefed it itself.
if (UsingDifferentAllocators())
{
    pms->Release();
}
```

```
        return hr;
}

HRESULT CSampleGrabber::Transform ( IMediaSample * pms )
{
    CheckPointer(pms,E_POINTER);
    CAutoLock lock( &m_Lock );

    if( m_callback )
    {
        REFERENCE_TIME StartTime, StopTime;
        pms->GetTime( &StartTime, &StopTime);

        StartTime += m_pInput->CurrentStartTime( );
        StopTime  += m_pInput->CurrentStartTime( );

        BOOL * pTypeChanged =
            &((CSampleGrabberInPin*) m_pInput)->m_bMediaTypeChanged;

        HRESULT hr =
          m_callback( pms, &StartTime, &StopTime, *pTypeChanged );

        *pTypeChanged = FALSE; // now that we notified user, can clear it

        return hr;
    }

    return NOERROR;
}
```

The *CheckInputType* method implements a series of comparisons against the media type that was specified by the application instancing the Grabber Sample. If no local type has been set for the *CSampleGrabber* object—implying that the application did not call *SetAcceptedMediaType* when initializing the filter—anything passed to *CheckInputType* will return without an error. If a media type is defined, the major type must match, and the subtype and format must match if they've been defined. Like the Sample Grabber, the Grabber Sample checks only the major type, subtype, and format type. It doesn't examine the details of the format (for example, sample rate on an audio stream, or image width and height in a video stream), so it's possible that the filter will accept a connection to a media stream that the application can't work with.

The *Receive* method is, in many ways, the heart of the filter class implementation. It overrides *CTransInPlaceFilter::Receive*, which is called by the input pin's *IMemInputPin::Receive* method. The method examines the properties of the sample that has been presented on the input pin by calling the *CBaseInputPin::SampleProps* method, which returns an *AM_SAMPLE2_PROPERTIES* data structure. The method then examines the *dwStreamId* field of the structure. If this field contains the value *AM_STREAM_MEDIA*, the sample presented on the input pin is stream data and needs to be processed by the method. If the field contains anything else, the sample on the input pin contains stream control data and is immediately passed along to the *Deliver* method on the output pin if the output pin is connected to anything downstream.

Next the method calls the *CTransInPlaceFilter::UsingDifferentAllocators* method. This method returns *true* if the input and output buffers are different. The *Receive* method then copies the buffers from the input to output pin buffer using the *CTransInPlaceFilter::Copy* method, which is necessary because in some cases a transform-in-place filter is forced to act like a copy transform filter with two allocators. (This situation is described exhaustively in the DirectX SDK documentation for the *CTransInPlaceFilter* class.) Once the buffer has been copied (if necessary), the class's *Transform* method is invoked, which performs any necessary manipulations of the stream data as it passes from input to output pin. If the *Transform* completes successfully, the buffer is sent along to the output pin with a call to the output pin's *Deliver* method. The buffer allocated in the *Copy* method call (if any) is released, and the method exits.

The *Transform* method doesn't do anything to the data in the buffer, so in this sense, this transform filter doesn't transform anything. However, this method is where the call to the user-defined callback is made. (This arrangement of filter and callback is similar to the relationship between the Histogram application and the Sample Grabber given earlier in this chapter.) If there's a user-defined callback set up through an invocation of the *SetCallback* method, it's called. The callback is passed a pointer to the stream buffer, the sample's start time and stop time (in *REFERENCE_TIME* units of 100 nanoseconds), and a flag indicating whether the media's type has changed. (Your own filters should check for a type change in either the *Receive* or the *Transform* method.) Once that's done, *Transform* exits.

Now let's look at the implementation of the class constructor and the methods that COM needs to publish through the *IGrabberSample* interface:

```
CUnknown * WINAPI CSampleGrabber::CreateInstance(LPUNKNOWN punk, HRESULT *phr)
{
    ASSERT(phr);

    // assuming we don't want to modify the data
    CSampleGrabber *pNewObject = new CSampleGrabber(punk, phr, FALSE);

    if(pNewObject == NULL) {
        if (phr)
            *phr = E_OUTOFMEMORY;
    }
```

```
        return pNewObject;

}


CSampleGrabber::CSampleGrabber( IUnknown * pOuter, HRESULT * phr,
                                BOOL ModifiesData )
            : CTransInPlaceFilter( TEXT("SampleGrabber"),
                    (IUnknown*) pOuter, CLSID_GrabberSample,
                    phr, (BOOL)ModifiesData )
            , m_callback( NULL )
{
    // this is used to override the input pin with our own
    m_pInput = (CTransInPlaceInputPin*) new CSampleGrabberInPin( this, phr );
    if( !m_pInput )
    {
        if (phr)
            *phr = E_OUTOFMEMORY;
    }

    // Ensure that the output pin gets created.
    // This is necessary because our
    // SetDeliveryBuffer() method assumes
    // that the input/output pins are created, but
    // the output pin isn't created until GetPin() is called.  The
    // CTransInPlaceFilter::GetPin() method will create the output pin,
    // since we have not already created one.
    IPin *pOutput = GetPin(1);
    // The pointer is not AddRef'ed by GetPin(), so don't release it
}

STDMETHODIMP CSampleGrabber::NonDelegatingQueryInterface( REFIID riid,
                                                          void ** ppv)
{
    CheckPointer(ppv,E_POINTER);

    if(riid == IID_IGrabberSample) {
        return GetInterface((IGrabberSample *) this, ppv);
    }
    else {
        return CTransInPlaceFilter::NonDelegatingQueryInterface(riid, ppv);
    }
}
```

These methods translate neatly into COM methods that we're already familiar with. The *CreateInstance* method is normally invoked by a COM call to *CoCreateInstance*, and it instantiates and then returns a *CSampleGrabber* object. The *CSampleGrabber::CSampleGrabber* constructor method calls its parent's constructor *CTransInPlaceFilter::CTransInPlaceFilter* for initialization. It then creates a new input pin with a call to the constructor for *CSampleGrabber-InPin* and an output pin with a call to the parent method *CTransInPlace-Filter::GetPin*. Finally the *NonDelegatingQueryInterface* method handles the particulars of the *QueryInterface* COM method and returns an *IGrabberSample* interface to a passed object, if that's what's requested, or passes the request up the inheritance chain to *CTransInPlaceFilter::NonDelegatingQueryInterface*.

Now all that's left are the few functions that implement the published interfaces on *IGrabberSample*: *SetAcceptedMediaType*, *GetConnectedMedia-Type*, *SetCallback*, and *SetDeliveryBuffer*. Here's the implementation of these four methods:

```
STDMETHODIMP CSampleGrabber::SetAcceptedMediaType( const CMediaType * pmt )
{
    CAutoLock lock( &m_Lock );

    if( !pmt )
    {
        m_mtAccept = CMediaType( );
        return NOERROR;
    }

    HRESULT hr;
    hr = CopyMediaType( &m_mtAccept, pmt );

    return hr;
}


STDMETHODIMP CSampleGrabber::GetConnectedMediaType( CMediaType * pmt )
{
    if( !m_pInput || !m_pInput->IsConnected( ) )
    {
        return VFW_E_NOT_CONNECTED;
    }

    return m_pInput->ConnectionMediaType( pmt );
}


STDMETHODIMP CSampleGrabber::SetCallback( SAMPLECALLBACK Callback )
{
    CAutoLock lock( &m_Lock );

    m_callback = Callback;

    return NOERROR;
}
```

```
STDMETHODIMP CSampleGrabber::SetDeliveryBuffer( ALLOCATOR_PROPERTIES props,
                                                BYTE * m_pBuffer )
{
    // have the input/output pins been created?
    if( !InputPin( ) || !OutputPin( ) )
    {
        return E_POINTER;
    }

// they can't be connected
// if we're going to be changing delivery buffers
    if( InputPin( )->IsConnected( ) || OutputPin( )->IsConnected( ) )
    {
        return E_INVALIDARG;
    }

    return ((CSampleGrabberInPin*)m_pInput)->SetDeliveryBuffer( props,
        m_pBuffer );
}
```

The *SetAcceptedMediaType* method establishes the media type acceptable to the filter. If *NULL* is passed, an empty *CMediaType* object is instantiated; otherwise, the object is copied locally using the DirectX function *CopyMediaType*. The *GetConnectedMediaType* method will return the media type specified on the filter's input pin if that pin is connected. *SetCallback* sets the member variable *m_callback* to the value of the supplied parameter. This value, if it exists, will be used when the *Transform* method is invoked.

Finally the *SetDeliveryBuffer* method defines the allocator properties and buffer to be used by the filter. If either the input or output pin does not exist, the method fails, which is a defense against a bad pointer and unlikely to happen. Alternatively, if both exist but either is connected, the function fails because if either of the pins is connected, it has already negotiated an allocator. If all these tests pass successfully, the actual work is passed off to *CSampleGrabberInPin::SetDeliveryBuffer*.

Defining and Implementing the Allocator Class

Although the Grabber Sample is descended from *CTransInPlaceFilter* and doesn't need to copy input or output buffers, it requires a custom allocator implementation because the Grabber Sample has a feature that allows the application hooked into it to allocate the memory for the sample buffers. This feature gives the application even greater control over the Grabber Sample, as it creates and owns the memory pool that the Grabber Sample uses for its *IMediaSample* objects. The application can set up this pool by calling *CSampleGrabber::Set-DeliveryBuffer*. Here's the implementation of the custom allocator methods:

```
class CSampleGrabberAllocator : public CMemAllocator
{
    friend class CSampleGrabberInPin;
    friend class CSampleGrabber;

protected:

    // our pin who created us
    CSampleGrabberInPin * m_pPin;

public:

    CSampleGrabberAllocator( CSampleGrabberInPin * pParent, HRESULT *phr )
        : CMemAllocator( TEXT("SampleGrabberAllocator\0"), NULL, phr )
        , m_pPin( pParent )
    {
    };

    ~CSampleGrabberAllocator( )
    {
        // wipe out m_pBuffer before we try to delete it.
        // It's not an allocated buffer,
        // and the default destructor will try to free it!
        m_pBuffer = NULL;
    }

    HRESULT Alloc( );

    void ReallyFree();

    // Override to reject anything that does not match the actual buffer
    // that was created by the application
    STDMETHODIMP SetProperties(ALLOCATOR_PROPERTIES *pRequest,
        ALLOCATOR_PROPERTIES *pActual);

};
```

The *CSampleGrabberAllocator* object is a descendant of *CMemAllocator*, which is a DirectX-defined object that allocates storage for media samples, such as DirectShow streams. This definition overrides the constructor *CSample-GrabberAllocator::CSampleGrabberAllocator*, which does little more than invoke the parent method in *CMemAllocator* and the destructor *CSample-GrabberAllocator::~CSampleGrabberAllocator*, which sets the buffer pointer to

NULL, ensuring that a buffer created by the application is released by the application and not by the Grabber Sample. The real work takes place in the three *CSampleGrabberAllocator* methods: *Alloc*, *ReallyFree*, and *SetProperties*. Here's the implementation of those methods:

```
HRESULT CSampleGrabberAllocator::Alloc( )
{
    // look at the base class code to see where this came from!

    CAutoLock lck(this);

    // Check he has called SetProperties
    HRESULT hr = CBaseAllocator::Alloc();
    if (FAILED(hr)) {
        return hr;
    }

    // If the requirements haven't changed then don't reallocate
    if (hr == S_FALSE) {
        ASSERT(m_pBuffer);
        return NOERROR;
    }
    ASSERT(hr == S_OK); // we use this fact in the loop below

    // Free the old resources
    if (m_pBuffer) {
        ReallyFree();
    }

    // Compute the aligned size
    LONG lAlignedSize = m_lSize + m_lPrefix;
    if (m_lAlignment > 1)
    {
        LONG lRemainder = lAlignedSize % m_lAlignment;
        if (lRemainder != 0)
        {
            lAlignedSize += (m_lAlignment - lRemainder);
        }
    }

    ASSERT(lAlignedSize % m_lAlignment == 0);

    // don't create the buffer - use what was passed to us
    //
    m_pBuffer = m_pPin->m_pBuffer;
```

```
    if (m_pBuffer == NULL) {
        return E_OUTOFMEMORY;
    }

    LPBYTE pNext = m_pBuffer;
    CMediaSample *pSample;

    ASSERT(m_lAllocated == 0);

    // Create the new samples -
    // we have allocated m_lSize bytes for each sample
    // plus m_lPrefix bytes per sample as a prefix. We set the pointer to
    // the memory after the prefix -
    // so that GetPointer() will return a pointer to m_lSize bytes.
    for (; m_lAllocated < m_lCount; m_lAllocated++, pNext += lAlignedSize)
    {
        pSample = new CMediaSample(
                            NAME("Sample Grabber memory media sample"),
                            this,
                            &hr,
                            pNext + m_lPrefix,   // GetPointer() value
                            m_lSize);            // not including prefix

        ASSERT(SUCCEEDED(hr));
        if (pSample == NULL)
            return E_OUTOFMEMORY;

        // This CANNOT fail
        m_lFree.Add(pSample);
    }

    m_bChanged = FALSE;
    return NOERROR;
}

void CSampleGrabberAllocator::ReallyFree()
{
    // look at the base class code to see where this came from!
    // Should never be deleting this unless all buffers are freed

    ASSERT(m_lAllocated == m_lFree.GetCount());

    // Free up all the CMediaSamples

    CMediaSample *pSample;
    for (;;)
    {
        pSample = m_lFree.RemoveHead();
```

```
        if (pSample != NULL)
        {
            delete pSample;
        }
        else
        {
            break;
        }
    }

    m_lAllocated = 0;

    // don't free the buffer - let the app do it
}

HRESULT CSampleGrabberAllocator::SetProperties(
    ALLOCATOR_PROPERTIES *pRequest,
    ALLOCATOR_PROPERTIES *pActual
)
{
    HRESULT hr = CMemAllocator::SetProperties(pRequest, pActual);

    if (FAILED(hr))
    {
        return hr;
    }

    ALLOCATOR_PROPERTIES *pRequired = &(m_pPin->m_allocprops);
    if (pRequest->cbAlign != pRequired->cbAlign)
    {
        return VFW_E_BADALIGN;
    }
    if (pRequest->cbPrefix != pRequired->cbPrefix)
    {
        return E_FAIL;
    }
    if (pRequest->cbBuffer > pRequired->cbBuffer)
    {
        return E_FAIL;
    }
    if (pRequest->cBuffers > pRequired->cBuffers)
    {
        return E_FAIL;
    }

    *pActual = *pRequired;
```

```
m_lCount = pRequired->cBuffers;
m_lSize = pRequired->cbBuffer;
m_lAlignment = pRequired->cbAlign;
m_lPrefix = pRequired->cbPrefix;

return S_OK;
}
```

The *Alloc* method is called when the allocator object needs to allocate the media samples. For this allocator, the application provides the memory buffer, so the allocator object doesn't need to allocate any buffer memory. However, the allocator object does need to create the media sample objects. An *IMedia-Sample* object manages a pointer to a block of memory, but the block is allocated and released independently.

The *Alloc* method determines whether storage has already been allocated for the media samples; if the requirements haven't changed since the previous call to *Alloc*, the method returns without doing anything. Otherwise, the media samples are released and a new series of *CMediaSample* objects are created. Each *CMediaSample* holds a pointer that points to a section of the memory buffer.

The *ReallyFree* method has a deceptive name. Although this method is supposed to free the buffers allocated by the allocator object, in this case it won't because those buffers haven't been allocated by this object. However, because *Alloc* did create *m_lAllocated CMediaSample* objects, the *ReallyFree* method must release those objects.

Finally the *SetProperties* method specifies the number of buffers to be allocated and the size of each buffer. This is a request, not a command, so *Set-Properties* returns the actual number and size of buffers allocated by the call, which might be at variance with the number requested. You should always check the returned value. The parameters are passed in an *ALLOCATOR_PROPERTIES* structure, which has the following definition:

```
typedef struct _AllocatorProperties {
    long cBuffers;
    long cbBuffer;
    long cbAlign;
    long cbPrefix;
} ALLOCATOR_PROPERTIES;
```

The *cBuffers* field specifies the number of buffers to be created by the allocator, while *cbBuffer* specifies the size of each buffer in bytes. The *cbAlign* field specifies the byte alignment of each buffer, and *cbPrefix* allocates a prefix of a specific number of bytes before each buffer, which is useful for buffer header information. Because no allocation is taking place inside this allocator, *SetProperties* passes the allocation request to its parent class, *CMemAllocator*, and then performs a series of checks to ensure that the allocations have been performed successfully. Because the allocator properties are set by the application, the request can't exceed these properties. If any of these checks fail, a failure is reported to the caller. If all the checks passed successfully, *SetProperties* returns the actual allocation values to the caller.

Defining and Implementing the Input Pin Class

The DirectShow filter implementation provides an overridden implementation of the class *CTransInPlaceInputPin*, which implements all the methods required for handling input pin connections on *CTransInPlaceFilter* objects. Here's the definition of that class, *CSampleGrabberInPin*:

```
class CSampleGrabberInPin : public CTransInPlaceInputPin
{
    friend class CSampleGrabberAllocator;
    friend class CSampleGrabber;

    CSampleGrabberAllocator * m_pPrivateAllocator;
    ALLOCATOR_PROPERTIES m_allocprops;
    BYTE * m_pBuffer;
    BOOL m_bMediaTypeChanged;

protected:

    CSampleGrabber * SampleGrabber( ) { return (CSampleGrabber*) m_pFilter; }
    HRESULT SetDeliveryBuffer( ALLOCATOR_PROPERTIES props, BYTE * m_pBuffer );

public:

    CSampleGrabberInPin( CTransInPlaceFilter * pFilter, HRESULT * pHr )
        : CTransInPlaceInputPin( TEXT("GrabberSampleInputPin\0"), pFilter,
                                 pHr, L"Input\0" )
        , m_pPrivateAllocator( NULL )
        , m_pBuffer( NULL )
        , m_bMediaTypeChanged( FALSE )
    {
        memset( &m_allocprops, 0, sizeof( m_allocprops ) );
    }


    ~CSampleGrabberInPin( )
    {
        if( m_pPrivateAllocator ) delete m_pPrivateAllocator;
    }
```

```
// override to provide major media type for fast connects
HRESULT GetMediaType( int iPosition, CMediaType *pMediaType );

// override this or GetMediaType is never called
STDMETHODIMP EnumMediaTypes( IEnumMediaTypes **ppEnum );

// override this to refuse any allocators besides
// the one the user wants, if this is set
STDMETHODIMP NotifyAllocator( IMemAllocator *pAllocator, BOOL bReadOnly );

// override this so we always return the special allocator,
// if necessary
STDMETHODIMP GetAllocator( IMemAllocator **ppAllocator );

HRESULT SetMediaType( const CMediaType *pmt );

// we override this to tell whoever's upstream of us what kind of
// properties we're going to demand to have
STDMETHODIMP GetAllocatorRequirements( ALLOCATOR_PROPERTIES *pProps );

};
```

Most of the variables and methods in *CSampleGrabberInPin* concern the allocation of buffers for stream data transfer with an upstream pin, but three methods, *GetMediaType*, *EnumMediaTypes*, and *SetMediaType*, are used during the negotiation of the media type in the pin-to-pin connection process. The constructor, *CSampleGrabberInPin::CSampleGrabberInPin*, calls its parent's constructor, *CTransInPlaceInputPin::CTransInPlaceInputPin*, clears a few variables, and zeroes some memory, while the destructor simply frees an associated *CSampleGrabberAllocator* object if one was created by the pin. Here are the method implementations for the rest of the class:

```
HRESULT CSampleGrabberInPin::GetMediaType( int iPosition,
                                           CMediaType * pMediaType )
{
    CheckPointer(pMediaType,E_POINTER);

    if (iPosition < 0) {
        return E_INVALIDARG;
    }
    if (iPosition > 0) {
        return VFW_S_NO_MORE_ITEMS;
    }

    *pMediaType = CMediaType( );
```

```
        pMediaType->SetType( ((CSampleGrabber*)m_pFilter)->m_mtAccept.Type( ) );

    return S_OK;
}


STDMETHODIMP CSampleGrabberInPin::EnumMediaTypes( IEnumMediaTypes **ppEnum )
{
    CheckPointer(ppEnum,E_POINTER);
    ValidateReadWritePtr(ppEnum,sizeof(IEnumMediaTypes *));

    // if the output pin isn't connected yet, offer the possibly
    // partially specified media type that has been set by the user

    if( !((CSampleGrabber*)m_pTIPFilter)->OutputPin( )->IsConnected() )
    {
        // Create a new reference counted enumerator

        *ppEnum = new CEnumMediaTypes( this, NULL );

        return (*ppEnum) ? NOERROR : E_OUTOFMEMORY;
    }

    // if the output pin is connected,
    // offer it's fully qualified media type

    return ((CSampleGrabber*)m_pTIPFilter)->OutputPin( )->
        GetConnected()->EnumMediaTypes( ppEnum );
}


STDMETHODIMP CSampleGrabberInPin::NotifyAllocator
    ( IMemAllocator *pAllocator, BOOL bReadOnly )
{
    if( m_pPrivateAllocator )
    {
        if( pAllocator != m_pPrivateAllocator )
        {
            return E_FAIL;
        }
        else
        {
            // if the upstream guy wants to be read only and we don't,
            // then that's bad
            // if the upstream guy doesn't request read only,
            // but we do, that's okay
            if( bReadOnly && !SampleGrabber( )->IsReadOnly( ) )
            {
                return E_FAIL;
            }
        }
```

```
            }
        }

        return CTransInPlaceInputPin::NotifyAllocator( pAllocator, bReadOnly );
    }

    STDMETHODIMP CSampleGrabberInPin::GetAllocator( IMemAllocator **ppAllocator )
    {
        if( m_pPrivateAllocator )
        {
            CheckPointer(ppAllocator,E_POINTER);

            *ppAllocator = m_pPrivateAllocator;
            m_pPrivateAllocator->AddRef( );
            return NOERROR;
        }
        else
        {
            return CTransInPlaceInputPin::GetAllocator( ppAllocator );
        }
    }


    HRESULT CSampleGrabberInPin::GetAllocatorRequirements
        ( ALLOCATOR_PROPERTIES *pProps )
    {
        CheckPointer(pProps,E_POINTER);

        if (m_pPrivateAllocator)
        {
            *pProps = m_allocprops;
            return S_OK;
        }
        else
        {
            return CTransInPlaceInputPin::GetAllocatorRequirements(pProps);
        }
    }


    HRESULT CSampleGrabberInPin::SetDeliveryBuffer( ALLOCATOR_PROPERTIES props,
                                                    BYTE * pBuffer )
    {
        // don't allow more than one buffer

        if( props.cBuffers != 1 )
        {
            return E_INVALIDARG;
        }
        if( !pBuffer )
```

```
    {
        return E_POINTER;
    }

    m_allocprops = props;
    m_pBuffer = pBuffer;

    // If there is an existing allocator, make sure that it is released
    // to prevent a memory leak
    if (m_pPrivateAllocator)
    {
        m_pPrivateAllocator->Release();
        m_pPrivateAllocator = NULL;
    }

    HRESULT hr = S_OK;

    m_pPrivateAllocator = new CSampleGrabberAllocator( this, &hr );
    if( !m_pPrivateAllocator )
    {
        return E_OUTOFMEMORY;
    }

    m_pPrivateAllocator->AddRef( );
    return hr;
}


HRESULT CSampleGrabberInPin::SetMediaType( const CMediaType *pmt )
{
    m_bMediaTypeChanged = TRUE;

    return CTransInPlaceInputPin::SetMediaType( pmt );
}
```

The *GetMediaType* method returns a pointer to a *CMediaType* object. We haven't covered this class before. The *CMediaType* class is a wrapper for the *AM_MEDIA_TYPE* structure, which provides accessor methods (such as *SetType*, *SetSubtype*, and *GetSampleSize*) for the fields in the *AM_MEDIA_TYPE* structure. In addition, the class overrides the assignment operator = and comparison operators *!=* and *==*, so when testing one instance of a *CMediaType* object with another, a test is made of each of the fields within the *AM_MEDIA_TYPE* structure.

The *EnumMediaTypes* method returns an enumerated list within an *IEnumMediaTypes* object of all the media types that the input pin will propose for the connection. Although *CBasePin* (the ancestor class for all pin objects) implements this functionality, *CTransInPlaceInputPin* (the ancestor class for this pin) overrides this behavior, so no types are returned when the input pin is unconnected. The Grabber Sample overrides this (yet again) so that media types are always returned, whether the pin is connected or unconnected.

If the output pin on the filter has already been connected, it has already negotiated its media type with a downstream filter. In that situation, the media type of the output pin is returned by *EnumMediaTypes* as the type required by the input pin. If the output pin isn't connected, the method instantiates an object of class *CEnumMediaTypes* (*IEnumMediaTypes* is an interface to *CEnumMediaTypes*) and returns a pointer to it. Because the constructor is passed with a reference to the *CSampleGrabberInPin* object, any media type established on the pin—perhaps by an earlier invocation of the *SetMediaTypes* method—will be returned in the enumeration.

The next few methods handle stream buffer allocation for the pin. The *NotifyAllocator* method determines whether the allocation is private—does it belong to the filter? If the application has allocated the memory for the pool of samples, the Grabber Sample must insist on using that allocator. If so, it then determines whether the upstream filter's output pin is requesting a read-only buffer. A read-only buffer is acceptable only if the Grabber Sample filter is not modifying the data. (The *m_bModifiesData* flag is set in the constructor if the buffer will be changed during the callback function.) If that test passes successfully or if the buffer is not private, the method is handed off to the parent, *CTransInPlaceInputPin::NotifyAllocator*. The *GetAllocator* method returns a pointer to the *IMemAllocator* object owned by the *CSampleGrabberInPin* object if the allocator is private; otherwise, it passes the request to the parent method, *CTransInPlaceInputPin::GetAllocator*. Much the same happens in the *Get-AllocatorRequirements* method. If the allocation is private, a pointer to *m_allocprops* is returned; otherwise, the request is passed to *CTransInPlace-InputPin::GetAllocatorRequirements*.

Allocation for the pin is handled through the *SetDeliveryBuffer* method, which stores its passed parameters in the *m_allocprops* and *m_pBuffer* variables within the *CSampleGrabberInPin* object. The method then releases any private allocators and instances a new private allocator, creating a new *CSampleGrabberAllocator*. In this case, the memory allocation is handled by the application, which passes a pointer to the buffer in *pBuffer*. Finally the media type for the input pin is set through a call to *SetMediaType*, which simply sets the local Boolean variable *m_bMediaTypeChanged* to *true* and then calls the parent method *CTransInPlaceInputPin::SetMediaType*. The parent classes do all the media type checking, which eventually resolves into a call to

CGrabberSample::CheckInputType. The implementation of the input pin is now complete. Together with the allocator, we have everything in place to implement the filter class.

There's just a little more definition work required to finish the entire specification of the filter. Here it is:

```
const AMOVIESETUP_PIN psudSampleGrabberPins[] =
{ { L"Input"              // strName
  , FALSE                 // bRendered
  , FALSE                 // bOutput
  , FALSE                 // bZero
  , FALSE                 // bMany
  , &CLSID_NULL           // clsConnectsToFilter
  , L""                   // strConnectsToPin
  , 0                     // nTypes
  , NULL                  // lpTypes
  }
, { L"Output"             // strName
  , FALSE                 // bRendered
  , TRUE                  // bOutput
  , FALSE                 // bZero
  , FALSE                 // bMany
  , &CLSID_NULL           // clsConnectsToFilter
  , L""                   // strConnectsToPin
  , 0                     // nTypes
  , NULL                  // lpTypes
  }
};


const AMOVIESETUP_FILTER sudSampleGrabber =
{ &CLSID_GrabberSample         // clsID
, L"Grabber Example Filter"    // strName
, MERIT_DO_NOT_USE             // dwMerit
, 2                            // nPins
, psudSampleGrabberPins };     // lpPin



// Needed for the CreateInstance mechanism
CFactoryTemplate g_Templates[]=
{
    { L"Grabber Example Filter"
        , &CLSID_GrabberSample
        , CSampleGrabber::CreateInstance
        , NULL
        , &sudSampleGrabber }

};
```

These data structures—*AMOVIESETUP_PIN* and *AMOVIESETUP_FILTER*—are used to identify the specifics of the filter to DirectShow. For example, the *strName* field of *AMOVIESETUP_FILTER* is the filter name as it shows up in GraphEdit or in any DirectShow enumeration of available filters. Changing that field will change the name as it appears in GraphEdit and across DirectShow.

Now, because we're creating a system-wide object, we need to add some entry points common to Microsoft Windows dynamic-link libraries (DLLs).

```
STDAPI DllRegisterServer()
{
    return AMovieDllRegisterServer2(TRUE);
}


STDAPI DllUnregisterServer()
{
    return AMovieDllRegisterServer2(FALSE);
}


//
// DllEntryPoint
//
extern "C" BOOL WINAPI DllEntryPoint(HINSTANCE, ULONG, LPVOID);

BOOL APIENTRY DllMain(HANDLE hModule,
                      DWORD  dwReason,
                      LPVOID lpReserved)
{
    return DllEntryPoint((HINSTANCE)(hModule), dwReason, lpReserved);
}
```

Finally, in a separate file, grabber.def, we define the DLL entry points for our filter.

```
LIBRARY     grabber

EXPORTS
            DllMain              PRIVATE
            DllGetClassObject    PRIVATE
            DllCanUnloadNow      PRIVATE
            DllRegisterServer    PRIVATE
            DllUnregisterServer  PRIVATE
```

When the project is compiled, you'll end up with a module named grabber.ax, which is a DLL object that must be registered with the system using the regsvr32.exe command. At the command line (and in the directory containing grabber.ax), type **regsvr32 grabber.ax**.

If all goes smoothly, you'll be informed that the DLL was successfully installed. The Grabber Sample filter is now available to all applications, including GraphEdit. Because you also have the class ID and interface ID for the filter, you can begin to use it in all your DirectShow applications.

Summary

In this chapter, we've covered the Sample Grabber from both the application side—that is, the use of the Sample Grabber to provide access to the media stream in your own DirectShow applications—and the Sample Grabber architecture. The design of the Sample Grabber is unusual, but it casts a lot of light on the internal design of DirectShow, the filter graph, and filters. With the Grabber Sample, you've begun to explore how application and filter come together in a synergistic way. Now we'll move on to a source filter and learn how media samples are created.

12

Writing DirectShow Source Filters

Of the three classes of Microsoft DirectShow filters—source, transform, and renderer—the source filter is the one that generates the stream data manipulated by the filter graph. Every filter graph has at least one source filter, and by its nature the source filter occupies the ultimate upstream position in the filter graph, coming before any other filters. The source filter is responsible for generating a continuous stream of media samples, beginning when the Filter Graph Manager runs the filter graph and ceasing when the filter graph is paused or stopped.

Source Filter Types

In a broad sense, there are three types of source filters used in DirectShow filter graphs—capture source filters, file source filters, and "creator" source filters. We're already quite familiar with capture source filters, such as the Microsoft DV Camcorder and VCR filter and the Logitech QuickCam Web filter, which we've used in numerous DirectShow applications. A capture source filter captures a live sample, converts it to a stream of media samples, and presents that stream on its output pins. Capture source filters are nearly always associated with devices, and in general, there's rarely a need for DirectShow programmers to write their own capture source filters. Any device that has a correctly written Windows Driver Model (WDM) driver will automatically appear as a filter available to DirectShow applications. DirectShow puts a filter wrapper around WDM and Video for Windows (VFW) device drivers so that the capture device, for example, can be used in a filter graph as a capture source filter. (See Figure 12-1.) If you really want or need to write your own capture driver filter, you can find the gory details in the Microsoft DirectX SDK documentation and Windows DDK documentation.

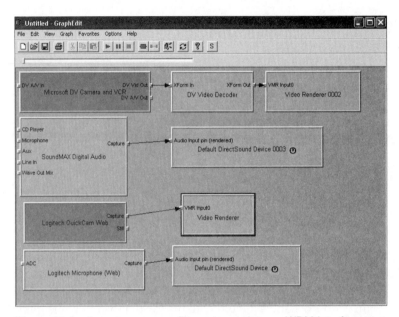

Figure 12-1   A capture source filter encapsulates a WDM interface to a hardware device

A file source filter acts as an interface between the world outside a Direct-Show filter graph and the filter graph. The File Source filter, for example, makes the Microsoft Windows file system available to DirectShow; it allows the contents of a disk-based file to be read into the filter graph. (See Figure 12-2.) Another filter, the File Source URL filter, takes a URL as its parameter and allows Web-based files to be read into a filter graph. (This is a technique that could potentially be very powerful.) We've already used the Stream Buffer Engine's source filter, a file source filter that reads stream data from files created by the Stream Buffer Engine's sink filter. The ASF Reader filter takes an ASF file and generates media streams from its contents.

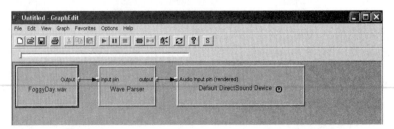

Figure 12-2   The File Source filter followed by a Wave Parser filter

With the notable exceptions of the SBE source filter and the ASF Reader, a file source filter normally sits upstream from a transform filter that acts as a file parser, translating the raw data read in by the file source filter into a series of media samples. The Wave Parser filter, for example, translates the WAV file format into a series of PCM media samples. Because the relationship between a file source filter and a parser filter is driven by the parser filter, the parser filter usually pulls the data from the file source filter. This is the reverse of the situation for capture ("live") source filters, which produce a regular stream of media samples and then push them to a pin on a downstream filter. Unless you're adding your own unique file media type to DirectShow, it's unlikely you'll need a custom parser transform filter. (You're a bit on your own here. There aren't any good examples of parser filters in the DirectX SDK samples.)

Finally there are source filters that create media samples in their entirety. This means that the sample data originates in the filter, based upon the internal settings and state of the filter. You can imagine a creator source filter acting as a "tone generator," for example, producing a stream of PCM data reflecting a waveform of a particular frequency. (If it were designed correctly, the COM interfaces on such a filter would allow you to adjust the frequency on the fly with a method invocation.) Another creator source filter could produce the color bars that video professionals use to help them adjust their equipment, which would clearly be useful in a DirectShow application targeted at videographers.

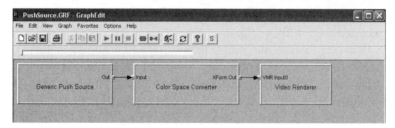

Figure 12-3   The Generic Push Source filter creates its own media stream

The PushSource filter example explored in this chapter (and shown in Figure 12-3) is a creator source filter that produces a media stream with a numbered series of video frames and that stops automatically when a certain number of frames have been generated. (When a source filter runs dry, all filters downstream of it eventually stop, waiting for more stream data.) PushSource is not complicated and only scratches the surface of what's possible with source filters. An excellent teaching example, PushSource exposes the internals of the source filter and, through that, much of how DirectShow handles the execution of the filter graph.

Source Filter Basics

As explained in the previous section, a source filter usually pushes its media samples to the input pin of a downstream filter. (The exception is file source filters.) Live sources, such as capture source filters, are always push sources because the data is generated somewhere outside the filter graph (such as in a camera or a microphone) and presented through a driver to the filter as a continuous stream of data. The PushSource filter covered in this chapter also pushes media samples to downstream filters, but these samples are generated in system memory rather than from a capture device.

A source filter generally doesn't have any input pins, but it can have as many output pins as desired. As an example, a source filter could have both capture and preview pins, or video and audio pins, or color and black-and-white pins. Because the output pins on a source filter are the ultimate source of media samples in the filter graph, the source filter fundamentally controls the execution of the filter graph. Filters downstream of a source filter will not begin execution until they receive samples from the source filter. If the source filter stops pushing samples downstream, the downstream filters will empty their buffers of media samples and then wait for more media samples to arrive.

The DirectShow filter graph has at least two execution threads: one or more streaming threads and the application thread. The application thread is created by the Filter Graph Manager and handles messages associated with filter graph execution, such as run, pause, and stop. You'll have one streaming thread per source filter in the filter graph, so a filter graph with separate source filters to capture audio and video would have at least two streaming threads. A streaming thread is typically shared by all the filters downstream of the source filter that creates it (although downstream filters can create their own threads for special processing needs, as parsers do regularly), and it's on these threads that transforms and rendering occur.

Once the streaming thread has been created, it enters a loop with the following steps. A free (that is, empty) sample is acquired from the allocator. This sample is then filled with data, timestamped, and delivered downstream. If no samples are available, the thread blocks until a sample becomes available. This loop is iterated as quickly as possible while the filter graph is executing, but the renderer filter can throttle execution of the filter graph. If a renderer's sample buffers fill up, filters upstream are forced to wait while their buffers fill up, a delay that could eventually propagate all the way back to the source filter. A renderer might block the streaming thread for one of two reasons: the filter graph could be paused, in which case the renderer is not rendering media samples (and the graph backs up with samples); or the renderer could be purposely slowing the flow of samples through the filter graph to ensure that each sample is presented at the appropriate time. When the renderer doesn't care about presentation time—such as in the case of a filter that renders to a file—the streaming thread runs as quickly as possible.

Seeking functionality should be implemented by the source filters where appropriate. Downstream filters and the Filter Graph Manager can use the *IMediaSeeking* interface to rewind or fast-forward through a stream. Seeking a live stream doesn't have to be implemented (it could be useful, such as in the case of a TV broadcast), but source filters should be able to seek as appropriate. When a seek command is issued, the Filter Graph Manager distributes it to all the filters in the filter graph. The command propagates upstream across the filter graph, from input pin to output pin, until a filter that can accept and process the seek command is found. Typically, the filter that creates the streaming thread implements the seek command because that filter is the one providing the graph with media samples and therefore can be sent requests for earlier or later samples. This is generally a source filter, although it can also be a parser transform filter.

When a source filter responds to a seek command, the media samples flowing through the filter graph change abruptly and discontinuously. The filter graph needs to flush all the data residing in the buffers of all downstream filters because all the data in the filter graph has become "stale"; that is, no longer synchronized with the new position in the media stream. The source filter flushes the data by issuing an *IPin::BeginFlush* call on the pin immediately downstream of the filter. This command forces the downstream filter to flush its buffers, and that downstream filter propagates the *IPin::BeginFlush* command further downstream until it encounters a renderer filter. The whole process of seeking and flushing looks like that shown in Figure 12-4. Both seek and flush commands are executed on the application thread, independent of the streaming thread.

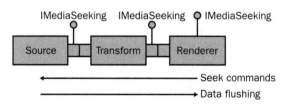

Figure 12-4   Seek and flush commands move in opposite directions across the filter graph

PushSource Source Filter

The PushSource source filter example generates a stream of black video frames (in RGB32 format) that have yellow frame numbers printed on them. The Push-Source filter generates frames at a rate of 30 per second at standard video speed, and it will keep going for 10 seconds (the value set by the *DEFAULT_DURATION* constant) for a total of 300 frames. In operation, the Push-Source filter—which appears in the list of DirectShow filters under the name "Generic Push Source"—looks like Figure 12-5.

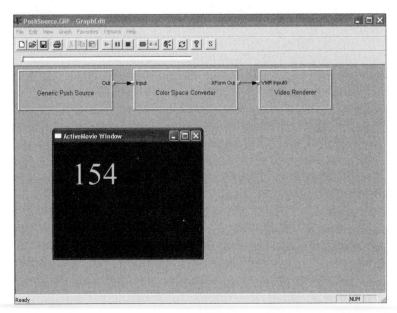

Figure 12-5   The PushSource filter creating a video stream with numbered frames

The DirectShow C++ base classes include three classes that are instrumental in implementing PushSource: *CSource*, which implements a basic source filter; *CSourceStream*, which implements the presentation of a stream on the source filter's output pin; and *CSourceSeeking*, which implements the seek command on the output pin of the source filter. If your source filter has more than one output pin (some do, most don't), you can't use *CSourceSeeking* as a basis for an implementation of the seek command. In that case, you'd need to coordinate between the two pins, which requires careful thread synchronization that *CSourceSeeking* doesn't handle. (You can use *CSourceStream* for multiple output pins.) In a simple source filter, such as PushSource, only a minimal implementation is required and nearly all of that is in the implementation of methods in *CSourceStream* and *CSourceSeeking*.

Implementing the Source Filter Class

The implementation of the source filter class *CPushSource* for the PushSource example is entirely straightforward. Only two methods need to be overridden: the class constructor, which creates the output pin, and *CPushSource::Create-Instance*, which calls the class constructor to create an instance of the filter. Here's the complete implementation of *CPushSource*:

```
// CPushSource class: Our source filter.

class CPushSource : public CSource
{

private:
    // Constructor is private
    // You have to use CreateInstance to create it.
    CPushSource(IUnknown *pUnk, HRESULT *phr);

public:
    static CUnknown * WINAPI CreateInstance(IUnknown *pUnk, HRESULT *phr);
};

CPushSource::CPushSource(IUnknown *pUnk, HRESULT *phr)
: CSource(NAME("PushSource"), pUnk, CLSID_PushSource)
{
    // Create the output pin.
    // The pin magically adds itself to the pin array.
    CPushPin *pPin = new CPushPin(phr, this);

    if (pPin == NULL)
    {
        *phr = E_OUTOFMEMORY;
    }
}

CUnknown * WINAPI CPushSource::CreateInstance(IUnknown *pUnk, HRESULT *phr)
{
    CPushSource *pNewFilter = new CPushSource(pUnk, phr );
    if (pNewFilter == NULL)
    {
        *phr = E_OUTOFMEMORY;
    }
    return pNewFilter;
}
```

This is all the code required to create the source filter object.

Implementing the Source Filter Output Pin Class

All the real work in the PushSource filter takes place inside the filter's output pin. The output pin class, *CPushPin*, is declared as a descendant of both the *CSourceStream* and *CSourceSeeking* classes, as shown in the following code:

```
class CPushPin : public CSourceStream, public CSourceSeeking
{
private:

    REFERENCE_TIME m_rtStreamTime;     // Stream time (relative to
                                       // when the graph started)
    REFERENCE_TIME m_rtSourceTime;     // Source time (relative to
                                       // ourselves)

    // A note about seeking and time stamps:

    // Suppose you have a file source that is N seconds long.
    // If you play the file from
    // the beginning at normal playback rate (1x),
    // the presentation time for each frame
    // will match the source file:

    // Frame:  0    1    2 ... N
    // Time:   0    1    2 ... N

    // Now suppose you seek in the file to an arbitrary spot,
    // frame i. After the seek
    // command, the graph's clock resets to zero.
    // Therefore, the first frame delivered
    // after the seek has a presentation time of zero:

    // Frame:  i    i+1  i+2 ...
    // Time:   0    1    2 ...

    // Therefore we have to track
    // stream time and source time independently.
    // (If you do not support seeking,
    // then source time always equals presentation time.)

    REFERENCE_TIME m_rtFrameLength;    // Frame length
    int m_iFrameNumber;  // Current frame number that we are rendering

    BOOL m_bDiscontinuity; // If true, set the discontinuity flag

    CCritSec m_cSharedState;  // Protects our internal state
    ULONG_PTR m_gdiplusToken; // GDI+ initialization token
```

```
        // Private function to draw our bitmaps.
        HRESULT WriteToBuffer(LPWSTR wszText, BYTE *pData,
                            VIDEOINFOHEADER *pVih);


        // Update our internal state after a seek command.
        void UpdateFromSeek();


        // The following methods support seeking
        // using other time formats besides
        // reference time. If you want to support only
        // seek-by-reference-time, you
        // do not have to override these methods.
        STDMETHODIMP SetTimeFormat(const GUID *pFormat);
        STDMETHODIMP GetTimeFormat(GUID *pFormat);
        STDMETHODIMP IsUsingTimeFormat(const GUID *pFormat);
        STDMETHODIMP IsFormatSupported(const GUID *pFormat);
        STDMETHODIMP QueryPreferredFormat(GUID *pFormat);
        STDMETHODIMP ConvertTimeFormat(LONGLONG *pTarget,
                                    const GUID *pTargetFormat,
                                    LONGLONG Source,
                                    const GUID *pSourceFormat );
        STDMETHODIMP SetPositions(LONGLONG *pCurrent, DWORD CurrentFlags,
                                LONGLONG *pStop, DWORD StopFlags);
        STDMETHODIMP GetDuration(LONGLONG *pDuration);
        STDMETHODIMP GetStopPosition(LONGLONG *pStop);


        // Conversions between reference times and frame numbers.
        LONGLONG FrameToTime(LONGLONG frame) {
            LONGLONG f = frame * m_rtFrameLength;
            return f;
        }
        LONGLONG TimeToFrame(LONGLONG rt) { return rt / m_rtFrameLength; }


        GUID m_TimeFormat;  // Which time format is currently active

protected:
    // Override CSourceStream methods.
    HRESULT GetMediaType(CMediaType *pMediaType);
    HRESULT CheckMediaType(const CMediaType *pMediaType);
    HRESULT DecideBufferSize(IMemAllocator *pAlloc,
                            ALLOCATOR_PROPERTIES *pRequest);
    HRESULT FillBuffer(IMediaSample *pSample);


    // The following methods support seeking.
    HRESULT OnThreadStartPlay();
    HRESULT ChangeStart();
    HRESULT ChangeStop();
    HRESULT ChangeRate();
    STDMETHODIMP SetRate(double dRate);
```

```
public:

    CPushPin(HRESULT *phr, CSource *pFilter);
    ~CPushPin();

    // Override this to expose ImediaSeeking.
    STDMETHODIMP NonDelegatingQueryInterface(REFIID riid, void **ppv);

    // We don't support any quality control.
    STDMETHODIMP Notify(IBaseFilter *pSelf, Quality q)
    {
        return E_FAIL;
    }

};
```

Let's begin with an examination of the three public methods defined in *CPushPin* and implemented in the following code: the class constructor, the destructor, and *CPushPin::NonDelegatingQueryInterface*.

```
CPushPin::CPushPin(HRESULT *phr, CSource *pFilter)
: CSourceStream(NAME("CPushPin"), phr, pFilter, L"Out"),
  CSourceSeeking(NAME("PushPin2Seek"), (IPin*)this, phr, &m_cSharedState),
  m_rtStreamTime(0),
  m_rtSourceTime(0),
  m_iFrameNumber(0),
  m_rtFrameLength(Fps2FrameLength(DEFAULT_FRAME_RATE))
{
    // Initialize GDI+.
    GdiplusStartupInput gdiplusStartupInput;
    Status s = GdiplusStartup(&m_gdiplusToken, &gdiplusStartupInput, NULL);
    if (s != Ok)
    {
        *phr = E_FAIL;
    }

    // SEEKING: Set the source duration and the initial stop time.
    m_rtDuration = m_rtStop = DEFAULT_DURATION;
}

CPushPin::~CPushPin()
{
    // Shut down GDI+.
    GdiplusShutdown(m_gdiplusToken);
}

STDMETHODIMP CPushPin::NonDelegatingQueryInterface(REFIID riid, void **ppv)
{
```

```
if( riid == IID_IMediaSeeking )
{
    return CSourceSeeking::NonDelegatingQueryInterface( riid, ppv );
}
return CSourceStream::NonDelegatingQueryInterface(riid, ppv);
}
```

The class constructor invokes the constructors for the two ancestor classes of *CPushPin*, *CSourceStream* and *CSourceSeeking*, and then the GDI+ (Microsoft's 2D graphics library) is initialized. GDI+ will create the numbered video frames streamed over the pin. The class destructor shuts down GDI+, and *CPushPin::NonDelegatingQueryInterface* determines whether a *QueryInterface* call issued to the PushSource filter object is handled by *CSourceStream* or *CSourceSeeking*. Because only seek commands are handled by *CSourceSeeking*, only those commands are passed to that implementation.

Negotiating Connections on a Source Filter

CPushPin has two methods to handle the media type negotiation, *CPushPin::GetMediaType* and *CPushPin::CheckMediaType*. These methods, together with the method *CPushPin::DecideBufferSize*, handle pin-to-pin connection negotiation, as implemented in the following code:

```
HRESULT CPushPin::GetMediaType(CMediaType *pMediaType)
{
    CheckPointer(pMediaType, E_POINTER);

    CAutoLock cAutoLock(m_pFilter->pStateLock());

    // Call our helper function that fills in the media type.
    return CreateRGBVideoType(pMediaType, 32, DEFAULT_WIDTH,
                              DEFAULT_HEIGHT, DEFAULT_FRAME_RATE);
}


HRESULT CPushPin::CheckMediaType(const CMediaType *pMediaType)
{
    CAutoLock lock(m_pFilter->pStateLock());

    // Is it a video type?
    if (pMediaType->majortype != MEDIATYPE_Video)
    {
        return E_FAIL;
    }

    // Is it 32-bit RGB?
    if ((pMediaType->subtype != MEDIASUBTYPE_RGB32))
```

```
        {
            return E_FAIL;
        }

        // Is it a VIDEOINFOHEADER type?
        if ((pMediaType->formattype == FORMAT_VideoInfo) &&
            (pMediaType->cbFormat >= sizeof(VIDEOINFOHEADER)) &&
            (pMediaType->pbFormat != NULL))
        {

            VIDEOINFOHEADER *pVih = (VIDEOINFOHEADER*)pMediaType->pbFormat;

            // We don't do source rects.
            if (!IsRectEmpty(&(pVih->rcSource)))
            {
                return E_FAIL;
            }

            // Valid frame rate?
            if (pVih->AvgTimePerFrame != m_rtFrameLength)
            {
                return E_FAIL;
            }

            // Everything checked out.
            return S_OK;
        }

        return E_FAIL;
}

HRESULT CPushPin::DecideBufferSize(IMemAllocator *pAlloc,
                                   ALLOCATOR_PROPERTIES *pRequest)
{
    CAutoLock cAutoLock(m_pFilter->pStateLock());

    HRESULT hr;

    VIDEOINFO *pvi = (VIDEOINFO*) m_mt.Format();
    ASSERT(pvi != NULL);

    if (pRequest->cBuffers == 0)
    {
        pRequest->cBuffers = 1;  // We need at least one buffer
    }

    // Buffer size must be at least big enough to hold our image.
    if ((long)pvi->bmiHeader.biSizeImage > pRequest->cBuffer)
    {
```

```
        pRequest->cbBuffer = pvi->bmiHeader.biSizeImage;
    }

    // Try to set these properties.
    ALLOCATOR_PROPERTIES Actual;
    hr = pAlloc->SetProperties(pRequest, &Actual);

    if (FAILED(hr))
    {
        return hr;
    }

    // Check what we actually got.

    if (Actual.cbBuffer < pRequest->cbBuffer)
    {
        return E_FAIL;
    }

    return S_OK;
}
```

All three methods begin with the inline creation of a *CAutoLock* object, a class DirectShow uses to lock a critical section of code. The lock is released when *CAutoLock*'s destructor is called—in this case, when the object goes out of scope when the method exits. This is a clever and simple way to implement critical sections of code. *CPushPin::GetMediaType* always returns a media type for RGB32 video because that's the only type it supports. The media type is built in a call to *CreateRGBVideoType*, a helper function that can be easily rewritten to handle the creation of a broader array of media types. *CPush-Pin::CheckMediaType* ensures that any presented media type exactly matches the RGB32 type supported by the pin; any deviation from the one media type supported by the pin results in failure. Finally, *CPushPin::DecideBufferSize* examines the size of each sample (in this case, a video frame) and requests at least one buffer of that size. The method will accept more storage if offered but will settle for no less than that minimum amount. These three methods must be implemented by every source filter.

Implementing Media Sample Creation Methods

One media sample creation method must be implemented with *CPushPin*. This is the method by which video frames are created and passed along as media samples. When the streaming thread is created, it goes into a loop, and *CPush-Pin::FillBuffer* is called every time through the loop as long as the filter is active (either paused or running). In *CPushPin*, this method is combined with another, internal, method, *CPushPin::WriteToBuffer*, which actually creates the image, as shown in the following code:

```
HRESULT CPushPin::FillBuffer(IMediaSample *pSample)
{
    HRESULT hr;

    BYTE *pData;
    long cbData;

    WCHAR msg[256];

    // Get a pointer to the buffer.
    pSample->GetPointer(&pData);
    cbData = pSample->GetSize();

    // Check if the downstream filter is changing the format.
    CMediaType *pmt;
    hr = pSample->GetMediaType((AM_MEDIA_TYPE**)&pmt);
    if (hr == S_OK)
    {
        SetMediaType(pmt);
        DeleteMediaType(pmt);
    }

    // Get our format information
    ASSERT(m_mt.formattype == FORMAT_VideoInfo);
    ASSERT(m_mt.cbFormat >= sizeof(VIDEOINFOHEADER));

    VIDEOINFOHEADER *pVih = (VIDEOINFOHEADER*)m_mt.pbFormat;

    {
        // Scope for the state lock,
        // which protects the frame number and ref times.
        CAutoLock cAutoLockShared(&m_cSharedState);

        // Have we reached the stop time yet?
        if (m_rtSourceTime >= m_rtStop)
        {
            // This will cause the base class
            // to send an EndOfStream downstream.
            return S_FALSE;
        }

        // Time stamp the sample.
        REFERENCE_TIME rtStart, rtStop;
```

```
        rtStart = (REFERENCE_TIME)(m_rtStreamTime / m_dRateSeeking);
        rtStop  = rtStart + (REFERENCE_TIME)(pVih->AvgTimePerFrame /
                                             m_dRateSeeking);

        pSample->SetTime(&rtStart, &rtStop);

        // Write the frame number into our text buffer.
        swprintf(msg, L"%d", m_iFrameNumber);

        // Increment the frame number
        // and ref times for the next time through the loop.
        m_iFrameNumber++;
        m_rtSourceTime += pVih->AvgTimePerFrame;
        m_rtStreamTime += pVih->AvgTimePerFrame;

    }

    // Private method to draw the image.
    hr = WriteToBuffer(msg, pData, pVih);

    if (FAILED(hr))
    {
        return hr;
    }

    // Every frame is a key frame.
    pSample->SetSyncPoint(TRUE);

    return S_OK;
}

HRESULT CPushPin::WriteToBuffer(LPWSTR wszText, BYTE *pData,
                                VIDEOINFOHEADER *pVih)
{
    ASSERT(pVih->bmiHeader.biBitCount == 32);

    DWORD dwWidth, dwHeight;
    long lStride;
    BYTE *pbTop;

    // Get the width, height, top row of pixels, and stride.
    GetVideoInfoParameters(pVih, pData, &dwWidth, &dwHeight,
                           &lStride, &pbTop, false);

    // Create a GDI+ bitmap object to manage our image buffer.
    Bitmap bitmap((int)dwWidth, (int)dwHeight, abs(lStride),
                  PixelFormat32bppRGB, pData);
```

```
// Create a GDI+ graphics object to manage the drawing.
Graphics g(&bitmap);

// Turn on anti-aliasing.
g.SetSmoothingMode(SmoothingModeAntiAlias);
g.SetTextRenderingHint(TextRenderingHintAntiAlias);

// Erase the background.
g.Clear(Color(0x0, 0, 0, 0));

// GDI+ is top-down by default,
// so if our image format is bottom-up, we need
// to set a transform on the Graphics object to flip the image.
if (pVih->bmiHeader.biHeight > 0)
{
    // Flip the image around the X axis.
    g.ScaleTransform(1.0, -1.0);
    // Move it back into place.
    g.TranslateTransform(0, (float)dwHeight, MatrixOrderAppend);
}

SolidBrush brush(Color(0xFF, 0xFF, 0xFF, 0));   // Yellow brush
Font       font(FontFamily::GenericSerif(), 48); // Big serif type
RectF      rcBounds(30, 30, (float)dwWidth,
                    (float)dwHeight);  // Bounding rectangle

// Draw the text
g.DrawString(
    wszText, -1,
    &font,
    rcBounds,
    StringFormat::GenericDefault(),
    &brush);

    return S_OK;
}
```

Upon entering *CPushPin::FillBuffer*, the media sample is examined for a valid media type. Then a thread lock is executed, and the method determines whether the source filter's stop time has been reached. If it has, the routine returns *S_FALSE*, indicating that a media sample will not be generated by the method. This will cause the downstream buffers to empty, leaving filters waiting for media samples from the source filter.

If the filter stop time has not been reached, the sample's timestamp is set with a call to *IMediaSample::SetTime*. This timestamp is composed of two pieces (both in *REFERENCE_TIME* format of 100-nanosecond intervals), indicating the sample's start time and stop time. The calculation here creates a series of timestamps separated by the time per frame (in this case, one thirtieth of a second). At this point, the frame number is written to a string stored in the object and then incremented.

That frame number is put to work in *CPushPin::WriteToBuffer*, which creates the RGB32-based video frame using GDI+. The method makes a call to the helper function *GetVideoInfoParameters*, retrieving the video parameters it uses to create a bitmap of appropriate width and height. With a few GDI+ calls, *CPushPin::WriteToBuffer* clears the background (to black) and then inverts the drawing image if the video format is bottom-up rather than top-down (the default for GDI+). A brush and then a font are selected, and the frame number is drawn to the bitmap inside a bounding rectangle.

Seek Functionality on a Source Filter

CPushPin inherits from both *CSourceStream* and *CSourceSeeking*. *CSourceSeeking* allows the source filter's output pin to process and respond to seek commands. In the case of the PushSource filter, a seek command causes the frame count to rewind or fast-forward to a new value. Because this filter is *frame-seekable* (meaning we can position it to any arbitrary frame within the legal range), it needs to implement a number of other methods. The following code shows the basic methods that implement seek functionality:

```
void CPushPin::UpdateFromSeek()
{
    if (ThreadExists())    // Filter is active?
    {
        DeliverBeginFlush();

        // Shut down the thread and stop pushing data.
        Stop();
        DeliverEndFlush();

        // Restart the thread and start pushing data again.
        Pause();

        // We'll set the discontinuity flag on the next sample.
    }
}


HRESULT CPushPin::OnThreadStartPlay()
{
    m_bDiscontinuity = TRUE; // Set the discontinuity flag on the next sample
```

```
        // Send a NewSegment call downstream.
        return DeliverNewSegment(m_rtStart, m_rtStop, m_dRateSeeking);
    }

    HRESULT CPushPin::ChangeStart( )
    {
        // Reset stream time to zero and the source time to m_rtStart.
        {
            CAutoLock lock(CSourceSeeking::m_pLock);
            m_rtStreamTime = 0;
            m_rtSourceTime = m_rtStart;
            m_iFrameNumber = (int)(m_rtStart / m_rtFrameLength);
        }
        UpdateFromSeek();
        return S_OK;
    }


    HRESULT CPushPin::ChangeStop( )
    {
        {
            CAutoLock lock(CSourceSeeking::m_pLock);
            if (m_rtSourceTime < m_rtStop)
            {
                return S_OK;
            }
        }

        // We're already past the new stop time. Flush the graph.
        UpdateFromSeek();
        return S_OK;
    }


    //----------------------------------------------------------------------
    HRESULT CPushPin::SetRate(double dRate)
    {
        if (dRate <= 0.0)
        {
            return E_INVALIDARG;
        }
        {
            CAutoLock lock(CSourceSeeking::m_pLock);
            m_dRateSeeking = dRate;
        }
        UpdateFromSeek();
        return S_OK;
    }
```

```
// Because we override SetRate,
// the ChangeRate method won't ever be called. (It is only
// ever called by SetRate.)
// But it's pure virtual, so it needs a dummy implementation.
HRESULT CPushPin::ChangeRate() { return S_OK; }
```

CPushPin::UpdateFromSeek forces the flush of the filter graph that needs to take place every time a seek is performed on the source filter. The buffer flushing process has four steps. Flushing begins (on the downstream pin) when *DeliverBeginFlush* is invoked. Next the streaming thread is stopped, suspending buffer processing throughout the filter graph. Then *DeliverEndFlush* is invoked; this sets up the downstream filters to receive new media samples. The streaming thread is then restarted. When restarted, *CPushPin::OnThreadStartPlay* is called, and any processing associated with starting the filter must be performed here. The new start, stop, and rate values for the stream are delivered downstream. If the filter does anything complicated to the threads, it's not hard to create a deadlock situation in which the entire filter graph seizes up, waiting for a lock that will never be released. Filter developers are strongly encouraged to read "Threads and Critical Sections" under "Writing DirectShow Filters" in the DirectX SDK documentation.

When the start position of the stream changes, *CPushPin::ChangeStart* is invoked. This method resets the stream time to zero (the current time, relatively, as the stream time counts upward while the filter runs) and changes the source time to the requested start time. This translates into a new frame number, which is calculated. *CPushPin::UpdateFromSeek* is called at the end of the routine so that any buffers in the filter graph can be flushed to make way for the new stream data.

When the filter receives a seek command that resets the stop position of the stream, *CPushPin::ChangeStop* is invoked. This method checks to see whether the new stop time is past the current time. If it is, the graph is flushed with a call to *CPushPin::UpdateFromSeek*.

The playback rate of a stream can be adjusted through a call to the *IMediaSeeking* interface. The playback rate of the PushSource filter, for example, is 30 frames a second (fps), but it could be adjusted to 15 or 60 fps or any other value. When the playback rate is changed, *CPushPin::SetRate* is invoked. It modifies the internal variable containing the playback rate and then calls *CPushPin::UpdateFromSeek* to flush the downstream filters. It's not necessary to override *CSourceSeeking::SetRate*, but we've overridden it here in *CPushPin* because this version includes a parameter check on the rate value to ensure its validity.

All the routines discussed thus far handle seeking from a base of the DirectShow reference time, in units of 100 nanoseconds. DirectShow filters can also support other time formats. This can be handy when dealing with video, which is parceled out in units of frames, or fields. A source filter doesn't need to implement multiple time formats for seeking, but the PushSource filter does. These *CPushPin* methods, overridden from *CSourceSeeking*, allow the Push-Source filter to work in a time base of frames, as shown in the following code:

```
STDMETHODIMP CPushPin::SetTimeFormat(const GUID *pFormat)
{
    CAutoLock cAutoLock(m_pFilter->pStateLock());
    CheckPointer(pFormat, E_POINTER);

    if (m_pFilter->IsActive())
    {
        // Cannot switch formats while running.
        return VFW_E_WRONG_STATE;
    }

    if (S_OK != IsFormatSupported(pFormat))
    {
        // We don't support this time format.
        return E_INVALIDARG;
    }
    m_TimeFormat = *pFormat;
    return S_OK;
}


STDMETHODIMP CPushPin::GetTimeFormat(GUID *pFormat)
{
    CAutoLock cAutoLock(m_pFilter->pStateLock());
    CheckPointer(pFormat, E_POINTER);
    *pFormat = m_TimeFormat;
    return S_OK;
}


STDMETHODIMP CPushPin::IsUsingTimeFormat(const GUID *pFormat)
{
    CAutoLock cAutoLock(m_pFilter->pStateLock());
    CheckPointer(pFormat, E_POINTER);
    return (*pFormat == m_TimeFormat ? S_OK : S_FALSE);
}


STDMETHODIMP CPushPin::IsFormatSupported( const GUID * pFormat)
{
    CheckPointer(pFormat, E_POINTER);
    if (*pFormat == TIME_FORMAT_MEDIA_TIME)
    {
        return S_OK;
    }
```

```
        else if (*pFormat == TIME_FORMAT_FRAME)
        {
            return S_OK;
        }
        else
        {
            return S_FALSE;
        }
    }


STDMETHODIMP CPushPin::QueryPreferredFormat(GUID *pFormat)
{
    CheckPointer(pFormat, E_POINTER);
    *pFormat = TIME_FORMAT_FRAME; // Doesn't really matter which we prefer
    return S_OK;
}


STDMETHODIMP CPushPin::ConvertTimeFormat(
    LONGLONG *pTarget,             // Receives the converted time value.
    const GUID *pTargetFormat,     // Specifies the target format
                                   // for the conversion.
    LONGLONG Source,               // Time value to convert.
    const GUID *pSourceFormat)     // Time format for the Source time.
{
    CheckPointer(pTarget, E_POINTER);

    // Either of the format GUIDs can be NULL,
    // which means "use the current time format"
    GUID TargetFormat, SourceFormat;
    TargetFormat = (pTargetFormat == NULL ? m_TimeFormat : *pTargetFormat );
    SourceFormat = (pSourceFormat == NULL ? m_TimeFormat : *pSourceFormat );

    if (TargetFormat == TIME_FORMAT_MEDIA_TIME)
    {
        if (SourceFormat == TIME_FORMAT_FRAME)
        {
            *pTarget = FrameToTime(Source);
            return S_OK;
        }
        if (SourceFormat == TIME_FORMAT_MEDIA_TIME)
        {
            // no-op
            *pTarget = Source;
            return S_OK;
        }
        return E_INVALIDARG;  // Invalid source format.
    }
```

```
        if (TargetFormat == TIME_FORMAT_FRAME)
        {
            if (SourceFormat == TIME_FORMAT_MEDIA_TIME)
            {
                *pTarget = TimeToFrame(Source);
                return S_OK;
            }
            if (SourceFormat == TIME_FORMAT_FRAME)
            {
                // no-op
                *pTarget = Source;
                return S_OK;
            }
            return E_INVALIDARG;  // Invalid source format.
        }

        return E_INVALIDARG;  // Invalid target format.
    }


    STDMETHODIMP CPushPin::SetPositions(
        LONGLONG *pCurrent,  // New current position (can be NULL!)
        DWORD CurrentFlags,
        LONGLONG *pStop,      // New stop position (can be NULL!)
        DWORD StopFlags)
    {
        HRESULT hr;

        if (m_TimeFormat == TIME_FORMAT_FRAME)
        {
            REFERENCE_TIME rtCurrent = 0, rtStop = 0;
            if (pCurrent)
            {
                rtCurrent = FrameToTime(*pCurrent);
            }
            if (pStop)
            {
                rtStop = FrameToTime(*pStop);
            }
            hr = CSourceSeeking::SetPositions(&rtCurrent, CurrentFlags,
                                              &rtStop, StopFlags);
            if (SUCCEEDED(hr))
            {
                // The AM_SEEKING_ReturnTime flag
                // means the caller wants the input times
                // converted to the current time format.
                if (pCurrent && (CurrentFlags & AM_SEEKING_ReturnTime))
                {
                    *pCurrent = rtCurrent;
```

```
            }
            if (pStop && (StopFlags & AM_SEEKING_ReturnTime))
            {
                *pStop = rtStop;
            }
        }
    }
    else
    {
        // Simple pass thru'
        hr = CSourceSeeking::SetPositions(pCurrent, CurrentFlags,
                                          pStop, StopFlags);
    }
    return hr;
}


STDMETHODIMP CPushPin::GetDuration(LONGLONG *pDuration)
{
    HRESULT hr = CSourceSeeking::GetDuration(pDuration);
    if (SUCCEEDED(hr))
    {
        if (m_TimeFormat == TIME_FORMAT_FRAME)
        {
            *pDuration = TimeToFrame(*pDuration);
        }
    }
    return S_OK;
}


STDMETHODIMP CPushPin::GetStopPosition(LONGLONG *pStop)
{
    HRESULT hr = CSourceSeeking::GetStopPosition(pStop);
    if (SUCCEEDED(hr))
    {
        if (m_TimeFormat == TIME_FORMAT_FRAME)
        {
            *pStop = TimeToFrame(*pStop);
        }
    }
    return S_OK;
}
```

A request to change the time format can be set with a call to *CPush-Pin::SetTimeFormat*; the passed parameter is a GUID, which describes the time format. (The list of time format GUIDs can be found in the DirectX SDK documentation.) If *CPushPin::IsSupportedFormat* reports that the time format is supported, the format is changed. The two supported formats for *CPushPin* are *TIME_FORMAT_MEDIA_TIME*, which is the reference time of 100-nanosecond units, and *TIME_FORMAT_FRAME*, in which each unit constitutes one video frame.

Conversions between time formats are performed in *CPushPin::ConvertTimeFormat*. Because PushSource supports two time formats, the routine must perform conversions between *TIME_FORMAT_MEDIA_TIME* and *TIME_FORMAT_FRAME*. *CPushPin::GetDuration*, *CPushPin::GetStopPosition*, and *CPushPin::SetPositions* are overridden because their return values must reflect the current time format. (Imagine what would happen if the Filter Graph Manager, expecting frames, was informed there were 300,000,000 of them!)

There's just a bit more C++ code needed to handle the COM interfaces, which we've seen previously in the YUVGray and SampleGrabber filters. When compiled and registered (which should happen automatically), the "Generic Push Source" filter will appear in the list of DirectShow filters in GraphEdit.

Summary

Source filters are absolutely essential because they generate the media samples that pass through the filter graph until rendered. Most hardware devices don't need custom DirectShow filters because DirectShow has wrappers to "automagically" make WDM and VFW device drivers appear as filters to DirectShow applications. Other source filters can read data from a file, from a URL, and so forth. Some source filters, such as the PushSource example explored in this chapter, create their own media streams. In large part, control of the filter graph is driven by the source filters it contains. In the implementation of PushSource, we've explored how the different operating states of the filter graph are reflected in the design of a source filter. Therefore, a detailed study of source filters reveals how DirectShow executes a filter graph.

13

Creating and Working with DirectX Media Objects

Microsoft DirectShow filters provide a flexible and extensible interface to add features to DirectShow applications, but they also have a lot of overhead, in both design and implementation, beyond the requirements that serve their basic functionality. DirectShow filters must handle buffer allocation, media type negotiation, and filter connection methods, and much of the implementation deals with these necessary features of a filter. Fortunately, there is another option: the Microsoft DirectX Media Object (DMO), which offers the most important feature of a transform filter—the ability to manipulate a media stream—without the overhead of a filter implementation. Although DMOs are an important feature of DirectShow, they are *portable*, which means that they do not require a filter graph for operation and can be used in non-DirectShow applications. Within DirectShow, the only restriction on DMOs is that they can't be used as transitions or effects in conjunction with the DirectShow Editing Services (DES) covered in Chapter 8. A separate architecture is required for DES transitions and effects; more information on that topic can be found in the DirectX SDK documentation.

DMOs were introduced with DirectX 8 as a way to speed the development of plug-in video and audio effects within the DirectX architecture. Although technically less sophisticated than DirectShow filters, DMOs can be brought into a filter graph and used like filters. DirectShow wraps DMOs in a filter, which makes DMOs appear as though they are fully functional DirectShow filters. Through this wrapper, DMOs can be instantiated, connected, and manipulated just like any other filter in the filter graph.

Most DMOs perform some basic audio or video processing on a stream, such as taking an audio stream and adding a delay effect to the signal. These effects are sometimes performed *in place* (that is, on an existing buffer of stream data without any need to copy it to a separate location) and don't require any input from the filter graph. DMOs are entirely self-contained and don't handle even the basic task of acquiring or sending along buffers of data. Instead, the DMO is called by the client, which presents a buffer to it. The client receives the processed data when the DMO's operation is complete.

All of this means that DMOs represent a lightweight approach for the development of DirectShow effects, encoders, and decoders. DMO audio effects can also be used by DirectSound, the audio component of the DirectX multimedia API. You can write an audio effect DMO—perhaps for a DirectShow application—and use it later in a DirectSound application. Because both DirectShow and DirectSound are important technologies for PC gaming development, using DMOs could potentially save a lot of time. In addition, any other application can use a DMO directly because DMOs aren't tied to any DirectX technology.

Looking Inside a DMO

A DMO is a COM object that takes an input stream and produces one or more output streams. Most commonly, a DMO will have one input stream and one output stream, but this isn't an absolute rule. A DMO must define the number of its input and output streams at compile time, and these can not change during execution of the DMO object. Unlike DirectShow filters, DMOs can't add input or output pins as they're needed.

Like a DirectShow filter, a DMO supports media types. The DMO wrapper for DirectShow handles media type negotiation with other filters, but the DMO itself can specify what media types it's prepared to support. Before any stream data can be processed by the DMO, its input and output media types must be set by the client application using the DMO. (Again, this is done by the DMO wrapper in DirectShow.)

DMOs don't allocate buffer pools to handle data processing, nor do they arbitrate who owns buffers of data. DMOs operate on buffers presented to them by the client application. Some DMOs perform in-place transformations of data, passing along the same buffer that they were given. Otherwise, the DMO will copy the input buffer to an output buffer during the transformation process.

Minimal overhead is required to implement a DMO architecture. The DMO interacts only minimally with the application that instantiates and controls it. These interactions are defined by the COM interfaces presented by the DMO. All DMOs must support at least one COM interface, *IMediaObject*. If the DMO is going to be used from DirectShow, the DMO must support the COM aggregation. If the DMO is going to be used within DirectSound applications, another interface must be implemented and supported: *IMediaObjectInPlace*, which handles in-place transformations of buffer data.

Using an Audio Delay DMO Within a DirectShow Application

Before we explore the implementation specifics of a DMO, it'll be useful to examine how a DMO is instantiated, connected, and executed within a DirectShow filter graph. In this chapter, we'll be working with a very simple audio DMO, SimpleDelay, which adds a measured audio delay to an audio stream passed through it. The duration of the delay, 2000 milliseconds, is hard-coded into the DMO, as is the *wet/dry mix* (the mix ratio between the delayed signal and the original signal), which is set at 25 percent. A full-featured DMO would have COM interfaces to allow you to change these parameters in real time, but SimpleDelay doesn't have them. (At this point, you should compile the SimpleDelay sample DMO, along with the DShowDemo application that's supplied with it.)

When you launch the DShowDemo (which uses the DMO), the application will allow you to select a valid WAV file. After a WAV file has been located, the Play button will be enabled, as shown in Figure 13-1.

Figure 13-1   The DShowDemo application that uses the SimpleDelay DMO

During WAV playback, you'll be able to hear the delayed audio signal, mixed in with the main audio signal. It'll be somewhat faint because the wet/dry mix is set at 25 percent. You can change that value by opening the Delay.h file and recompiling the SimpleDelay DMO. You can also do the same thing with the delay time. It's not real-time adjustment, but it's better than nothing.

The source code for DShowDemo is very brief. It does little more than manage the dialog box and build the filter graph. The filter graph building takes place in the *LoadWavFile* function, as shown here:

```
HRESULT LoadWavFile(HWND hwnd, LPTSTR szFileName)
{
    IBaseFilter  *pDmoFilter = NULL;
```

```
        HRESULT hr;

        CleanUp(); // Restore to original state

        // Create the Filter Graph Manager and query for interfaces.
        hr = CoCreateInstance(CLSID_FilterGraph, NULL, CLSCTX_INPROC_SERVER,
                IID_IGraphBuilder, (void **)&g_pGraph);

        if (FAILED(hr))
        {
            return hr;
        }

        g_pGraph->QueryInterface(IID_IMediaControl, (void **)&g_pMediaControl);
        g_pGraph->QueryInterface(IID_IMediaEventEx, (void **)&g_pEvent);

        g_pEvent->SetNotifyWindow((OAHWND)hwnd, WM_GRAPHNOTIFY, 0);

        // Create the DMO Wrapper filter.
        hr = CoCreateInstance(CLSID_DMOWrapperFilter, NULL,
            CLSCTX_INPROC, IID_IBaseFilter, (void **)&pDmoFilter);

        if (FAILED(hr))
        {
            return hr;
        }

        IDMOWrapperFilter *pWrap;
        pDmoFilter->QueryInterface(IID_IDMOWrapperFilter, (void **)&pWrap);

        hr = pWrap->Init(CLSID_Delay, DMOCATEGORY_AUDIO_EFFECT);
        pWrap->Release();

        if (SUCCEEDED(hr))
        {
            hr = g_pGraph->AddFilter(pDmoFilter, L"SimpleDelay DMOî);

#ifdef _UNICODE
    hr = g_pGraph->RenderFile(szFileName, NULL);
#else
    WCHAR wszFile[MAX_PATH];
    int result = MultiByteToWideChar(CP_ACP, 0, szFileName, -1,
        wszFile, MAX_PATH);
    if (result == 0)
    {
        hr = E_FAIL;
    }
    else
```

```
    {
        hr = g_pGraph->RenderFile(wszFile, NULL);
    }
#endif

    }

    pDmoFilter->Release();

    return hr;
}
```

In this function, a filter graph builder object is instantiated, and its media control and event interfaces are queried. Once that overhead is complete, the function makes a *CoCreateInstance* call with a class ID of *CLSID_DMO-WrapperFilter*. This call instantiates a DMO wrapper filter, the generic wrapper for all DMO objects. Once the function has queried for the *IDMOWrapperFilter* interface, it invokes the interface's *Init* method, passing the GUID of the requested DMO. This operation assigns the appropriate DMO to the Direct-Show wrapper filter. The second parameter on the *Init* call is a category identi-fier used by DirectShow when it enumerates the DMOs looking for one that matches the passed GUID.

At this point, the DMO is treated like any other DirectShow filter. It's added to the filter graph with a call to *AddFilter*, and it's put into the render path as a transform filter when the *RenderFile* method is executed, resulting in a filter graph that looks like Figure 13-2.

Figure 13-2   The SimpleDelay DMO, which looks like any other Direct-Show filter when invisibly wrapped inside the DirectShow Wrapper filter

Although this is a very simple exploration of an audio DMO inside a filter graph, this code contains everything you'll need to use DMOs within your own DirectShow applications. If you need to learn which DMOs are available for use, you can enumerate them using the System Device Enumerator, which was explored in Chapter 4. (There's also a DMOEnum sample program in the DirectX SDK that does much the same thing.) Instead of passing the GUID for classes of DirectShow filters in the call, pass a DMO enumerator. The DMO audio effects can be enumerated with the value *DMOCATEGORY_AUDIO_EFFECT*, while video effects can be enumerated with the value *DMOCATEGORY_VIDEO_EFFECT*. Table 13-1 lists the DMO enumerators.

Table 13-1 DMO Enumerator GUIDs

GUID	Description
DMOCATEGORY_AUDIO_DECODER	Audio decoder
DMOCATEGORY_AUDIO_EFFECT	Audio effect
DMOCATEGORY_AUDIO_ENCODER	Audio encoder
DMOCATEGORY_VIDEO_DECODER	Video decoder
DMOCATEGORY_VIDEO_EFFECT	Video effect
DMOCATEGORY_VIDEO_ENCODER	Video encoder
DMOCATEGORY_AUDIO_CAPTURE_EFFECT	Audio capture effect

Designing and Coding the SimpleDelay DMO

The design of the SimpleDelay DMO is straightforward. Input samples enter the DMO, are held for a specific length of time (as defined in the header file), are mixed with later input samples, and are passed to the output. When the DMO begins operation, silence is sent as output samples until sufficient time has passed for the input samples to appear as output samples. This process iterates until no more input samples are presented; once all remaining output samples have been sent to the DMO's caller, operation of the DMO ceases.

The definition and internal structure of a DMO is analogous to that of a DirectShow filter. There are methods to negotiate media type, negotiate buffer size, and perform data transformations. However, whereas DirectShow filters are defined as descendants of *CBaseFilter* or perhaps *CTransformFilter*, DMOs are declared as descendants from a class template, *IMediaObjectImpl*. That template provides the framework for functionality—such as sanity checks on input parameters and setting and storing the media type—but the public methods call equivalent internal methods where the real work gets done, and these need to be overridden by the programmer. Here's the class definition for the Simple-Delay class *CDelay*:

```
class ATL_NO_VTABLE CDelay :
    public IMediaObjectImpl<CDelay, 1, 1>, // DMO Template 1 input, 1 output
    public CComObjectRootEx<CComMultiThreadModel>,
    public CComCoClass<CDelay, &CLSID_Delay>,
    public IMediaObjectInPlace
{
public:
    CDelay() :
        m_nWet(DEFAULT_WET_DRY_MIX),
        m_dwDelay(DEFAULT_DELAY)
```

```
    {
        m_pUnkMarshaler = NULL;
    }


DECLARE_REGISTRY_RESOURCEID(IDR_DELAY)
DECLARE_GET_CONTROLLING_UNKNOWN()

DECLARE_PROTECT_FINAL_CONSTRUCT()

BEGIN_COM_MAP(CDelay)
    COM_INTERFACE_ENTRY(IMediaObject)
    COM_INTERFACE_ENTRY(IMediaObjectInPlace)
    COM_INTERFACE_ENTRY_AGGREGATE(IID_IMarshal, m_pUnkMarshaler.p)
END_COM_MAP()

    HRESULT FinalConstruct()
    {
        return CoCreateFreeThreadedMarshaler(
            GetControllingUnknown(), &m_pUnkMarshaler.p);
    }

    void FinalRelease()
    {
        FreeStreamingResources();  // In case client does not call this
        m_pUnkMarshaler.Release();
    }

    CComPtr<IUnknown> m_pUnkMarshaler;

public:
    // Declare internal methods required by ImediaObjectImpl.
    HRESULT InternalGetInputStreamInfo(DWORD dwInputStreamIndex,
        DWORD *pdwFlags);
    HRESULT InternalGetOutputStreamInfo(DWORD dwOutputStreamIndex,
        DWORD *pdwFlags);
    HRESULT InternalCheckInputType(DWORD dwInputStreamIndex,
        const DMO_MEDIA_TYPE *pmt);
    HRESULT InternalCheckOutputType(DWORD dwOutputStreamIndex,
        const DMO_MEDIA_TYPE *pmt);
    HRESULT InternalGetInputType(DWORD dwInputStreamIndex,
        DWORD dwTypeIndex, DMO_MEDIA_TYPE *pmt);
    HRESULT InternalGetOutputType(DWORD dwOutputStreamIndex,
        DWORD dwTypeIndex, DMO_MEDIA_TYPE *pmt);
    HRESULT InternalGetInputSizeInfo(DWORD dwInputStreamIndex,
        DWORD *pcbSize, DWORD *pcbMaxLookahead, DWORD *pcbAlignment);
    HRESULT InternalGetOutputSizeInfo(DWORD dwOutputStreamIndex,
        DWORD *pcbSize, DWORD *pcbAlignment);
    HRESULT InternalGetInputMaxLatency(DWORD dwInputStreamIndex,
```

```cpp
                REFERENCE_TIME *prtMaxLatency);
        HRESULT InternalSetInputMaxLatency(DWORD dwInputStreamIndex,
            REFERENCE_TIME rtMaxLatency);
        HRESULT InternalFlush();
        HRESULT InternalDiscontinuity(DWORD dwInputStreamIndex);
        HRESULT InternalAllocateStreamingResources();
        HRESULT InternalFreeStreamingResources();

        HRESULT InternalProcessInput(DWORD dwInputStreamIndex,
            IMediaBuffer *pBuffer, DWORD dwFlags,
            REFERENCE_TIME rtTimestamp, REFERENCE_TIME rtTimelength);

        HRESULT InternalProcessOutput(DWORD dwFlags, DWORD cOutputBufferCount,
            DMO_OUTPUT_DATA_BUFFER *pOutputBuffers, DWORD *pdwStatus);

        HRESULT InternalAcceptingInput(DWORD dwInputStreamIndex);

        // IMediaObjectInPlace methods.
        STDMETHOD(Process)(ULONG ulSize, BYTE *pData,
            REFERENCE_TIME refTimeStart, DWORD dwFlags);
        STDMETHOD(Clone)(IMediaObjectInPlace **ppMediaObject);
        STDMETHOD(GetLatency)(REFERENCE_TIME *pLatencyTime);

    private:
        // TypesMatch: Return true if all the required fields match.
        bool  TypesMatch(const DMO_MEDIA_TYPE *pmt1,
                const DMO_MEDIA_TYPE *pmt2);

        // CheckPcmFormat: Return S_OK if pmt is a valid PCM audio type.
        HRESULT CheckPcmFormat(const DMO_MEDIA_TYPE *pmt);

        // DoProcessOutput: Process data.
        HRESULT DoProcessOutput(
            BYTE *pbData,            // Pointer to the output buffer
            const BYTE *pbInputData, // Pointer to the input buffer
            DWORD dwQuantaToProcess  // Number of quanta to process
            );

        void FillBufferWithSilence(void);

        // GetPcmType: Get our only preferred PCM type
        HRESULT GetPcmType(DMO_MEDIA_TYPE *pmt);

        // Members
        CComPtr<IMediaBuffer> m_pBuffer;  // Pointer to current input buffer

        BYTE      *m_pbInputData;      // Pointer to data in input buffer
        DWORD      m_cbInputLength;    // Length of the data
```

```
REFERENCE_TIME  m_rtTimestamp;    // Most recent timestamp
bool        m_bValidTime;         // Is timestamp valid?

WAVEFORMATEX    *m_pWave;         // Pointer to WAVEFORMATEX struct

BYTE        *m_pbDelayBuffer;     // circular buffer for delay samples
DWORD       m_cbDelayBuffer;      // size of the delay buffer
BYTE        *m_pbDelayPtr;        // ptr to next delay sample

long        m_nWet;              // Wet portion of wet/dry mix
DWORD       m_dwDelay;           // Delay in ms

bool Is8Bit()  { return (m_pWave->wBitsPerSample == 8); }

// Moves the delay pointer around the circular buffer.
void IncrementDelayPtr(size_t size)
{
    m_pbDelayPtr += size;
    if (m_pbDelayPtr + size > m_pbDelayBuffer + m_cbDelayBuffer)
    {
        m_pbDelayPtr = m_pbDelayBuffer;
    }
}


};
```

The class definition of *CDelay* begins with a declaration of the four ancestor classes. *IMediaObjectImpl*, as previously explained, provides the basic framework for the DMO. Its initialization parameters define the *CDelay* DMO as possessing one input and one output. *CComObjectRootEx* defines the interfaces required by COM to make the object visible across the operating system. The COM map defined in the first part of the class definition is managed by *CComObjectRootEx*. *CComCoClass* is used by the class factory, which creates instances of the DMO based on its GUID. Both *CoComObjectRootEx* and *CComCoClass* are Active Template Library (ATL) constructs; they're by-products of an ATL wizard that was used to implement SimpleDelay. *IMediaObjectImpl* doesn't require ATL, but ATL does handle a lot of the COM details for you and is more convenient.

IMediaObjectInPlace implements a DMO that performs in-place transformations on buffer data. The in-place transform means that this object needs to implement a *Process* method, which transforms the buffer data without moving it to a separate output buffer. All DMOs, whether they do in-place transformations or not, need to implement separate *ProcessInput* and *ProcessOutput* methods, which are part of the *IMediaObject* interface, and copy data from the input to output buffer during the transform process, much like a DirectShow transform filter does.

Implementing the DMO Media and Buffer Negotiation Methods

Two methods declared in *CDelay*, *CDelay::InternalGetInputStreamInfo* and *CDelay::InternalGetOutputStreamInfo*, are methods required by the *IMediaObjectImpl* class template. They correspond to the *GetInputStreamInfo* and *GetOutputStreamInfo* methods on the *IMediaObject* interface. Calls to these methods use bit fields to signal information about the input and output streams. For the input stream, here are the possible values given by *DMO_INPUT_STREAM_INFO_FLAGS*:

```
enum _DMO_INPUT_STREAM_INFO_FLAGS {
    DMO_INPUT_STREAMF_WHOLE_SAMPLES            = 0x00000001,
    DMO_INPUT_STREAMF_SINGLE_SAMPLE_PER_BUFFER = 0x00000002,
    DMO_INPUT_STREAMF_FIXED_SAMPLE_SIZE        = 0x00000004,
    DMO_INPUT_STREAMF_HOLDS_BUFFERS            = 0x00000008
};
```

The output stream values are defined by *DMO_OUTPUT_STREAM_INFO_FLAGS*.

```
enum _DMO_OUTPUT_STREAM_INFO_FLAGS {
    DMO_OUTPUT_STREAMF_WHOLE_SAMPLES            = 0x00000001,
    DMO_OUTPUT_STREAMF_SINGLE_SAMPLE_PER_BUFFER = 0x00000002,
    DMO_OUTPUT_STREAMF_FIXED_SAMPLE_SIZE        = 0x00000004,
    DMO_OUTPUT_STREAMF_DISCARDABLE              = 0x00000008,
    DMO_OUTPUT_STREAMF_OPTIONAL                 = 0x00000010
};
```

In the implementation of *CDelay::InternalGetInputStreamInfo*, *CDelay* informs callers that it's expecting an input stream that consists of whole samples and that these samples must have a fixed size. The same flags are set for *CDelay::InternalGetOutputStreamInfo*, indicating that it will send streams consisting of whole samples of a fixed size. The functions of other bits in the *DMO_INPUT_STREAM_INFO_FLAGS* and *DMO_OUTPUT_STREAM_INFO_FLAGS* enumerations are given in the DirectX SDK documentation.

Four *CDelay* methods directly handle media type negotiation: *CDelay::InternalCheckInputType*, *CDelay::InternalCheckOutputType*, *CDelay::InternalGetInputType*, and *CDelay::InternalGetOutputType*. The *Get* methods query the DMO for its preferred media types, and the *Check* methods determine whether the DMO will accept a media type. As is true for DirectShow filters, DMOs can negotiate the media types they can accept by sending a list of possible types back to the caller. In the case of the SimpleDelay DMO, that list consists only of PCM audio, so these methods ensure that only a valid media stream—validated by the *CDelay::CheckPcmFormat* method—is received by the DMO for processing. Any other media types are rejected by the DMO. Here's the implementation of *CDelay::CheckPcmFormat*:

```
HRESULT CDelay::CheckPcmFormat(const DMO_MEDIA_TYPE *pmt)
{
    if (pmt->majortype    == MEDIATYPE_Audio    &&
        pmt->subtype      == MEDIASUBTYPE_PCM    &&
        pmt->formattype   == FORMAT_WaveFormatEx &&
        pmt->cbFormat     == sizeof(WAVEFORMATEX) &&
        pmt->pbFormat != NULL)
    {
        // Check the format block

        WAVEFORMATEX *pWave = (WAVEFORMATEX*)pmt->pbFormat;

        if ((pWave->wFormatTag == WAVE_FORMAT_PCM) &&
            (pWave->wBitsPerSample == 8 || pWave->wBitsPerSample == 16) &&
            (pWave->nBlockAlign ==
                pWave->nChannels * pWave->wBitsPerSample / 8) &&
            (pWave->nAvgBytesPerSec ==
                pWave->nSamplesPerSec * pWave->nBlockAlign))
        {
            return S_OK;
        }
    }
    return DMO_E_INVALIDTYPE;
}
```

The SimpleDelay DMO isn't very picky about the kind of audio stream it wants to receive, but the input and output types must match. (This is a requirement for any DMO that supports in-place processing.) The stream must be PCM audio, and it must be either 8 or 16 bits per sample. The fields of the passed *DMO_MEDIA_TYPE* structure are examined within *CDelay::CheckPcmFormat*. Here's the composition of *DMO_MEDIA_TYPE*:

```
typedef struct _DMOMediaType {
    GUID      majortype;
    GUID      subtype;
    BOOL      bFixedSizeSamples;
    BOOL      bTemporalCompression;
    ULONG     lSampleSize;
    GUID      formattype;
    IUnknown *pUnk;
    ULONG     cbFormat;
    [size_is(cbFormat)] BYTE * pbFormat;
} DMO_MEDIA_TYPE;
```

The fields within a *DMO_MEDIA_TYPE* structure have the same names and the same purposes as the equivalent fields within the *AM_MEDIA_TYPE* structure, which was covered in Chapter 10. As with *AM_MEDIA_TYPE*, it's important to remember that *cbFormat* must hold the size of the data structure pointed to by *pbFormat*, if any.

```
HRESULT CDelay::InternalGetInputSizeInfo(DWORD dwInputStreamIndex,
DWORD *pcbSize, DWORD *pcbMaxLookahead, DWORD *pcbAlignment)
{

    // IMediaObjectImpl validates this for us...
    _ASSERTE(InputTypeSet(dwInputStreamIndex));

    // And we expect only PCM audio types.
    _ASSERTE(InputType(dwInputStreamIndex)->formattype ==
        FORMAT_WaveFormatEx);

    WAVEFORMATEX *pWave =
        (WAVEFORMATEX*)InputType(dwInputStreamIndex)->pbFormat;

    *pcbSize = pWave->nBlockAlign;
        *pcbMaxLookahead = 0;
        *pcbAlignment = 1;

    return S_OK;
}

HRESULT CDelay::InternalGetOutputSizeInfo(DWORD dwOutputStreamIndex,
DWORD *pcbSize, DWORD *pcbAlignment)
{
    // IMediaObjectImpl validates this for us...
    _ASSERTE(OutputTypeSet(dwOutputStreamIndex));

    // And we expect only PCM audio types.
    _ASSERTE(OutputType(dwOutputStreamIndex)->formattype ==
        FORMAT_WaveFormatEx);

    WAVEFORMATEX *pWave =
        (WAVEFORMATEX*)OutputType(dwOutputStreamIndex)->pbFormat;

    *pcbSize = pWave->nBlockAlign;
        *pcbAlignment = 1;

    return S_OK;
}
```

The *CDelay* DMO implements two methods crucial to the buffer allocation process: *CDelay::InternalGetInputSizeInfo* and *CDelay::InternalGetOutput-SizeInfo*. Both methods use the *DMO_MEDIA_TYPE* data structure to calculate the total buffer size needed—the size of one full sample of audio data. Because this is an in-place transformation of buffer data, both methods should return the same values.

Two other methods, *CDelay::InternalGetInputMaxLatency* and *CDelay::InternalSetInputMaxLatency*, establish latency values on the input stream. *Latency* is the difference between the input timestamp on a stream as it enters a DMO and the output timestamp on the transformed stream. DMOs allow their latency values to be read and set so that other processing elements can properly synchronize their streams with the DMO. In the case of *CDelay*, both methods return the error message *E_NOTIMPL*, which means that latency is not implemented in this DMO and zero latency can be assumed.

Implementing DMO Internal Methods

Four methods handle states and conditions internal to the DMO. Two of these methods, *CDelay::InternalAllocateStreamingResources* and *CDelay::InternalFreeStreamingResources*, simply allocate and free a sample buffer used to create the sample delay. If your own DMO has resource allocation requirements to handle a media stream, these routines manage the allocation and release of those resources. The client might not call the public versions of these methods, but the *IMediaObjectImpl* class template will invoke them if the client doesn't.

Two other methods, *CDelay::InternalFlush* and *CDelay::InternalDiscontinuity*, handle states generated by the client in its normal operation. When *CDelay::InternalFlush* is executed, all data held by the DMO is released and any sound samples are wiped out with a call to *CDelay::FillBufferWithSilence*, which resets the delay buffer.

```
void CDelay::FillBufferWithSilence()
{
    if (Is8Bit())
        FillMemory(m_pbDelayBuffer, m_cbDelayBuffer, 0x80);
    else
        ZeroMemory(m_pbDelayBuffer, m_cbDelayBuffer);
}
```

There are two ways to clear the sample buffer, depending on the number of bits per sample. If the PCM waveform is composed of 8-bit samples, the entire buffer of byte values must be set to 128—silence for 8-bit PCM. If the waveform is composed of 16-bit samples, the entire buffer is zeroed.

When the media stream ceases flowing to a DMO or the media type of the stream changes, the condition is signaled with a *discontinuity*. A discontinuity indicates that there's a forthcoming break in the stream. Some DMOs will need to continue to provide output data until their internal buffers empty, but they can use the discontinuity signal to reject any input buffers until such time as their output buffers have emptied. At this point, the DMO is ready, waiting for stream input to begin again. The *CDelay::InternalDiscontinuity* method doesn't do anything in the SimpleDelay DMO beyond returning an *S_OK* response, but in the case of a more complex DMO, this method could be used to trigger a number of state-driven events, such as tracking whether the DMO is ready to receive more input.

Another method, *CDelay::InternalAcceptingInput*, is queried when the client wants to know whether the DMO's input stream can accept more input. If a buffer pool is allocated to a DMO, the implementation of the *InternalAcceptingInput* method can determine whether the DMO can accept another input buffer. In this case, we return *S_FALSE* if the DMO can't accept an input buffer (we're full, thank you very much) or *S_OK* if the DMO is able to receive another input buffer.

Implementing DMO Data Processing Methods

An in-place DMO must have publicly accessible *ProcessInput* and *ProcessOutput* methods. The *CDelay* DMO has two similar internal methods, *CDelay::InternalProcessInput* and *CDelay::InternalProcessOutput*. Here's the implementation of both methods:

```
HRESULT CDelay::InternalProcessInput(DWORD dwInputStreamIndex,
    IMediaBuffer *pBuffer, DWORD dwFlags, REFERENCE_TIME rtTimestamp,
    REFERENCE_TIME rtTimelength)
{
    _ASSERTE(m_pBuffer == NULL);

    HRESULT hr = pBuffer->GetBufferAndLength(&m_pbInputData,
        &m_cbInputLength);
    if (FAILED(hr))
    {
        return hr;
    }

    if (m_cbInputLength <= 0)
        return E_FAIL;

    m_pBuffer = pBuffer;

    if (dwFlags & DMO_INPUT_DATA_BUFFERF_TIME)
    {
        m_bValidTime = true;
        m_rtTimestamp = rtTimestamp;
    }
    else
    {
        m_bValidTime = false;
    }
```

```
        return S_OK;
}

HRESULT CDelay::InternalProcessOutput(DWORD dwFlags,
    DWORD cOutputBufferCount, DMO_OUTPUT_DATA_BUFFER *pOutputBuffers,
    DWORD *pdwStatus)
{
    BYTE   *pbData;
    DWORD   cbData;
    DWORD   cbOutputLength;
    DWORD   cbBytesProcessed;

    CComPtr<IMediaBuffer> pOutputBuffer = pOutputBuffers[0].pBuffer;

    if (!m_pBuffer || !pOutputBuffer)
    {
        return S_FALSE;  // Did not produce output
    }

    // Get the size of our output buffer.
    HRESULT hr = pOutputBuffer->GetBufferAndLength(&pbData, &cbData);

    hr = pOutputBuffer->GetMaxLength(&cbOutputLength);
    if (FAILED(hr))
    {
        return hr;
    }

    // Skip past any valid data in the output buffer.
    pbData += cbData;
    cbOutputLength -= cbData;

    if (cbOutputLength < m_pWave->nBlockAlign)
    {
        return E_FAIL;
    }

    // Calculate how many quanta we can process.
    bool  bComplete = false;

    if (m_cbInputLength > cbOutputLength)
    {
        cbBytesProcessed = cbOutputLength;
    }
    else
    {
        cbBytesProcessed = m_cbInputLength;
        bComplete = true;
    }
```

```
            DWORD dwQuanta = cbBytesProcessed / m_pWave->nBlockAlign;

            // The actual data we write may be
            // less than the available buffer length
            // due to the block alignment.
            cbBytesProcessed = dwQuanta * m_pWave->nBlockAlign;

            hr = DoProcessOutput(pbData, m_pbInputData, dwQuanta);
            if (FAILED(hr))
            {
                return hr;
            }

            hr = pOutputBuffer->SetLength(cbBytesProcessed + cbData);

            if (m_bValidTime)
            {
                pOutputBuffers[0].dwStatus |= DMO_OUTPUT_DATA_BUFFERF_TIME;
                pOutputBuffers[0].rtTimestamp = m_rtTimestamp;

                // Estimate how far along we are...
                pOutputBuffers[0].dwStatus |= DMO_OUTPUT_DATA_BUFFERF_TIMELENGTH;
                pOutputBuffers[0].rtTimelength =
                    (cbBytesProcessed / m_pWave->nAvgBytesPerSec) * UNITS;
            }

            if (bComplete)
            {
                m_pBuffer = NULL;  // Release input buffer
            }
            else
            {
                pOutputBuffers[0].dwStatus |= DMO_OUTPUT_DATA_BUFFERF_INCOMPLETE;
                m_cbInputLength -= cbBytesProcessed;
                m_pbInputData += cbBytesProcessed;
                m_rtTimestamp += pOutputBuffers[0].rtTimelength;

            }

    return S_OK;
}
```

The *CDelay::InternalProcessInput* method receives a pointer to the *IMediaBuffer* interface that manages the sample data buffer. The method verifies that the length of the data in the buffer is greater than zero. If the timestamp is expected to be valid on the sample—because the appropriate *DMO_INPUT_DATA_BUFFER_FLAG* bit is set—a class variable is set and the sample's timestamp is stored.

Although the DMO receives one call to *CDelay::InternalProcessInput* for every buffer presented to it, the DMO can process one buffer per stream on each call to its corresponding output method, *CDelay::InternalProcessOutput*. If you have more than one output stream from a DMO, each stream's buffer will be processed with each call to *CDelay::InternalProcessOutput*. This method is passed the number of buffers to be processed and a list of pointers to *DMO_OUTPUT_DATA_BUFFER* structures that hold pointers to the *IMedia-Buffer* interfaces for each sample and timestamp information. (In our case, the *CDelay* DMO has only one output stream.)

The method sets up the information it needs to make a method call to *CDelay::DoProcessOutput*, which performs the in-place transform of the buffer data. Here's the implementation of that private method:

```
HRESULT CDelay::DoProcessOutput(BYTE *pbData, const BYTE *pbInputData,
    DWORD dwQuanta)
{
    DWORD sample, channel, num_channels;

    num_channels = m_pWave->nChannels;

    if (Is8Bit())
    {
        for (sample = 0; sample < dwQuanta; ++sample)
        {
            for (channel = 0; channel < num_channels; ++channel)
            {
                // 8-bit sound is 0..255 with 128 == silence.

                // Get the input sample and normalize to -128..127.
                int i = pbInputData[sample * num_channels + channel] - 128;

                // Get the delay sample and normalize to -128..127.
                int delay = m_pbDelayPtr[0] - 128;

                m_pbDelayPtr[0] = i + 128;
                IncrementDelayPtr(sizeof(unsigned char));

                i = (i * (100 - m_nWet)) / 100 + (delay * m_nWet) / 100;

                // Truncate.
                if (i > 127)
                    i = 127;
                if (i < -128)
                    i = -128;
```

```
                    pbData[sample * num_channels + channel] =
                        (unsigned char)(i+128);

                }
            }
    }
    else // 16-bit
    {
        for (sample = 0; sample < dwQuanta; ++sample)
        {
            for (channel = 0; channel < num_channels; ++channel)
            {
                int i =
                    ((short*)pbInputData)[sample * num_channels + channel];

                int delay = ((short*)m_pbDelayPtr)[0];

                ((short*)m_pbDelayPtr)[0] = i;
                IncrementDelayPtr(sizeof(short));

                i = (i * (100 - m_nWet)) / 100 + (delay * m_nWet) / 100;

                // Truncate.
                if (i > 32767)
                    i = 32767;
                if (i < -32768)
                    i = -32768;

                ((short*)pbData)[sample * num_channels + channel] =
                    (short)i;

            }
        }
    }
    return S_OK;
}
```

This method manipulates the sound data in the buffer passed to it, mixing it together with sound data in another buffer (this is how you get a 2-second delay) and then producing an output from the mixture of the sound data. There are different pathways for 8-bit sound and 16-bit sound because the arithmetic involved in each is slightly different, but the basic algorithm is the same for both: input sample + delay sample = output sample.

Implementing the *IMediaObjectInPlace* Methods

Three methods must be overridden as part of the implementation of any class descendent from *IMediaObjectInPlace*: *Process*, *Clone*, and *GetLatency*. Here is the method that, in normal circumstances, performs the data transform for the SimpleDelay DMO, *CDelay::Process*:

```
STDMETHODIMP CDelay::Process(ULONG ulSize, BYTE *pData,
    REFERENCE_TIME refTimeStart, DWORD dwFlags)
{
    if (dwFlags &= ~DMO_INPLACE_ZERO)
        return E_INVALIDARG;

    if (!pData)
    {
        return E_POINTER;
    }

    LockIt lock(this);

    if (!InputTypeSet(0) || !OutputTypeSet(0))
    {
        return DMO_E_TYPE_NOT_SET;
    }

    // Make sure all streams have media types set
    // and resources are allocated.
    HRESULT hr = AllocateStreamingResources();

    if (SUCCEEDED(hr))
        hr = DoProcessOutput(pData, pData, ulSize / m_pWave->nBlockAlign);

    return hr;
}
```

The method determines that the pointers are valid, that in-place data transformations are allowed, and that the input and output types have been set (which implies that the DMO is connected to something outside itself). This parameter validation is not performed for *IMediaObjectInPlace* methods (although it is for *IMediaObject* methods), so we have to do it ourselves. The method invokes *CDelay::AllocateStreamingResources* to ensure that memory is available for the transform operation and then calls *CDelay::DoProcessOutput* to handle the actual data transform. The *CDelay::Clone* method is an implementation of the base class method that creates new copies of objects. In this implementation, the media type information for both the input and output streams is copied to the new object. Finally *CDelay::GetLatency* should return the actual time it takes the DMO to process buffer data. In this case, *CDelay::GetLatency* returns a value of zero, or no latency, which is consistent with the value returned by *CDelay::InternalGetLatency*.

Summary

Although a number of methods need to be implemented, even within a basic DMO such as SimpleDelay, the implementation details are not difficult. Simple-Delay could be used as a basis for your own DMOs—provided that you generated another GUID for your DMO. DMOs can be freely used in your filter graphs, with one exception: audio and video effects created by DMOs can't be used by DES in the effects track. That's a minor drawback, and DMOs do allow you to create a reusable code object that can be used in DirectSound as well as Direct-Show, multiplying the utility of one code module across multiple applications.

Part IV

Advanced Topics

14

Understanding the AVI File Format

On the Microsoft Windows platform, the most common file format for storage of digital video capture is the venerable AVI format. DV-encoded audio/video files are normally stored in AVI format, and files encoded in any of a number of other compression formats can also be stored in AVI format. Perhaps the most common use of AVI today is for the storage of "raw," uncompressed video streams—such as those captured by a digital camcorder—which will be edited, analyzed, or processed at some later time. The internal structure of an AVI file reveals how many media streams are stored in the file and the media types of these streams. AVI is a generic container format; it's entirely neutral as to what kind of data it contains.

In the context of this book, you're most likely to encounter AVI files when they contain captured audio and video streams from a digital video (DV) device—such as a DV camcorder or a webcam. Although Microsoft DirectShow will allow you to process those streams through the use of the AVI Splitter filter, which creates separate audio and video streams from a single, multiplexed stream of data, it's occasionally necessary to delve into the internals of an AVI file. You might also be interested in creating an AVI file from scratch, although normally you'd create AVI files by placing the AVI Mux transform filter immediately before the File Writer renderer filter in your filter graph.

This chapter is designed to help you learn how AVI files are constructed. It's meant to complement the "AVI RIFF File Reference" and "DV Data in AVI File Format" entries located in the appendixes of the DirectShow documentation in the Microsoft DirectX SDK. Those documents contain basic information about the structure of an AVI file, which this chapter will expand on.

The AVI File Header

AVI file format is based on the Resource Interchange File Format (RIFF). RIFF is a versatile format used for WAV files (and several other file formats) in addition to AVI files. Every RIFF file begins with a four-character code—or FOURCC, a series of four byte-wide character values—that spells out *RIFF*. This code is followed by a 32-bit value indicating the length of the file—excluding the RIFF header and length value, so really, it's the length of the rest of the file. In earlier versions of AVI files, the file size was limited to 4 gigabytes (GB), which is the maximum file size on Windows operating systems earlier than Windows 2000. Given that an hour of DV-encoded video runs to 13.5 GB, it was necessary to extend the AVI file format to work with very large files. To this end, the latest version of the AVI file format allows multiple RIFF headers to be concatenated sequentially. Each of these RIFF files-within-a-file can be up to 4 GB in length. The extended AVI file format looks like Figure 14-1.

Figure 14-1   Second-generation AVI file format, which handles file sizes much longer than 4 GB

Following the 32-bit length-of-file value, another FOURCC value defines the type of the RIFF file. In the case of AVI files, the value is "*AVI* ". (Note that a trailing space is necessary to pad the value to four characters.) If the RIFF file had PCM audio data inside, the FOURCC type would be "*WAV* ", a WAV file.

Chunks and Lists

Following the RIFF header, which identifies the file as containing AVI data, the file is broken into a series of data areas, known as *chunks* and *lists*. Within an AVI file, both chunks and lists can either occur sequentially (one after another), or nested (one within another). There's no practical limit to the number of chunks or lists in an AVI file—although the maximum file size for AVI files is a whopping 48 terabytes. Chunks can be nested within chunks that are within lists that are within chunks, which might themselves be part of a series of sequential lists, and so forth. The structure of a typical AVI file might look something like Figure 14-2.

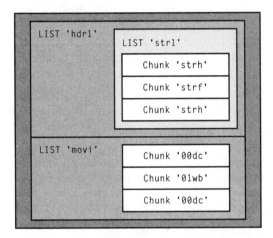

Figure 14-2   Nested and sequential lists and chunks within an AVI file

Chunks and lists are distinguished between themselves by their formats. A chunk has a FOURCC header, identifying the chunk type, followed by a 32-bit value for the length of the chunk data, followed by the chunk data. Chunk data is always padded to the nearest 16-bit (word) boundary to maintain alignment with other chunks. A list has a FOURCC header of "LIST", followed by a 32-bit value for the length of the list data, then another FOURCC code with the list type (in other words, what kind of list is it?), followed by the list data. Every AVI file contains at least two lists. The first of these defines the format of the streams contained in the file, and the second contains the actual stream data.

The AVI Header Chunk

The AVI file always opens with a header list, identified by the FOURCC value *hdrl*. The list type for AVI files is *avih*, or AVI header. The AVI header chunk has the following definition:

```
typedef struct _avimainheader {
    FOURCC fcc;
    DWORD  cb;
    DWORD  dwMicroSecPerFrame;
    DWORD  dwMaxBytesPerSec;
    DWORD  dwPaddingGranularity;
    DWORD  dwFlags;
    DWORD  dwTotalFrames;
    DWORD  dwInitialFrames;
    DWORD  dwStreams;
    DWORD  dwSuggestedBufferSize;
    DWORD  dwWidth;
    DWORD  dwHeight;
    DWORD  dwReserved[4];
} AVIMAINHEADER;
```

The *AVIMAINHEADER* structure (which includes the FOURCC and chunk length values as the first two fields in its definition) provides basic parameters needed for file playback. The *dwMicroSecPerFrame* field specifies the number of microseconds between frames. (For NTSC video, for example, this figure would be approximately 18000 because there are roughly 18 milliseconds between each field, assuming this is interleaved data.) The *dwMaxBytesPerSec* field specifies the maximum data rate of the file—in other words, the number of bytes per second the system must be prepared to process when it presents the AVI movie. If the system can't guarantee that throughput, frames could be dropped. The byte-alignment of the data is given in *dwPaddingGranularity*; many AVI files are aligned on multiples of 4 bytes. The *dwFlags* field holds five bit values in a single field, as described in Table 14-1.

Table 14-1   AVI Header Flags

Value	Description
AVIF_HASINDEX	The AVI file has an index. (We'll cover the index later.)
AVIF_MUSTUSEINDEX	The application should use the index, rather than the physical ordering of the chunks in the file, to determine the presentation order of the data.
AVIF_ISINTERLEAVED	The AVI file contains interleaved data.
AVIF_WASCAPTUREFILE	The file is a specially allocated file used for capturing real-time video.
AVIF_COPYRIGHTED	The file contains copyrighted data and should not be duplicated.

The *dwTotalFrames* field specifies the total number of frames in the file, which can be used to calculate the running time of a movie. To do so, multiply the number of frames by the time per frame. The *dwInitialFrames* value contains zero, unless the data in the AVI file is interleaved. When the data is interleaved, the *dwInitialFrames* value specifies the number of frames by which the audio leads the video, which gives the audio some extra samples as a "head start," typically around three-quarters of second.

The number of streams in the file is given in the *dwStreams* field. A file with both audio and video has two streams. (It's possible to have more than two streams in an AVI file. You could have one video stream and two separate audio streams, perhaps for different languages or for a "director's cut.") The *dwSuggestedBufferSize* field contains a suggested buffer size for any application reading the AVI file. This value is generally large enough to contain the largest chunk in the AVI file. If this value is set incorrectly (or to zero), an application might have to reallocate its buffers during operation, which would impair AVI playback performance. Finally, the width and height of the AVI movie, in pixels, are given in *dwWidth* and *dwHeight*.

The Stream Header Chunk

Following the AVI header comes the stream header list, which is identified by the FOURCC value *strl*. The list is populated with stream header chunks, which are identified with *strh*. (FOURCC values are case sensitive.) The stream headers are used to define the specifics of each stream, as follows:

```
typedef struct _avistreamheader {
    FOURCC fcc;
    DWORD  cb;
    FOURCC fccType;
    FOURCC fccHandler;
    DWORD  dwFlags;
    WORD   wPriority;
    WORD   wLanguage;
    DWORD  dwInitialFrames;
    DWORD  dwScale;
    DWORD  dwRate;
    DWORD  dwStart;
    DWORD  dwLength;
    DWORD  dwSuggestedBufferSize;
    DWORD  dwQuality;
    DWORD  dwSampleSize;
    struct {
        short int left;
        short int top;
        short int right;
        short int bottom;
    } rcFrame;
} AVISTREAMHEADER;
```

The *fccType* field is key to the AVI stream header. It has one of four possible FOURCC values, as described in Table 14-2.

Table 14-2   FOURCC Values of the *fccType* Field

FOURCC Value	Description
auds	Audio stream
mids	MIDI stream
txts	Text stream
vids	Video stream

The *fccHandler* field is another FOURCC code; it describes the preferred handler for the stream. In the case of audio or video streams, it specifies the codec for decoding the stream. If the stream is DV video, this field will usually be set to *dvds*. The *dwFlags* bit field indicates whether the stream is disabled (*AVISF_DISABLED*) or whether the video palette animates throughout the stream (*AVISF_VIDEO_PALCHANGES*). The *dwPriority* field specifies the priority of the stream. In a file with multiple audio or video streams, the stream with the highest priority might be the default stream, while the others could be alternate streams, for use at different times. In this way, a single AVI file could keep multiple "paths" of video and audio bundled together. The *dwInitialFrames* field has information necessary for working with interleaved streams. This field specifies how far ahead of the video data the audio data runs (that is, how many frames of audio must appear in the file before the first frame of video), just as the *dwInitialFrames* field does in the AVI header chunk.

The stream's playback speed is controlled with the next two fields, *dwScale* and *dwRate*. Dividing *dwRate* by *dwScale* gives the number of samples per second, which is the frame rate if it's a video stream. Standard AVI files don't include any timestamps, so these values are needed to specify the playback rate per stream. The *dwStart* field specifies a start time (in units of *dwRate* divided by *dwScale*) for the stream. Usually, this time is zero—meaning the start of the stream—but it can be any value up to the value in the next field, *dwLength*, which is the entire stream length, given in the same units as *dwStart*. As in the AVI header, *dwSuggestedBufferSize* specifies how large a buffer a client reading the stream should allocate to read the stream.

The *dwQuality* field provides an indicator of the quality of the data in the stream. This value is in the range 0 to 10000, and in the case of compressed streams, this value represents a quality value passed to the compression software. The *dwSampleSize* field specifies the size of each sample in the stream in bytes. If this field is set to zero, the samples can vary in size, although each sample must reside in its own chunk. Finally, the *rcFrame* field defines a destination rectangle (four points) within the rectangle defined by the *dwWidth* and *dwHeight* of the AVI header. This field is used to coordinate multiple video streams, which can be combined and presented as a single video output.

The Stream Format Chunk

The stream header is followed by another chunk, *strf*, which defines the format of the data in the stream. Because that data is format-dependent, it can have any of a number of legal formats. The two most common formats for these fields are *BITMAPINFO*, a descriptor for video streams, and *WAVEFORMATEX*, a descriptor for audio streams. Here's the structure of *BITMAPINFOHEADER*, which comprises the first fields in the *BITMAPINFO* structure:

```
typedef struct tagBITMAPINFOHEADER {
    DWORD  biSize;
    LONG   biWidth;
    LONG   biHeight;
    WORD   biPlanes;
    WORD   biBitCount;
    DWORD  biCompression;
    DWORD  biSizeImage;
    LONG   biXPelsPerMeter;
    LONG   biYPelsPerMeter;
    DWORD  biClrUsed;
    DWORD  biClrImportant;
} BITMAPINFOHEADER;
```

The size of the structure is defined in *biSize*. The *biWidth* field specifies the width of the bitmap. For RGB and YUV bitmaps, this figure is given in pixels, except where the YUV depth is not an even power of two, in which case, it's given in bytes. The *biHeight* field specifies the height of the image and the image direction. If the image is RGB and *biHeight* is negative, a bottom-up image is specified. Otherwise, a top-down image is specified. YUV images are always top down.

The number of bits per pixel is specified in *biBitCount*, and if the bitmap is compressed, the FOURCC field *biCompression* specifies the compression format. Otherwise, the legal values are *BI_RGB* for RGB bitmaps and *BI_BITFIELDS* for RGB bitmaps with color masks. The *BI_BITFIELDS* flag is valid for 16-bit-depth and 32-bit-depth RGB images and when set means that the R, G, and B (red, green, and blue) values for each pixel can be found using three bitmasks. You can get the R, G, and B portions of a pixel by applying the appropriate mask to the value of the pixel. For 16-bit RGB, *BI_BITFIELDS* allows you to distinguish between 565 RGB and 555 RGB. *BI_RGB* is valid for all uncompressed RGB bit depths. For 16-bit color depths, *BI_RGB* always means 555. For other bit depths, there's no ambiguity. For 24-bit and 32-bit color, *BI_RGB* always means 8 bits per color. Anything less than or equal to 8 bits per color is always palettized.

The *biSizeImage* field defines the image size in bytes, while *biXPelsPerMeter* and *biYPelsPerMeter* specify the horizontal and vertical resolution, respectively, in pixels per meter, of the target device. Therefore, an image can be scaled up or down to meet the output capabilities of a display device. The *biClrUsed* field defines the number of palette entries used by the video sequence. For palettized video formats (with 8 or fewer bits of color per pixel), if this value is zero, it means the maximum size color table (the number of bits of color, raised to the power of two, so an 8-bit color table would have 256 entries). For non-palettized formats (greater than 16 bits of color per pixel), the color table is optional, so zero really means zero. In these days of supercomputer-class graphics cards and cinema-sized displays, we don't see much palettized video. The *biClrImportant* field defines how many of the colors in the color table are "important," a feature used by some palette-processing software.

Following the *BITMAPINFOHEADER* might be a color table and/or the three color masks for *BI_BITFIELDS* formats. It's up to the application to calculate the size for these additional elements because they're not included in the *biSize* field. The *BITMAPINFO* structure is a *BITMAPINFOHEADER* plus a field for the first entry in the color table, which is simply a convenience for easily accessing the color table from a structure definition.

The *WAVEFORMATEX* structure, used to describe audio data, looks like this:

```
typedef struct {
    WORD  wFormatTag;
    WORD  nChannels;
    DWORD nSamplesPerSec;
    DWORD nAvgBytesPerSec;
    WORD  nBlockAlign;
    WORD  wBitsPerSample;
    WORD  cbSize;
} WAVEFORMATEX;
```

The *wFormatTag* field is a value that describes the audio format type. For PCM data, this value will be *WAVE_FORMAT_PCM*. (Other values are registered with Microsoft.) The number of audio channels (2 for stereo) is defined in *nChannels*, and the number of samples per second is defined in *nSamplesPerSec*. The average data-transfer rate required to read and play the sample in real time is given in *nAvgBytesPerSec*, and the byte alignment of the sample data is specified in *nBlockAlign*. The number of bits per sample (generally 8 or 16, but could be 12, 24, or even 32) is given in *wBitsPerSample*. If the audio stream is not a *WAVE_FORMAT_PCM* type, additional format data might follow the *WAVFORMATEX* structure. In this case, the *cbSize* field will define how many bytes of additional format data follow. If there's no additional data or if the audio stream is *WAVE_FORMAT_PCM*, this field is set to zero.

An AVI file will have at least one stream format chunk and will most likely have two, one for audio and one for video. These streams, in the order they are presented in the stream header list, are used to reference entries in another list, which actually contains the stream data. Figure 14-3 shows how the lists and chunks should look inside the AVI header.

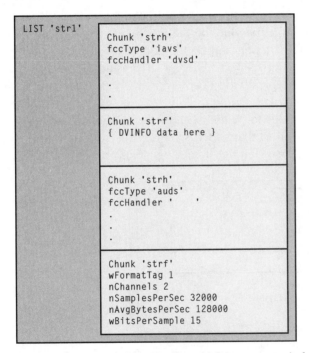

Figure 14-3   The AVI header list, which is composed of stream headers and stream formats

The Stream Data List

Immediately following the header list comes another list, the stream data list with the FOURCC code *movi*. This list is then followed by a series of chunks—that is, the audio and video samples—which compose the stream. Each chunk in the stream is identified by a FOURCC code. The FOURCC value comprises a stream number, plus one of the two-character codes shown in Table 14-3.

Table 14-3   Stream Data Chunk Identifiers

Two-Character Code	Description
db	Uncompressed video
dc	Compressed video
pc	Palette change
wb	Audio data

The stream number and the code are concatenated to create a FOURCC value. For example, the video in stream 0 would be identified as either *00db* or *00dc*, and the audio track on stream 1 would be identified as *01wb*. The internal structure of each sample, beyond the FOURCC code that identifies it as a stream sample, varies widely, depending on the compression techniques used for the sample. In general, samples from different streams are interleaved in the stream data list. Consider a typical video capture, with both video and audio components. Each video sample is the equivalent of one frame (or one thirtieth of a second) of video and needs to be associated with an audio sample. Audio samples can be longer (or shorter) than video samples, but they are interleaved to maintain synchronization between the streams, generally as shown in Figure 14-4.

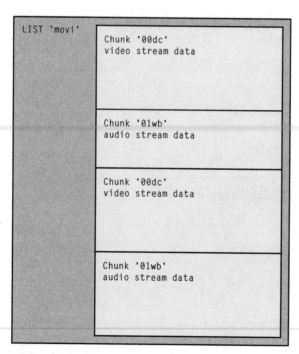

LIST 'movi'

Chunk '00dc'
video stream data

Chunk '01wb'
audio stream data

Chunk '00dc'
video stream data

Chunk '01wb'
audio stream data

Figure 14-4   The stream data list, which is interleaved to keep video and audio in sync

Alternately, the *movi* list can contain within it a list of *"rec"* chunks. The *"rec"* FOURCC code identifies stream data chunks that are meant to be read as a unit at the same time, which is useful when reading tightly interleaved data from a CD-ROM, when any delay in reading the next chunk could cause frames to drop in the playback.

AVI Index Entries

Following the stream data list, there can be an additional chunk, the index chunk, *idx1*. This chunk is an index that points to the stream data chunks within the AVI file. This feature is very useful because it allows you to locate any stream data chunk at random, rather than have to search from the beginning of the stream data list for a particular chunk.

It's also possible that the index chunk has the FOURCC value *indx*, as defined in the OpenDML AVI File Format specification. The *indx* index is preferable to the older *idx1* index because it includes support for files bigger than 4 GB. It's also broken into smaller subindexes, which makes it more efficient to work with than the monolithic *idx1* index. By default, the AVI Mux filter writes AVI files with the *indx* chunk. It will also write an *idx1* index for backward compatibility with older software. This functionality can be disabled with a call to *IConfigAviMux::SetOutputCompatibilityIndex*. The structure of the *idx1* chunk is as follows:

```
typedef struct _avioldindex {
    FOURCC fcc;
    DWORD  cb;
    struct _avioldindex_entry {
        DWORD dwChunkId;
        DWORD dwFlags;
        DWORD dwOffset;
        DWORD dwSize;
    } aIndex[];
} AVIOLDINDEX;
```

The *fcc* field is always *idx1*, and the *cb* field gives the length of the entire index, minus the *fcc* and *cb* fields. An arbitrary number of index entries follows. (You should be able to calculate the total number by dividing the total length of the index by the size of each entry.) Each entry has a *dwChunkId*, which refers to the stream number plus the two-character code used by the stream data list. Next is *dwFlags*, a bit field that signals the presence of key-frame and other information. The *dwOffset* field specifies the start of the chunk as an offset, either from the beginning of the file or from the beginning of the *movi* list. (It should be from the beginning of the *movi* list, but some AVI files don't observe this convention. You'll have to test the value in your code and decide.) Finally, the *dwSize* field specifies the size of the stream data chunk in bytes.

For an AVI movie three frames in length, with sound, the index chunk might appear like Figure 14-5.

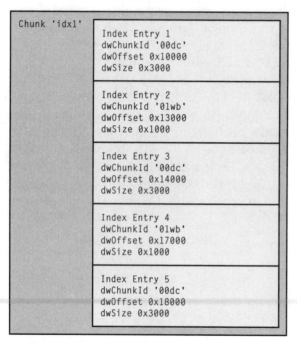

Figure 14-5 The AVI index, which points to all the samples in the AVI stream

When all these lists and chunks are combined into a single unit, you get the structure of a complete AVI file, as shown in Figure 14-6. This figure is just a sample AVI file structure, with one video and one audio stream, which is typical of the structure you'd see for DV-encoded AVI files.

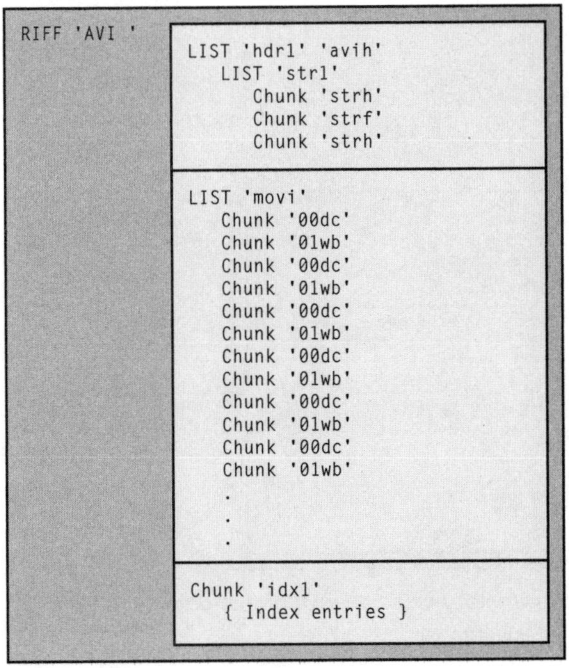

```
RIFF 'AVI '
            LIST 'hdrl' 'avih'
                LIST 'strl'
                    Chunk 'strh'
                    Chunk 'strf'
                    Chunk 'strh'

            LIST 'movi'
                Chunk '00dc'
                Chunk '01wb'
                Chunk '00dc'
                Chunk '01wb'
                Chunk '00dc'
                Chunk '01wb'
                Chunk '00dc'
                Chunk '01wb'
                Chunk '00dc'
                Chunk '01wb'
                Chunk '00dc'
                Chunk '01wb'
                    .
                    .
                    .

            Chunk 'idxl'
                { Index entries }
```

Figure 14-6   The complete AVI file, with an AVI header, chunks of data, and an index

DV Video in the AVI Format

DV stream data is received from the digital camcorder as a single, multiplexed stream of audio and video data. When stored inside an AVI file, this multiplexed stream can be stored as a single stream, or the stream can be demultiplexed into separate audio and video streams. When a multiplexed stream is stored within an AVI file, it's known as a Type 1 AVI file. When the stream is stored as a demultiplexed stream, it's known as a Type 2 AVI file. Although the two types are functionally identical, in that each contains the same DV stream data, Type 1 AVI files have a restriction: they will not work with Video for Windows applications, which expect demultiplexed streams of audio and video data. Therefore, Type 1 AVI files are not backward-compatible with VFW applications. However, using the DV Muxer filter, Type 1 AVI files can be created in DirectShow and demultiplexed into separate streams with the DV Splitter filter. Figure 14-7 shows the structure of a Type 1 AVI file.

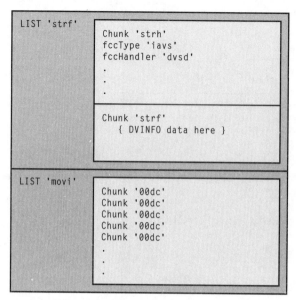

Figure 14-7 A Type 1 AVI file, which has only one stream containing multiplexed audio and video streams

A Type 1 AVI file is identified by a unique *fccType* in its stream header chunk, *iavs*, that is, "interleaved audio-video stream." There are three possible values in the *fccHandler* field of the stream header chunk: *dvsd*, which indicates that the file contains an SD-DVCR stream (as discussed in Chapter 6) from a digital camcorder; *dvhd*, which indicates a HD-DVCR high-definition digital stream; and *dvsl*, which indicates an SDL-DVCR high-compression digital stream. In any case, the stream header chunk is followed by a *DVINFO* stream format chunk (without any FOURCC chunk header or length). The *DVINFO* chunk has the following structure:

```
typedef struct tag_DVINFO {
    DWORD dwDVAAuxSrc;
    DWORD dwDVAAuxCtl;
    DWORD dwDVAAuxSrc1;
    DWORD dwDVAAuxCtl1;
    DWORD dwDVVAuxSrc;
    DWORD dwDVVAuxCtl;
    DWORD dwDVReserved[2];
} DVINFO, *PDVINFO;
```

The *dwDVAAuxSrc* and *dwDVAAuxCtl* fields specify the Audio Auxiliary Data Source Pack and Audio Auxiliary Data Source Control for the first audio block of the frame, and *dwDVAAuxSrc1* and *dwDVAAuxCtl1* define the same for the second audio block. The *dwDVVAuxSrc* and *dwDVAuxCtl* fields specify the Video Auxiliary Data Source Pack and Video Auxiliary Data Source Control. (If you need to learn what these fields do, check out "The Pack Header Table and Contents of Packs" from the *Specification of Consumer-Use Digital VCRs* (the "Blue Book"). These fields are the arcana of DV, and it's unlikely you'll ever use these fields yourself.) The last field, *dwDVReserved*, must be set to zero. All the stream data chunks in the *movi* list are identified with the FOURCC code *##dc*, where ## is the stream number.

In a Type 2 AVI file, the structure of the file is very much as we've already covered, with one or more audio streams and a video stream combined into a single AVI file, but with the various stream data maintained in separate chunks in the stream data list. The stream header for the audio stream has an *fccType* of *auds* but doesn't need any *fccHandler* value, so that field is set to four blanks. Both Type 1 and Type 2 AVI files can have index chunks.

Summary

The AVI file format is an older but still widely used format for the storage of DV on the Windows platform. Although AVI is somewhat complex in its nested structure of chunks and lists, it's easy to write applications or DirectShow filters that "walk" an existing AVI file or create an AVI file from scratch. AVI is a generic container format for a variety of types of stream data, including video, audio, MIDI, and text. Although particularly well suited to the storage of uncompressed video data, the AVI format can also be used with a variety of the video or audio codecs on the Windows platform (including Windows Media 9 Series) to produce compact files. However, AVI has limitations, so Microsoft has developed a new container format named ASF that's suitable for digital media content that is to be streamed over a network, as well as for content to be played back or stored on a local machine. Microsoft itself uses the ASF format as the container for digital media content compressed using its state-of-the-art Windows Media Audio and Windows Media Video codecs. Therefore, before we conclude our examination of DirectShow, we need to explore the new generation of Windows Media technologies and how they're used in DirectShow.

15

Windows Media Applications

Throughout this book, whenever we've wanted to reduce the size of an audio or video file, we've used the Microsoft Windows Media Audio and Video codecs through the WM ASF Writer. The reason is obvious: Windows Media provides state-of-the-art compression quality, and the format is supported by Windows Media Player, which ships with every PC. (Windows Media Player is also available for the Macintosh operating system, and Microsoft is trying to ensure that all major computing platforms support Windows Media playback.)

Just before this book went to press, Microsoft introduced Windows Media 9 Series (code-named "Corona"), which sets a new industry standard for audio and video compression. The core of Windows Media 9 Series is a new suite of codecs, including the WMA Pro codec for cinema-quality compression, the Image Codec for pan-and-scan imagery (à la Ken Burns's documentaries), and codecs that deliver improved performance on low bit-rate audio and video streams. Windows Media 9 Series allows you to encode high-quality audio or video samples at very low bit rates (comparatively) with little loss in quality. It thus opens up a whole new level of applications. For example, using Windows Media 9 Series encoding, a single DVD can contain a whole feature-length movie in high-definition (1280 × 768) resolution—something that's impossible with standard MPEG-2-encoded DVDs.

How good is the compression in Windows Media 9 Series? It can be as much as 30 percent better than MPEG-4, which is considered the benchmark standard for compression techniques. This means we're likely to see Windows Media–encoded files become ubiquitous on computers and on the Internet. Many CD and MP3 players already support Windows Media formats for audio compression. (For full stats, check out the details on the Microsoft Windows Media Web site at *http://www.microsoft.com/windows/windowsmedia/9series /nextwave/quality.aspx*.) With the release of Windows Media 9 Series, Microsoft announced new licensing terms that effectively allow third parties to use certain components of Windows Media Technologies independently of other components. Most significantly, the new terms allow third parties to place audio or video encoded with Windows Media codecs into any file container. This means the ASF file format and the Windows Media codecs are independent of each other, and you can program directly to the codec Microsoft DirectX Media Objects (DMOs) without going through the Windows Media Format SDK. (See "Windows Media Audio and Video Codec Interfaces" on MSDN for more information.)

DirectShow supports Windows Media 9 Series through two filters, the WM ASF Reader and the WM ASF Writer. You don't need to know much about Windows Media and its API to play back a Windows Media–encoded file within a DirectShow application; you can use a Filter Graph Manager to do the work. Just call the *IGraphBuilder* method *RenderFile*, and let it build the filter graph for you. If you add the Video Mixing Renderer (VMR) filter to the graph, it will be used as the renderer, opening up further possibilities for on-the-fly processing at playback time.

WM ASF Reader vs. Windows Media Source Filter

ASF, Windows Media Video, and Windows Media Audio go back a few years. Before the Windows Media Format SDK was released, DirectShow support for Windows Media playback was provided through the Windows Media Source Filter. This filter is used by Windows Media Player 6.4, which still ships with Windows and is widely used on Web pages around the world. To not break existing applications, the Windows Media Source Filter was maintained as the default source filter in both DirectX 8 and DirectX 9. In other words, if you called *RenderFile* with myVideo.wmv, the Filter Graph Manager used that filter as the source filter. If you wanted to use the newer WM ASF Reader, you had to add it explicitly to the graph. This situation was not ideal; with Windows Media Format 9 Series SDK, the developers made the WM ASF Reader the default filter for ASF files, without breaking existing applications. This means that with Windows Media 9 Series runtimes installed, if your application calls *RenderFile* with myVideo.wmv, the WM ASF Reader is used, but if Windows Media Player 6.4 is hosting the filter graph, the Windows Media Source filter is used.

Using the WM ASF Writer to create ASF files containing Windows Media–based content is only a bit more complex because of certain options available to you before you encode a file. We've used the WM ASF Writer previously in this book, but we've used only its default settings for the sake of simplicity; in the process, we've glossed over some of the more sophisticated features of Windows Media. This chapter covers all the techniques you'll need to master to create a full range of Windows Media files from within Microsoft DirectShow applications. Now that you've mastered the secrets of audio and video capture using DirectShow, Windows Media 9 Series can provide an extremely high-quality and efficient output, storage, and distribution format for your work.

ASF Files

When you use DirectShow or the Windows Media Format SDK to compress audio and video, the end result is an ASF file. ASF stands for Advanced Systems Format. Like AVI, ASF is a neutral container format that can be used to store any type of data. Also like AVI, ASF is an open specification. You can download the specification from the Microsoft Web site, and you can create ASF files using your own custom tools.

Naming Conventions in Windows Media

Microsoft's recommendations on ASF file name extensions are as follows: an ASF file that contains only audio streams and is compressed with one of the Windows Media Audio codecs should have the .WMA extension. A video-only or audio-video ASF file in which all the streams are compressed using Windows Media should have the .WMV extension. An ASF file that does not meet these requirements should have the .ASF extension.

The primary advantage of ASF over AVI is its packetized structure, which enables it to be streamed efficiently over networks. An ASF file can contain several streams with the same content encoded at various bit rates, which enables a client and a server to choose the rate that is most appropriate for a given network connection. ASF, as you might expect, also has excellent support for metadata.

Another big advantage of the ASF format over the AVI format is its support for a scheme for digital rights management (DRM). DRM is naturally a contentious issue in today's environment of rampant music copying. It enables content producers or distributors, such as record labels, to encrypt files so they cannot be played back or in some cases cannot even be copied to another machine without a license. The license contains a numerical key that enables a DRM-enabled player to decrypt the file at playback time. The license, which an end-user typically obtains separately from the media file itself, also contains conditions of use known as *rights*. The Microsoft DRM implementation enables you to specify such things as the number of times the file can be played (from one to infinity), whether it can be copied to a CD, and whether it can be copied to a portable device. The restrictiveness and cost (if any) of the license are up to the content owner or distributor; however, Microsoft requires that license issuers adhere to Microsoft's privacy policy in their license terms.

A multitude of DRM techniques are in use, although Microsoft's is the only one in wide use as of this writing. DRM is more politics and social engineering than technology because it enforces usage and copyright restrictions; ASF can support any DRM scheme, not just Microsoft's. (We won't cover DRM in this book; for more general information on Microsoft's DRM implementation, see the Windows Media site on Microsoft's Web site. For more detailed technical information, see the documentation for the Windows Media Format SDK and the Windows Media Rights Manager SDK.)

The ASF format is fully extensible; if you need a data type with your media stream that's not one of the six types defined by the SDK, you can add a custom stream to the ASF file that's capable of holding any stream of binary stream. Of course, if you add a custom stream type, you probably need to write your own DirectShow filter that can handle that stream. You can find more information on how to add custom streams to an ASF file in the Windows Media SDK documentation.

Windows Media Profiles

Before a media file can be encoded using Windows Media, the codecs must be configured with a set of parameters that tell them what kind of compression to apply, the relationships of the streams (audio and video, for example), how to share limited bandwidth, and so forth. In the Windows Media Format SDK, these parameters are grouped together into an object called a *profile*, which is translated into the header of an ASF file that has had the profile applied to it. Profiles are needed because of the increasingly large number of possible combinations of audio encoding, video encoding, and script encoding, all of which must be grouped into a logical and internally consistent whole.

Profiles are container-driven; they describe the qualities of the streams in their compressed state. A high-end profile can specify better-than-DVD quality for streaming high-definition video, and the low-end profiles can create files suitable for streaming audio-video over a 28.8-Kbps modem connection. (Profiles can be stored in XML files, which have the .PRX extension, but you never work with the XML files directly in your application; you always work with profile objects using the methods of the Windows Media Format SDK.)

A profile must specify all compression settings. The audio encoding parameters include settings such as bit rate, bandwidth, and constant or variable bit-rate encoding. (Variable bit-rate encoding allows the bits per second used to encode a stream to fluctuate based on the compressibility of that sample of a stream; variable bit-rate encoding takes longer, but it generally leads to higher fidelity at a given bit rate.) Video encoding parameters include settings for image width and height, frame rate, variable or constant bit rate, buffer size (how many seconds of "preroll" to have on hand when playing the video), and keyframe interval. Windows Media allows very fine control of each of these settings. The video bit rate, for example, can be tuned in integer units all the way from 1 bit per second to many gigabits per second. The encoder will match the requirements spelled out in the profile as closely as possible.

Windows Media SDK and Encoding Tools

Thus far in this book, we've been able to compile and build all our examples using only Microsoft Visual Studio .NET and version 9 of the DirectX SDK. In this final chapter, you'll have to download and install two more packages from Microsoft's Web site: the Windows Media Format SDK and the Windows Media Encoder, a tool that provides a GUI for conversion of existing media files into Windows Media. (Both of these can be found at *http://www.microsoft.com/windows/windowsmedia/download*.) We need the Windows Media Encoder application only for the convenient Profile Editor tool that comes with it. For our application development, only the Windows Media Format SDK is actually required because it contains both the Windows Media 9 Series codecs and the latest versions of the DirectShow WM ASF Reader and WM ASF Writer.

Although we could integrate complete profile editing capabilities into our application using the Windows Media Format SDK, for our purposes it is much more convenient to use the one provided by Microsoft. Once you install both the Windows Media SDK and Windows Media Encoder, launch the Windows Media Profile Editor. Load an existing profile (these should be installed along with the Encoder), and you should see something like that shown in Figure 15-1.

Figure 15-1 The Windows Media Profile Editor, which allows you to examine and edit all the settings in a profile

The profile loaded in the figure (with the filename d0_vbr_hd.prx) defines a high-definition, high-quality video stream with variable bit-rate encoding. To view the specifics of the encoding, click on the tab that displays the bit-rate value, as shown in Figure 15-2.

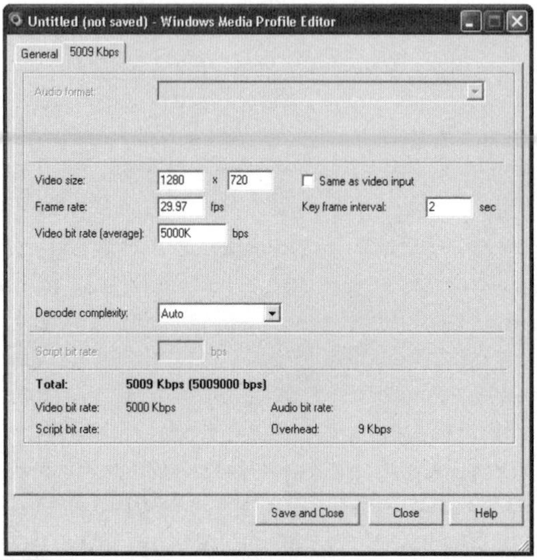

Figure 15-2 The tab where specific encoding preferences are set

You can see that a 5009-Kbps video stream is configured for 1280 × 720, HD dimensions, with a frame rate of 29.97 fps, which is standard for broadcast television. This is definitely adequate for playback of a video—it exceeds the standards for DVD video—but no audio channel is defined. To define an audio channel, select the General tab again, select the Audio check box, and select a mode and codec for the audio stream, as shown in Figure 15-3.

Figure 15-3   Adding an audio stream to the profile

Note that once the basic features of the stream have been established, the bit rate of the combined stream changes and the name of the bit-rate tab changes to match. The bit-rate tab allows you to fine-tune the format of the audio stream. You can select a bit rate from 320 Kbps (for better-than-CD quality) down to 5 Kbps, which would sound like a very bad mobile phone call! Once you select the encoding particulars for the audio stream, you can write this profile back to disk by selecting the General tab and clicking Save And Close. If you want to save these settings as a new profile, you can select Export.

A single profile can define encoding that delivers multiple streams. This might be useful, for example, if a single file (such as a news clip) is aimed at a variety of users who are connected over modems, mobile links, ISDN, and high-speed broadband links. When you load a multiple bit-rate profile (d2_cbr_film.prx) into the Profile Editor, you get a tab for each bit rate in the stream, as shown in Figure 15-4.

Figure 15-4   Defining multiple streams and multiple bit rates in a single profile to target streaming content to a variety of connections and devices

Once again, you can modify the characteristics of any bit rate in the profile, or you can add new bit rates to the profile by clicking the Add button on the General tab. When you click the Add button, a dialog box will ask you for the target bit rate. You can give any value you like, all the way from 1 bps to 100 Gbps—although neither extreme is likely to work well! If you specify a bit rate that is too low relative to other variables, such as video rectangle size and key frame interval, the end result might be less than satisfactory, assuming the Windows Media Format SDK even accepts the profile as valid and tries to compress a file based on it. Creating profiles is an art, and you'll probably spend some time tweaking yours until they yield the best results.

DirectShow and Windows Media

To integrate most efficiently with the Windows Media Format SDK, the Direct-Show development team chose to implement the WM ASF Reader and Writer filters as "thin wrappers" of the Windows Media Format SDK. The filters act as a bridge between the reader and writer objects in that SDK and the rest of the DirectShow filter graph. They make it very easy, relatively speaking, to stream data into and out of the Windows Media reader and writer objects, using all the power of DirectShow to handle format conversion, intermediate transforms, and stream synchronization. For non-streaming functionality, such as profile creation, metadata insertion, and certain other configuration tasks, the application can talk directly to the Windows Media Format SDK.

You can also build graphs automatically using Intelligent Connect to create ASF file transcoding graphs with the WM ASF Writer object as the renderer; this filter creates ASF files from any number of input streams. The *IFilterGraph2* method *RenderEx* renders only to renderer filters that already exist in the graph when the call is made if you specify the flag *AM_RENDEREX_RENDERTO-EXISTINGRENDERERS*. You build this filter graph by first adding the WM ASF Writer filter to the filter graph. This filter has a default configuration for encoding streams passed to it by the filter graph. We used that default configuration when we used the filter in previous chapters, but as I explained earlier in this chapter, the filter's default profile uses the Windows Media 8 codecs. Therefore, to use the Windows Media 9 Series codecs, you must configure the filter with a custom Windows Media profile, as part of the filter initialization process, before file encoding can commence.

To configure the WM ASF Writer filter, you must query it for its *IConfigAsfWriter2* interface. (Because this interface exists only on the latest version of the filter, which ships with the Windows Media Format SDK, it is documented there rather than in DirectX.) *IConfigAsfWriter2* inherits much of its functionality from the *IConfigAsfWriter* interface (which exists on earlier versions of the filter and is documented in the DirectX SDK documentation). *IConfigAsfWriter* has several methods that allow a profile to be applied to the filter, including *ConfigureFilterUsingProfile*, which takes a pointer to an *IWMProfile* interface, using that profile to configure the filter. To instantiate the profile object, you can either create it from scratch or load it from a .PRX file using the Windows Media Format SDK method *LoadProfile*. We're using the latter method for the sake of convenience, which is why we downloaded the Windows Media Profile Editor. *LoadProfile* returns a *IWMProfile* interface on the object; through this and related interfaces, your application works with the profile.

The *IWMProfile* interface has a rich set of methods that allow you to manually adjust each of the parameters of the profile—just as we did with a GUI in the Windows Media Profile Editor. However, using the *IWMProfile* interface means you can build a profile that might be rejected by the Windows Media Format SDK, so you have to guard against errors your profile might generate when you put it to work. The upside of this power is that the *IWMProfile* methods offer greater functionality than the Profile Editor. (A caveat: for audio streams, you can't arbitrarily change the stream encoding; you must retrieve the list of formats using *IWMCodecInfo3* and select an entry from that list.)

As mentioned earlier, the DirectShow filters for reading and writing Windows Media files are implemented as a thin wrapper. These filters allow DirectShow applications to program directly to the Windows Media Format SDK if necessary. When you use the Windows Media Format SDK from within a DirectShow application, your operations will likely be confined to one of these interfaces:

■ *IWMReaderAdvanced*, which handles the parsing of ASF files and is provided as an interface on the WM ASF Reader filter.

■ *IWMWriterAdvanced2*, which manages the creation and composition of ASF files and is available through the *IServiceProvider* interface on the WM ASF Writer filter.

■ *IWMHeaderInfo3*, which adds or modifies metadata information. You can obtain this interface only in a roundabout way, by calling *Query-Interface* using a *IWMWriterAdvanced2* pointer that you obtain using a *QueryService* call.

■ *IWMMetadataEditor*, which allows you to open Windows Media file and manipulate the header information within it.

■ *IWMProfileManager*, which allows you to create, load, and save profiles.

■ *IWMCodecInfo3*, which provides the configuration of supported formats for the Windows Media codecs. If you want to change the parameters of an audio stream, you must obtain the stream configuration information using the methods of this interface.

■ *IWMProfile3*, which provides access to the information in a profile object.

■ *IWMStreamConfig3*, which enables configuration of individual media streams.

■ *IWMMutualExclusion2*, which enables you to configure mutually exclusive streams (such as those created for multiple bit-rate profiles).

■ *IWMMediaProps*, which provides access to basic media properties for streams.

Full documentation on these interfaces and their methods can be found in the Windows Media Format SDK documentation.

With these COM-based interfaces to Windows Media, you can have very fine-grained control over the creation, encoding, and parsing of ASF files. Each interface works in conjunction with one of the two DirectShow filters, WM ASF Reader or WM ASF Writer, to expose low-level controls not provided in the standard filter interfaces.

The most difficult aspects of streaming media file creation, such as dealing with timing and synchronization issues among multiple streams with different encoding rules, are handled invisibly by DirectShow's WM ASF Reader and WM ASF Writer filters. Yet again, DirectShow hides the complexity of the Windows Media API behind a few very simple components.

MakeASF: Using DirectShow and Windows Media in an Application

The two most common tasks DirectShow applications perform on Windows Media files are decoding (playback) and encoding. Decoding can be handled with the *RenderFile* method on the *IFilterGraph* interface, but encoding is a more sophisticated procedure, involving Windows Media profile creation and manipulation. MakeASF is a GUI-based application that "transcodes" (decodes and then encodes) a media file from any format understood by DirectShow (and that's a lot of formats) into a Windows Media–format ASF file. In this sense, MakeASF is a "universal translator" that you can use to produce Windows Media files from almost any media file you encounter. The interface elements in MakeASF are simple and straightforward, as shown in Figure 15-5.

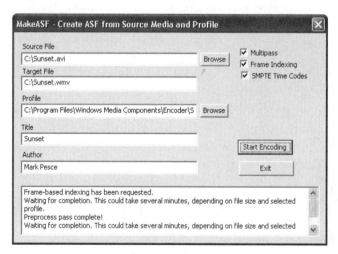

Figure 15-5   The MakeASF application, which accepts nearly any media file as input and outputs a Windows Media ASF file

The application's window allows you to browse for the source media file. It automatically creates an output file name based on the source file name, but the user can edit this field. Next you select a profile file (with the .PRX extension), which specifies the encoding parameters for the output file. Finally, you can add output file metadata by typing in the Title and Author fields. Three encoding options are available. The Multipass option allows the Windows Media codec to review and preprocess the entire media sample before beginning the encoding process. This requires more processing time but generally improves stream quality at a given bit rate. Frame Indexing adds index numbers to the frames, which allows the created file to respond to frame-addressable seek commands. SMPTE Time Codes adds timecode information (as described in Chapter 6) to data unit extensions for the file. (Don't confuse these optional timecodes with the timestamps that will be applied to each media sample in the file.)

After you specify all the parameters, click Start Encoding to begin the transcoding process. This process takes some time, and you won't see any progress dialog box or thermometer-type visual feedback, but an output field at the bottom of the window gives up-to-date progress information as the encoding process proceeds. The transcoding process isn't speedy—a lot of work is going on even though it all looks simple enough—but eventually the field will report "Encoding complete!" Next we'll take a detailed look at how MakeASF works.

Constructing the Filter Graph

The filter graph is constructed and executed in one monolithic function, *Make-AsfFile*. *MakeAsfFile* is a big function, but it breaks into the following discrete steps:

1. Load a profile from disk. (This step is required unless you choose to create a profile from scratch.)

2. If the profile specifies a display window of zero dimensions for video, adjust the video dimension in the profile to a temporary valid value until you can determine the native dimensions of the input stream. (This step, together with step 9, is optional.)

3. Create the filter graph.

4. Add the WM ASF Writer filter to the graph.

5. Apply the loaded profile to the WM ASF Writer filter.

6. Set configuration parameters on the WM ASF Writer based on UI selections.

7. Add the File Source filter to the graph.

8. Connect all output pins of the File Source filter to corresponding input pins on the WM ASF Writer filter.

9. Readjust the dimensions of the video rectangle in the profile, if necessary. (Optional, together with step 2.)

10. Add data unit extensions for SMPTE timecode, if selected in the UI, and install a callback routine that will add the SMPTE timecode data to every sample as it passes through the WM ASF Writer. (Optional.)

11. Add the title and author metadata. (Optional.)

12. Run the filter graph, and stop it when it completes.

13. If multipass encoding has been selected in the UI, rewind the source to the beginning and run the filter graph again, stopping it when complete. (Optional.)

14. Run the frame indexing functions, if selected in the UI. (Optional.)

15. Release everything and exit.

This is a lot of work for just one function to perform, so *MakeAsfFile* makes calls to other local functions to perform some of the tasks. Here's the function's first portion, where it loads the profile:

```
HRESULT MakeAsfFile(_TCHAR* szSource, _TCHAR* szTarget, _TCHAR* szProfile)
{
    HRESULT hr;
    WCHAR wszTargetFile[_MAX_PATH] = {'\0'};
    WCHAR wszSourceFile[_MAX_PATH] = {'\0'};
    WCHAR wszAuthor[_MAX_PATH] = {'\0'};
    WCHAR wszTitle[_MAX_PATH] = {'\0'};

    CComPtr <IGraphBuilder>    pGraph;
    CComPtr <IBaseFilter>      pSourceFilter;
    CComPtr <IBaseFilter>      pASFWriter;

    CASFCallback*                         pASFCallback = NULL;
    CComPtr <IAMWMBufferPassCallback> pSMPTECallback;

    // Convert target filename,
    // title and author metadata fields to a wide character string.
    wcsncpy(wszTargetFile, szTarget, NUMELMS(wszTargetFile));
    wcsncpy(wszAuthor, szAuthor, NUMELMS(wszAuthor));
    wcsncpy(wszTitle, szTitle, NUMELMS(wszTitle));

    // Load the prx file into memory
    // and tell us whether it is a special case profile with a zero-sized
    // video rectangle. If it is, we'll have to adjust the profile later,
    // to specify the native video size before running the graph.
    // This is how the Windows Media Encoder works with profiles created
    // by the Profile Editor.
```

```
CComPtr<IWMProfile> pProfile1;
BOOL bZeroSizedVidRect = FALSE;

// Load the data in the prx file into a WMProfile object.
hr = LoadCustomProfile((LPCSTR)szProfile, &pProfile1,
    bZeroSizedVidRect);
if(FAILED(hr))
{
    DbgLog((LOG_TRACE, 3,
        _T("Failed to load profile!  hr=0x%x\n"), hr));
    return hr;
}


if(bZeroSizedVidRect)
{
    OutputMsg(_T("The profile has a zero-sized rectangle. This will be →
    interpreted as an instruction to use the native video size.\r\n"));
    DbgLog((LOG_TRACE, 3, _T("Zero-sized rectangle!\n")));

    // Now we need to insert some dummy values
    // for the output rectangle in order to avoid an
    // unhandled exception when we first configure the filter
    // with this profile.
    // Later, after we connect the filter,
    // we will be able to determine the upstream rectangle size, and
    // then adjust profile's rectangle values to match it.

    hr = SetNativeVideoSize(pASFWriter, pProfile1, TRUE);
    if(FAILED(hr))
    {
        DbgLog((LOG_TRACE, 3,
            _T("Failed to SetNativeVideoSize with dummy values!  →
                hr=0x%x\n"), hr));
        return hr;
    }
}
```

The MakeASF application uses ATL smart pointers to handle the instantiation and management of COM objects. A smart pointer to an *IWMProfile* interface is created to manage the profile for the transcoding. It is then loaded from disk, in the function *LoadCustomProfile* (taken from the Windows Media Format SDK samples):

```
HRESULT LoadCustomProfile( LPCTSTR ptszProfileFileName,
                    IWMProfile ** ppIWMProfile, BOOL& bEmptyVidRect )
{
    HRESULT             hr = S_OK;
    DWORD               dwLength = 0;
```

```
DWORD             dwBytesRead = 0;
IWMProfileManager * pProfileManager = NULL;
HANDLE            hFile = INVALID_HANDLE_VALUE;
LPWSTR            pwszProfile = NULL;

if( NULL == ptszProfileFileName || NULL == ptszProfileFileName )
{
    return( E_POINTER );
}

do
{
    //
    // Create profile manager.
    //
    hr = CreateProfileManager( &pProfileManager );
    if( FAILED( hr ) )
    {
        break;
    }


    //
    // Open the profile file.
    //
    hFile = CreateFile( ptszProfileFileName,
                        GENERIC_READ,
                        FILE_SHARE_READ,
                        NULL,
                        OPEN_EXISTING,
                        FILE_ATTRIBUTE_NORMAL,
                        NULL );
    if( INVALID_HANDLE_VALUE == hFile )
    {
        hr = HRESULT_FROM_WIN32( GetLastError() );
        break;
    }

    if( FILE_TYPE_DISK != GetFileType( hFile ) )
    {
        hr = NS_E_INVALID_NAME;
        break;
    }

    dwLength = GetFileSize( hFile, NULL );
    if( -1 == dwLength )
    {
        hr = HRESULT_FROM_WIN32( GetLastError() );
```

```
                break;
            }


            //
            // Allocate memory to hold profile XML file.
            //
            pwszProfile = (WCHAR *)new BYTE[ dwLength + sizeof(WCHAR) ];
            if( NULL == pwszProfile )
            {
                hr = E_OUTOFMEMORY;
                break;
            }

            // The buffer must be null-terminated.
            ZeroMemory(pwszProfile, dwLength + sizeof(WCHAR) ) ;

            //
            // Read the profile to a buffer.
            //
            if( !ReadFile( hFile, pwszProfile, dwLength, &dwBytesRead, NULL ) )
            {
                hr = HRESULT_FROM_WIN32( GetLastError() );
                break;
            }


            //
            // Load the profile from the buffer
            //
            hr = pProfileManager->LoadProfileByData( pwszProfile,
                                                     ppIWMProfile );
            if( FAILED(hr) )
            {
                break;
            }
        }
    }
    while( FALSE );


    // The WM Profile Editor uses empty rectangles
    // as a signal to the Windows Media Encoder
    // to use the native video size.
    // Our application will do the same thing.
    // Here we cheat for the sake of efficiency. In general, do not
    // get into the habit of manipulating the XML profile string directly.
    // Here we are just peeking to see
    // if we have an empty video rectangle.
    // If we do have one,
    // we won't attempt to modify the XML string directly, but
    // instead will just set a flag now
    // and modify the profile object later using the SDK methods.
```

```
if(SUCCEEDED(hr))
{
    if( wcsstr( pwszProfile , L"biwidth=\"0\"" ) !=
        NULL || wcsstr( pwszProfile , L"biheight=\"0\"" ) != NULL )
    {
        bEmptyVidRect = TRUE;
    }
}

//
// Release all resources.
//
SAFE_ARRAYDELETE( pwszProfile );
SAFE_CLOSEHANDLE( hFile );
SAFE_RELEASE( pProfileManager );

return( hr );
}
```

LoadCustomProfile is our first example of how a DirectShow application programs directly to the Windows Media Format SDK. It instantiates a Windows Media Profile Manager object in the call to *CreateProfileManager*, which is just a wrapper around a call to *WMCreateProfileManager*. The specified file containing the XML schema for the profile is opened and read into memory. The XML is parsed and returned in a pointer to an *IWMProfile* interface in the Profile Manager method *LoadProfileByData*. Although the profile has been loaded successfully, the function takes the extra (optional) step of examining the XML of the profile for the *biwidth* and *biheight* values contained in the schema. The Windows Media Encoder application knows what this means, but the Windows Media Format SDK does not. To be as smart as the Encoder, we check the rectangle, and if it is empty, the global flag *bEmptyVidRect* is set. If, on return, the flag is set, the function *SetNativeVideoSize* is called:

```
HRESULT SetNativeVideoSize(IBaseFilter* pASFWriter, IWMProfile* pProfile,
    BOOL bUseDummyValues)
{
    HRESULT hr = S_OK;

    // Get the native rectangle size from the video pin.
    SIZE nativeRect;

    if( TRUE == bUseDummyValues)
    {
        nativeRect.cx = 640;
        nativeRect.cy = 480;
    }
```

```
        else
        {
            nativeRect = GetVideoSizeFromPin(pASFWriter);
        }
        // For the profile,
        // get the IWMStreamConfig interface for the video stream.
        DWORD dwStreams = 0;
        DWORD dwMediaTypeSize = 0;
        hr = pProfile->GetStreamCount(&dwStreams);
        if ( FAILED( hr ) )
        {
            DbgLog((LOG_TRACE, 3, _T("Failed GetStreamCount (hr=0x%08x)!\n"),
                hr));
            return hr;
        }

        for(WORD j = 1; j <= dwStreams ; j++)
        {
            CComPtr<IWMStreamConfig> pWMStreamConfig;
            hr = pProfile->GetStreamByNumber(j, &pWMStreamConfig);
            if ( FAILED( hr ) )
            {
                DbgLog((LOG_TRACE, 3,
                    _T("Failed GetStreamByNumber (hr=0x%08x)!\n"), hr ));
                return hr;
            }

            // Get the stream's major type.
            // Note that we assume only one video stream in the file.
            GUID guidStreamType;
            hr = pWMStreamConfig->GetStreamType(&guidStreamType);
            if ( FAILED( hr ) )
            {
                DbgLog((LOG_TRACE, 3,
                    _T("Failed GetStreamType (hr=0x%08x)!\n"), hr ));
                return hr;
            }

            if(IsEqualGUID(WMMEDIATYPE_Video, guidStreamType))
            {
                CComQIPtr<IWMMediaProps, &IID_IWMMediaProps>
                    pMediaProps (pWMStreamConfig);
                if(!pMediaProps)
                {
                    DbgLog((LOG_TRACE, 3,
                        _T("Failed to QI for IWMMediaProps (hr=0x%08x)!\n"),
                        hr ));
```

```
        return hr;
    }


    //Retrieve the amount of memory required
    // to hold the returned structure.
    hr = pMediaProps->GetMediaType(NULL, &dwMediaTypeSize);
    if(FAILED( hr ) )
    {
        DbgLog((LOG_TRACE, 3,
            _T("Failed GetMediaType first call(hr=0x%08x)!\n"),
            hr ));
        return hr;
    }


    //Allocate the memory.
    BYTE *pData = 0;
    do
    {
        pData = new BYTE[ dwMediaTypeSize ];

        if ( NULL == pData )
        {
            hr = E_OUTOFMEMORY;
            DbgLog((LOG_TRACE, 3,
                _T( " Out of memory: (hr=0x%08x)\n" ), hr ));
            break;
        }

        ZeroMemory( pData, dwMediaTypeSize );

        // Retrieve the actual WM_MEDIA_TYPE structure
        // and format block.
        hr = pMediaProps->GetMediaType( ( WM_MEDIA_TYPE *) pData,
            &dwMediaTypeSize );
        if ( FAILED( hr ) )
        {
            DbgLog((LOG_TRACE, 3,
                _T( " GetMediatype second call failed: →
                (hr=0x%08x)\n" ), hr ));
            break;
        }

        WM_MEDIA_TYPE* pMT =
            ( WM_MEDIA_TYPE *) pData; // pMT is easier to read

        // Set the native video rectangle size
        // on the BITMAPINFOHEADER.
        if(IsEqualGUID(pMT->formattype, WMFORMAT_VideoInfo))
```

```
            {
                WMVIDEOINFOHEADER* pWMVih =
                    (WMVIDEOINFOHEADER*) pMT->pbFormat;
                pWMVih->bmiHeader.biHeight = nativeRect.cy;
                pWMVih->bmiHeader.biWidth = nativeRect.cx;
            }
            else
            {
                // We only handle WMFORMAT_VideoInfo.
                DbgLog((LOG_TRACE, 3,
                    _T( "Video Media Type is not WMFORMAT_VideoInfo\n" )
                    ));
                break;
            }

            hr = pMediaProps->SetMediaType(pMT);
            if ( FAILED( hr ) )
            {
                DbgLog((LOG_TRACE, 3,
                    _T( " SetMediaType failed: (hr=0x%08x)\n" ), hr ));
                break;
            }
            hr = pProfile->ReconfigStream(pWMStreamConfig);
            if ( FAILED( hr ) )
            {
                DbgLog((LOG_TRACE, 3,
                    _T( " ReconfigStream failed: (hr=0x%08x)\n" ), hr ));
                break;
            }

        }while (FALSE);

        SAFE_ARRAYDELETE(pData);

    }//end ifIsEqualGUID

    }

    return hr;

}
```

SetNativeVideoSize examines the *IWMProfile* pointer passed to it, and it determines the number of streams in the profile. The function assumes that there is only one video stream in the file and iterates through the streams, calling the *IWMProfile* interface method *GetStreamByNumber*, which returns a pointer to an *IWMStreamConfig* interface. The stream's media major type is returned in a call to the *IWMStreamConfig* method *GetStreamType*. This returns a GUID value, which is then compared to *WMMEDIATYPE_Video*, the GUID for Windows Media video streams.

Now that we know we're working with a video stream, we can query for the *IWMMediaProps* interface on the *IWMStreamConfig* interface. This interface allows us to examine the media type–specific properties of the stream with a call to its method *GetMediaType*. The first call passes a null pointer, so it returns the size of the buffer needed to hold the media type. When allocated, a second call to *GetMediaType* returns a pointer to the *WM_MEDIA_TYPE* structure. The definition of this structure is identical to the definition of the *AM_MEDIA_TYPE* structure we've used throughout the last several chapters. (The format block is allocated as part of the memory for the media type.) Once we have that structure in memory, we modify it with the new temporary video size (a default of 640 x 480, because it's a standard video size) and then commit these changes to the stream with a call to the *IWMMediaProps* method *SetMediaType*.

Finally, the profile must be reconfigured to accommodate the media type change to one of its streams. We do this with a call to the *IWMProfile* method *ReconfigStream*, which is passed a pointer to the modified *IWMStreamConfig* object. We must do this to accommodate a scenario where the user wants to keep the native video size but doesn't know that size in advance. When you have more control over the encoding settings and you know in advance the input size or the desired output size, or if you simply disallow zero-sized video rectangles, you can delete *SetNativeVideoSize* and its related code from your application.

Now that the profile has been loaded and adjusted, we can return to *MakeAsfFile*, where we now build the filter graph:

```
// Create an empty DirectShow filter graph.
hr = CreateFilterGraph(&pGraph);
if(FAILED(hr))
{
    DbgLog((LOG_TRACE, 3,
        _T("Couldn't create filter graph! hr=0x%x"), hr));
    return hr;
}

// Create the WS ASF Writer Filter.
hr = CreateFilter(CLSID_WMAsfWriter, &pASFWriter);
if(FAILED(hr))
{
    DbgLog((LOG_TRACE, 3,
        _T("Failed to create WMAsfWriter filter!  hr=0x%x\n"), hr));
    return hr;
}
```

```
// Get a file sink filter interface from the ASF Writer filter
// and set the output file name.
CComQIPtr<IFileSinkFilter, &IID_IFileSinkFilter>
    pFileSink (pASFWriter);
if(!pFileSink)
{
    DbgLog((LOG_TRACE, 3,
        _T("Failed to create QI IFileSinkFilter!  hr=0x%x\n"), hr));
    return hr;
}


hr = pFileSink->SetFileName(wszTargetFile, NULL);
if(FAILED(hr))
{
    DbgLog((LOG_TRACE, 3,
        _T("Failed to set target filename!  hr=0x%x\n"), hr));
    return hr;
}

// Add the WM ASF writer to the graph.
hr = pGraph->AddFilter(pASFWriter, L"ASF Writer");
if(FAILED(hr))
{
    DbgLog((LOG_TRACE, 3,
        _T("Failed to add ASF Writer filter to graph!  hr=0x%x\n"), hr));
    return hr;
}


// Obtain the interface we will use to configure the WM ASF Writer.
CComQIPtr<IConfigAsfWriter2, &IID_IConfigAsfWriter2>
    pConfigAsfWriter2(pASFWriter);
if(!pConfigAsfWriter2)
{
    DbgLog((LOG_TRACE, 3,
        _T("Failed to QI for IConfigAsfWriter2!  hr=0x%x\n"), hr));
    return hr;
}

// Configure the filter with the profile.
hr = pConfigAsfWriter2->ConfigureFilterUsingProfile(pProfile1);
if(FAILED(hr))
{
    DbgLog((LOG_TRACE, 3,
        _T("Failed to configure filter to use profile1!  hr=0x%08x\n"),
            hr));
    return hr;
}
```

```
// If frame-based indexing was requested, disable the default
// time-based (temporal) indexing.
if (g_fFrameIndexing)
{
    hr = pConfigAsfWriter2->SetIndexMode(FALSE);
    if(FAILED(hr))
    {
        DbgLog((LOG_TRACE, 3,
            _T("Failed to disable time-based indexing!  hr=0x%08x\n"),
            hr));
        return hr;
    }
    OutputMsg(_T("Frame-based indexing has been requested.\r\n"));
}

// Enable multipass encoding if requested.
if (g_fMultipassEncode)
{
    hr = pConfigAsfWriter2->SetParam(AM_CONFIGASFWRITER_PARAM_MULTIPASS,
        TRUE, 0);
    if (FAILED(hr))
    {
        DbgLog((LOG_TRACE, 3,
            _T("Failed to enable multipass encoding param!  ⇥
            hr=0x%x\n"), hr));
        return hr;
    }
}
// Set sync source to NULL to encode as fast as possible.
SetNoClock(pGraph);

// Convert the source file into WCHARs for DirectShow.
wcsncpy(wszSourceFile, szSource, NUMELMS(wszSourceFile));
DbgLog((LOG_TRACE, 3, _T("\nCopying [%ls] to [%ls]\n"),
    wszSourceFile, wszTargetFile));

// Let DirectShow render the source file.
// We use "AddSourceFilter" and then
// render its output pins using IFilterGraph2::RenderEx
// in order to force the
// Filter Graph Manager to always use the
// WM ASF Writer as the renderer.

hr = pGraph->AddSourceFilter(wszSourceFile, L"Source Filter",
    &pSourceFilter);
if(FAILED(hr))
{
    DbgLog((LOG_TRACE, 3,
```

```
            _T("Failed to add source filter!  hr=0x%x\n"), hr));
        return hr;
    }

    // Render all output pins on source filter using RenderEx.
    hr = RenderOutputPins(pSourceFilter, pGraph);
    if(FAILED(hr))
    {
        DbgLog((LOG_TRACE, 3,
            _T("Failed RenderOutputPins!  hr=0x%x\n"), hr));
        return hr;
    }
```

The filter graph building is a straightforward affair: a filter graph is created, and the WM ASF Writer and File Source filters are instantiated and added to the filter graph. The *IFileSink* interface on the WM ASF Writer is used to call *SetFile-Name* on the output file. The WM ASF Writer also presents an *IConfigAsfWriter2* interface (which is documented only in the Windows Media Format SDK, although it inherits most of its methods from *IConfigAsfWriter*, which is documented in the DirectX SDK), and the Windows Media profile is applied to the filter, using the *IConfigAsfWriter* interface method *ConfigureFilterUsingProfile*.

Two of the user settings, for multipass encoding and frame indexing, are implemented in calls to *IConfigAsfWriter* methods. These are user options, so they are obviously not required steps. First, a call to *SetIndexMode* turns off automatic indexing of the ASF file. We want frame-based indexing, not temporal indexing (based against the *REFERENCE_TIME* of the samples), so we have to turn off the latter to prevent automatic index generation. (We'll turn on frame indexing just as we finish the entire transcoding process.) Next, we call the *Set-Param* method, with a parameter value of *AM_CONFIGASFWRITER_MULTPASS* to tell the filter that multipass encoding will be used. As you'll see later, when multipass encoding is enabled, the filter graph is run twice, sequentially, so the encoder can process the streams twice.

The source filter is added with a call to the *IGraphBuilder* method *AddSourceFilter*, and then control passes to the local function *RenderOutput-Pins*, which attempts to detect all the streams presented by the source filter and connects them to the WM ASF Writer filter:

```
HRESULT RenderOutputPins(IBaseFilter *pFilter, IGraphBuilder* pGB)
{

    CComPtr <IEnumPins>     pEnum;
    CComPtr <IPin>          pPin;
    CComQIPtr<IFilterGraph2, &IID_IFilterGraph2> pFilterGraph2(pGB);

    HRESULT hr = pFilter->EnumPins(&pEnum);
```

```
    if (FAILED(hr))
    {
        return hr;
    }

    while(pEnum->Next(1, &pPin, 0) == S_OK)
    {
        PIN_DIRECTION PinDirThis;
        pPin->QueryDirection(&PinDirThis);
        if (PINDIR_OUTPUT == PinDirThis)
        {
            pFilterGraph2->RenderEx(pPin,
                AM_RENDEREX_RENDERTOEXISTINGRENDERERS, NULL);
            if (FAILED(hr))
            {
                DbgLog((LOG_TRACE, 3,
                    _T("Failed to render source filter pin (hr=0x%08x)!\n"),
                    hr));
                return hr;
            }
        }
        pPin.Release();
    }

    return hr;
}
```

RenderOutputPins enumerates the pins on the source filter; for each output pin, the *IFilterGraph2* method *RenderEx* is invoked. *RenderEx* forces rendering of a media stream through to renderer filters already present in the filter graph. In this case, this can only mean the WM ASF Writer filter because it's the only renderer filter in the filter graph. Every stream presented by the source filter is connected—perhaps through some intermediate conversion filters (using Intelligent Connect)—to the WM ASF Writer filter. With the connections made, control passes back to *MakeAsfFile*:

```
    // Verify that all of our input pins are connected.
    // If the profile specifies more streams
    // than are actually contained in the source file,
    // the filter will not run. So here we check
    // for the condition ourselves and fail gracefully if necessary.

    hr = VerifyInputsConnected(pASFWriter);
    if(FAILED(hr))
    {
        OutputMsg(_T("Cannot encode this file because not all input pins ➔
            were connected. The profile specifies more input streams than ➔
            the file contains. Aborting copy operation. \r\n"));
```

```
            DbgLog((LOG_TRACE, 3,
                _T("Not all inputs connected!  hr=0x%x\n"), hr));
            return hr;
        }


        // To support profiles that were created
        // in the Windows Media Profile Editor, we need to
        // handle the case where the user selected
        // the "Video Size Same as Input" option. This causes
        // the video rectangle in the profile to be set to zero.
        // The WM Encoder understands the "zero" value
        // and obtains the source video size before encoding.
        // If we don't do the same thing, we will create a
        // valid ASF file but it will have no video frames.
        // We have waited until now to check the input rectangle
        // size because it is most efficient to do this
        // after the filter graph has been built.

        if(bZeroSizedVidRect)
        {
            hr = SetNativeVideoSize(pASFWriter, pProfile1, FALSE);
            if(FAILED(hr))
            {
                DbgLog((LOG_TRACE, 3,
                    _T("Failed to SetNativeVideoSize!  hr=0x%x\n"), hr));
                return hr;
            }

            hr = pConfigAsfWriter2->ConfigureFilterUsingProfile(pProfile1);
            if(FAILED(hr))
            {
                DbgLog((LOG_TRACE, 3,
                    _T("Failed ConfigureFilterUsingProfile-2-!  hr=0x%x\n"),
                    hr));
                return hr;
            }

            OutputMsg(_T("Filter was successfully reconfigured ⮐
                for native video size.\r\n"));
        }
```

VerifyInputsConnected walks through the list of input pins on the WM ASF Writer filter, verifying that all the inputs are connected. If any input pins are left unconnected, a mismatch of some sort has occurred between the media streams presented by the File Source filter on its output pins and the number of streams expected by the WM ASF Writer filter based on the profile we gave it. The output profile must match the input media streams exactly, or the filter graph won't execute. *VerifyInputsConnected* lets us fail gracefully if a problem is found. (Strictly speaking, this step is optional, but the application could crash without this check!)

Now that we have a filter graph, we can discover what our input stream looks like, so once again we call *SetNativeVideoSize*—this time modifying the profile not with dummy values but with the dimnsions of the actual video stream. We pass FALSE as the final parameter, which forces *SetNativeVideoSize* to issue a call to the local function *GetVideoSizeFromPin*. *GetVideoSizeFromPin* retrieves the *AM_MEDIA_TYPE* associated with all pins on a filter, looks for a *FORMAT_VideoInfo* or *FORMAT_VideoInfo2* format type, and extracts the video size from the fields associated with those formats.

Adding Data Unit Extensions to Windows Media

The Windows Media Format SDK allows you to add supplemental data to the streams within a Windows Media file using *data unit extensions* (also known as *payload extension systems*). A data unit extension is simply a name that is paired with some data that's attached to a sample (or series of samples) in the Windows Media file. You can add data unit extensions while the Windows Media file is being created and then extract them from the file during playback.

The data unit extensions are sometimes confused with metadata. Like the data unit extensions, metadata is extra data added to an ASF file; unlike data unit extensions, metadata generally appears at the head of the file and is unconnected with any particular stream. Title and author information, for example, are both metadata types, while timecode information, which occurs on a per-sample basis, is a data unit extension.

In MakeASF, the author and title information are added once, to the file headers. The SMPTE timecode, on the other hand, is added on a per-sample basis, throughout the entire length of the sample. This requires a callback mechanism so the timecode information can be added to each sample just before the sample is encoded. Here's how we set up SMPTE timecoding in *MakeAsfFile*:

```
// When adding Data Unit Extensions,
// the order of operations is very important.

if (TRUE == g_SMPTETimecodes)
{
    // (1) Set the DUE on the profile stream.
    hr = AddSmpteDataUnitExtension(pProfile1);
    if(FAILED(hr))
```

```
    {
        DbgLog((LOG_TRACE, 3,
            _T("Failed AddSmpteDataUnitExtension!  hr=0x%x\n"), hr));
        return hr;
    }


    // (2) Update the filter with the new profile.
    hr = pConfigAsfWriter2->ConfigureFilterUsingProfile(pProfile1);
    if(FAILED(hr))
    {
        DbgLog((LOG_TRACE, 3,
            _T("Failed ConfigureFilterUsingProfile-3-!  hr=0x%x\n"),
            hr));
        return hr;
    }


    // (3) Find the video pin and register our callback.
    // Note here we use the same object to handle DUE callbacks
    // and index callbacks. So we create the object
    // on the heap , which is how COM objects should be created anyway.

    pASFCallback = new CASFCallback();
    if(!pASFCallback)
    {
        return E_OUTOFMEMORY;
    }

    DbgLog((LOG_TRACE, 3,
        _T("About to QI for IAMWMBufferPassCallback!\n")));
    hr = pASFCallback->QueryInterface( IID_IAMWMBufferPassCallback ,
        (void**) &pSMPTECallback);
    if(FAILED(hr))
    {
        DbgLog((LOG_TRACE, 3,
            _T("Failed to QI for IAMWMBufferPassCallback!  hr=0x%x\n"),
            hr));
        return hr;
    }


    // Find the video pin.
    CComPtr<IPin> pVideoPin;
    hr = GetPinByMajorType(pASFWriter, PINDIR_INPUT, MEDIATYPE_Video,
        &pVideoPin);
    if(FAILED(hr))
    {
        DbgLog((LOG_TRACE, 3,
            _T("Failed to GetPinByMajorType(pVideoPin)!  hr=0x%x\n"),
            hr));
```

```
        return hr;
    }


    // Get its IAMWMBufferPass interface.
    CComQIPtr<IAMWMBufferPass, &IID_IAMWMBufferPass>
        pBufferPass( pVideoPin ) ;

    DbgLog((LOG_TRACE, 3, _T("About to set callback!  hr=0x%x\n"), hr)) ;
    // Give it the pointer to our object.
    hr = pBufferPass->SetNotify( (IAMWMBufferPassCallback*)
        pSMPTECallback) ;
    if(FAILED(hr))
    {
        DbgLog((LOG_TRACE, 3,
            _T("Failed to set callback!  hr=0x%x\n"), hr)) ;
        return hr;
    }


}
// Now that we have set the final profile,
// we can safely add the metadata.
hr = AddMetadata(pASFWriter, wszAuthor, wszTitle);
if(FAILED(hr))
    {
        DbgLog((LOG_TRACE, 3,
            _T("Failed to set AddMetadata!  hr=0x%x\n"), hr));
        return hr;
    }
```

In the first step, the profile is updated with the SMPTE timecode information in a call to *AddSmpteDataUnitExtension*. The profile must be updated because the SMPTE timecode information is being added to the stream data, and this will affect the overall bandwidth requirements of the stream:

```
HRESULT AddSmpteDataUnitExtension(IWMProfile *pProfile)
{
    HRESULT hr;

    DWORD dwStreams = 0;
    DWORD dwMediaTypeSize = 0;
    hr = pProfile->GetStreamCount(&dwStreams);
    if ( FAILED( hr ) )
    {
        DbgLog((LOG_TRACE, 3,
            _T("Failed GetStreamCount (hr=0x%08x)!\n"), hr ));
        return hr;
    }
```

```
// First, find the profile's video stream.
for(WORD j = 1; j <= dwStreams ; j++)
{
    CComPtr<IWMStreamConfig> pWMStreamConfig;
    hr = pProfile->GetStreamByNumber(j, &pWMStreamConfig);
    if ( FAILED( hr ) )
    {
        DbgLog((LOG_TRACE, 3,
            _T("Failed GetStreamByNumber (hr=0x%08x)!\n"), hr ));
        return hr;
    }

    // Get the stream's major type. Note that in this example we assume
    // that there is only one video stream in the file.
    GUID guidStreamType;
    hr = pWMStreamConfig->GetStreamType(&guidStreamType);
    if ( FAILED( hr ) )
    {
        DbgLog((LOG_TRACE, 3,
            _T("Failed GetStreamType (hr=0x%08x)!\n"), hr ));
        return hr;
    }

    // If this is the video stream, then set the DUE on it.
    if(IsEqualGUID(WMMEDIATYPE_Video, guidStreamType))
    {
        CComQIPtr<IWMStreamConfig2, &IID_IWMStreamConfig2>
            pWMStreamConfig2 (pWMStreamConfig);

        hr = pWMStreamConfig2->AddDataUnitExtension(
            WM_SampleExtensionGUID_Timecode,
            WM_SampleExtension_Timecode_Size, NULL, 0);

        if ( FAILED( hr ) )
        {
            DbgLog((LOG_TRACE, 3,
                _T("Failed to set SMPTE DUE (hr=0x%08x)!\n"), hr ));
            return hr;
        }
        else
        {
            DbgLog((LOG_TRACE, 3,
                _T("AddDataUnitExtension for SMPTE succeeded ->
                (hr=0x%08x)!\n"), hr ));
        }

    // Don't forget to call this,
    // or else none of the changes will go into effect!
```

```
        hr = pProfile->ReconfigStream(pWMStreamConfig);
        if ( FAILED( hr ) )
        {
            DbgLog((LOG_TRACE, 3,
                _T("Failed to reconfig stream (hr=0x%08x)!\n"), hr ));
            return hr;
        }

        return S_OK;

    }

}

// We didn't find a video stream in the profile
// so just fail without trying anything heroic.
return E_FAIL;
}
```

AddSmpteDataUnitExtension walks through the profile (a technique you saw in *SetNativeVideoSize*) looking for the video stream. (If you need to handle profiles with more than one video stream, you have to do some extra work here.) Once it locates the video stream, it acquires the *IWMStreamConfig2* interface for the stream and calls its *AddDataUnitExtension* method. The method is passed a GUID indicating that a timecode will be added, and it passes a size for the timecode data. (A list of the permissible GUIDs for data unit extensions can be found in the Windows Media Format SDK.) *AddDataUnitExtension* adjusts the profile to reflect the timecode data now inserted into the stream. The changes are committed to the profile with another call to the *IWMProfile* method *ReconfigStream*.

Note   Adding data unit extensions to a stream can make the stream much larger, depending on how much data you carry with every sample. This data will need to be streamed—along with any audio and video streams—to the client for playback. If you're not careful, you can add so much data using data unit extensions that it becomes impossible to play your streams over low-bandwidth connections.

Upon the return to *MakeAsfFile*, the new profile is applied to the filter with another call to *ConfigureFilterUsingProfile*. (Using the Windows Media Format SDK, we could have added these data unit extensions to the profile when we created it, but the Windows Media Profile Editor doesn't let you do this. Now you know how to add data unit extensions to a profile on the fly.)

A callback method must be registered on the video input pin of the WM ASF Writer so the SMPTE timecode can be updated as each media sample arrives at the filter. A callback object is instantiated and is queried for its *IAMWMBufferPassCallback* interface, which it inherits as a descendent. The video input pin on the WM ASF Writer filter is located with a call to the local function *GetPinByMajorType*, and using the returned *IPin* pointer, its *IAMWMBufferPass* interface is acquired. This interface is implemented only on the input pins of the WM ASF Writer and output pins of the WM ASF Reader; it is used to register callbacks on those pins. It has one method, *SetNotify*, which is passed a pointer to the *IAMWMBufferPassCallback* object. (The implementation of the callback object is discussed in a later section.) The callback has now been set; on every video sample received by the WM ASF Writer, the callback will be invoked. With the SMPTE timecode metadata callback installed, we can go through the simpler process of adding some author and title metadata to the output file with a call to the local function *AddMetadata*:

```
HRESULT AddMetadata(IBaseFilter* pFilter, WCHAR* pwszAuthor,
    WCHAR* pwszTitle)
{
    HRESULT hr = S_OK;
    CComQIPtr<IServiceProvider, &IID_IServiceProvider>
        pServiceProvider(pFilter);
    if(!pServiceProvider)
    {
        return E_FAIL;
    }

    CComPtr<IWMWriterAdvanced2> pWriterAdvanced2;
    hr = pServiceProvider->QueryService(IID_IWMWriterAdvanced2,
        &pWriterAdvanced2);

    if(FAILED(hr))
    {
        return hr;
    }

    CComQIPtr<IWMHeaderInfo3, &IID_IWMHeaderInfo3>
        pWMHeaderInfo3 (pWriterAdvanced2);
    if (!pWMHeaderInfo3)
    {
        return E_FAIL;
    }
```

```
// If we wanted the ability to modify these attributes later
// in our session, we would store this value.
WORD pwIndex = 0;
DWORD length = (DWORD) (wcslen(pwszAuthor)* sizeof(WCHAR)) ;

//Set the author that the user entered.
hr = pWMHeaderInfo3->AddAttribute(0, g_wszWMAuthor, &pwIndex,
    WMT_TYPE_STRING, 0, (BYTE*) pwszAuthor, length);
if(FAILED(hr))
{
    return hr;
}

//Set the title that the user entered.
length = (DWORD)(wcslen(pwszTitle)* sizeof(WCHAR)) ;
hr = pWMHeaderInfo3->AddAttribute(0, g_wszWMTitle, &pwIndex,
    WMT_TYPE_STRING, 0, (BYTE*) pwszTitle, length);

return hr;
}
```

AddMetadata acquires the *IServiceProvider* interface on the WM ASF
Writer filter. This interface offers a *QueryService* method, which is used to
acquire the *IWMWriterAdvanced2* interface. That interface is queried for its
IWMHeaderInfo3 interface; it has the *AddAttribute* method, which is used to
add metadata to a Windows Media file. The method is passed a stream number
(stream 0, as passed here, means file-level metadata, but metadata can be
applied on a per-stream basis), the name of the metadata attribute (*Author* or
Title in this case), a data type, the data itself, and a length value for the data.
The possible data types for metadata are listed in Table 15-1.

Table 15-1   Data Types for Metadata

Metadata Type	Description
WMT_TYPE_DWORD	32-bit DWORD value
WMT_TYPE_STRING	Null-terminated Unicode string
WMT_TYPE_BINARY	An array of bytes of arbitrary length
WMT_TYPE_BOOL	4-byte Boolean value
WMT_TYPE_QWORD	64-bit QWORD value
WMT_TYPE_WORD	16-bit WORD value
WMT_TYPE_GUID	128-bit GUID value

The File Source and WM ASF Writer filters have been added to the filter graph and interconnected properly. A callback for SMPTE metadata has been added to the WM ASF Writer, if needed, and any author and title metadata has been added to the output file. Now *MakeAsfFile* is ready to run the filter graph:

```
// Now we are ready to run the filter graph and start encoding.
// First we need the IMediaControl interface.
CComQIPtr<IMediaControl, &IID_IMediaControl> pMC(pGraph);

if(!pMC)
{
    DbgLog((LOG_TRACE, 3,
        _T("Failed to QI for IMediaControl!  hr=0x%x\n"), hr));
    return hr;
}

hr = pMC->Run();
if(FAILED(hr))
{
    DbgLog((LOG_TRACE, 3,
        _T("Failed to run the graph!  hr=0x%x\nCopy aborted.\n\n"),
        hr));
    DbgLog((LOG_TRACE, 3,
        _T("Please check that you have selected the correct profile ⮑
        for copying.\n")
        _T("Note that if your source ASF file is audio-only, ⮑
        then selecting a\n")
        _T("video profile will cause a failure when running ⮑
        the graph.\n\n")));
    return hr;
}
```

```
// Wait for the event signaling that we have reached the end
// of the input file. We listen for the
// EC_COMPLETE event here rather than in the app's message loop
// in order to keep the order of operations
// as straightforward as possible. The downside is that
// we cannot stop or pause the graph once it starts.

int nEvent = WaitForCompletion(g_hwnd, pGraph);

// Stop the graph. If we are doing one-pass encoding, then we are done.
// If doing two-pass, then we still have work to do.
hr = pMC->Stop();
if (FAILED(hr))
    DbgLog((LOG_TRACE, 3,
        _T("Failed to stop filter graph!  hr=0x%x\n"), hr));
```

```
// We should never really encounter these two conditions together.
if (g_fMultipassEncode && (nEvent != EC_PREPROCESS_COMPLETE))
{
    DbgLog((LOG_TRACE, 3,
        _T("ERROR: Failed to receive expected EC_PREPROCESSCOMPLETE.\n")));
    return E_FAIL;
}

// If we're using multipass encode, run again.
if (g_fMultipassEncode)
{
    DbgLog((LOG_TRACE, 3, _T("Preprocessing complete.\n")));

    // Seek to beginning of file.
    CComQIPtr<IMediaSeeking, &IID_IMediaSeeking> pMS(pMC);
    if (!pMS)
    {
        DbgLog((LOG_TRACE, 3,
            _T("Failed to QI for IMediaSeeking!\n")));
        return E_FAIL;
    }

    LONGLONG pos=0;
    hr = pMS->SetPositions(&pos, AM_SEEKING_AbsolutePositioning ,
                           NULL, AM_SEEKING_NoPositioning);

    // Run the graph again to perform the actual encoding based on
    // the information gathered by the codec during the first pass.
    hr = pMC->Run();
    if (FAILED(hr))
    {
        DbgLog((LOG_TRACE, 3,
            _T("Failed to run the graph!  hr=0x%x\n"), hr));
        return hr;
    }

    nEvent = WaitForCompletion(g_hwnd, pGraph);
    hr = pMC->Stop();
    if (FAILED(hr))
    {
        DbgLog((LOG_TRACE, 3,
            _T("Failed to stop filter graph after completion!
            hr=0x%x\n"), hr));
        return hr;
    }

    DbgLog((LOG_TRACE, 3, _T("Copy complete.\n")));
```

```
                // Turn off multipass encoding.
                hr = pConfigAsfWriter2->SetParam(AM_CONFIGASFWRITER_PARAM_MULTIPASS,
                    FALSE, 0);
                if (FAILED(hr))
                {
                    DbgLog((LOG_TRACE, 3,
                        _T("Failed to disable multipass encoding!  hr=0x%x\n"), hr));
                    return hr;
                }
            } // end if g_fMultipassEncode
```

The filter graph interface *IMediaControl* receives the Run message, and the filter graph begins execution. The *WaitForCompletion* local function interprets messages sent to the application. If single-pass encoding was specified, the function should return the value *EC_COMPLETE*. If multipass encoding was specified, the function returns *EC_PREPROCESS_COMPLETE*, indicating that the first of the two passes required to encode the streams has completed successfully.

If multipass encoding has been enabled, we need to rewind the source to its beginning so it can play a second time through the filter graph. We do this by acquiring the *IMediaSeeking* interface from the *IMediaControl* interface. We invoke its *SetPositions* method with parameters that specify a rewind to the beginning of the stream. This forces the File Source filter to seek to the beginning of the input file. Once the stream is rewound, the *Run* method is called again, and the filter graph again executes. This time, *WaitForCompletion* should return *EC_COMPLETE*, indicating that the multipass encoding process has completed successfully. When the encoding has completed (successfully or not) the multipass parameter on the WM ASF Writer is turned off with a call to the *IConfigAsfWriter2* method *SetParam*.

There's only a little bit of *MakeAsfFile* left; it handles the frame indexing if that feature was enabled in the application's UI:

```
// Finally, if frame-based indexing was requested,
// this must be performed manually after the file is created.
// Theoretically, frame based indexing
// can be performed on any type of video data in an ASF file.

if (g_fFrameIndexing)
{
    if(!pASFCallback) // We didn't ask for SMPTE
                      // so we need to create the callback object here
    {
        DbgLog((LOG_TRACE, 3,
            _T("Creating a new callback obj for Frame Indexing\n")));
        pASFCallback = new CASFCallback();
        if(!pASFCallback)
```

```
                    {
                        return E_OUTOFMEMORY;
                    }
                }

                hr = IndexFileByFrames(wszTargetFile, pASFCallback);
                if (FAILED(hr))
                {
                    DbgLog((LOG_TRACE, 3,
                        _T("IndexFileByFrames failed! hr=0x%x\n"), hr));
                    return hr;
                }

                OutputMsg(_T("A frame-based index was added to the file.\r\n"));
            }

            // Note: Our callback object is automatically cleaned up
            // when we exit here because we only addref'd
            // using CComPtrs in our app,
            // which call Release automatically when they go out of scope. The
            // WM ASF Writer filter also AddRef's the object
            // when it gets the SetNotify call, and it correctly
            // releases its pointers when its done with them.

            return hr;
        }
```

The application's UI permits two types of indexing: SMPTE indexing, which is implemented in a callback on the WM ASF Writer filter's input pin, and frame indexing. Once again, a callback object is instantiated, and it is passed to the local function *IndexFileByFrames*:

```
HRESULT IndexFileByFrames(WCHAR *wszTargetFile, CASFCallback* pCallback)
{
    HRESULT hr;
    CComPtr<IWMIndexer> pIndexer;
    hr = WMCreateIndexer(&pIndexer);
    CASFCallback myCallback2;

    if (SUCCEEDED(hr))
    {
        // Get an IWMIndexer2 interface to configure for frame indexing.
        CComQIPtr<IWMIndexer2, &IID_IWMIndexer2> pIndexer2(pIndexer);

        if(!pIndexer2)
        {
            DbgLog((LOG_TRACE, 3,
                _T("CopyASF: Failed to QI for IWMIndexer2!  hr=0x%x\n"),
                hr));
```

```
            return hr;
        }

        // Configure for frame-based indexing.
        WORD wIndexType = WMT_IT_NEAREST_CLEAN_POINT;

        hr = pIndexer2->Configure(0, WMT_IT_FRAME_NUMBERS, NULL,
                                  &wIndexType);
        if (SUCCEEDED(hr))
        {
            HANDLE hIndexEvent = CreateEvent( NULL, FALSE, FALSE,
                WMVCOPY_INDEX_EVENT );
            if ( NULL == hIndexEvent )
            {
                DbgLog((LOG_TRACE, 3,
                    _T("Failed to create index event!\n")));
                return E_FAIL;
            }

            HRESULT hrIndex = S_OK;

            //CASFCallback
            pCallback->hEvent = hIndexEvent;
            pCallback->phr = &hrIndex;

            DbgLog((LOG_TRACE, 3,
                _T("About to QI for IWMStatusCallback\n")));
            CComPtr<IWMStatusCallback> pIndexCallback;
            pCallback->QueryInterface(IID_IWMStatusCallback,
                (void**) &pIndexCallback);

            if (fVerbose)
                DbgLog((LOG_TRACE, 3,
                    _T("\nStarting the frame indexing process.\n")));

            hr = pIndexer->StartIndexing(wszTargetFile, pIndexCallback,
                NULL);
            if (SUCCEEDED(hr))
            {
                // Wait for indexing operation to complete.
                WaitForSingleObject( hIndexEvent, INFINITE );
                if ( FAILED( hrIndex ) )
                {
                    DbgLog((LOG_TRACE, 3,
                        _T("Indexing Failed (hr=0x%08x)!\n"), hrIndex ));
                    return hr;
                }
```

```
                //else
                    DbgLog((LOG_TRACE, 3,
                        _T("Frame indexing completed.\n")));
            }
            else
            {
                DbgLog((LOG_TRACE, 3,
                    _T("StartIndexing failed (hr=0x%08x)!\n"), hr));
                return hr;
            }
        }
        else
        {
            DbgLog((LOG_TRACE, 3,
                _T("Failed to configure frame indexer! hr=0x%x\n"), hr));
            return hr;
        }
    }


    return hr;
}
```

The Windows Media Format API function *WMCreateIndexer* returns a pointer to an *IWMIndexer* interface, which is immediately queried for its *IWMIndexer2* interface. *IWMIndexer2* is configured with a call to its *Configure* method, specifying the stream to be indexed (only video streams can be indexed), the indexer type, the desired interval between index entries (*NULL* means use the default), and a pointer to the type of object associated with the index. Table 15-2 lists the possible values for the indexer type. Table 15-3 lists the permissible values for the index object type.

Table 15-2   Values for the Indexer Type

Indexer Value	Description
WM_IT_PRESENTATION_TIME	Indexer will build its index using presentation times as indexes.
WMT_IT_FRAME_NUMBERS	Indexer will build its index using frame numbers as indexes.
WM_IT_TIMECODE	Indexer will build its index using SMPTE timecodes as indexes.

Table 15-3 Values for the Index Object Type

Index Object Value	Description
WMT_IT_NEAREST_DATA_UNIT	The index will associate indexes with the nearest data unit, or packet, in the Windows Media file.
WMT_IT_NEAREST_OBJECT	The index will associate indexes with the nearest data object, or compressed sample, in the Windows Media file.
WMT_IT_NEAREST_CLEAN_POINT	The index will associate indexes with the nearest keyframe in the Windows Media file. This is the default index type.

Once the *IWMIndexer2* interface has been configured, a callback is set up using the *IWMStatusCallback* interface, which the callback object inherits. The *IWMIndexer* method *StartIndexing* is invoked. The indexing takes place on its own thread, so the call to the Windows function *WaitForSingleObject* allows us to wait until the indexing operation is complete. During the indexing process, every time an index point is located by the indexer, the callback method is called. When complete, the entire index will have been added to the Windows Media file.

Implementing Callback Objects for Windows Media

The callback class, *CASFCallback*, is implemented entirely inside its class definition. It inherits interfaces from both *IWMStatusCallback*, which is used during frame indexing, and *IAMWMBufferPassCallback*, which is used when adding SMPTE timecode metadata to the file:

```
class CASFCallback : public IWMStatusCallback,
    public IAMWMBufferPassCallback
{
public:
    // We create the object with a ref count of zero
    // because we know that no one
    // will try to use it before we call QI.
    CASFCallback(): m_refCount(0)
    {
        phr = NULL ;
        hEvent = NULL;
    }

    ~CASFCallback()
    {
```

```
        DbgLog((LOG_TRACE, 3,
            _T("Deleting CASFCallback!  refCount=0x%x\n"), m_refCount));
}


// IAMWMBufferPassCallback
// This method is called by the WM ASF Writer's video input pin
// after it receives each sample but before the sample is encoded.
// In this example we only set the timecode property.
// You can extend this to set or get any number of properties
// on the sample.
virtual HRESULT STDMETHODCALLTYPE Notify(INSSBuffer3* pNSSBuffer3,
                                         IPin* pPin,
                                         REFERENCE_TIME*  prtStart,
                                         REFERENCE_TIME*  prtEnd
                                         )
{

    WMT_TIMECODE_EXTENSION_DATA SMPTEExtData;
    ZeroMemory( &SMPTEExtData, sizeof( SMPTEExtData ) );

    // wRange is already zero,
    // but we set it explicitly here to show that
    // in this example, we just have one range for the entire file.
    SMPTEExtData.wRange = 0;

    DWORD carryOver = 0;

    // Convert REFERENCE_TIME to seconds for convenience.
    DWORD dwStartTimeInSeconds = (DWORD)(*prtStart / 10000000 );
    DWORD dwSeconds = dwStartTimeInSeconds % 60;
    DWORD dwHours = dwStartTimeInSeconds / 3600;
    DWORD dwMinutes = dwStartTimeInSeconds / 60;

    // If we are at > 60 minutes then we do one additional calculation
    // so that minutes correctly starts back at zero after 59.
    if (dwHours)
    {
        dwMinutes = dwMinutes % 60;
    }

    // SMPTE frames are 0-based.
    // Also, our sample is hard-coded for 30 fps.
    DWORD dwFrames = (DWORD) ((*prtStart % 10000000) / 333333);

    //
    // The timecode values are stored in the ANSI SMPTE format.
    //
    // BYTE  MSB                LSB
```

```
// -----------------------------------------------
// 1      Tens of hour      Hour
// 2      Tens of minute  Minute
// 3      Tens of second  Second
// 4      Tens of frame    Frame
//
// For example, 01:19:30:01 would be represented as 0x01193001.

SMPTEExtData.dwTimecode =
    ( ( dwFrames / 10 ) << 4 ) | ( dwFrames % 10 );
SMPTEExtData.dwTimecode |=
    ( ( dwSeconds / 10 ) << 12 ) | ( ( dwSeconds % 10 ) << 8 );
SMPTEExtData.dwTimecode |=
    ( ( dwMinutes / 10 ) << 20 ) | ( ( dwMinutes % 10 ) << 16 );
SMPTEExtData.dwTimecode |=
    ( ( dwHours / 10 ) << 28 ) | ( ( dwHours % 10 ) << 24 );

HRESULT hr =
    pNSSBuffer3->SetProperty(WM_SampleExtensionGUID_Timecode,
    (void*) &SMPTEExtData, WM_SampleExtension_Timecode_Size);
if(FAILED(hr))
{
    DbgLog((LOG_TRACE, 3,
        _T("Failed to SetProperty!  hr=0x%x\n"), hr));
}

// The calling pin ignores the HRESULT.
return hr;
}

// IWMStatusCallback
virtual HRESULT STDMETHODCALLTYPE OnStatus(
                    /* [in] */ WMT_STATUS Status,
                    /* [in] */ HRESULT hr,
                    /* [in] */ WMT_ATTR_DATATYPE dwType,
                    /* [in] */ BYTE __RPC_FAR *pValue,
                    /* [in] */ void __RPC_FAR *pvContext)
{
    switch ( Status )
    {
        case WMT_INDEX_PROGRESS:
            // Display the indexing progress as a percentage.
            // Use "carriage return" (\r) to reuse the status line.
            DbgLog((LOG_TRACE, 3,
                _T("Indexing in progress (%d%%)\r"), *pValue));
            break ;
```

```
        case WMT_CLOSED:
            *phr = hr;
            SetEvent(hEvent) ;
            DbgLog((LOG_TRACE, 3, _T("\n")));
            break;

        case WMT_ERROR:
            *phr = hr;
            SetEvent(hEvent) ;
            DbgLog((LOG_TRACE, 3,
                _T("\nError during indexing operation! hr=0x%x\n"), hr));
            break;

        // Ignore these messages.
        case WMT_OPENED:
        case WMT_STARTED:
        case WMT_STOPPED:
            break;
    }
    return S_OK;
}


ULONG STDMETHODCALLTYPE AddRef( void )
{
    m_refCount++;
    DbgLog((LOG_TRACE, 3, _T("CASFCallback::AddRef!  refCount=0x%x\n"),
        m_refCount));
    return 1;
}


ULONG STDMETHODCALLTYPE Release( void )
{
    m_refCount--;
    DbgLog((LOG_TRACE, 3,
        _T("CASFCallback::Release!  refCount=0x%x\n"), m_refCount));
    if(m_refCount == 0)
        delete this;
    return 1;
}


HRESULT STDMETHODCALLTYPE QueryInterface(
            /* [in] */ REFIID riid,
            /* [iid_is][out] */ void __RPC_FAR *__RPC_FAR *ppvObject)
{
    if ( riid == IID_IWMStatusCallback )
    {
        *ppvObject = ( IWMStatusCallback * ) this;
    }
```

```
            else if (riid == IID_IAMWMBufferPassCallback)
            {
                *ppvObject = ( IAMWMBufferPassCallback * ) this;
            }
            else
            {
                return E_NOINTERFACE;
            }
            AddRef();
            return S_OK;
        }

public:
    HANDLE      hEvent ;
    HRESULT     *phr ;
    int         m_refCount;

};
```

Because the *CASFCallback* object has ancestors in both *IWMStatus-Callback* and *IAMWMBufferPassCallback*, it must implement its *QueryInterface* method so it can disambiguate between calls on each interface, returning the correct interface while maintaining the reference count. The *IWMStatus-Callback* interface must have an implementation of its callback method, *OnStatus*, and *IAMWMBufferPassCallback* must implement the *Notify* method. The *OnStatus* method tracks the progress of the indexing operation, informing the application when the index has been completed (or, alternately, if it fails).

The *Notify* method handles the SMPTE timecode data unit extension generation. The callback receives a pointer to an *INSSBuffer3* interface. This interface allows you to set or read properties on an individual sample (in this case, a video frame). The timecode string is generated (in the weird ANSI format discussed in Chapter 6) and then applied to the sample with the *INSSBuffer3* method *SetProperty*. This method is supplied with the GUID of the property (which matches the GUID of the property as initialized in *AddSmpteDataUnit-Extention*), a pointer to the SMPTE data, and the length of the data. Every time the callback executes—that is, every time a sample is received by the WM ASF Writer—another SMPTE timecode data packet is inserted into the stream.

Summary

The Windows Media architecture is a powerful and flexible API for the implementation of a wide range of streaming media, including high-quality, low-bandwidth audio and video streams. Although it is easy to play Windows Media streams within DirectShow applications, encoding Windows Media streams from within DirectShow applications requires at least a basic knowledge of the Windows Media API. As encapsulated by the WM ASF Reader and WM ASF Writer filters, Windows Media presents a simple interface to DirectShow—one that hides most of the sophisticated capabilities of the Windows Media API. Some of these capabilities, such as the assignment of Windows Media profiles to the WM ASF Writer, are absolutely essential skills for any DirectShow programmer who wants to work with Windows Media. Other features, such as DRM and metadata insertion in streams, allow you to create custom media streams with minimal work.

Appendix A

MPEG Format Support in DirectShow

DirectShow includes support for several video compression formats, including those defined by the Motion Picture Experts Group, or MPEG. There are several MPEG standards. MPEG-1 is commonly used for video CDs, and the audio encoding standard, known as MPEG Layer 3, or MP3, has become the de-facto standard for audio compression. MPEG-2 was introduced with the DVD, and includes capabilities for very high-quality encoding of video signals. In 2002, MPEG-4 was released. It provides for better encoding quality than MPEG-2 and has features designed for interactivity and delivery over data networks. Here's a brief exploration of the MPEG features in DirectShow.

MPEG-1

Microsoft DirectShow provides native filters for MPEG-1 demultiplexing and audio/video decoding. These decoders ship with the DirectX redistributable package, whereas most of the decoders available through DirectShow are actually operating system components that are installed with Microsoft Windows. For MPEG-1 encoding, several good filters are available from independent software vendors.

MPEG Layer 3 Audio (MP3)

Microsoft licenses two versions of an MP3 decoder from the Fraunhofer Institute, which holds the patents on MP3 encoding. DirectShow uses a decoder implemented as a native DirectShow filter, and Windows Media Player and the

Windows Media Format SDK use a decoder implemented as an Audio Compression Manager (ACM) codec. The ACM version is more recent than the filter version. DirectShow applications can use the ACM version through the ACM Wrapper filter. Windows also includes an MP3 encoder, but it can create only low-bit-rate files. Several high-quality MP3 encoders are available from independent software vendors. Windows Media Player requires one of these encoders to create MP3 content; the help documentation for Windows Media Player provides a link to MP3 encoder vendors. In that documentation, the encoders are referred to as "MP3 Creation Plug-Ins," but they are simply DirectShow filters.

MPEG-2

As the compression format for both DVD and digital television (both ATSC and DVB), as well as for some consumer camcorders and other PC peripherals, MPEG-2 is a major feature of the digital media landscape and will continue to be so for some time.

For DVD playback, DirectShow provides the DVD Navigator filter, which demultiplexes the MPEG-2 program streams and passes them down to the decoder for decrypting and decoding. For demultiplexing of MPEG-2 transport streams and program streams from any source except DVDs, DirectShow provides the MPEG-2 Demultiplexer. This filter works with regular DirectShow filter graphs (such as file playback or capture from non-BDA-compliant devices) as well as Microsoft Broadcast Driver Architecture (BDA) digital TV graphs.

For digital television, Microsoft provides a set of filters and related components collectively referred to as Microsoft TV Technologies. (This set of Direct-Show components should not be confused with Microsoft TV, which develops Windows CE–based software for set-top boxes.) The Microsoft TV Technologies components are designed to be used with digital TV tuner cards whose drivers are compliant with BDA. As of this writing, such devices are not widely available, but the DirectShow support exists for ATSC, DVB-T (terrestrial), DVB-S (satellite) and DVB-C (cable) transport streams.

For MPEG-2 playback from any source including DVD, you'll need to obtain an MPEG-2 decoder from an independent software vendor, unless you have Windows XP Media Center Edition. Although some hardware decoders work with DirectShow, these devices are rapidly becoming obsolete. Software decoders for MPEG-2 are highly recommended. Several good software decoders are available; if you have a choice, get one that supports Microsoft DirectX Video Acceleration. MPEG-2 encoding and multiplexing is also possible through DirectShow, but as with MPEG-2 decoders, you'll need the necessary filters (and possibly hardware) from third-party vendors.

MPEG-4

Microsoft has been an active contributor to the development of MPEG-4 since 1994 and is one of the patent holders of the International Organization for Standardization (ISO) MPEG-4 Visual Standard. Various implementations of MPEG-4 encoders and decoders have been made available through releases of Windows Media Technologies, through the codec download feature in Windows Media Player, and in recent versions of Windows.

Early releases of Windows Media Technologies contained implementations of MPEG-4 video encoders and decoders that were completed before the ISO standard was finalized. These earlier implementations are known as versions 1, 2, and 3 of the Microsoft MPEG-4 Video Codecs. They are visible in GraphEdit as the Microsoft MPEG-4 Video Decompressor Filter (versions 1, 2, and 3), the Mpeg4 Decoder DMO (versions 1 and 2), and the Mpeg43 Decoder DMO (version 3). After the standard was completed, Microsoft shipped the ISO-compliant MPEG-4 Video Codec version 1 (encoder and decoder) and version 1.1 (decoder). This codec interoperates with devices created by several companies.

DirectShow applications can access these codecs through the WM ASF Writer and the WM ASF Reader filters. Although the decoders will be maintained for backward compatibility with legacy content, the encoders are being phased out because of licensing issues. No MPEG-4 encoder ships with Windows Media 9 Series, and it's not guaranteed that the encoders will still be present in future versions of Windows. Nevertheless, if a MPEG-4 encoder is in the system (for example, if Windows Media 7.1 was previously installed), the Windows Media 9 Series components will pick it up. To be more concrete, the encoder will show up in the Windows Media Encoder 9 Series, and it will be available to applications based on the Windows Media Format 9 Series SDK. It will also be visible in GraphEdit.

Multiple companies own patents on the ISO MPEG-4 Visual Standard, and fees are associated with the standard. Microsoft will cover any required fees for shipping MPEG-4 codecs in future Microsoft products, but other fees might apply. (For example, the content provider might need to pay a per-minute fee when streaming content.) Third-party MPEG-4 encoders might be available as DirectShow filters or DMOs, but you might still be subject to license fees for using them in your application. For additional questions, please contact MPEG LA, L.L.C., at 250 Steele Street, Suite 300, Denver, Colorado USA 80206; by telephone at (303) 331-1880; by fax at (303) 331-1879; or on the Web at *http://www.mpegla.com/.*

For the official Microsoft position on MPEG-4, see the white paper at *http://www.microsoft.com/windows/windowsmedia/wm7/mpeg4.aspx.*

Appendix B

The DirectShow Transform Filter Wizard

To ease the job of creating Microsoft DirectShow Transform filters, Microsoft's Ross Cutler has written the Transform Filter Wizard for Microsoft Visual Studio .NET. With a few clicks, this wizard will create most of the code you need to support either a transform filter or an in-place transform filter, producing a Visual Studio .NET project as output. The wizard creates the class definitions and method implementations for a filter that does nothing, so you'll need to implement some methods yourself if you want it to do something useful.

Requirements

- Microsoft DirectX 9.0 SDK
- Microsoft Visual Studio .NET

Installing the Transform Filter Wizards

To install the transform filter wizards, copy the contents of the VCProjects folder from the CD that accompanies this book to C:\Program Files\Microsoft Visual Studio .NET\Vc7\vcprojects. To complete installation, copy the VCWizards\ DSWizard folder from the CD to C:\Program Files\Microsoft Visual Studio .NET\Vc7\VCWizards.

Using the DirectShow Filter Wizard

To use the DirectShow Filter Wizard, run Visual Studio .NET and choose New Project from the File menu. In the New Project dialog box, select Visual C++ Projects. You should see a list of the available wizards, including the Direct-Show Filter Wizard, as shown in Figure B-1.

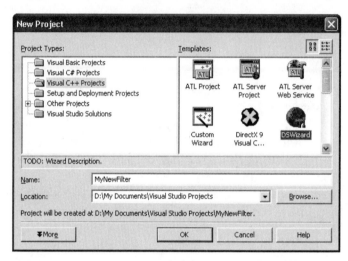

Figure B-1   The DSWizard used to create DirectShow filters

Select the DSWizard, type a name for the filter you want to create, select a directory within which the project will be created, and click OK. You will be asked to select the type of transform filter you want to create, as shown in Figure B-2.

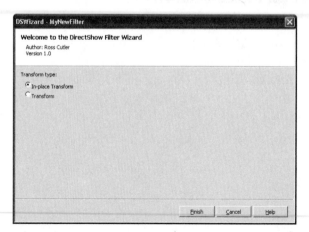

Figure B-2   Selecting either a transform or an in-place transform filter in DSWizard

As discussed in Chapters 10 and 11, a transform filter uses its own internal buffers for media sample processing and can change the media type of a sample as it passes through the filter. An in-place transform preserves the buffers passed through it and can't change the media type of the sample as it passes through the filter, nor can it perform any other operation that would modify the size of the sample buffer.

When you click the Finish button, Visual Studio .NET will load the project, as shown in Figure B-3. You can open any of the code modules and begin to make the changes specific to your filter's needs.

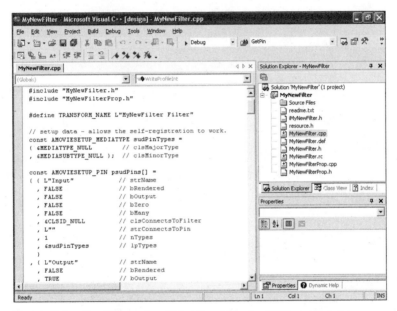

Figure B-3   The filter code within Visual Studio .NET, ready to be modified for your specific needs

Implementing Your Filter

The specifics of a transform filter will vary from application to application. The DirectShow Transform Filter Wizard creates stub code for a number of methods that you must implement to create the specific functionality for your filter. For a transform filter, the *Transform*, *CheckInputType*, *CheckTransform*, *DecideBufferSize*, *GetMediaType*, and *CheckTransform* methods must be reimplemented to meet the specific needs of your filter design. (Each of these methods and their functions are covered in Chapter 10.) For an in-place transform filter, the *CheckInputType* and *CheckTransform* methods must be reimplemented in your own filter designs. You will also want to implement the *Transform* method so that the filter actually does something interesting.

Installing the Filter

Once you've gotten the filter to compile without errors in Visual Studio .NET, you must register the filter with the operating system, using the regsvr32.exe command, which is discussed in Chapter 10. To test your filter, launch GraphEdit and look for your filter in the list of available DirectShow filters. If the filter has been properly implemented, you should be able to instantiate your filter and make connections to it.

Appendix C

Optimizing File Input and Output in Digital Media Applications

Two general areas affect the efficiency with which you can store and edit digital media files: how an application is written and how a computer is configured. This appendix provides information for application developers to optimize file I/O and information for users to be able to take advantage of those optimizations.

Developer Considerations

A developer needs to consider the size of each file I/O data block that an application writes, the mode in which the application passes those blocks to the file system, and the technique the application uses to extend the file size during a write operation.

Blocks and Clusters

Sectors are the smallest storage unit in a file storage medium such as a hard disk volume. The disk driver handles data in sector-size blocks. The sector size is a feature of the physical storage medium.

Written by Jim Gray, Distinguished Engineer, Microsoft Corporation

Clusters are the smallest data block that a file system handles, and they are a whole multiple of the volume sector size. Users specify the file system cluster size when they format a hard disk.

Applications are capable of writing file I/O data blocks of arbitrary size. However, an application writes data most efficiently when it passes I/O data blocks that are whole multiples of the file system cluster size (itself a whole multiple of the volume sector size) and begins a write operation at a position on a cluster boundary.

Consider what happens when an application writes 100-byte I/O blocks to 4-kilobyte (KB) file system clusters. The application will have to provide about 40 data blocks to actually fill one cluster. For each data block, the following actions take place:

1. The file system updates its internal mapping table and directs the disk driver to read the data from certain volume sectors into the file system cache.

2. The disk heads move from the file system data, typically at the beginning of the physical disk, to the location of the file system cluster containing the first sector.

3. The disk driver can handle data in sectors, but the file system must handle data in clusters. The disk driver therefore reads all the sectors in the cluster—that is, 4 KB of existing data.

4. The file system modifies the existing data to include the 100 bytes of new data.

5. The disk driver writes the modified 4 KB of data back to the file system cluster.

Obviously, you can improve the performance of this scenario by writing larger I/O data blocks. However, if the blocks are 5 KB, for example, the application still incurs additional overhead by almost always writing to partial file system clusters.

If the application writes an I/O data block the same size as a file system cluster (or a whole multiple of that size), the disk driver doesn't need to read the existing cluster and modify it. It simply writes the I/O data block into the file system cache and later writes it to the on-disk cluster.

You can't change the fact that it will take about ten times longer to write a 10-GB file than it takes to write a 1-GB file. Your opportunity for optimization is with the system overhead—the amount of time spent handling metadata and moving the physical parts of the disk. That time is most affected by the number of calls to the file system.

An application that writes digital media files should follow these guidelines:

■   Always start write operations at the beginning of a cluster, which is also the beginning of a sector.

■   Write file I/O data blocks that are at least 64 KB, and preferably 256 KB, in size. Writing extremely large files to a file system configured to use large clusters will benefit from data blocks as large as 1 MB.

Writing Data Blocks

An application can open a file for buffered or unbuffered I/O. Buffered I/O means that the operating system first copies the I/O data block to one or more system cache buffers. Data being read is then copied to the application address space; data being written is then copied to the disk. Buffered I/O benefits applications performing many small I/O operations but degrades the reading or writing of very large files.

When you implement unbuffered file I/O, you're required to read and write data blocks that are a multiple of the file system cluster size and are aligned on block boundaries.

> **Note**   Programmatic requirements for unbuffered file I/O are very specific. Read the "Remarks" section of the documentation for the Microsoft Windows kernel functions *WriteFile* or *WriteFileEx* for more information.

When correctly implemented, unbuffered I/O reduces the amount of time required to write each data block because it's not necessary to copy the data block to the system cache buffers. Unbuffered I/O also assures that the application doesn't incur the overhead of reading unmodified data from the disk and then writing it back again.

One of the benefits of a larger data block is to reduce the system overhead of NTFS logging. The log file is updated once for every allocation request, not for every volume sector or file system cluster. If you use buffered I/O, you won't have definite control over the number of requests it takes to write the file. An application that reads or writes digital media files should open them for unbuffered file I/O.

Extending Files

Programmers generally take one of two approaches to extending a file: they either seek to a new end-point location, or they call the Windows kernel functions *SetFilePointer* and *SetEndOfFile*. You should avoid both of these approaches.

When you use the seek approach, the file system allocates the new space and then writes zeroes into each file system cluster. (This technique, called *cleaning*, is a requirement for C2-level security as defined by the U.S. National Computer Security Center.) Each cluster actually has data written into it twice: first during the cleaning operation that follows the seek-and-write operation, and then again when the application sends a data block to that cluster.

When you call *SetEndOfFile* and the file system is NTFS, you gain a significant performance benefit over the seek-and-write approach because NTFS simply reduces the free-cluster counter and updates the file size. NTFS doesn't clean the new space, although it does mark the clusters as belonging to the file. Therefore, each cluster receives data only once—when the application writes a data block.

Note   When you call *SetEndOfFile* and the file system is FAT32, no performance gain occurs over seek-and-write because FAT32 allocates the new space and then cleans it. You should recommend that your customers use NTFS.

To take full advantage of this technique, you must also take care to write data sequentially. Whenever you actually write to a cluster that is beyond the current end of the file (as opposed to merely notifying the system that you plan to write beyond the current end), the file system always cleans the intervening clusters.

Instead of using either of these approaches, applications that write digital media files should extend files during the write operation by writing I/O data blocks sequentially. If the file system is NTFS, the effect is the same as if the application had called *SetEndOfFile*, and it's also more efficient. Therefore, you should also recommend that your customers format their hard disks using NTFS.

Developer Summary

To achieve the best file I/O performance in applications that handle digital media files, programmers should follow these guidelines:

- Use unbuffered file I/O.

- Write and read I/O data blocks sequentially.

- Start all write operations on a 64-KB boundary.

- Write and read I/O data blocks that are at least 64 KB and preferably 256 KB in size.

- Recommend that customers configure their computers to use NTFS and follow the other suggestions in the following section, "User Considerations."

User Considerations

The hard disk partition, file system, and cluster size all affect the efficiency with which an application can write digital media files. A user configuring a computer that will run such an application needs to consider these issues.

Hard Disk Partition

If you install the operating system in one partition and write files in a different partition in the same physical drive, the performance of your applications might degrade. Performance degrades because of the additional time it takes to move between one partition (for access to the file system log file, the operating system modules, and so on) and the other partition (for file I/O access).

On the other hand, separate partitions in separate drives can improve the performance of your applications. In this scenario, you install the operating system, the operating system paging file, and your applications in one drive and use the other drive for application data. This approach reduces file I/O time because the movements of the disk heads in each drive are completely independent.

You gain the most benefit when the two hard disk drives are not using a single IDE controller, configured as master and slave; such drives cannot work in parallel. But even this arrangement gives better performance than you can achieve with multiple partitions in a single physical drive.

You should configure one partition per hard disk drive and place separate disk drives on separate IDE controllers if at all possible. (Several SCSI drives can share the same controller.)

File System

When you install Microsoft Windows NT, Windows 2000, or Windows XP, you select whether to use the NTFS or the FAT32 file system. When an application is writing a file to a disk, these file systems extend the file in different ways and the difference affects performance. You should use NTFS.

If an application is written to do so, it can extend a file much more quickly on NTFS than on FAT32, which is important, for example, when you are capturing real-time digital media and writing it to the hard disk. Typically, the file must be repeatedly extended.

The two file systems differ in another way. Every time NTFS changes file metadata (such as the particular clusters that a file occupies), it also logs the change. Doing so guarantees that even in the case of power failure, the file system will be accurate.

Logging takes measurable time, which makes file I/O technically faster on FAT32 than on NTFS. The difference is negligible, however, especially with the larger data blocks that we recommend to developers. When writing 8-KB blocks, NTFS is typically 3 to 5 percent slower than FAT32. When writing 64-KB blocks, NTFS is only 1 to 3 percent slower than FAT32. When writing 256-KB or larger blocks, there is no measurable difference between the file systems because the file metadata changes so slowly.

For computers that use a digital media application that has been optimized for extending files, you should use NTFS. You should also regularly defragment the partition, which will ensure that very large files can be written and read as quickly as possible.

> **Note**   Do not use NTFS compression on the folder or on the entire drive where you store digital media files. First, using compression would require additional processing time for reading and writing the files, which would particularly degrade the writing of streaming media content. Second, the general compression algorithm used by the operating system does not compress digital media content very well. Third, you gain no benefit at all when you read or write files that are already compressed by the application.

Cluster Size

When you format a hard disk volume, you specify the size of the clusters that the file system uses. The size of these clusters also affects performance. It's much faster to write very large files using large clusters than using the default cluster size of 4 KB.

As an application is writing a very large file to the disk, it must frequently extend the size of the file. If the application requests, for example, an additional 64 KB of space for the file, the file system must locate 64 KB of free clusters. If each cluster is 4 KB, the file system must carry out 16 searches in its data structures to locate 16 free clusters. On the other hand, if each cluster is 64 KB, the file system must search only once in its data structures to locate one free cluster. The larger the cluster size, the less time the file system requires to allocate additional space for a very large file.

Larger clusters also reduce file fragmentation. Suppose again that the file system uses the default 4-KB clusters and the application writes data in 64-KB blocks. When the application writes a block of data, the file system tries to put the entire block in contiguous free clusters. In this example, it tries to locate 16 contiguous free clusters.

The file system is much more likely to locate two contiguous 32-KB clusters or one 64-KB cluster immediately following the current end of the file data than it is to locate 16 contiguous free clusters. The larger the cluster size, the less fragmentation of a given file.

However, one drawback to larger cluster sizes is the risk of wasted space on the disk. A cluster is the smallest data unit that the file system handles, and a given cluster can contain data from only a single file. If an application writes a 123-byte file to a file system configured with 64-KB clusters, an entire cluster must be assigned to that file even though almost all of it is empty. Similarly, if the application writes a file that is 64 KB plus one byte, that file must be assigned two entire clusters.

You must consider this tradeoff between performance and wasted space when you configure a hard disk volume. If the volume will have many small files, it should use smaller clusters. If it will have many very large files, it should use larger clusters. If at all possible, you should use different hard disk drives for files that will benefit from very different cluster sizes. For example, install the operating system and applications on a volume with the default cluster size and use a volume with a large cluster size to store large digital media files.

For a hard disk that will store and manipulate very large digital media files, you should configure the file system to use clusters of at least 8 KB, with 64 KB preferred.

Hardware

Hardware considerations do not lead to a choice between NTFS and FAT32. An application that uses carefully implemented, asynchronous, non-buffered, sequential file I/O can easily reach the transfer rate of the hardware. This is true for both file systems.

User Summary

To achieve the best file I/O performance in applications that handle digital media files, users should take these steps:

- Format each physical hard disk drive with only one partition.

- If you have a separate hard disk drive for data files, try to use a separate IDE controller.

- Format the drive where you will store multimedia files using NTFS. Do not use FAT32.

- Format the drive where you will store multimedia files with the largest cluster size that is practical. If it's a separate drive used only to store multimedia files, use clusters at least 64 KB in size.

- Regularly defragment the partition. Do not use NTFS compression on the partition.

Index

Mark Pesce

Internationally recognized as the man who invented the Virtual Reality Modeling Language (VRML), bringing 3-D graphics onto the World Wide Web, Mark Pesce has been exploring the frontiers of the future for nearly two decades. A professional software engineer since 1982, he began writing professionally in 1992. In 1995, Pesce published the first of three books on VRML, *VRML: Browsing and Building Cyberspace*, which sold 70,000 copies in six languages. It was followed by *VRML: Flying Through the Web* in 1996 and *Learning VRML 2.0: Design for Cyberspace* in 1997. In 2000, Random House published *The Playful World: How Technology Is Transforming Our Imagination*. Pesce has also written for magazines such as *WIRED*, *PC Magazine*, *Salon*, and *FEED*. This is his first book for Microsoft Press.

In 1995, Pesce accepted a teaching position in San Francisco State University's Multimedia Studies Program, where he codesigned the curriculum for the certificate program in 3D Arts. In 1998, Pesce received a two-year appointment as Visiting Professor and Chair of the Interactive Media Program at the University of Southern California's world-renowned School of Cinema-Television. His mandate—to bring cinema and broadcast television into the interactive era—led him to create a program heavily reliant on digital video, and it is already producing a generation of entertainment professionals shaping the media of the next century.

Pesce has worked with and consulted for numerous high-technology companies, including Silicon Graphics, Apple, Sega, and Microsoft. This is his fifth book.

At Microsoft Press, we use tools to illustrate our books for software developers and IT professionals. Tools very simply and powerfully symbolize human inventiveness. They're a metaphor for people extending their capabilities, precision, and reach. From simple calipers and pliers to digital micrometers and lasers, these stylized illustrations give each book a visual identity and add personality to the series. With tools and knowledge, there's no limit to creativity and innovation. Our tag line says it all: *the tools you need to put technology to work.*

The manuscript for this book was prepared and galleyed using Microsoft Word. Pages were composed by Microsoft Press using Adobe FrameMaker+SGML for Windows, with text in Garamond and display type in Helvetica Condensed. Composed pages were delivered to the printer as electronic prepress files.

Cover Designer: Methodologie, Inc.
Interior Graphic Designer: James D. Kramer
Principal Compositor: Gina Cassill
Electronic Artist: Rob Nance
Principal Copyeditor: Holly M. Viola
Indexer: Richard Shrout

Learn how to develop software at your own pace with the proven Microsoft STEP BY STEP *method!*

**Microsoft® Visual Basic®
.NET Step by Step**
ISBN: 0-7356-1374-5
U.S.A. $39.99
Canada $57.99

**Web Database
Development Step by
Step .NET Edition**
ISBN: 0-7356-1637-X
U.S.A. $39.99
Canada $57.99

**Microsoft Visual C#™
.NET Step by Step**
ISBN: 0-7356-1289-7
U.S.A. $39.99
Canada $57.99

**Microsoft Visual C++®
.NET Step by Step**
ISBN: 0-7356-1567-5
U.S.A. $39.99
Canada $57.99

Learn core programming skills with these hands-on, tutorial-based guides—all of them designed to walk any developer through the fundamentals of Microsoft's programming languages. Work through every lesson to complete the full course, or do just the lessons you want to learn exactly the skills you need. Either way, you receive professional development training at your own pace, with real-world examples and practice files to help you master core skills with the world's most popular programming languages and technologies. Throughout, you'll find insightful tips and expert explanations for rapid application development, increased productivity, and more powerful results.

Microsoft Press has other STEP BY STEP titles to help you master core programming skills:

Microsoft ASP.NET Step by Step
ISBN: 0-7356-1287-0

Microsoft ADO.NET Step by Step
ISBN: 0-7356-1236-6

**Microsoft .NET XML Web Services
Step by Step**
ISBN: 0-7356-1720-1

**OOP with Microsoft Visual Basic .NET and
Microsoft Visual C# Step by Step**
ISBN: 0-7356-1568-3

XML Step by Step, Second Edition
ISBN: 0-7356-1465-2

**Microsoft Visual Basic 6.0 Professional
Step by Step, Second Edition**
ISBN: 0-7356-1883-6

**Microsoft Excel 2002 Visual Basic for
Applications Step by Step**
ISBN: 0-7356-1359-1

**Microsoft Access 2002 Visual Basic for
Applications Step by Step**
ISBN: 0-7356-1358-3

To learn more about the full line of Microsoft Press® products for developers, please visit us at:

microsoft.com/mspress/developer

Learn how to *build dynamic, scalable Web applications* with *ASP.NET!*

Designing Microsoft® ASP.NET Applications
ISBN 0-7356-1348-6

Get expert guidance on how to use the powerful new functionality of ASP.NET! ASP.NET, the next generation of Active Server Pages, provides a new programming model based on the Microsoft .NET Framework for writing Web applications. Learn about ASP.NET development—with reusable code samples in languages such as Microsoft Visual Basic® .NET and Microsoft Visual C#™—in DESIGNING MICROSOFT ASP.NET APPLICATIONS. This book provides an in-depth look at how to create ASP.NET applications and how they work under the covers. You'll learn how to create Web Forms and reusable components, and how to develop XML Web services. You'll also learn how to create database-enabled ASP.NET applications that use XML (Extensible Markup Language) and ADO.NET (the next generation of Microsoft ActiveX® Data Objects).

Building Web Solutions with ASP.NET and ADO.NET
ISBN 0-7356-1578-0

Take your Web programming skills to the next level. Most Web applications follow a simple "3F" pattern: fetch, format, and forward to the browser. With this in-depth guide, you'll take your ASP.NET and ADO.NET skills to the next level and learn key techniques to develop more functional Web applications. Discover how to build applications for ad hoc and effective Web reporting, applications that work disconnected from the data source and use XML to communicate with non-.NET systems, and general-purpose applications that take advantage of the data abstraction of ADO.NET. Along the way, you'll learn how to take advantage of code reusability, user controls, code-behind, custom Web controls, and other timesaving techniques employed by ASP.NET experts.

Microsoft ASP.NET Step by Step
ISBN 0-7356-1287-0

Master ASP.NET with the proven Microsoft STEP BY STEP learning method. Get a solid handle on this revolutionary new programming framework and its underlying technologies with this accessible, modular primer. You'll quickly learn how to put together the basic building blocks to get working in ASP.NET and find examples drawn from the real-world challenges that both beginning and experienced developers face every day. Easy-to-grasp instructions help you understand fundamental tools and technologies such as the common language runtime, Web Forms, XML Web services, and the Microsoft .NET Framework. Throughout the book, you'll find insightful tips about best practices to follow while using ASP.NET to create scalable, high-performance Web applications.

Microsoft Press has many other titles to help you put development tools and technologies to work. To learn more about the full line of Microsoft Press® products for developers, please visit:

microsoft.com/mspress/developer

Microsoft Press products are available worldwide wherever quality computer books are sold. For more information, contact your book or computer retailer, software reseller, or local Microsoft Sales Office, or visit our Web site at **microsoft.com/mspress**. To locate your nearest source for Microsoft Press products, or to order directly, call 1-800-MSPRESS in the U.S. (In Canada, call 1-800-268-2222).

Get a **Free**
e-mail newsletter, updates,
special offers, links to related books,
and more when you

register on line!

Register your Microsoft Press® title on our Web site and you'll get a FREE subscription to our e-mail newsletter, *Microsoft Press Book Connections*. You'll find out about newly released and upcoming books and learning tools, online events, software downloads, special offers and coupons for Microsoft Press customers, and information about major Microsoft® product releases. You can also read useful additional information about all the titles we publish, such as detailed book descriptions, tables of contents and indexes, sample chapters, links to related books and book series, author biographies, and reviews by other customers.

Registration is easy. Just visit this Web page and fill in your information:

http://www.microsoft.com/mspress/register

Microsoft®

Proof of Purchase

Use this page as proof of purchase if participating in a promotion or rebate offer on this title. Proof of purchase must be used in conjunction with other proof(s) of payment such as your dated sales receipt—see offer details.

Programming Microsoft® DirectShow® for Digital Video and Television
0-7356-1821-6

CUSTOMER NAME

Microsoft Press, PO Box 97017, Redmond, WA 98073-9830

MICROSOFT LICENSE AGREEMENT

Book Companion CD

- **Support Services.** Microsoft may, but is not obligated to, provide you with support services related to the SOFTWARE PRODUCT ("Support Services"). Use of Support Services is governed by the Microsoft policies and programs described in the user manual, in "online" documentation, and/or in other Microsoft-provided materials. Any supplemental software code provided to you as part of the Support Services shall be considered part of the SOFTWARE PRODUCT and subject to the terms and conditions of this EULA. With respect to technical information you provide to Microsoft as part of the Support Services, Microsoft may use such information for its business purposes, including for product support and development. Microsoft will not utilize such technical information in a form that personally identifies you.

- **Software Transfer.** You may permanently transfer all of your rights under this EULA, provided you retain no copies, you transfer all of the SOFTWARE PRODUCT (including all component parts, the media and printed materials, any upgrades, this EULA, and, if applicable, the Certificate of Authenticity), **and** the recipient agrees to the terms of this EULA.

- **Termination.** Without prejudice to any other rights, Microsoft may terminate this EULA if you fail to comply with the terms and conditions of this EULA. In such event, you must destroy all copies of the SOFTWARE PRODUCT and all of its component parts.

3. **COPYRIGHT.** All title and copyrights in and to the SOFTWARE PRODUCT (including but not limited to any images, photographs, animations, video, audio, music, text, SAMPLE CODE, REDISTRIBUTABLES, and "applets" incorporated into the SOFTWARE PRODUCT) and any copies of the SOFTWARE PRODUCT are owned by Microsoft or its suppliers. The SOFT-WARE PRODUCT is protected by copyright laws and international treaty provisions. Therefore, you must treat the SOFTWARE PRODUCT like any other copyrighted material **except** that you may install the SOFTWARE PRODUCT on a single computer provided you keep the original solely for backup or archival purposes. You may not copy the printed materials accompanying the SOFTWARE PRODUCT.

4. **U.S. GOVERNMENT RESTRICTED RIGHTS.** The SOFTWARE PRODUCT and documentation are provided with RESTRICTED RIGHTS. Use, duplication, or disclosure by the Government is subject to restrictions as set forth in subparagraph (c)(1)(ii) of the Rights in Technical Data and Computer Software clause at DFARS 252.227-7013 or subparagraphs (c)(1) and (2) of the Commercial Computer Software—Restricted Rights at 48 CFR 52.227-19, as applicable. Manufacturer is Microsoft Corporation/One Microsoft Way/Redmond, WA 98052-6399.

5. **EXPORT RESTRICTIONS.** You agree that you will not export or re-export the SOFTWARE PRODUCT, any part thereof, or any process or service that is the direct product of the SOFTWARE PRODUCT (the foregoing collectively referred to as the "Restricted Components"), to any country, person, entity, or end user subject to U.S. export restrictions. You specifically agree not to export or re-export any of the Restricted Components (i) to any country to which the U.S. has embargoed or restricted the export of goods or services, which currently include, but are not necessarily limited to, Cuba, Iran, Iraq, Libya, North Korea, Sudan, and Syria, or to any national of any such country, wherever located, who intends to transmit or transport the Restricted Components back to such country; (ii) to any end user who you know or have reason to know will utilize the Restricted Components in the design, development, or production of nuclear, chemical, or biological weapons; or (iii) to any end user who has been prohibited from participating in U.S. export transactions by any federal agency of the U.S. government. You warrant and represent that neither the BXA nor any other U.S. federal agency has suspended, revoked, or denied your export privileges.

DISCLAIMER OF WARRANTY

NO WARRANTIES OR CONDITIONS. MICROSOFT EXPRESSLY DISCLAIMS ANY WARRANTY OR CONDITION FOR THE SOFTWARE PRODUCT. THE SOFTWARE PRODUCT AND ANY RELATED DOCUMENTATION ARE PROVIDED "AS IS" WITHOUT WARRANTY OR CONDITION OF ANY KIND, EITHER EXPRESS OR IMPLIED, INCLUDING, WITHOUT LIMITA-TION, THE IMPLIED WARRANTIES OF MERCHANTABILITY, FITNESS FOR A PARTICULAR PURPOSE, OR NONINFRINGEMENT. THE ENTIRE RISK ARISING OUT OF USE OR PERFORMANCE OF THE SOFTWARE PRODUCT REMAINS WITH YOU.

LIMITATION OF LIABILITY. TO THE MAXIMUM EXTENT PERMITTED BY APPLICABLE LAW, IN NO EVENT SHALL MICROSOFT OR ITS SUPPLIERS BE LIABLE FOR ANY SPECIAL, INCIDENTAL, INDIRECT, OR CONSEQUENTIAL DAM-AGES WHATSOEVER (INCLUDING, WITHOUT LIMITATION, DAMAGES FOR LOSS OF BUSINESS PROFITS, BUSINESS INTERRUPTION, LOSS OF BUSINESS INFORMATION, OR ANY OTHER PECUNIARY LOSS) ARISING OUT OF THE USE OF OR INABILITY TO USE THE SOFTWARE PRODUCT OR THE PROVISION OF OR FAILURE TO PROVIDE SUPPORT SERVICES, EVEN IF MICROSOFT HAS BEEN ADVISED OF THE POSSIBILITY OF SUCH DAMAGES. IN ANY CASE, MICROSOFT'S ENTIRE LIABILITY UNDER ANY PROVISION OF THIS EULA SHALL BE LIMITED TO THE GREATER OF THE AMOUNT ACTUALLY PAID BY YOU FOR THE SOFTWARE PRODUCT OR US$5.00; PROVIDED, HOWEVER, IF YOU HAVE ENTERED INTO A MICROSOFT SUPPORT SERVICES AGREEMENT, MICROSOFT'S ENTIRE LIABILITY REGARDING SUPPORT SERVICES SHALL BE GOVERNED BY THE TERMS OF THAT AGREEMENT. BECAUSE SOME STATES AND JURISDICTIONS DO NOT ALLOW THE EXCLUSION OR LIMITATION OF LIABILITY, THE ABOVE LIMITATION MAY NOT APPLY TO YOU.

MISCELLANEOUS

This EULA is governed by the laws of the State of Washington USA, except and only to the extent that applicable law mandates govern-ing law of a different jurisdiction.

Should you have any questions concerning this EULA, or if you desire to contact Microsoft for any reason, please contact the Microsoft subsidiary serving your country, or write: Microsoft Sales Information Center/One Microsoft Way/Redmond, WA 98052-6399.